Doing Life

Doing Life
BRIAN DIBBLE

A Biography of
Elizabeth Jolley

*To Bill & Jean
With thanks, more thanks.
Brian & Barbara
19 October 08*

University of Western Australia Press

First published in 2008 by
University of Western Australia Press
Crawley, Western Australia 6009
www.uwapress.uwa.edu.au

This book is copyright. Apart from any fair dealing for the purpose of private study, research, criticism or review, as permitted under the *Copyright Act 1968*, no part may be reproduced by any process without written permission. Enquiries should be made to the publisher.

Copyright © Brian Dibble, 2008

The moral right of the author has been asserted.

National Library of Australia
Cataloguing-in-Publication entry:

Dibble, Brian.

Doing life: a biography of Elizabeth Jolley / Brian Dibble.

1st ed.

9781921401060 (pbk.)

Jolley, Elizabeth, 1923–2007.
Women authors, Australian–Biography.

A823.3

Cover image by Frances Andrijich, www.andrijich.com.au
Edited by Terri-ann White
Designed by Anna Maley-Fadgyas, Perth
Typeset in 10pt Janson Text by Midland Typesetters, Australia
Printed by McPherson's Printing Group, Victoria

To Barbara
The Sufficient Cause when the Necessary Cause is not enough,
in art and life—and in biography . . .

CONTENTS

Introduction—That little art which is family life . . .   ix

The British Years
1. 'Flowermead'—The fury haunting the family . . .   1
2. Sibford—If she can swim, it does not matter how deep the water is . . .   39
3. Pyrford—A nurse should be unable to make a mistake . . .   63
4. Birmingham—The most powerful thing in this life . . .   76
5. Pinewood—Herts requires staff: Matron, Teacher, Handyman/gardner . . .   97
6. Scotland—The horror of marriage lies in its 'dailiness' . . .   114

The Australian Years
7. 1960s—After the flight of the cockatoos . . .   137
8. 1970s—I was sort of on the market . . .   157
9. 1980–84—The inside of people's survival . . .   183
10. 1985–89—Optimistic and fond . . .   202
11. 1990–2007—Who talks of victory . . .   220

Epilogue—Friendship has a meaning that goes both ways . . .   249
Notes   254
Acknowledgements   285
List of Illustrations   298
Works Cited   302
Index   328

Introduction—That little art which is family life . . .

Should a book, that is a novel, have a message, I am not clear about this, but if my experiences and feelings are of any help to any one then let a message be found for then I shall feel that I am at least doing something in a wider sphere than the domestic routine within the walls of the little house. I shall start in the early years of my life and try and make things take some sort of order but order is not a strong point with me and I shall write with all my heart so that there will be the noise of my children in these pages and the sounds from my own childhood, the people I hope will come alive and the warmth of them be felt. Then there is my school, and afterwards the hospitals where I trained, it is even easier to remember the antiseptic fragrance from the later years as people and feelings were becoming more distinct and more urgent.
A Feast of Life[1]

If we love what does not yet love us
Can we not give it love . . .
'Great Branches Fall', *Diary of a Weekend Farmer* (87)

'"What Sins to Me Unknown Dipped Me in Ink?"' is the opening essay of *Central Mischief*, Caroline Lurie's first collection of Elizabeth Jolley's essays. The title alludes to a couplet from Alexander Pope's 'An Epistle to Dr Arbuthnot':

Introduction

> Why did I write? What sin to me unknown
> Dipt me in ink, my parents, or my own? (lines 125-6)

Elizabeth Jolley's use of those lines signals the fact that her experiences in her family of origin inform her essays and shape her fiction. Her books are full of details from her own life, occasionally even the names and addresses of people she has known. As her prose passage quoted above suggests, she is constantly preoccupied with the family and various analogues of it, like schools, hospitals, and nursing homes, all of them institutions she lived and worked in. This is not to say that her novels are romans à clef or novels with a 'key' to them because, except for her last one, they are not.

Her essays, stories, and novels are meditations on the family and, by extension, the community, communion, and other terms derived from the Latin word *commūnis* which refers to what people have in common. She is especially preoccupied with love, its possibility, and its potential, including the potential failure of it and what happens then. Thus, sometimes provocatively, she addresses relationships between a couple or among a threesome, like a love triangle, or parents and their child. In Jolley's fictional geometry, if the relationship between a couple is the simplest one that can be imagined, the relationship among three people is the most complex. And so I address myself to the family unit in Jolley's life and work, using as touchstones the originary relationships that existed in her youth between and among her parents, Wilfrid Knight and Margarete Fehr Knight and Kenneth Berrington, whom Jolley called, in italics, *'The Friend of the Family'* ('Mr Berrington' 33).

Jolley often recurred to Leo Tolstoy's dictum that serves as the opening line of *Anna Karenina*—'All happy families resemble one another but each unhappy family is unhappy in its own way'. This is a study of Elizabeth Jolley and her various families. The first half of the book focuses relatively more on her personal life in England and the second half more on her professional life in Australia.

Hazel Rowley has said that a biographer is part historian, part detective and part novelist.[2] For me, the most interesting historical discoveries in researching and writing this book were also the most productive ones for interpretive purposes, especially those explaining the factual bases of the stories that Jolley's mother told about herself and her Austrian Fehr family. A most sombre historical discovery, not described in this book, occurred while reading the black scrawls in a large, more-than-hundred-year-old folio of births, deaths, and marriages in the archives of the Votivkirche in Vienna, close to Jolley's mother's family home. Having determined the date of the death of Margarete Fehr's great-grandfather, as I fanned the remaining pages of the book in closing it, I noticed minute, quarter-inch-wide, blue marks in the right-hand margins. Returning to the entries for 26 July 1874, where Joseph Deri Fehr's death at noon was recorded, I saw the tiny notation 'Z11733 26/8/38' and the word *arisch*, Hitler's neologism for his Aryan *Übermensch*. Thus, within five months of the Anschluss whereby Germany annexed Austria in March of 1938, some agent of the state, like the Gauleiter in Jolley's story 'Paper Children', was checking to see if one of Margarete Fehr's relatives was fit to fight and die for the Third Reich. Perhaps the suspect person was her cousin Günther Fehr who was killed while serving as a doctor in the Battle of Stalingrad four or five years later.

Richard Ellmann's virtually minute-by-minute, womb-to-tomb approach to Joyce, Yeats, and Wilde, once a gold standard for biography, no longer dominates for a variety of practical and theoretical reasons. If I have not employed Ellmann's approach, I have tried to emulate his commitment to detailed biographical and bibliographical research. One reason for doing so is that my position was a privileged one in that I had special access to materials and people and ample time to conduct my research. Another is that, for me, it is necessary to learn as much as possible in order finally to determine what information is to be excluded or included, foregrounded or not. When someone's name came up, I would note it and, if it came up again, would investigate and evaluate any recurrence. Marie Stapf Kemmeter is a good example of a person who became more important with each mention of her name, even though references to her were far apart: as Marie Stapf, she figured in Jolley's childhood, affiliating Jolley to Stapf's Austrian Uncle Otto; as Marie Kemmeter, she influenced Jolley again when they met in Germany in 1939; in World War II, she was the go-between for a German prisoner of war who contacted Jolley's family in Birmingham; and she appears in one of Jolley's juvenile stories as well. If that research commitment makes the biography data-dense, I am hopeful that my defining and contextualising such information will make it meaningful for current and future readers and scholars of Jolley's work.

At the same time, mindful of Rowley's reference to the novelist, I wanted to create a 'good read', and thus chose not to foreground theory or critical jargon. Put positively, I chose three strategies for telling my story of Elizabeth Jolley's life and work. The first is to begin with a Knight family history with three embedded 'pen-and-ink' portraits, one of each of Jolley's parents from the time before they met, and one of the older friend of the family who figured directly in their lives for twenty years and in Jolley's until he died when she was thirty. They are people who have invited an unusual amount of speculation from Jolley's general and academic audiences, and so beginning with their stories obviated the need to try to insert them into subsequent chapters. Although the rationale for the portraits and the history is that the family unit is the ground that Jolley continually reworks in her poetry, fiction, plays, and essays—often recycling her own family events and always addressing topics integral to her Knight–Jolley family—readers not interested in details of Jolley's remote and proximate, real and virtual family (including the pivotal 'Mr B', the ubiquitous Anti Mote, the nudist Uncle Acheson) should not be seriously disadvantaged by just skimming the 'Flowermead' chapter or skipping it altogether.

The second strategy is, within chapters, to employ a chronological but discontinuous narrative technique I have come to call 'layering', which consists of overlapping, separated, or contiguous dramatically developed *morceaux choisis* or slices of life. James Boswell, Samuel Johnson's biographer, called them 'scenes'.[3] According to one critic, the result of Boswell's technique was 'biography as intimate epic—strong narrative with a glamorous supporting cast and the loquacious warts-and-all hero at centre stage'. I do not aim for the scope of an epic, but hope that layering carefully chosen facts, images, and the words of others can suggest the plenitude and complexity of the subject's life.

The last strategy relates to the second. It is to facilitate reading by using prose that favours the concrete and descriptive. A concomitant technique is to imply my position by means of prefacing statements at the beginning of chapters (and sometimes within the text) and, especially, in not-always-contextualised indented quotations throughout, by Jolley and others, like the ones at the head of this Introduction. I intend by the facts and details to document and illustrate—the noise of children, the sounds of childhood, antiseptic fragrances, the sense of people and feelings becoming more distinct and urgent—and by layering to imply their scope, whether the supporting cast is glamorous or homely, whether or not the scope becomes epic. I did not look for warts but included them when I found them, literally in the Sibford chapter and metaphorically elsewhere.

I am fascinated by detective work, by direction or indirection. It is thrilling when it answers central questions, like how many wives Jolley's maternal grandfather had and whether he was a general, a judge, both, or neither. It is frustrating when it hits dead ends: I was able to identify Jolley's colourful Anti Mote as one of her paternal grandmother's half-sisters, and I identified the boarding house where she lived in the 1920s, but I can only speculate on why Jolley represents her as having a German accent in 'One Christmas Knitting'. I found Jolley's mother's paternal grandfather's will, a key document, in the Rathaus in Vienna, unopened because it is fire-damaged and awaiting the development of preservation technologies that will one day make it available. And I could not locate, dead or alive, someone important to Jolley's life in Glasgow in the late 1950s, and so do not refer to that person by name here. Such detective work led me to realise how birth, marriage, death, census and voting records are to a biographer what DNA analysis is to a modern-day detective.

But detective work is always incomplete, its results always provisional and contingent. Biographers need to keep in mind that, even after long, careful, and fruitful research, what they know about the subject is not all there is to know nor even a very large percentage of what might be known. (My work on Kenneth Berrington is a good example of research that became more obviously incomplete the more I learned.) The greater part of the job involves deduction and induction, commonsensical and even counter-intuitive reasoning—biographers are not unlike a palaeontologist or zoologist with a few bones and a handful of teeth trying to determine the anatomy and physiology of some unknown animal. Thus the importance of learning to tolerate and even value certain unresolved questions, discontinuities and contradictions in order to draw a more nuanced portrait than that made by, so to speak, connecting all the dots to reveal one possible picture and then erasing all the other dots. A biographer's job is not to eliminate complexity but to contextualise it. As Vikram Seth writes in his biography of his uncle and aunt, he wanted them to be 'complexly remembered'.[4]

That detective work was facilitated by the personal and professional assistance of scores of people who generously helped me in the research and writing of this book, providing information by fax and phone, mail and email, and face-to-face interviews, often several of them. They include people as far-flung in space as the 1960s badminton champion of Borneo and an Iraqi orthopaedic surgeon now in Saudi Arabia. And they include people far-flung in time, as it were: I was blessed to be able to interview Leonard Jolley's university love-from-afar from the mid-1930s as well as Elizabeth Jolley's English and Art teachers from the late 1930s.

My debt to such people, including many octogenarians and several nonagenarians, is immeasurable, for telling their stories was a matter of sooner or never, an example being the widow of a professor at the University of Western Australia who, knowing that she was dying, asked to be interviewed immediately, to say that neither she nor the other UWA faculty wives envied Jolley her success. Half of the people interviewed were seventy or older, and nearly half of those people are now dead. Without their generosity and, often, special trust, many facts, stories and myths would not now be known or, if known, understood. Those who helped are recorded in the Acknowledgements section.

I am pleased to acknowledge Curtin University with thanks for several Australian Research Council and other grants awarded me over the course of my work; Paul Brunton, Senior Curator at the Mitchell Library of the State Library of New South Wales, for kindness and material assistance he and his colleagues provided to me over the years I worked on Elizabeth Jolley materials in their possession; Margaret Allen, State Librarian for Western Australia, for permission to quote from the Battye Library transcript of Stuart Reid's 1988 interviews with Elizabeth Jolley; Bob and Jean Hazlehurst of Wolverhampton for their friendship and for helping me discover things about Wilfrid Knight and Kenneth Berrington I would never have found on my own; Sylvia Eisenreich, my translator and researcher in Vienna, whose genius was never to take yes for an answer; Caroline Lurie in Sydney, Elizabeth Jolley's first agent as well as her friend and confidante, whose subtle advice was invaluable; and Terri-ann White, Director of the University of Western Australia Press and friend of Elizabeth Jolley, whose continued support and enthusiasm for the project was critical; and her colleague Kate McLeod, editorial Manager, whose always-insightful advice was equally critical.

I record my special gratitude to Madelaine Knight Blackmore, Elizabeth Jolley's sister. For years she patiently answered my questions, sometimes the same ones over and over, and always provided valuable information and new leads; she contributed photographs for the illustrations, and she also read the chapters on Jolley's British years and critiqued them for fact and meaning. Having been her sister's partner in making up childhood stories in the 1920s and 1930s, in the past decade she was invaluable in helping to reconstruct that childhood and its sequel. Time and again she refocused my vision by insisting how the two sisters had two different experiences in the Knight household; and, through telling me hers, she helped me to gain perspectives and correctives on Jolley's versions. Madelaine Blackmore had, I should note, a great love of music and literature and had three stories broadcast over the BBC in recent years (see Works Cited). I am sorry she did not live to see this book in print after having contributed so much to it. She died 27 October 2007.

I must also thank Richard Jolley and Ruth Jolley Radley, Elizabeth Jolley's son and younger daughter, for generously answering questions about their family's time in Western Australia. Richard helped with photographs and was particularly helpful in relation to details of his mother's final illness. Ruth told of her early days in Perth with her mother, including the times when she sometimes worked with her in other people's homes.

It is not possible to thank Elizabeth Jolley who early on gave me to-whom-it-may concern letters in English and German as well as specific letters of introduction requesting those people I approached with them to share with me their memories and opinions along with supporting materials like letters and photographs; provided me with published and unpublished visual, written and taped materials (hers, her husband's, her parents', et al); and granted me access to her private papers, diaries, notebooks and letters in the Mitchell Library. Perhaps to encourage my work, she also gave me as a birthday present the William Makepeace Thackeray and Robert Louis Stevenson books that Kenneth Berrington's father gave him a hundred years ago and Berrington subsequently gave to Jolley. She always helped when I asked questions, but I tried to refrain from doing so.

Finally I must thank Barbara Milech, my partner and colleague, who participated in a decade of Elizabeth Jolley research with me, a labour of love. Her work on Jolley's writing formed the ballast of the critical discussions in this book, and her contribution to its final rewriting and editing was likewise a labour of love.

I followed the recommendation an anthropologist gave Isobel Fonseca when she told him that she wanted to conduct research on her Romany ancestors for a book about them, *Bury Me Standing*. 'Never ask any questions', he advised. 'Asking is no way to get answers'.[5] If mine was at least a foolhardy and more time-consuming technique than its obvious alternatives, it uncovered much information and elicited many insights that direct probing might have driven underground, perhaps forever. Although Jolley read or listened to drafts of the British years presented in this book, and occasionally corrected details, she never sought to change matters of substance. While fully supportive, she maintained an arm's-length relationship to this project. Although Elizabeth Jolley was my friend and colleague for thirty years, this is neither a hagiography nor a panegyric: she would not want one, and I would not write one. This is my thanks to her.

When I began this work I imagined the result would be a history of Elizabeth Jolley's life which documented, among other things, what she wrote, if and when/where it was published, and what was the critical and popular reaction to it. It became clear that her bibliography would be long, as would be the list of her literary awards and public commendations for her work. What I had not anticipated was how inextricably interrelated her life and work were. Nor had I anticipated the complexity of the relationship between Elizabeth and Leonard Jolley. I came to think of them as like a couple in a three-legged race: they might have looked mismatched, their progress proceeding by fits and starts, but they got on, they stayed the course, and neither could have done it without the other.

From her earliest days her parents modelled love, often heroically and usually badly. Jolley's behaviour mimicked theirs to the finest details of their passions, from their different ways of being charitable, to their enactment of love in unconventional circumstances. But her writing did more. It minutely reflected on her behaviour and that of others, intuiting extraordinary ways of loving by ordinary people. She became a chronicler and a philosopher of love against all odds.

The title *Doing Life* comes from her story '"Surprise! Surprise!" from Matron' in her first book, *Five Acre Virgin*. There, 100-year-old Mrs Morgan who lives in a nursing home explains the absence of her imprisoned 100-year-old husband by saying that he is 'doing life'.

All along, I have been mindful of Sigmund Freud's saying, 'Work and love, love and work—*Arbeit und Lieben*—that is all there is'. For Elizabeth Jolley, working and loving and writing were 'doing life'.

Brian Dibble
Curtin University

Introduction

Note regarding names, spelling, formatting and quoting in the text:

Elizabeth Jolley, born Monica Elizabeth Knight, was always known as Bunti by her father and Bunty by her mother and her sister Madelaine (and also Bun by Madelaine); at school in the 1930s she was called Monica and various nicknames (especially Beaky); and during nurse training in the early 1940s she was usually called Knight; for a year or more after she left nursing she was Monica Fielding, having changed her name by deed poll, and then in the early 1950s she was Monica Jolley, having changed Fielding to Jolley on her ration books and identity card. She became Monica Elizabeth Jolley in December 1952 when she married Leonard Jolley and some time after that Elizabeth Jolley at the encouragement of Leonard Jolley. What she is called across these chapters changes with those name changes.

She called him Leonard or Leo to friends and, more directly to him, especially in her letters and diary, Sticks (variously spelled Stiks, Stxe, Styx and Stx), not referring the cane or stick he sometimes used for walking, but meaning clever as in the epithet Cleversticks used by British children. His nickname for her was Fish.

The spelling used here accords with the preferences of the *Macquarie Dictionary*, as does the use of italics on foreign words and phrases.

Elizabeth Jolley's private papers in the Mitchell Library in Sydney are embargoed until 2028 or until the death of all of her children, whichever is sooner. Although I sometimes rely on those papers, I do not quote directly from them here. The chronology of the narrative should provide sufficient direction for later researchers who might want to consult the letters/diaries relevant to the events, thoughts and actions referred to in the narrative. Any materials quoted in the text are not part of the embargoed materials in the Mitchell.

1

'Flowermead'—The fury haunting the family...

> *I suppose I loved him.*
> Wilfred Knight's student

> *I wanted to be just like her.*
> Margarete Knight's neighbour

> *What kind of marriage can spring from the moving sight of Goethe's Werther first observing the youthful and charming Lotte distributing slices of bread at dusk to the small children in her care? My father first beheld my mother in a similar pose but in very different circumstances. She was sharing out soup and bread amongst her near-starving pupils in a school in Vienna...He was distributing food and clothes.*
> '"What Sins to Me Unknown Dipped Me in Ink?"' (2)

Elizabeth Jolley—Monica Elizabeth Knight—was a normal child, if her first letter to Father Christmas is any indication, for she asked that her pillow case be filled to the top. She also showed an early interest in arts and crafts when her second Christmas letter asked for a paint box, a children's book, a school book, a skipping rope, another book, and a carpenter set. And the Knight family was a normal one, if intimacy problems between husband and wife were normal in their day. But it was not a happy family.

What tightly bound Charles Wilfrid Knight—called Wilfrid—and Margarete Fehr Knight was their lack of self-esteem deriving from their different family-of-origin experiences. Her sense of worthlessness related to her feeling of abandonment caused by her mother's early death and by her father's devotion to two successive stepmothers, the second driving her out of the household. His related to his rejection by a self-centred father and an at least complicit mother who favoured their daughter and threw him out of the house for what others might have regarded as his selfless, if not heroic, commitment to the Seventh Commandment.

It was not a marriage of opposites but rather one of diabolically complementary personalities. Margarete Knight's way of dealing with her lack of self-esteem was to attract attention through flamboyance, flattery, and unpredictable bursts of anger. Wilfrid Knight's was to seek approval through self-effacement and service to others. Both did so through their teaching, she through her friendship circle and he through his pastoral work—she baked cakes to put on the table, and he cast bread upon the waters. She endured his absence while ministering to people they did not even know, and he tolerated her over-familiarity or rejective behaviour with visitors, friends, and family, attempting to mediate between and among them—she was narcissistic, and he was placatory. He suppressed anger, and she withheld affection. The whole time they worked to maintain the appearance of a normal middle-class household, and they were largely successful in doing so. Each was remembered with admiration and often affection by many people who knew them, and only a few detected signs of conflict and distress.

Kenneth Berrington played an important role in the Knight household. For more than twenty years his presence functioned like the central wall in the family structure, acknowledged but not questioned for the fact that, while holding it up, it also kept family members apart. After Berrington's death in 1953, with both Knight daughters moved away from the Midlands, the parents had to live together as if for the first time. By then their behaviour had become ritualised, and they accepted their relationship as normal, although they both knew that it was not perfect. Long before that, their daughters knew that it was more like a marriage made in Hell than Heaven, but that realisation only came after their participation in the family constellation, the experiences of two sisters seeming almost as if they lived in different families.

A similarity for each was trying to reconcile the double message resulting from the fact that Berrington sometimes acted like their father's brother and sometimes like their mother's lover, making the father look like a good friend or a great fool. And a difference was the experience of trying to mediate between their parents' attempts at triangulation whereby Wilfrid or Margarete Knight would strive, consciously or unconsciously, to enlist one of the children as an ally in opposition to the other parent. In '"What Sins"' she wrote, 'My mother was given to moods. Storms blew up unexpectedly, were savage and disappeared again as quickly ... I became by nature and circumstance a placator and learned to read every change in the eye, every crease in the brow. I am still a placator' (6). Her sister likewise became a placator in her own way.

It was with reason that, having described Margarete as Lotte and Wilfrid as Werther in Goethe's novel *The Sorrows of Young Werther*, she wrote in '"What Sins"' that it was a 'deeply moving scene but not a good guide to marriage' (2).

Wilfrid Knight was an introspective, serious-minded man descended from no-nonsense Methodist dawn-to-dusk dairying people from Winterslow, near Salisbury. He told a story of himself as a boy coming across sparrows trapped in a strawberry net and, on impulse, beating them to death with a stick. Unlike Shakespeare's boys who blithely pulled the wings off flies, he reflected deeply on the event, he said, and made his first significant life-changing decision: he renounced evil and determined to live a life based on the concept of the good. That seriousness is also reflected in another story he told, of knocking on the door of Berggasse 19 in Vienna and asking Sigmund Freud to make him a psychoanalyst.[1] His idealism was attentive to soul and psyche equally.

Wilfrid's father, also Charles Knight, was a dairyman-cum-Methodist lay preacher who married Martha 'Patti' Thrippleton from Leeds, a schoolmistress. They lived in Wells, Somerset, where he sold watered-down milk and delivered full-strength sermons. Wilfrid, born in 1890, and his sister Daisy, born two years later, attended the Blue School as charity cases, their blue uniforms signifying humility and gratitude to the Society for Promoting Christian Knowledge which ran the school. Terribly shy and badly bullied at school, he became ill every day at the prospect of having to go there, his mother solving the problem by asking if he wanted to go before or after she belted him. He and Daisy were good enough students to become pupil-teachers, a practice of the time whereby some older students were chosen to teach classes of younger ones. By 1912, at twenty-two, he had progressed to being a student-teacher at the Wells Elementary School where he had more than fifty students in his classroom. In his twenties he was also a Methodist lay preacher.

At twenty-seven, when he was drafted into the army, he made a second life-changing decision: handed a soldier's uniform, he would not put it on. Tried for refusing an order, he declared himself a pacifist, declining to serve on the grounds of conscientious objection. As a result he was sentenced to nine months of hard labour wearing His Majesty's Prison Wormwood Scrubs number 5018 on his uniform, prisoner 5016 ironically given only six months for being 'an unauthorised person wearing [a] military uniform'. Later he explained that 'The Sermon on the Mount shows that ALL war is wrong whatever the special circumstances may be'.[2]

He was placed in solitary confinement for a fortnight and after that had to work in silence, forbidden from looking out the window, on a diet formulated to strip prisoners of their body fat so that they could better appreciate their freezing conditions. Each time his sentence expired, he was handed a uniform to put on, again declining, until he had served two years or more, and they discharged him nonetheless. Perhaps the Governor was embarrassed by a guest who, refusing to call him 'Sir', pointed out that all men were equal in the eyes of God. Or perhaps he eventually discharged his obstinate inmate because Knight, impressed by the Quaker chaplain, made his third life-changing decision, to commit to the principles of the Society of Friends (although her never officially became a Quaker). The Governor did not need any more friends like that.

Released from prison, he went straight to the home of his parents who were living at 7 Claremont Road, Sparkbrook, three miles southeast of Birmingham, where he might have hoped to be welcomed after his principled sacrifice to the sanctity of human life. Instead his father disowned him and, as Patti Knight stood by, threw him into the street with a shilling for good riddance. Unable to free himself from the powerful grip of his family, he took a room with the Rose family at 24 Claremont Road.

Eventually he found a teaching job in Caernarvon, Wales, a stroke of luck, since COs were despised at large, the authorities threatening to send whole platoons of them to the European front as cannon fodder. In Wales he fell in love with his landlady's daughter, an affair that eventually went bad—later, whenever he referred to someone as Welsh, he was being disparaging. When they broke up, he set off to meet Freud in Austria.

> *'Young man, I do not have the time and you do not have the money'.*
> Sigmund Freud to Wilfrid Knight

In Vienna he met his wife-to-be while she was teaching kindergarten in an experimental class being run by the University of Vienna. She was Margarete 'Grete' Johanna Carolina Fehr, born in 1896, by some accounts as Baroness von Fehr.[3] Six years younger than Wilfrid Knight, she was a romantic young woman who at twelve had followed a tall, blond, athletic-looking man through the wintry streets of Vienna's Town Hall and Museum Quarters, becoming lost until she saw 'the church with two spires'. The man was Fridtjof Nansen, the Norwegian scientist then famous for his exploration of Greenland and his Arctic Ocean experiments, and Votivkirche, the church with two spires, stood a few hundred yards from Margarete Fehr's home. It was a large residential building at the intersection of Florianigasse and Landesgerichtestrasse in the Josephstadt District, on the northwest quadrant of Vienna's elegant Ringstrasse, just a few hundred yards from the Rathaus.

Wilfrid Knight was no Nansen but rather an out-of-work schoolteacher whose prospects were limited on account of his having been a conscientious objector. But he was tall, handsome and athletic, a man who enjoyed hiking, cycling and boxing. Referred to in Austria as 'Professor', he was intelligent, high-minded and well educated, with a Bachelor of Science degree from the University of London and plans for further study. His interest in theology complemented hers in philosophy (she admired Seneca); they both enjoyed learning languages, his being French and German—his German good enough to converse with her—and hers French and Italian. And, like Nansen, he was a foreigner. She had a penchant for foreign, exotic or high-achieving men, like her Czech boyfriend of whom her brother disapproved and of whom she eventually tired, later saying *'Trau shau Wen, / Aber nur kein Böhm'* ('Trust, but watch whom, and never a Bohemian').

Her father, Walter Fehr, was a general and a judge, she said, her ancestors members of the Swiss court in the 1600s. The family's wealth and status were reflected in the apartment building at Florianigasse 2 in central Vienna, but the truth of the Fehrs was more like that of the eponymous Buddenbrooks family in Thomas Mann's 1901 novel. According to the Buddenbrooks Principle, one generation makes a fortune, the second consolidates it, and the third loses it, in the Fehr's case three generations of Josephs. In the eighteenth century Joseph Xavier Fehr started a weaving business that produced 'Manchester' goods in Fischamend, southeast of Vienna, enabling him to purchase Florianigasse 2 as his second residence; his son Joseph Deri Fehr moved the business from Fischamend to Vienna where he made value-added *Modewaren* (finished garments and accessories); and the last Joseph was Grete Fehr's grandfather Joseph Edward Fehr, once called *ein stadtbekannter Sonderling*—a widely known eccentric.[4] By the time of her father's generation, remnants of the family, like his older sister Johanna Fehr Bukowsky and her husband, were living, perhaps by usufruct, in one of the twenty once-elegant apartments in the still-elegant Florianigasse building.

Walter Fehr was neither a general nor a judge. He gained his engineering degree but failed his medical examination for military service, and so was a *Kaiserlich und Koeniglicher Oberrevident der Bundesbahnen* or state railway station worker during World War I. There was no general. But that did not stop Grete Fehr from fashioning one in her mind out of her grandfather's two brothers, Karl and Alexander. In 1854, as a young man, Karl served on a ship commanded by Austria's iconic Admiral Wilhelm von Tegetthoff, but not in battle, and he never rose higher than lieutenant—Tegetthoff said he should not be promoted until he had more experience and enthusiasm. But just having served with Tegetthoff would lend a man considerable reflected glory.[5] As for Alexander, he had a chestful of medals when he concluded his career as General-Commissär in charge of Department VIII of the War Ministry's Marine Section in Vienna. But his main service was in an accounts area, he never saw battle, and his awards were of the kind, naval historians joke, given to anyone who does not commit suicide. He was only adjectivally a general rather than substantively an admiral, although he was the equivalent of an Australian rear admiral.[6] It seems that near enough was close enough for Grete Fehr to amalgamate two of her grandfather's naval brothers into one army general.

Nor was her father a judge. But his father, Joseph Edward Fehr, held a doctorate in jurisprudence and (another in philosophy) from the University of Vienna, and was briefly a lawyer during his two years in the navy in the 1860s. Although if he actually practiced law in civilian life, he never served on the bench.[7] He likened himself to Diogenes the Cynic, the anti-establishment Greek philosopher who went about Athens with a lantern during the day looking for an honest man—except that, especially as he grew older, Joseph Fehr kept to his room by day and only came out at night. The title of Doctor of Law, his impressive central-city residence of seven rooms on two floors, and the fact that Florianigasse 2 was immediately around the corner from the Landesgericht or Provincial Court might have sustained his being called 'judge' as a term of affectionate respect, or even pity, by some family members or neighbours.[8]

Grete Fehr's symbolic elevation of her father Walter to the bridge and the bench accorded with his being an intellectual and glamorous figure. Rudolph Steiner, the anthroposophist, was his friend. He gave the eulogy at the funeral of Walter's father, Joseph Edward Fehr, and was in love with Walter's younger sister Radegunde whom he alluded to in one of his plays—after they broke up, he wrote to her saying 'we both very well knew it, but we could not overcome the timidity to say that we loved each other. And so love lived between the words we spoke with each other, but not in those words'.[9] Walter Fehr and Steiner parted because of some quarrel over theology.[10]

And a drama unfolded as Walter Fehr serially married three women progressively younger than himself, the last one twenty-nine when he was forty-eight. The first produced Grete's brother Walter, the second a stepbrother, and the third a stepsister. The first two wives died of illness early in their marriages, thereby depriving Grete of maternal affection and leaving her to compete with her brother and a stepbrother for her father's attention. Bad blood existed between Grete and her second stepmother from the beginning: when she was the flower girl at Walter Fehr's marriage to Aloisia Noster, fourteen-year-old Grete vomited on the altar; after the birth of Aloisia's baby, they quarrelled to the point that Noster struck her, sending her to board with nuns in a *Klosterschule*; and after that she lived with Tante Johanna Bukowsky at Florianigasse 2. Indeed, bad blood existed between Walter Fehr and his wife Aloisia to the extent that, according to one record, she divorced him before their child Johanna 'Hansi' Fehr was born or, according to another, two years after his death . . . In Oedipal terms, Grete was progressively displaced from the centre of her father's affections, not only by two stepmothers of the wicked variety, but also by their siblings. As a result, in adult life she had difficulty sharing her household with women and always sought the attention of men rather than women.

She was living with Tante Joh in apartment #20 at Florianigasse 2 and teaching at the University of Vienna when Wilfrid Knight visited, having been working with Quakers who were running post-World War I relief programs in a ruined Vienna. The poor and the rich alike suffered from the contagious diseases spread by turn-of-the century urbanisation—scarlet fever, diphtheria, tuberculosis—a situation accentuated by the privations and dangers of World War I, the influenza pandemic of 1918 which killed 30 million people worldwide, and the famine that killed thousands in Vienna. Even disregarding deaths in infancy, the average life span of Margarete Fehr's extended family was just under fifty. She and her bourgeois family also experienced wartime privation—her brother became tubercular, and many of the kindergarten pupils she was teaching when she met Wilfrid Knight were afflicted with rickets, angrily called *die englische Kranhkeit*, the English disease.

They were married 13 July 1922 (the feast of Saint Margaret of Antioch), when he was thirty-two and she was twenty-six, in the First Methodist Church in Vienna. She is not listed as a Baroness, her name recorded simply as Margareta [sic] Fehr.[11] Handwritten in the Knight family bible are the words, '*Ich will dich segnen, und du vollst ein Segen sein*': 'I will bless you, and you will be blessed'.[12]

> *Be kind to her, because she is young and very spoiled.*
> Johanna Fehr Bukowsky to Wilfrid Knight[13]

Wilfrid Knight brought his new bride to the West Midlands by the end of the summer of 1922 where he had the good fortune to secure a teaching job for the fall term in the day school of the Sir Josiah Mason Orphanage in Erdington, about five miles northeast of central Birmingham. They lived nearby at 'The Ferns' with a Mrs Margaret Moore, a widow with two young children, from whom they rented rooms.[14]

They were still living at 'The Ferns' when Monica Elizabeth Knight was born at The Norlands Maternity and Surgical Nursing Home on 4 June 1923. And they were there when her sister Madelaine Winifred was born at The Norlands on 20 August 1924, although her birth certificate shows their home as 23 Harman Road, Erdington. That was the address of the Wynns, friends whose doctor Margarete used, the doctor believing Madelaine would die; she was so frail because of an oesophageal problem that she had to be fed intravenously. So the Wynns welcomed the mother and baby into their home, and they stayed there for several months while Madelaine gained strength.

Madelaine's nickname was 'Baba', after what Monica first called her. Monica's nickname was 'Bunti' (Wilfrid's spelling) or 'Bunty' (Margarete's), from the old nursery rhyme:

> Bye, baby bunting,
>   Daddy's gone a-hunting,
> To get a little rabbit's skin
>   To wrap a baby bunting in.

Years later Wilfrid Knight wrote, 'You were named Monica, after Monica Ewer, who was a well-known writer at the time of your birth', but then he added, 'M[other] says NO, you were named after Monica Mother of Saint Augustine'.[15] He later added that Elizabeth was chosen because it was the name of the mother of John the Baptist and also of the thirteenth-century Landgräfin or Countess of Thuringa. More prosaically, Madelaine always assumed her sister's second name referred to their grandmother, Martha Elizabeth Thrippleton.

When Monica was seven months old, Margarete Knight took her to meet the Fehr family in Vienna where she visited with her few remaining relatives, her beloved Tante Joh, her father Walter, and her brother Walter. She would not see any of them on the two subsequent trips she took to Vienna in the 1930s, for Johanna died in 1927 and her father in 1928, and she became estranged from her brother who, whatever the will might have said, refused to share their father's estate with her. She had been jealous of him since his birth and later angry that her father put so much money into his son/her brother, paying for Walter's horse, sword, uniform and lodging when he was a dragoon in the army. Effectively, her family connection to Austria was severed on her return to England in 1924.

Upon the birth of Monica Knight, her grandfather Charles Knight's controlling and judgemental nature continued to make itself felt, his first Christmas letter enclosing ten shillings with an exhortation to save, one with a sting in the tail: '<u>Waste</u> not, <u>want</u> not', he wrote, telling Monica that 'to be clever without being good is disappointing, so you must try to be both, like your father <u>used to be</u>'. Later letters indirectly told her father to resume his work as a Methodist lay preacher, and not to have more children: he was using her like a ventriloquist's dummy in order to address her parents, infantilising his son and delivering outrageous opinions about his wife—'I expect she was born naughty; tell her whilst it is "never too late to mend" it is better to <u>mend early than late</u>'.[16] Virtually from birth, Monica seems to have been conditioned to become a placator, a repeated self-description of hers.

Her grandfather's letters are symptomatic of Wilfred Knight's powerfully conflicted family. There were titanic shouting matches between them all when Daisy was young and, after the parents' death, comparable ones between the never-married Daisy and the live-in housekeeper Mrs Clayton. In later years, Wilfrid Knight found it difficult to visit Daisy because it was so emotionally draining for him to do so.

Margarete Knight had problems with Daisy too, finding her spoiled, dogmatic, and self-absorbed, like Charles Knight. When Daisy died peacefully in her chair in 1965, Margarete said that her will 'was all over the place', making bequests to fourteen people, which was true but none of her business; and she said Daisy gave away silverware meant for Monica, which was untrue. But her feelings are made quite clear in 'One Christmas Knitting', when she says 'Anti Daisy should have drowned slowly with all her sins floating in front of her and herself weighted down with Grannie's silver spoons . . . ' (118). The strength of those feelings reveals that she did not feel part of the Knight family, and not without reason. That feeling of being like an orphan was magnified by her memory of being symbolically excluded from her natal family at the time of her father's death when her brother refused to share the estate with her.

> *My father with his fine white teeth and thick hair suggested, in his appearance, a life in England which would restore prosperity and social status. My mother confessed later to imagining that she would live in a large country house set in its own park. The England of her hopes did not turn out to be as expected. My father was a teacher in the heart of England's Industrial Midlands, the Black Country, an area of coal mines, brick works, iron and steel foundries, factories and rows of mean little houses in narrow streets.*
>
> '"What Sins to Me Unknown Dipped Me in Ink"' (4)

After their children were born, the Knights moved to 'Flowermead', so named by the grandfather. The closest Margarete would ever come to a large country home, it was a newly built bungalow on a half-acre block in the triangle formed by Walmley, Hollyfield and Reddicap Heath Roads in Sutton Coldfield. It was not a country house with its own park but rather one built on clay that Margarete Knight said caused the girls earaches; it did not have electricity, but used gas lamps and had a gas ring in the fireplace for cooking. But it had a nice garden and a small pool.[17]

In '"What Sins"' 'Flowermead' is remembered as a very small house but with a big garden, cherry trees, blackcurrant bushes and raspberry canes. There was piano music and Schubert Lieder, '[t]hen the music changed and someone sang *"How do you feel when you marry your ideal / Ever so goosey goosey goosey"*. And someone else sang "The Wedding of the Painted Doll"'. [The] mother 'danced twirling her beads, strings of them; she danced kicking her feet out to the sides, heels up, toes down and turned in. Across the room she danced, across the room and back' (8). But there was a void in what should have been a happy scene, Monica and Madelaine often told to be quiet because their father was writing a book.[18] At other times, 'My father sat with one hand shading his eyes but I saw his tears' (8)—he later told them that his prison experiences gave him a persecution complex, making him feel unworthy to own a home, and even causing him frequently to change lodgings when travelling. The experience went back to his time in Wormwood Scrubs and his father's subsequently humiliating him, not for Wilfrid's pacifism but for Charles' belief, 'in the disgrace of being in prison' (4). Wilfrid Knight was often caught in a double bind.

Life at 'Flowermead' was a rite of passage with several trials for Margarete Knight who had no household skills, little English, and socialisation only within her own conflicted family before and after the war. Ilse Gaugusch, an Austrian family friend, once suggested any woman from the continent could pass as good cook in England, but the result of Margarete's first effort, frying a roast, was such a disaster that even Mrs Moore's dog would not eat it. And sometimes her language and culinary efforts got confused, as when she told a German girl staying with them to add an eye to the soup, *ei* being 'egg' in German. But pride and determination soon turned her into a competent cook whose specialty was *guglhupf*, a rich cake baked in a *bundt* pan, an elixir and catholicon. Likewise, her facility at languages enabled her to improve her English rapidly, and ultimately she became highly fluent (although she retained an accent); she went on to study Hebrew to converse with refugees during World War II and, much later, took up Norwegian. Her home, particularly her kitchen and dining room, became a place of power from which she could dispense or withhold both nurture and nutriment.

At first her social circle was her family of marriage, not a circle in which one would want to be trapped forever: her father-in-law referred to her as 'that foreign woman', her mother-in-law would not allow her to use the shampoo (it was reserved for Daisy), and Daisy was unpleasant to everyone. They not only treated their daughter-in-law like a migrant from a country England was at war with but like the enemy itself. Of course, Bunty and Baba perceived Charles Knight differently: '[m]y grandfather in the heyday of his hernia walked, to save the fare, from Birmingham to Sutton Coldfield carrying a cot and a mattress on his back. Setting down the cot at the back door he brought, straight from his boots, cracked hazel-nuts which he held out to me on the palm of his hand'—'[i]t is not everyone who has had an old man walking with nuts in his boots and carrying a cot' ('On War' 13).

Like Joseph Edward Fehr, that is the kind of grandfather who is remembered as a mythic figure but, whereas Fehr was eccentric, Knight was lugubrious. He would invite his granddaughters to look through the bedroom door at their sleeping grandmother, saying that she would be dead soon; he asked them to speculate on how many young girls were killed on the highways by runaway horses; and he encouraged them to contemplate how long, at the current rate of production, it would take before the streets would be completely blocked with horse manure'.[19] Nor were his attempts at humour any more cheering: he would hold out a farthing for each but, when they took them, he asked for them back—the grandmother explained he was just showing the coins to them, that 'it was his way of being funny'.[20] Charles Knight died at seventy-seven in 1937 as dramatically as he lived, by pouring boiling water from a kettle on himself during an epileptic fit, subsequently developing blood poisoning from which he died in hospital'.[21]

Fortunately, while they were at 'Flowermead', the Knights also made a number of acquaintances who welcomed Margarete Knight and who, if anything, celebrated her European background and culture. Their new social circle was a virtual menagerie of consanguineous, mysterious, ersatz and honorary relatives. As for the family, '[m]others may point at Aunty Daisy and say, "see for yourself the peculiarities which are bound to be repeated" and often, in hushed and dropped voices, poor cousin Dorothy will be mentioned but no one will say exactly what Aunt Daisy did or what happened to Dorothy' ('The Changing Family' 82).[22] Monica thought that Daisy taught embroidery and needlework, but Madelaine was certain it was art, and one cousin speculated that she taught languages since she studied for a year in Grenoble, while still another imagined that she was a mathematician since her will was split into fourteenths. Dorothy, 'said to be mad' in '"What Sins"' (1), was her grandfather's youngest brother Stanley's daughter, a sad, 'nervous' woman sometimes looked after by a cousin and sometimes by the Wolverhampton Knights: such troubled people, as well as ageing parents and grandparents, are movingly invoked in 'Dignity, Composure and Tranquility'.

Then there was Anti Mote, the former word being the girls' perverse version of 'Aunty', the latter Margarete Knight's Germanic pronunciation of Maud. She was an eccentric, if not mentally unwell, woman whom Monica or Madelaine would return home to find sleeping in the bed of one of them. Her visits inevitably enlivened the household and often scandalised the neighbourhood. Maud was brought home by policemen for stealing the timetables and passenger lists off buses or for sunbaking in the nude in a public park in winter; and Madelaine remembered their mother returning home on a cold day to see that Maud had set Madelaine, naked, in the open front window so that she too could enjoy the benefits of sunbaking. Most touchingly, there is the story of Maud trying to pick flowers off the hallway wallpaper when the family was moving from 'Flowermead' to their second home ('One Christmas' 125). Maud also found her way into the fiction, when one sister 'watched Anti Mote comb out and cut off Pretty's [the other sister's] hair till there was only a tuft on top like a turnip' ('Clever' 200).

Aunti Mote was one of their grandmother's younger, unmarried half-sisters, Annie Maud Thrippleton.[23] Women like Dorothy and Maud led the adult Monica Knight to wonder about mental instability in the family, another odd relative being Charles Knight's brother William's wife Sophia who went into 'emotional decline' around 1900. Her fears were probably genetically unfounded but nonetheless understandable, for histrionic real and pseudo family members lurched in and out of the Knights' family life.

The ersatz relatives were also called 'uncle' or 'aunt' for acting more like relatives than most neighbours or friends might do. Prominent among them were Acheson and Mary Sheldon of Erdington who had two daughters, Betty and Norah, about ten years older than the Knight girls. Wilfrid met the Sheldons through Betty who was his day student at Sir Josiah Mason's—they lived at 727 Chester Road, Erdington, just a few blocks from the orphanage, an address memorialised in 'Strange Regions There Are' (118-20). The Sheldons had an au pair girl living with them, Marie Stapf from Germany, and so they introduced her to newly arrived Margarete Knight. The Sheldons also introduced the Knights to their friends and neighbours the Wynns, William and Elsie and their daughter Margaret, who lived in the next street to the Sheldons at 23 Harmon Road. The Wynns were the people who took Margarete and Madelaine into their home for a few months after Madelaine was born.

The three men shared a passion for motorcycles, the families also joined by their various interests in and experiences with Quakerism, pacifism, music and languages: Sheldon was hounded from Nottingham University for being a pacifist, and a sympathetic Will Wynn, Head of Maths/Physics at Aston Technical College in Birmingham, hired him to teach electrical engineering to young men who, alas, would make and deploy munitions. Even their subsets generated lively conversation, Wynn and Sheldon both undergoing psychoanalysis and Sheldon a being a subset of one as a nudist. An older member of the group was Marie Stapf's actual uncle but otherwise an honorary Knight uncle, Viennese Dr Otto Stapf, Keeper of the Herbarium at Kew Gardens. His wife was the mysterious Aunt Martha whose air baths and ominous talk about the head-high watermark in the hallway from the Thames in flood kept Monica Knight awake when, as a four- or five-year-old girl, she stayed with them in London ('Silent Night' 80).

The Sheldon household then and later figured large in her imagination. She later said they 'were intellectual, intelligent, cultivated people and discussions in their homes "shaped" me even before I could understand'.[24] An example appears '727 Chester Road'[25] where she recalls puzzling over the brass plate by Aunt Mary's front door, imagining the abbreviation 'MusB(Singing)' to mean *'Must Be Singing'*. In the same essay she implies that the Sheldon household made her feel special in a way that her own did not, as when Mary Sheldon played Mussorgsky's *Gopak* for her:

> It seemed to me then, as it does now, to be very special—this having the piano played especially for me. I mean, my being the only person in the room and the piano player turning to me and smiling while she played. Not smiling only with her lips, smiling and smiling with her eyes and with her shoulders and with her hands. She said the music was a sort of little dance.
>
> 'Strange Regions There Are' (119)

In addition to music and 'a great deal of affection which continued during my life', she said that the Sheldon household 'gave me "more speech"'—she instanced Betty Sheldon's saying 'knickers' in the presence of her father, after seeing a woman they knew wearing a white summer dress through which her bright green underwear showed.

Biographical and autobiographical details from the 1920s and 1930s routinely appear in Monica Knight's juvenilia and in her adult fiction. In 'Her First Minuet', a story she wrote in Form IV when she was sixteen, sixteen-year-old Anne Kemmeter appears in her special dress, hair piled in ringlets and powdered: 'A more beautiful sight can hardly be imagined'—Kemmeter was the married surname of Marie Stapf whom Monica Knight visited in Hamburg in the summer of 1939, on the eve of World War II. Thirty years later, Betty Sheldon's green knickers appear in a never-published novel, one with a woman named Krammer as its main character, Krammer being Margarete Knight's mother's family name. And Mary Wynn's piano playing is given to staff nurse Ramsden in *My Father's Moon* (65).

After three or four years in 'Flowermead', from 1925 to 1928, when Monica and Madelaine attended the Reddicap Heath Infants School, the Knights moved three times in about as many years, each time some two–three miles from Wolverhampton. First they rented a semi-detached house in Coalway Road, Penn Fields, southwest of Wolverhampton, a house called 'Barclay' (named by the grandfather after the bank). After a year or so they moved to a house in Bunkers Hill Lane, Bilston, southeast of Wolverhampton, a house they called 'Newton' (after the physicist). There Wilfrid Knight taught at Bilston Boys' Central School, and Monica attended Bradmore School for a few weeks and Bilston Girls' School for a few months, both spells in 1931, after which home schooling commenced. Then, in 1932, they rented at 63 Wells Road, also southwest of Wolverhampton, a bungalow they once more called 'Newton'. Finally, in 1939, they rented 62 Wells Road, the house across the street; it was the one which Margarete Knight preferred because, she said, she had always liked the people who lived there. They lived there the rest of their lives, purchasing it in 1956 with Mr Berrington's money.

Saints are very nice in heaven but I am not sure that earth is the right place for them.
Ilse Gaugusch of Wilfrid Knight[26]

If Wilfrid and Margarete Knight's new circle of friends offered them the opportunity to socialise, sharing ideas and pleasantries, looking after each other's children and the like, their life at home soon revealed differences between them that their brief courtship in Vienna did not give them time to discover. Those differences related to culture, religion, politics and the myriad practices informed by them.

Wilfrid Knight's religious attitude was inclusive, optimistic, and progressive, endorsing reconciliation between Anglicans and Methodists, sure Satan could be saved if he existed, and believing we never knowingly choose evil but consciously or unconsciously rationalise our actions—he insisted, in Mme de Staël's phrase, that 'to know all is to forgive all'.

He cultivated Quaker openness to the 'inner light' which could be exasperating as well as awe-inspiring, as Ilse Gaugusch, an atheistic, straight-talking family friend, discovered: while rowing on the River Severn in the 1940s, their boat got stuck and so Knight, who could not push it off with his oar, closed his eyes and announced, 'I will pray'. As workmen looked down and laughed at them, Gaugusch gave the Lord a few minutes, then tucked her skirt into her knickers, got out of the boat, and pushed them off. She challenged, 'Your prayers didn't do much good, did they?' 'Oh yes', he said, 'because it was God who made you get out of the boat!'[27]

Ideologically, he was a Socialist who endorsed Marx's credo, 'From every one according to his ability. To every one according to his need'.[28] Politically, he was liberal, passionately opposed to racism and, in his own way, to sexism ('most people received their early education from a woman').[29] And his unequivocal pacifism was lifelong: when Ilse Gaugusch asked what he would do if someone attacked his granddaughter, he again said, 'I would pray'. She refrained from asking her next question, 'And if they killed her, what would you think afterwards?'[30]

By contrast, Margarete Knight, if not an atheist, was at least an agnostic.[31] She set definite limits on her religious tolerance, especially for Roman Catholics—she disapproved of the Irish Catholic man her daughter Madelaine married and was shocked in her old age to learn that a friend was Roman Catholic. She was openly critical of her husband's public displays of Christianity, which she considered 'overdone', and she was especially vocal about the amount of time and money he devoted to 'good works', his annually giving away his overcoat like Saint Martin of Tours making her furious.[32] One by one he also gave away both of his motorcycles to men he thought needed them more.

Politically, she was a right-wing conservative, a Royalist who witnessed the end of the Habsburg Empire in 1916. When she first arrived, she approved of Queen Victoria, but was irritated by the current royal family, and Churchill was *verboten*. 'I feel very sad that I had to experience the dissolution of the Austrian Empire . . . and later the one founded during the reign of Queen Victoria', she said. 'I adored Kaiser Franz Josef and I admired Queen Victoria + I am glad to live in a monarchy'.[33] During World War II she 'railed against [Churchill] in her Viennese accent, embarrassing us all dreadfully. She would tear up his photograph whenever it appeared on the front of the *Radio Times* and was once even seen stamping on a bit of him she had torn off a poster outside the newsagents' ('Good Knight' 126). Yet in her later years she watched the Queen's Message on television at Christmas, and she listened to Princess Anne's wedding on the radio, grumbling that no one invited her to watch it on television.[34] And when Churchill died in January 1965 she wept all the way through his funeral as she watched it on television. She said it was very moving and wrote to her daughter how important it was 'to really admire someone' ('Good Knight' 126).

She was succinct and unambiguous in her opinions on gender, ethnicity and race: she said, 'I'm not very fond of women altogether',[35] and she did not like the French, Poles, and Czechs. She warned her daughters not to marry Jews—perhaps an illustration of the epigram that Austrians made poor Nazis but first-class anti-Semites[36]—and worried about the possibility of 'coloured neighbours'.[37]

These differences caused constant tension and uncertainty in the home. Some were arguably less central, like his sympathising with striking dustmen and her noting with satisfaction when they went back to work.[38] But some went to core values, as when Wilfrid Knight wrote to Monica, concerned about what he called 'the Coloured Question', and Margarete Knight, who occasionally added postscripts to his letters, wrote, 'I am half dead but still strong enough to contradict some of D[addy]'s ideas'. She supported the ideas of the man she voted for, Enoch Powell, whose famous 'Rivers of Blood' speech, given on Hitler's birthday, argued that allowing people of colour to immigrate to the United Kingdom was 'heaping up its own funeral pyre'.[39]

Wilfrid Knight was frustrating because his ideas seemed too simplistic and unproblematic: he condemned sin, saw everyone as a sinner, and every sinner as deserving of forgiveness. She was frustrating because sometimes she projected mixed messages. For example, she once wrote to a Jewish former student that 'the chief aim in life must be "to be good", so good that other people feel happy in the presence of a "good" human being, no matter what religion or nationality', going on to tell him, 'if it were not for the <u>white man</u>, the Africans would still live in mud or bamboo huts, without roads, buildings, railways + airfields, schools + universities'. What was he to think of her concept of racism?[40] Yet her inconsistencies were not always a bad thing, as when her practices contradicted her prejudices, most conspicuously when she took Jewish refugees into her home and worked tirelessly to help them get back on their feet.

Hence a question that has been mooted elsewhere: How was Hitler regarded in the Knight household?[41]

Wilfrid Knight's response to the invasion of Poland on 1 September 1939 was to fall to his knees and spend the morning praying that 'nothing so evil would happen again', a scene imitated in the short story 'Clever and Pretty'. He mentioned Hitler in only one surviving letter, implying a desire to intervene to moderate Hitler's intentions: 'Mr Delaney . . . is willing to 'phone Hitler at his own expense if you [Monica] think that would be a good thing'.[42] In any case, he would have followed Saint Augustine's injunction to hate the sin and love the sinner.

Margarete Knight wrote to her daughter on 25 March 1938, a fortnight after Germany's annexation of Austria, saying that 'For years German Austrians have worked, hoped and suffered *für den Anschluss* + at last it has come about'. The following year she wrote to say that at noon on Friday 6 October 1939, the day Warsaw fell to Germany, she listened to Hitler's speech on the radio and 'enjoyed it'.[43] Then, a few weeks later, she wrote about a Mr Stanley who visited Wells Road to repair a lamp and who blew a fuse, literally, while talking politics, 'anti H—of course,' she noted parenthetically.[44] Those comments appear to be more approving of Hitler than otherwise.

The answer to the 'Hitler question' is likely that Margarete changed her allegiances if not her values. A woman who lived through the horror of World War I in Vienna and the privation and suffering that gripped it afterwards, during World War II, she came to recognise Germany's wrongs—perhaps war's wrongs, although that is not clear—but did not repudiate Hitler at any particular point. Although she gradually came to champion Churchill and support the British cause, she remained a cultural descendent of the Habsburg empire. Austria's commitment to German culture and language, once its strength, was finally its undoing. As Michael Ignatieff argues, 'The most influential anti-Semitic tradition in Austria . . . was pan-German, and the ideological roots of the hatred of the Jews were from the anti-capitalist, völkisch [ethnocentric], anti-feminist, anti-egalitarian political romanticism common to Central Europe. German-Austrians shared in it . . .[45] Perhaps her affection for and support of her Jewish student was subconsciously influenced by her knowledge of the Holocaust and her imagination of what it might have meant to his family.

Despite what her head told her about people of other races, she took in Jewish refugees because they were deracinated people and families in need. She could be hard-hearted, particularly when her pride was involved, but she was not heartless. Moreover, helping people fed her own ego, demonstrating her qualities and capabilities and helping her to find a place in society, something that was always an issue for her.

> *I think this fury described as long ago as 1750 is the particular thing which does not show on the outside of family life. It is the hidden unhappiness.*
> 'The Changing Family—Who Cares?' (83)

From 'Flowermead' onward, Wilfrid and Margarete led lives that did not much overlap within the home, something perhaps not uncommon, then as now. From the beginning he devoted a great deal of time to his study and writing, completing a Master of Science degree, and commencing a doctorate on the water cycle that he abandoned (doubting its worth), writing his two textbooks and helping friends write a local history of Penn.

At the same time he also devoted a great deal of time and thought to his teaching, becoming the Senior Science Master at Bilston Grammar School. Some colleagues thought he was remote because he was shy, others because he was arrogant and felt intellectually superior to them. But none doubted that he felt passionate about his work: during the Depression he organised after-school dinners for his working-class boys, hiring women to come in and cook, ostensibly to provide them with edifying social occasions but actually to make sure the boys were well fed; he introduced German to the curriculum in the 1930s, at the least suggesting that he had a different view of foreign affairs from most of his colleagues; and he took a group of boys on a trip to the Tyrol.[46] As well, he modelled his commitment to social justice when he participated in the ship-builders' 300-mile hunger crusade from

Jarrow to Parliament in London in October 1936.

He cared for each student, and he could be deeply personal about it. When he taught Religious Education, he treated it as a philosophical inquiry rather than an indoctrination, inviting the students to explore such questions such as 'Why should God exist?' He would also help his students on their quests, but discreetly, once kneeling with a troubled boy to pray with him after class. At the same time, he was an inflexible disciplinarian—the students called him 'The Czar' and 'Nase' (German for nose) for how, shoulders squared and close-cropped head tilted back, he would look along his nose at them in the classroom where his teaching could be literally explosive or electrifying—he would start the first Science class of the year with a bang, setting off explosions as an introduction to the topic of combustion, or he would command the attention of the boys with his Wimshurst machine that produced a prodigious electrical charge. His teaching also could be metaphorically explosive. Once he was writing on the blackboard when he turned to see a student at the back of the room flicking ink-soaked paper off his ruler: while the rest of the class sat rigid and silent, Knight strode to the back, whopped the boy, and then walked back to the front shaking with emotion. He turned around, smiled and apologised by telling of once boxing with a young man and suddenly realising that he actually liked hurting him, something so appalling to him that he never boxed again. If the apology was perplexing to the boys, it was nonetheless memorable to them.[47]

Such personal attention and public testimonies meant much to many of his students, some keeping in touch with him until his death, bringing him fish they caught in the Severn, introducing their new brides to him, and the like. Today one says, 'I suppose next to my Father he was the greatest influence in my life during my school years', attributing his university and professional success in large part to Wilfrid Knight's care. He remembers how '[h]e often seemed to be profoundly sad but when you broke upon his reverie he always lit up with a beaming smile and a twinkling eye'. He says, 'I suppose I loved him'.

Wilfrid Knight was a teacher who would 'make a lesson out of everything' ('Sort of Gift' 70), finding as much to analyse and appreciate in a brick as in a sunset. Believing most schools spoiled children's, innocence, he proposed starting a school in the Pennines with the help of his wife's friend Kenneth Berrington, but Berrington declined. So he sought and received approval from the authorities for his daughters to study at home under his tutelage and that of his wife, she supported by European au pairs. Studying with Margarete Knight and the continental girls who lived with them would introduce their daughters to cultures, languages and literatures. But there were several theoretical and practical problems with the idea, the insurmountable one being the fact that no one but he thought it was a good one.

From the beginning the arrangement caused problems. He never much involved himself in the program and, even if Margarete Knight were inclined to do so, she had neither the talent to teach across the arts-sciences curriculum nor the time to integrate such work with keeping house; and she did not have the inclination. Moreover, he had overlooked its short-term social implications: Monica and Madelaine were persecuted by neighbourhood children who envied their staying away from school weekdays and were intolerant of the fact that they spoke German at home. As a result, they 'were exiles in our own street' ('"What Sins"' 5).

Thinking no more highly of the idea than their mother, and wanting to go to school like other children, the two girls tried to avoid lessons and largely succeeded. They learned little from the curriculum their father had worked out, not even from the piano lessons they were supposed to take from a Mr Jones, an old piano tuner-cum-teacher. Monica and Madelaine only remembered Mr Jones later for his touching their thighs inappropriately as he sat beside them.[48] In addition to a spotty education, another result of their not attending school was a strong bonding between Monica and Madelaine: 'We retreated into fantasy. Our childhood was one long game of people. We were each other's nephews. "I'm her nephew", I told the postmistress, "and she's my nephew". With sofa cushions on our heads we said we were widows' ('"What Sins"' 5). Such experiences, coupled with the hothouse atmosphere in the home, led to extreme closeness between the two girls: when asked if they were twins, Monica replied that they were, once saying, 'I'm ten and she's nine', and another time, 'I'm Monica Elizabeth and she's Madelaine Winifred, we're boys' ('Mr Berrington' 31 and 'My Sister Dancing' 171).

They sang to each other in bed, wrote stories, enacted scenes in their doll houses or throughout the house. 'Quick Change Pearl' was a favourite game they played, appropriating a detective character from one of the magazines Mr Berrington brought them every week. 'We admired Quick Change Pearl and emulated her, stripping off our clothes in the cupboard under the stairs and putting on other things' ('Mr Berrington' 35). In 'Only Connect! (Part One)' she jokingly but tellingly relates those experiences to her formation as a writer, noting, 'I started work when very young. Nymphomaniacs and murderers, perplexed housewives, greedy spoiled children, unfaithful husbands and angry maiden aunts inhabited our dolls' houses . . . ' (21). One of the characters, Joan the cleaning lady 'with loose pink legs, too big to fit in any bed, sat on the wooden chair all night and later rattled about with her dust pan and brush from one room to the next. She began and ended each day with the most vital gossip'. Much later, when she finished her first novel, *The Newspaper of Claremont Street*, she realised that Joan was the forerunner of its main character, Weekly ('Only Connect' 21).

Their attachment was partly a response to one parent's attempt to get a daughter on side in opposition to the other. At first the pairings tended to be Monica and Margarete versus Madelaine and Wilfrid, at which times the mother and daughter would tease Madelaine by calling her 'Daisy! Daisy! Daisy!', Margarete hurtfully saying Madelaine reminded her of Daisy whom she disliked. Later there was a switch that resulted in Monica becoming much closer to her father.

Although Margarete Knight's angry outbursts were unpredictable and disturbing, and despite the infinitely benevolent image of her father reflected in the fiction and essays, in the 1920s and early 1930s he frequently displayed anger at home as well as at school. Monica later recalled it as deliberate and methodical, as if from an attempt to suppress or control it, but at the time it felt merely cruel: he would make one of the girls fetch the newspaper which he would roll up and use to strike her legs, making her feel abject and resentful, Madelaine recalling how his wedding ring hurt so much.[49] She was clear that this was not abuse but acceptable discipline, saying 'We were only ever smacked as children if we were rude or disobedient. We were never beaten'. At the same time, she insisted that the atmosphere in the household was alive with tension, that anger flared unpredictably from both parents, and that she and her sister felt they always had to be on the lookout.

Whether or not it was the result of such tension in the household, when Monica was ten she was having nightmares severe enough to cause her father to take her to see a psychoanalyst. She remembered a large, darkened room with heavy curtains and a diminutive Melanie Klein—Freud's sometime-disciple—who sat behind her desk and, after a few questions, declared, 'There is nothing wrong with the child'. Returning late from London, as they walked from the station to Wells Road, Monica marvelled as the sparks struck from the nails on the soles of her father's boots as they hit the pavement.[50]

That vivid memory bespeaks an awe for, and identification with, her father that was matched at home by disrespect for her mother that took the form of growing disobedience and rebellion against her: if Margarete struck out, Monica struck back. That rebellion might have been related to her nightmares which might, in turn, have been related to the ambiguous presence of Kenneth Berrington in the Knight household from 1933. In any event, Wilfrid Knight agreed to end the noble experiment and send her to school. With a bursary from Amy Sturge, a prominent Quaker philanthropist from Birmingham whom they knew from the Friends' meetings they attended in Wolverhampton, Monica Knight left for Sibford School near the Cotswolds, about fifty miles southeast of Birmingham, when she was eleven, in September of 1934.

While she was away at Sibford, her sister Madelaine was bereft. With all pretence of home schooling dropped, she spent her time eating biscuits and reading French fairy tales, lonely and bored. While Wilfrid Knight told his mother how well Madelaine was doing under their tutelage and that she would be ready to matriculate before the usual age, Madelaine grieved.[51] She believed she was not wanted at home, particularly by her mother, for she secretly read a letter from Otto Stapf to Margarete in which he alluded to her saying that Madelaine was the result of an unplanned pregnancy that she had hoped would at least produce a son rather than another daughter. Together, Monica and Madelaine had retreated into fantasy, but alone Madelaine felt lonely, unwanted, helpless and hopeless.

Wilfrid Knight had no close friends. He even kept his distance from his work colleagues, avoiding small talk and gossip, eating his lunchtime sandwich in the graveyard across from Bilston Grammar. Margarete Knight had few, if any, close friends but many acquaintances, not all of whom she got on well with. One exception was Doris Horobin, a young neighbour in Wells Road who looked up to her as a role model, visiting often and learning how cook from her, wanting to be just like her.[52]

Long-term household visitors inevitably fell foul of her, like the young women meant to help with the home-schooling experiment, such as her nineteen-year-old Austrian cousin, a country girl named Gretl Walli, the first in a series of German- or French-speaking young women who came to live with the Knights. Au pair girls or governesses, they never stayed long enough to know what they were supposed to be. If they were teachers, those efforts failed, and if they were household helpers, that prospect was doomed from the outset. Sooner rather than later Margarete Knight would quarrel with them and '[t]hey would usually leave the house crying'.[53]

It was a pattern that repeated. A school friend from Vienna, Hilda Vorwickl, left in tears after she bought special sausages as a gift for the table and Margarete Knight, insulted, roared, 'I buy the food in this house!'—a Hilde Vorwickl appears as the companion and possible lover of the wife in *The Sugar Mother*. Nor were relatives exempt, for when her fifteen-year-old niece, Ilse Fehr, toured England with other schoolgirls at the time of the 1948 Royal Silver Jubilee, Monica Knight, who had never met her before, found her in tears on the doorstep, crying about how badly she had been treated by her Tante Grete. Even Madelaine received similar treatment: after she gave the house a top-to-bottom cleaning in her mother's absence, a furious Margarete Knight screamed, 'You want to take *my* place in the house!'[54]

During the 1930s and 1940s Margarete and Wilfrid Knight welcomed a number of German-speaking refugees from Europe into their home and helped them to resettle. They often arrived without clothes, money, or a common language: 'Our house was always full of people who were on the move, who arrived and they were trying to find places for them to go', people crying and weeping, and who, because no one could afford taxis, would be taken to and from the train station by Wilfrid Knight, who helped them to carry their heavy cases.[55] Monica and Madelaine had to sleep downstairs in the front room while strangers often slept in their room and sometimes wore their clothes: 'We didn't like it and I'm ashamed that we didn't like it, but I suppose children are put out by an invasion in their home and in looking back I can see that my parents were really trying to do something good and useful'. Those experiences found their way into *Milk and Honey* with its 'shadows and the weeping of people my mother and father tried to help before and during the second world war' ('"What Sins"' 5).

Irma Roitman was one such person, although not Jewish. When her Jewish husband, anticipating trouble in Austria, decided that the family should leave Vienna, he went to the United States, the older son to India, the daughter to Holland, and Roitman and her younger son, Pauli, to Birmingham. The result was a titanomachy, Roitman's presence in the Knight home an equal challenge to both women. One was determined and the other indomitable, but it was not clear which was which. They had intelligence, language, nationality, class and age in common (though Roitman was four years older); each had experienced life as a young woman in wartime, and each had a young family to look after in another war. Some intimacy was possible between them, Margarete Knight confiding that she was not happy with England or with her marriage.[56] But if Margarete Knight had to tolerate a woman in her home, one with close Jewish connections at that, she was resolute in using her home-town advantage to determine outcomes, for example by trying to send Pauli Roitman to a boarding school of Knight's choice, against Roitman's wishes.

In the end, Irma found a job as a housekeeper and moved out, eventually returning to Vienna. The two women kept in touch until their deaths, Roitman visiting the Knights in Wolverhampton from time to time, and their daughter Monica in Australia in the 1970s. But the relationship between the two remained like that of superannuated generals who had served on opposite sides, the presence of each validating the self-worth of the other. A legacy of such relationships may be the Hilde and Irma who appear in the novel *Palomino*. Further, the central character in 'Paper Children', a story about a young Australian woman terrorised by a visit from her Viennese mother, named Clara Carolina Schultz (compare with [Margarete] Johanna Carolina Fehr) seems based on Irma Roitman, who in turn seems a metonym for Margarete Knight.

> *I had a very good teacher, the best teacher you can imagine, Mrs Knight.*
> Gottfried Leiser[57]

> *You were taking cups + saucers into the kitchen + you were singing:* zu Hilfe . . . sonst bin ich verloren!
> Margarete Fehr to ex-student Gabriel Horn[58]

For Margarete Knight, male acquaintances were quite another matter.

In the 1940s Gottfried Leiser, a paratrooper in the German Air Force who was captured by the Allies in March 1945, spent the next three years as a prisoner of war in various camps in the West Midlands. His industrious mother enlisted the aid of her family and friendship circle, her sister contacting a friend in Kitzingen—Marie Stapf Kemmeter—and then in July 1946 Leiser was visited in his camp by Margarete Knight. From then on she went to visit him on the last Saturday of each month.

She loaned the family piano to the German soldiers in the camp and, since POWs in England were let out of custody periodically, Leiser was able to visit the Knights at their home from May 1947, which he did about twice a month, on Sundays. Sometimes he did so with fellow-prisoner Max Knöfel, the two men riding bicycles the Knights had also provided. She would prepare a noontime meal and organise entertainment by way of visitors or an opera-listening session—Knöfel remembered one devoted to Mozart's *Die Zauberflöte*, and Leiser recalled an after-dinner conversation celebrating the BBC broadcast of 'The Adventures of George Henry the Caterpillar'. A children's short story written by Monica Knight, her first-ever professional publication was broadcast in August 1947.

Monica and Madelaine were uneasy that their mother referred to the handsome Leiser as 'Goldilocks'. Max Knöfel, friendlier with Wilfrid than Margarete, said she ruled the household, needing to be the centre of attention, especially the attention of male admirers—she inveigled him into helping her dry the dishes, a new and flattering experience for him. But, he said, the fuss she made over Leiser made him uncomfortable. Leiser, too, was aware of her controlling nature, remembering that Margarete Knight always was trying to get people married and that, when she later visited him in Schweinfurt, Germany, she seemed to be passing judgement on his new wife.[59]

During the same period as she was tutoring Leiser, Margarete Knight was also coaching Gabriel Horn, her favourite English student. After matriculating from Birmingham Tech, he decided that he wanted to read medicine, something that his education had not qualified him to do, and so he took extracurricular measures. They included his studying German with Margarete Knight at Aston Tech from the mid-1940s. It did not start off well because he and a schoolmate initially presented as smart alecs, but that did not faze Margarete who took them aside and sharply corrected them. Twenty-year-old Horn, at first affronted at being treated like a child, quickly came to regard her highly enough to send a belated card for her birthday in 1946 when she was fifty-two, having wheedled the birth date out of the departmental secretary.

Like Gottfried Leiser, Horn considered her an excellent teacher and recalls her using Lieder as an instructional device—as a result, *Die Zauberflöte* remained a favourite for him too. For the rest of her life, they maintained an epistolary relationship supplemented with occasional telephone contact or visits when Horn was in Birmingham. Now a medical doctor, professor, and past Master of Sidney Sussex College, Cambridge, Sir Gabriel Horn remains unsure what motivated her interest and what his role in the household was: when he dined in Wells Road, with Margarete Knight at the head of the table and Wilfrid Knight at the other end, saying little, she would tell him, 'you must not be unnerved by this—Wilfrid is communing with God'. He felt that she was neither bringing him into nor excluding him from the family, nor presenting as a mother-substitute; he cannot remember ever kissing her on the cheek, as he always did with his mother and father, 'but, again, that may be wrong. Maybe when we did meet I always gave her just a little peck on the cheek'. He imagined her feelings toward him were 'what a rather proud aunt or mother might say to her child. She had aspirations for me . . . she wanted me to succeed'. Still, there seems something over-determined on Margarete Knight's part. In 1948 she sent him the *Oxford Book of German Poetry*, quoting from it in subsequent letters. And thirty years later her letters continued to have a flirtatious edge, as when she wrote, 'NO woman is good enough for you', or when, in her eighties, she wrote after his recent visit, 'you looked so handsome, clever and no-one can resist your charming smile'.[60]

> *Falling in love and winning love are often difficult tasks to overbearing and rebellious spirits <u>but to keep in love is also a business of some importance, to which both man and wife must bring kindness and goodwill</u>'.*
> Robert Louis Stevenson, Virginibus Puerisque *and Other Papers*,
> underlined by Kenneth Berrington[61]

And then there was Mr B.

Madelaine Knight asked why he continued to visit Margarete Knight when she could be so unpleasant to him. He said, 'Because I do not need to, I can leave when I want, and I don't have to come back'. As an adult, Monica wrote: 'Looking back on the way she treated him towards the end I realise that it is only when people have been very close, intimate is perhaps the word, that they can hurt each other as my mother repeatedly hurt Mr Berrington'; and continued, 'he was for a very long time *The Friend of the Family*. Perhaps it would be more accurate to say he was my mother's Friend' ('Mr Berrington' 32, Jolley's emphases).

Kenneth Berrington was both more ordinary and extraordinary than he presented. For one thing, his father was not always Richard Evans Willoughby Berrington, Gentleman, of 'Rosehaugh', Copthorne, in Shrewsbury, Salop, as shown on Berrington's birth certificate. Welsh-born Richard Evans was a plumber who at sixteen married a twenty-year-old woman who was five months pregnant and who died soon after the birth of their son. He represented himself as a water works manager on the census, a canny official revising the entry to 'plumber'. But in time he became a wealthy engineer-entrepreneur with offices in London and Birmingham, Manager of the Wolverhampton Waterworks, and Mayor of Wolverhampton in 1904–1905. Somewhere between Wales and Wolverhampton his name expanded.

Kenneth Clunes Berrington (his middle name his mother's surname), born 19 February 1884, left Pembroke College with a Bachelor of Arts and a Bachelor of Law degree and was admitted as a barrister to Lincoln's Inn. From September 1915 to 1919 he served with the Royal Army Service Corps, then practiced law on the Oxford Circuit (sitting on an Appeals Tribunal for conscientious objectors during World War II) and, finally, in 1948, when he was sixty-four, became Chair of the Appeals Tribunal of the Dudley District of the Ministry of National Insurance.

His achievements are respectable but not outstanding. He became neither the judge his father wanted him to be nor the stockbroker he wanted to be. He was not unlike Robert Louis Stevenson, whose *Virginibus Puerisque and Other Papers* he read and underlined after his father gave it to him for Christmas in 1903: Stevenson's father, a civil engineer, wanted his son to become a lighthouse engineer, but he would not do so. They compromised on law which the son, who led a bohemian life and despised bourgeois hypocrisy, never practised. Berrington and his father compromised on his becoming a barrister and Berrington, although apparently a conservative barrister, like Stevenson also exhibited bohemian tendencies.

One can only guess what his thrice-married father had in mind when he gave him the book, which translates as *Maidens and Boys*. In the event, Berrington's behaviour did not imitate that of his high-achieving father. He graduated with an ordinary BA instead of the Honours degree he easily could have had; and received an LLB in 1906 but did not take out the MA which was available just by paying a small fee. Likewise, he declined a military commission, enlisting as a private, a conspicuous decision since hardly anyone from Pembroke College entered the army below the rank of second lieutenant. He told Madelaine that he objected to the class assumptions on which military ranks were based.[62] What he did not tell her was that the Royal Army Service Corps was a preferred option for pacifists to serve as truck-drivers, as Berrington did. Trucks being more valuable than men, they were kept well behind the front lines, and so pacifists who were not conscientious objectors could perform their patriotic duty without having to kill people in the process. Declining a commission also meant that he would not have to order men to kill or be killed. Those decisions might explain his later service on the tribunal that heard the appeals of conscientious objectors.

Margarete Knight was attracted to older, intelligent men of real or apparent accomplishment, like Nansen, her uncles Alexander and Karl, her grandfather Joseph Edward Fehr, and the young Wilfrid Knight. Thus, as she did with her father, Walter Fehr, she elevated Berrington. It was not difficult to make him a King's Council, since his name could be represented as Berrington, KC,[63] nor was it hard to make him into a military man, since he held the 1914–15 Star, the British War Medal and the Allied Victory Medal, although every soldier who was in the right places long enough received those same medals. Gottfried Leiser recalled her explaining the term King's Council to him by distinguishing it from a solicitor and a barrister. Both Madelaine and Monica believed the story too, and he is depicted that way in the essay 'Mr Berrington' (33).

They met when he became a student in her Thursday night German class at Aston Technical College in the early 1930s, and they got on well enough for her to offer him private tuition at the Knight home in Wells Road. Soon he began to visit for lessons on Thursday afternoons and, later, for the Sunday midday meal. He and Wilfrid Knight would discuss the weather and the sermons at his St Paul's Anglican Church and Knight's Beckminster Methodist Church. Then Berrington and Margarete Knight would repair to the living room for their German lesson, or perhaps to his home at 32 Copthorne Road, a mile away. He soon came to be known to the family as 'Mr B'.

Six years older than Wilfrid and twelve years older than Margarete Knight, Berrington was a calm, unassuming man, fastidious and reserved in his manners, tastes and dress, a member of the Conservative Party. No doubt he and Wilfrid Knight had serious conversations that tested their philosophical, ethical and political positions, and certainly he suffered political diatribes from Margarete Knight who challenged his pro-British point of view from her own European one. Likewise, twenty-one-year-old Monica Knight challenged him from her own disingenuous position. She imagined allowing Germany to invade England in order to create a United States of England. For England to 'win', she argued, would be history repeating itself without effecting any basic change.

Reserved or shy as well as prudish, he could not bring himself to ask his housekeeper, Mrs Bartlett, to buy toilet paper for him, and so he asked Margarete Knight to do so. He also slept with his bedroom door closed and locked, as Wilfrid Knight and the police discovered the morning they found him dead in bed of a cerebral haemorrhage on 10 July 1953, after he failed to visit the previous Sunday. He was sixty-nine.

Berrington was Margarete Knight's touchstone for what constituted genteel behaviour, a worshipful attitude mocked in 'Mr Berrington' when the mother instructs her daughter to hold her silverware like Berrington and also to speak like him: '"Barth", she said, "and parth, you must say are, barth and parth, not bath and path". "Don't make me laff", I said'. The older Monica was able to reflect that 'Mr Berrington was remarkably generous', and that 'his generosity enabled my mother to re-establish her own good taste which she had suppressed in order to fit in with the dreary surroundings in which she found herself. She had her own dressmaker and Mr Berrington gave the impression, without actually saying anything, that he liked to see her in good-quality clothes'. She goes on, 'I do not know if my father minded. I never heard him make a critical remark. He often paid my mother compliments, perhaps putting into words the things Mr Berrington did not say' (35-6).

Although he did not become so bohemian as Stevenson, nonetheless Berrington's conduct with Margarete Knight sometimes presented as scandalous, particularly when they went abroad together. In the summer of 1936 he took Margarete and Madelaine on a trip to Austria, and in July 1938 he took her and Monica to Germany, booking one room for himself and another for mother and daughter in expensive hotels. Nor were these day trips, for the 1938 trip lasted a month and ranged some 1200 miles, from Aachen to Köln, Mainz, Frankfurt, Würzburg, Stuttgart, Friedrichshafen, Lindau, Konstanz, Tuttlingen, Böblingen, Mannhein, Saarbrücken and back.

Still, Berrington was not heedless of appearances, for not only did he arrange separate hotel rooms, but he also arranged for mother and daughter to meet him in London; and, for her part, Margarete Knight insisted to her daughters that they not tell anyone about their going with him. 'Perhaps my first realisation that it was not usual for a family to have a Friend like Mr Berrington came during the long golden summer in 1938' (36).

Madelaine Knight's guess, then and later, is that the special friendship was not a sexual one. She said her mother was always flirtatious, 'but not in a sexy way . . . she wanted to get their admiration, and she had this attractive personality and lovely blue eyes too'. She added, 'I think sex was too close for her—I think she just wanted someone like Mr Berrington to admire her enormously'. Of Berrington, she remarked, 'only a cad would have had an affair with Mother, and Mr Berrington was not a cad!' Monica's original belief was the same as Madelaine's, but she later came to the conclusion that they were surreptitious lovers.[64]

Whatever the sisters' conclusions as adults, Berrington's presence was a source of tension in the Knight household, at least to begin with. In 1933 Wilfrid Knight banned him from visiting because of the relationship, but Margarete persuaded him to relent. The pain and humiliation it caused him, when Margarete Knight was at Berrington's in Copthorne Road for German lessons, is clear: 'My father prowled, white-faced, up and down the hall' ('Mr Berrington' 36). And when Berrington took Margarete and Monica in the first-class carriage of the train to London for the boat trip to the continent, Knight separately took the train on a platform ticket and met them at the other end, white-faced:

> *Mr Berrington moves his folded rain coat from one arm to the other and holds open the door of the compartment for my mother and me to climb up. Before following us he shakes hands with my father and hopes he will have a pleasant journey back to the Midlands.*
>
> *As the train begins to move my father walks alongside on the platform. The train gathers speed and my father runs smiling and waving. His face, anxious and sad behind his smile, is the last thing I see.*
>
> 'Mr Berrington' (38)

Sixty years later the situation in *An Innocent Gentleman* echoes the one in the Knight household: with the permission of the husband Mr Henry Bell,

Mr Hawthorne—called 'Mr H.'—meets Mrs Muriel Bell who travels from Birmingham to London and, with permission or not, shares a hotel room with her when they attend Beethoven's suggestively named opera *Fidelio*.

'Mr Berrington' encourages further speculation on the nature of the triangle when Berrington sings '*Mann und Weib, und Weib und Mann*' as he and Margarete Knight do the dishes in the kitchen. It is a line from Mozart's *Die Zauberflöte* where Papageno looks for a woman (*Weib*) to be his wife. Perhaps Berrington makes 'half-hidden declarations' (36). Then the question is given an added fillip: 'When they sat together over a text, even if it was only a grammar, it could be said *Galeotto fu il libro e chi lo scrisse* [Galeotto was the name of the book, and he who wrote it], but it was many years before I realised this' (34). The passage is suggestive for not being a German one that they might have been studying but rather one in Italian, from Dante's *Inferno* (Canto V, line 137).

That passage tells of Virgil and Dante in the Fifth Circle of Hell coming upon Paolo and Francesca. The couple explain that they were condemned to be there because they had been reading the love story of Lancelot and Guinevere, when, in effect, the meaning became the matter—that is, when, they enacted the love they had been reading about Francesca making love with her husband's brother.[65] Thus readers are encouraged to speculate whether or not Margarete and Berrington reading together, 'even if only a grammar', suggests that they are lovers.

Adi Wimmer argues 'Mr Berrington' is an essay devoted to 'Margarete's adulterous relationship, grudgingly tolerated by her husband'.[66] The question of whether or not they are lovers can be argued either way. On the one hand, Wilfrid Knight and Kenneth Berrington were religious men, and Berrington and Margarete Knight were solid bourgeois citizens, she with a strong dislike of being touched. On the other hand, why would Berrington pay Madelaine's school fees at Sibford, take Margarete Knight and her daughters on long, expensive trips to the continent, and buy her fine clothing? How to explain the fact that Monica Knight resolved to be like him ('Mr Berrington' 37), and that Madelaine was broken-hearted when he died? And how to account for nearly £27,000—more than $1,000,000 today—he bequeathed to Margarete Knight when he died?[67]

Cad or King's Council is a false alternative in more ways than one. Surely the prior question is about love, not sex. That is, Kenneth Berrington and Wilfrid Knight might have been very similar men, the pacifist and the conscientious objector, the one emphasising justice and fealty to the state, the other virtue and love for God, both of them in love with the same person. Thus the remarkable conclusion in 'Of Butchers and Bilberry Baskets' that 'I began to understand that all war is wrong and that both my father and Mr Berrington loved my mother very much' (45).

Berrington did not die forlorn, but neither did he follow the unheroic path of marriage. He kept in love with Margarete Knight for twenty years, a business of importance to him, as he obliquely averred by singing *Mann und Weib*. His presence in the Knight household lasted until his death because it satisfied each person's need and so ultimately was more cohesive than divisive. It could only have occurred in the first place if everyone—Berrington, parents and children—was more or less preconditioned for such an arrangement and thereby prepared to respond positively to his being among them.

> *I am ashamed to think what unkind thoughts I have nursed for so long. I am 'changed', girlie, and am so thankful.*
> Wilfrid Knight to Monica Knight, 3 October 1938

> *I now have the 'golden touch' (the gift of God).*
> Wilfrid Knight to Monica Knight, 13 March 1939

Four defining events changed the Knight household in 1938.

The first occurred in late January when Madelaine, not yet fourteen, was assaulted in a field near the family home by an older boy. She managed to get away and do what she had been told by her parents, namely, to go straight to the police station and report the offence. Thus she was shattered by their response, for they were more concerned with blaming the dog Bobby for not intervening and about what the neighbours would think if the assault were reported in the newspaper. When she later went bicycling with her father, from whom she already felt distant, he counselled her to forget about it all. 'Clever and Pretty' contains a scene that recalls the assault, as does *An Innocent Gentleman*.[68]

The second event took place in August when Wilfrid Knight took Madelaine for a holiday in Bournemouth where they stayed with his uncle William Knight and his wife Sophie, parents of Wilfrid's favourite cousin Ewart. Ewart Knight introduced him to the Oxford Group, something Patti Knight, Wilfrid's mother, had been hoping for.[69] The Oxford Group was a conservative protestant movement begun in the 1920s in the United States and popular in North America, parts of Europe and South Africa in the 1930s, from 1938 being called Moral Rearmament. At first Wilfrid Knight was not impressed, perhaps because of its revivalist features. However, on his return home he started attending meetings of the Wolverhampton branch where the Oxford Group's four key principles of absolute purity, complete unselfishness, total honesty and unconditional love fired his imagination. One of the first things he did was withdraw all of his savings and, despite the remonstrations of the bank manager, give the money to someone he thought needed it more.

The third defining event was Wilfrid Knight's re-conversion to Methodism that led to his studying to become a lay preacher. It was something he accomplished quickly, starting as a Methodist local or lay preacher in July 1940, being fully accredited by January of 1941. Nearly twenty years after the fact, he had more than fully complied with his father's wishes that he complete further study and return to Methodism.

The result of his two conversions was a sea change. Anyone who had previously found him to be arrogant and dominant now discovered him to be earnest, self-effacing and servile. Not surprisingly, the extremes of his new behaviour had drawbacks: when he held Oxford Group meetings in Wells Road, Margarete Knight was not only discomfited by the unwanted guests in her home but also put off by their expectation that people should be totally honest about their past actions and present thoughts and feelings, especially regarding sexual matters.

The fourth event is the result of this last change: after he discussed the situation with his Wolverhampton Oxford Group, Wilfrid Knight decided to send Madelaine to Sibford, something much hoped-for by her and long overdue. With Kenneth Berrington paying her school fees, Madelaine and her sister were united there for the Autumn term of the 1938–1939 school year.

> *I am afraid when I am dead there won't be any parcels. D[addy] does not seem to bother, prayers and bible reading is all that matters to him . . .*
> Margarete Knight, posting the card game Happy Families
> to the Jolley family in Australia, 25 March 1961

> *I can walk and run and cycle and read and understand. I find life more interesting every day.*
> Wilfrid Knight, nearly 80, to Elizabeth Jolley, 9 April 1970

During the 1940s Wilfrid Knight continued teaching and preaching. Margarete Knight continued teaching (although she had no German classes allocated to her for the start of 1939[70]), working with her refugees, being involved with several women's groups, and tutoring at home after her retirement. Kenneth Berrington remained a fixture in the household until his death in the early 1950s.

Following his conversions, Wilfrid Knight wrote to Monica at Sibford, '[s]ome of my boys used to hate me (my fault) consciously or unconsciously . . . Now, all that is over: I like them (or love them) + they like me + will do anything for me.'[71] He retired in 1956, at sixty-five, but taught part-time until he was seventy-five. A teacher-training student who did not know him remarked, 'He was a little old man in his seventies who cycled to college and who tied his case to his bicycle with pieces of string, but he held his students spellbound and he illustrated every point with visual aids that he produced from his case. He is really a brilliant teacher who has it all!'[72]

He continued the two pastoral activities that made him feel more at one with himself that anything else, preaching and visiting hospitals. Preaching reduced to one or two services per year, filling in for someone else. But his hospital work went on until he died—never once having missed a Sunday visit to the patients in New Cross Hospital. When in his eighties, he reported that Mrs Powis was a 'changed woman' in only eight weeks, because of his prayers, but he was certain he hastened an elderly, blind woman's death when she scalded herself drinking the hot tea he gave her.[73] In his eighties, he could be seen pushing Tony Goring in his wheelchair through the streets of Wolverhampton—Goring, a young man he helped to join the Congregational Church, said Knight was a sober but happy man, that they talked about peace and seeing the world becoming a better place.[74] Knight helped three such men, and people reported seeing him pushing their wheelchairs far from home, rain or shine, day or night. Margarete Knight would worry when he was late home from such ministrations, writing that 'I was frightened in case he got knocked down by a car'.[75]

She retired from formal teaching at Aston Tech but occasionally tutored students at home. One of them was the son of an Iraqi general, Zuhair al Kalbani, who went on to study medicine at the University of Mosul, graduating at the head of his class when he received his bachelor degrees in medicine and in surgery; as she was with Gabriel Horn, she was very proud of him. She aged in more debilitating and dramatic ways than her husband.

In her eighties aching joints made it difficult for her to get in and out of cars, she could not carry bags, and had to go down the stairs on all fours.[76] She would rest, read, write letters and listen to music. All along she would complain, about how Wilfrid Knight was forgetful, lost things, got angry, forgot to pay income tax on his savings, and 'does not mind if the house falls down'.[77] He neglected her, she said, despite of how ill she was and 'how weak I am'. She wished she died, she told the doctor, 'because I cannot cope with all my responsibilities'.[78]

On 5 October 1977 Wilfrid Knight wrote to his daughter in Australia about a program with an 'eloquent radio-speaker on heavy lorry [traffic] and the state of our roads'. A week later, on 12 October, he started another letter to her, leaving it unfinished because, he wrote, he had to be on time for a dental appointment.[79] The next day Margarete Knight wrote to Gabriel Horn, acknowledging in the first paragraph his postcard from Spain, in the third thanking him for a carnation in her garden, and in the fourth telling him the French saying about civilisation stopping at the Pyrenees. The second paragraph, remarkable for its lack of animation, begins, 'Now I have to tell you that my husband was knocked down by a heavy lorry on Penn Rd., and killed instantly'. It goes on to say how good the neighbours were and how marvellous the police but fails to make clear that the event took place the day before, as he was returning from the dentist.[80]

The Wolverhampton *Express and Star* of 12 October carried an article on Wilfrid Knight headlined 'Poor Hearing Led to Accident', and two days later an obituary notice advised of funeral services at Beckminster Methodist Church followed by cremation: 'No Flowers by request. Donations to the Institute for the Blind'.[81] He died with £13 in his bank account.

The unhappy family responded to Wilfrid Knight's death each in her own way. Margarete Knight improvised a melodrama starring herself as the tragic, romantic heroine, and the rest of her friends and family played their accustomed roles. In the first act, she quarrelled with Madelaine over all of the details—identifying the body, attending the inquest, making the funeral arrangements, and deciding who should ride in the funeral car. Characteristically, she positioned the house-helper Helen Marsh in the middle of it all.

In the second act she blamed the lorry driver for recklessly speeding on a wet road, even though an off-duty policeman travelling behind the lorry supported the driver's claim of having honked and swerved to miss

Wilfrid Knight. Since the policeman was attempting to pass the lorry, she reasoned, he was speeding too and would have been guilty if he had blamed the truck driver.

Then the volte-face for the third act: she turned on all her charm for another policeman who came to the house to escort her to the morgue to identify the body. 'He was like a son when he took me into the little room to see D[addy] through a glass window', she wrote. And when he visited again to ask how she was holding up, she was sure he was 'just going to invite me for Christmas (he asked what I was doing at Christmas)'. But a neighbour and the bank manager arrived, and '[s]o he had to leave but he said he was calling again'.[82] In the same letter she encouraged her daughter to write to the policeman, including his name, badge number and address. A note on the outside of the envelope, said, 'I think he would be more a grandson in age than a son! He is quite young'. Half a world away, Elizabeth Jolley resisted the bizarre request to write to the policeman. Ever the placator, she wrote a letter of sympathy to the lorry driver who, she imagined, must feel awful.

In 1978 Margarete Knight began to give away things, to burn letters and personal effects.[83] In September she spent time in The Woodlands, a Quaker home not far from Wells Road, which she enjoyed for the attention from staff and visitors. However, after a few weeks she left when she discovered she had to sell her house to remain in the Quaker home, and the staff were not unhappy to see their imperious resident leave.[84] In October she wrote to say that 'death seems to avoid me', but Death stopped avoiding Margarete Knight in less than a year, arriving in the form of congestive heart failure that took her on the morning of 13 August 1979. Although Madelaine and her husband Tony Blackmore went straight to Wells Road, when they arrived a hostile Mrs Morris blamed Madelaine for not being there earlier, even though no one had telephoned her—it was as if the disapproval she sensed from her parents had transferred to the neighbours. Still, she proceeded 'exactly according to instructions' and had Margarete Knight cremated without a ceremony and without flowers on Friday 17 August, to predictable criticism. The same neighbours seemed to doubt her when Madelaine told them she had written to tell her sister of their mother's death. Uncle Ewart wrote to complain that Margarete did not have a 'proper' funeral.

All criticism fell on fertile ground, for Madelaine was knotted with worry about not having visited her mother the day before, and about having recently written to her sister blaming the mother for inflicting so much misery on her (Madelaine). Not even seeing her helpless and lifeless released Madelaine from feeling her mother's grip on her life.

Monica did not get to see her mother helpless or lifeless, for she did not attend the funeral. It would have been difficult and expensive to fly from Australia, and she had little motivation. A contretemps between them had occurred two years before, at the time of their common birthday, when Margarete Knight had refused to believe something she said. She scrawled across the back of her mother's 17 July 1977 air letter, '<u>Mother I'd like to tell you that you cannot tell me what I remember only I can know what I remember. I know that I never want to see you again because if I did I would lose my temper. You have not changed</u>'.[85]

Twenty-five years later Madelaine Blackmore could say, 'I can forgive her now from the distance but I couldn't then, she hurt me so often'. Elizabeth Jolley remarked, 'It was as though she felt deprived, as though all the love of Mr Berrington and my father was not enough. And of course I think she was disappointed in her daughters'.[86]

2

Sibford—If she can swim, it does not matter how deep the water is . . .

Perhaps the summers were remarkable because, in their difference, in their contrasting and in their confluence, they made one threshold.
'Of Butchers and Bilberry Baskets' (45)

Monica Knight—'Beaky' because of a nose like her father's, or 'Four-eyes' because of her eyeglasses—received two postcards from Adolph Hitler in 1938. They were in response to a letter she and fellow Sibford scholars had written in the hope of getting his autograph.[1] Sibford encouraged such initiatives.

While she was there she also maintained a lively correspondence with several continental penfriends around her age, like Charles-Fleury 'Charly' Mews in Germany, a train porter and later a ship steward. He told her of his trips to the United States and South Africa and, aware of her travel to Germany, wondered if they might meet in Berlin. In November of 1938 he wrote, 'I am looking forward to your coming to Berlin on Christmas and I am sure we shall have a good time together. We shall also have a fine Christmas-tree which is a novelty for you as you have mistletoe in England', adding hopefully, 'You know the customs about the mistletoe!!!'

In her last year of school Monica and her friends also corresponded with Steffi Bauer, a young Jewish, Polish-born Austrian woman in a camp at 'La Distillerie', a cognac factory near Montguyon in Charente-Maritime in western France. France had been inundated from the east with Jews fleeing Hitler and from the south with international Republican freedom fighters fleeing Franco after he gained the upper hand in the Spanish Civil War. Sibford provided its students with a halfpenny a week for postage to write to such people in distress. Bauer said that their letter, although a joy to receive, made her reflect on how the winter that meant skating and sleighing to them—things she also previously delighted in—to her meant suffering. She knitted, she read, she slept on her straw palliasse and woke as tired as when she lay down. She worried for her parents who stayed in Austria when Hitler invaded, and she thought of relatives in other *Konzentrationslager*. And she concluded with the hope that their studies would prepare them to be people who worked to prevent others from having to live miserable and worry-filled lives.

Steffi Bauer's exhortation neatly previews a number of Monica Knight's future concerns: while 'doing life'—as a daughter, sister, wife, mother, grandmother, and as a nurse, writer and teacher of writing—she was, or soon would be, preoccupied with a world filled with people's miserable and worry-filled lives. Her schooling was the nexus that joined her home to that world, a world poised to enter the war that followed the recent one which was supposed to have ended all wars.

Monica Knight's stress in the previous year or two was different from Steffi Bauer's but nonetheless disorienting if not devastating in its own way. In the summer of 1933, when she turned ten, she had become aware that her mother's relationship with her 'Friend' Kenneth Berrington led her father to ban him from the household for a period. That awareness likely was a driver behind Monica's subsequent rebellious and disrespectful behaviour toward her mother that led to the decision to end her home schooling and send her to boarding school. As a result, Sibford served in loco parentis for her in much more than just the legal sense. In her memory the place and its people—the countryside and the school, the staff and the students, the formal and informal institutional and social interactions between and among them all—became her 'original' home, to be followed by two decades of institutions that served as pro tem homes.

Like many new students, she was homesick at first, perhaps more than many others, because she also felt an 'outsider' for not being a birthright Quaker, and also because she was unfamiliar with institutional schools' routines. Later she recalled standing, howling, in 'the changing light at the end of the autumn afternoon which reminded [me] of the time of day when my father would return, knock the carbide from his lamps on the doorstep and bring his bicycle into the safety of the scullery'.[2] At the same time, Sibford was ideally situated for her, at a distance she could cover on her bicycle on a fine day, perhaps staying overnight with her grandparents in Sparkbrook. Neither too close nor too far, it provided her with the separation she needed from the tension in her family, without the extreme sense of abandonment that some other students at Sibford might have felt. As hard as it was on her sister Madelaine to be kept at home, it was important for both of them to loosen that bond too.

A Quaker school near the Cotswolds, seven miles west of Banbury and about fifty miles south-southeast of Birmingham, Sibford was founded in 1842. Notes for a never-published centenary history say it was established as:

> *a school for the children of Friends disowned for 'marrying out', and for others not closely in membership of the Society. This in itself was a bold innovation. It was for many years an agricultural school, with a bias in its curriculum towards land work; later this became the famous Sibford trend to handicrafts, which provided in the scholastic world a valuable corrective to what became some years ago a dangerous tendency to over-emphasise the importance of bookwork and examination results, as against the training of hand and eye and character. Sibford has also been a co-educational school for a great many more years than most outside people will believe.*[3]

The school's motto is *Ye Menne of Sheep-Ford Wendath Whithersoever They Wilen*, or *Quo Volumus Vagamur* as it appears on the badge on Sibford scholars' jackets beneath a ship under sail, the image of an elm tree on its mainsail. And old scholars of Sibford School wandered far indeed. A hundred years after its establishment, some could be found in Australia—in Tasmania and New South Wales in the 1930s, and in Western Australia from the 1950s when Brian Southall and classmate Monica Knight independently immigrated there.

In its first hundred years, Sibford had only four Superintendents or Headmasters, each with a wife who played an active role in school life. From Sibford's beginning until 1880, Richard Routh gave it an agricultural emphasis, and then Robert B. Oddie enlarged the grounds and improved the facilities, attempting also to raise its educational standards. Next, in what Finch calls Sibford's 'golden age', there were James T. Harrod and his wife (1904–1930) as:

> the first truly academic Heads with a cultured and thoughtful outlook and an emphasis on developing the whole character of the child and to dispense education in its broadest possible sense. They understood very clearly the world at that time and introduced a great sense of international understanding to Sibford which it maintains until this day.[4]

Harrod came from fellow Friends school Sidcot near Bristol 'to work out an educational experiment at Sibford—education through handicraft—and brought such energy, enthusiasm and ability that he made of it a success that excited the great interest of the Board of Trade'.[5]

And then there were the Johnstones. E. Arthur and Jessie Johnstone—he called 'A. J.' or 'Tufty' and she 'Ma J.' by students—presided over Sibford in the 1930–1956 period. By that time the emphasis on agriculture had shifted to one on domestic and manual arts, like cooking and sewing and wood- and metalwork, subjects that were not treated as gendered activities at the school. To the extent that Arthur Johnstone was known and understood at all, he was not much liked and only grudgingly respected; Jessie Johnstone, better known, was less liked and not much respected by Monica's school mates.[6]

Michael Van Blankenstein damns with faint praise when he says the Headmaster 'could be labelled a somewhat eccentric autocrat but he did his best within his limitations, consistent with his personal philosophy and according to the standard of the day', going on to remark:

> It is impossible to say whether he had any strong social or political views and he seemed at times to lack intellectual acuity. His ex-pupils may recall him with curiosity and not a little fascination. He was certainly the boss, but he was no faceless bureaucrat. He probably did not engender much love or admiration, but it is very clear that deep down he really cared about Sibford, its pupils and its fortunes.[7]

And Monica Knight's fellow student Paul Eddington (later playing Jim Hacker in *Yes, Minister*) did not bother to pull his punches either when describing his first interview with Johnstone for his 1937 entry to Sibford:

> It was an interview calculated, I am sure, to instill in me a respect for A. J.'s authority. He appeared to be genuinely outraged by what he interpreted as my casual attitude. His ruddy complexion flushed purple, his eyes grew even smaller behind their gold-rimmed spectacles and his tuft of white hair quivered with anger. It would be

understating the case to write that I was dismayed; I was appalled and terrified. I had never, as a tenderly reared ten-year-old, been confronted by adult rage, particularly directed towards myself, and it set the tone of our relationship for the future.[8]

The result was the 'tremor of dread' he felt for Johnstone across all his six years at Sibford.

Still, Johnstone must be credited with promoting the creative arts at Sibford, a significant commitment given the fact that originally the Quaker school's down-to-earth ethic was set firmly against 'distractions'. Henry J. Randall, an early President of the Sibford Old Scholars' Association, wrote that in Routh's day 'a newspaper was looked upon as an evil thing, as was any musical instrument; even a Jew's harp was taken away from a boy, and another boy, Jonathan Chamber, was very severely punished for secreting a flute which he could play nicely'.[9] Johnstone's initiative met with approval by other old scholars of Routh's time, like E. Prideaux Lakeman who had left more than fifty years before: 'In reading some of the reports of the Old Scholars' meetings it rather staggers me to read of the dances, the music lessons, and, I presume, the boys and girls mixing together. I can hardly believe it . . . I am glad to see the changes that are now in vogue'.[10]

One of Johnstone's main accomplishments was to encourage staff to teach drama and otherwise to facilitate the students' appreciation of it. Thus Monica went on the school's trips to Stratford-on-Avon every term, seeing *She Stoops to Conquer* and half a dozen of Shakespeare's plays, *A Midsummer Night's Dream*, *As You Like It*, *Love's Labour's Lost*, *Twelfth Night*, *Julius Caesar*, and *Macbeth*, studying the latter for her leaving certificate. And Eddington recalls fondly 'austere' Miss Gladys M. Burgess, the English Mistress:

> *. . . at her hands I was seized by a passion for Shakespeare which has fortunately never left me. She also directed the school play, and it must have been her production of* The Wind in the Willows *that entranced me and reconciled me to the school in Penzance. I was later recruited for some of the plays myself and discovered that being on stage and making people laugh was the most tremendous fun and actually, it seemed to me, rather easy.*[11]

Monica too was cast in the production of *Toad of Toad Hall*, Sibford's version of *The Wind in the Willows*, as the neighing end of the horse, but she developed an inner-ear infection and had to be replaced. She had other opportunities for dramatic roles, though; in Hamburg in 1939 she was the other end of the beast, and later at Sibford she played Quince in *Pyramis and Thisby* and then Rapunzel in a 1940 play.[12]

Another of Johnstone's enthusiasms was to encourage the appreciation of music at Sibford. He employed two music teachers, Miss Dorothy G. Prior, ARCM, and Miss Ena Grubb, LRAM, and he would also invite students to listen to classical music records in his study or in the girls' Common Room in The Manor. That was an important experience for many of them, including Knight. She was alive to A. J.'s unpleasant ways and words, recalling that once, when he had the students on the lawn writing letters home, he announced that he 'could not stand that vulgar expanse of flesh'—meaning the space between the knee and the thigh—for, as he said, he feared something 'would raise its ugly head'.[13] But at the same time, she valued the great gift he gave her. More than fifty years later she wrote to her Sibford friend Edith Worrall, a fine singer, that 'I have always felt that my love of music came from his choral sessions [of hymns and carols]—when I listened with much pleasure to your voice singing solo—and those wonderful gramophone times when he played records and talked about music'.[14]

Moreover, she had special sympathy for Johnstone because she knew that, like her father, he had been a conscientious objector during World War I and had spent time breaking rocks in Dartmoor Prison. She believed that, as a result of that experience, he too carried on only with difficulty. 'Since then I have understood how a person can "put up with" difficulties and rise above them which is what he did all his life at Sibford. To me he has been an example of <u>endurance</u> which I have tried to emulate'.[15] It was characteristic of her to distinguish the motives of unpleasant behaviours, as well as to speak of endurance—endurance became a constant theme in her fiction, and something she would recur to in interviews.

Perhaps the best thing that can be said about the Johnstones is that their dour behaviour did not impede the transmission of a certain spirit which seems to have characterised the Sibford experience from Routh's time to Knight's. Sir Michael Sadler, an eminent educationalist, in his address 'The New Work of Sibford School' to the 1907 Friends' General Meeting, said students at Sibford benefitted from being among the men and women there who knew 'the secret of a quiet mind':

The distinctive marks of the Friendly tradition in education are naturalness, simplicity, and good sense. But the living power of that tradition lies in the principles which support and guide it, and those principles win their way to the heart by patience, by prayer, and through the persuasive power of personal example.[16]

It was the staff who did most to perpetuate that Sibford tradition among the 150 boarders and a handful of day students, boys and girls roughly equal in number, rising to more than 180 in 1940 with the influx of refugees from Europe.[17] They were a dedicated group of a dozen or so academics along with half a dozen office, grounds and catering staff. All of the teachers were single people who had to resign in order to get married. Most of the teachers were Friends, something unusual at the time, even in the other eight Quaker schools in England.

In 1935 there were thirteen teachers, counting Arthur Johnstone (Maths) and Jessie Johnstone (French). Three held diplomas, three held honours degrees and four held both, one had an associateship in Music and another a licentiate. Roland Herbert (Crafts [woodwork and metalwork]), who had no formal qualification, was nevertheless highly regarded as a teacher.[18] They ran a sound program of vocational and general academic disciplines, including Art, Biology, Chemistry, English, French, Geography, History, Mathematics, Metalwork, Music, Physics and Woodwork, along with a range of Domestic Science subjects, including Cookery, Gardening, Household and Personal Hygiene, Laundry, and Needlework. Fifth-form students were encouraged to sit the Oxford General School Certificate program, and all students were required to take Art, whether willing, gifted or not.

If most of the staff were Friends they were not necessarily friends as well.[19] They displayed the same range of temperaments and behaviours as would be found in any such group of older and younger men and women from different places who came to Sibford because times were tough and teaching jobs were scarce; if they held a qualification, their salary was £250 per year minus £60 for room and board. Misses Brigham and Prior tended to socialise together, but Pat Kenning was a loner who went for walks with her dog; Darlington was a respected academic and teacher who could be bad-tempered, Naylor was greatly admired, MacPherson much beloved, and Burgess was both.

Several of them particularly imprinted themselves on Monica Knight, especially Gladys Burgess (English Composition and Literature) with whom she remained in touch until Burgess died in 1988.[20] Burgess and Dorothy Brigham (History and Scripture) and Dorothy Prior (Music)—collectively 'The Big Three', individually 'The Bug', 'The Brig' and 'The Hag', all in their thirties—broadly inspired the Headmistress and her colleagues affectionately parodied in the novel *Miss Peabody's Inheritance*. Similarly, sixty years later she still was corresponding with Barrie Naylor and Sheila MacPherson Naylor, when they were in their nineties and their health was better than hers, Barrie still playing tennis. Naylor, MacPherson and the other teachers lived in the student residences, effectively serving as monitors and, if they were inclined, also as mentors. In addition, they each had a 'duty day' when they were responsible for the students' out-of-school behaviour, getting them up in the morning and putting them to bed. They had comparable weekend duty as well.

The rooms were freezing in winter because of what Eddington calls A. J.'s 'lunatic obsession with fresh air'. Predictably, the food—under Ma J.'s charge—was either bad or awful, depending on who described it: Eddington recalls supper as 'the most depressing meal of the day', saying that '[d]uring the hungriest part of the war it consisted of an enamel jug of watery cocoa and a trayful of pieces of bread and marge'.[21] His alarmed mother took him to a doctor who diagnosed clinical undernourishment. Years later Monica Knight wrote, 'we all thought that we were starving and the one thing we wanted was food', adding that '[a]ll the time I was at school I never had anything but dry bread for supper', but failing to say that they all had a snack before bed.[22] Both reported that the students would scavenge the fields for root vegetables—'Carrots were wonderful', he said, 'beetroot fine, turnips less so and raw potatoes quite unacceptable'. The perception of privation was not helped by seeing the staff at the head of each table served a different, specially cooked meal—an embarrassment to some of the staff—or by seeing the caretaker 'shoveling into the boiler out-of-date ration books'.

Upholding the long-standing tradition of boarding-school complaints, Theodora Sheppard, another Old Scholar who preceded Monica Knight by twenty years, implied that conditions were always thus at Sibford, and even worse during World War I: she made many of Knight's and Eddington's points about the food, including the transubstantiation of the butter into margarine.[23] She also remarked that in her day '[w]e generally had two eggs a year', in contrast to an egg per term recalled by Eddington or the egg per week reported by Sheila MacPherson Naylor—leading more cunning students to take the cooking class.[24] Though Margarete Knight urged her daughter to respect the value of clothes, stressing how difficult the times were, it would have been useless telling the hungry young scholars that Sibford was not a wealthy school, charging less than £100 per year for tuition, room and board in 1940, that the Depression had impoverished their parents, and that the war in Europe was taxing everything that was left. They could not help but recall, like Sheppard and Eddington, the apparition and the disappearance of an egg.

Monica and most of her female school friends seem especially to have appreciated Sibford's icons and traditions as counterbalances to its privations. Those icons included the ancient elm on the grounds that featured on the school crest and which was reverently replaced when it died. Another was one of the earliest indoor school swimming pools in England, at 15 by 30 feet considered immense when it was installed in 1862. In addition, there was a harmless unkempt local hermit, Theodore Lamb, who lived in a crudely made hut that had a penny-farthing bicycle as the gate in front—Monica once offered Lamb a comb, but he cryptically refused it as not being good enough. There were also two donkeys, Selena and Japheth, who pulled the gardener's cart and seemed always to have been there as the generations of students came and went. More bible-minded students remember Japheth as being named after one of Noah's three sons, others recalling the Japheth featured in 'The Noah Family', a 1920s British comic strip.

Sibford's emphasis on tradition fostered practices such as assigning nicknames that caricatured or ridiculed, like 'Beaky' and 'Four Eyes'. When Madelaine arrived, Monica called her 'Sancho' (pronounced 'Sank-o'), telling her that she would have to fetch and carry for her, like Don Quixote's offsider. Her other mates included 'Pecker', 'Barrel', 'Gleeb Glob' and 'Viola da Gamba', the latter referring unflatteringly to the girl's legs. Another tradition was the Pig Drive, Sunday walks through the countryside, junior students being accompanied by a staff member whereas senior students were allowed to go by themselves. And there were daily morning and evening prayers, along with Sunday meeting at the Friends' Meeting House in Sibford Gower—First- and Second-form students attending their own meetings in the school with a teacher in charge.

As age blurred the sharp edges and softened the strong contrasts of early experiences, many ex-students constructed Sibford as certain to please and sure to improve young people in need of mental or moral restoration. Its setting near the Cotswolds seemed an idyllic place where people led quiet uncomplicated lives in accord with basic Quaker principles related to simplicity, modesty and pacifism. For her part, after Monica Knight got over her homesickness and the Spartan conditions and came to know her teachers and to make some close friends, she became quite enthusiastic about Sibford's ethos and environs. That appreciation led her to write an undated hundred-word encomium on Sibford stationery in praise of its rural appeal, beginning:

> We have the most beautiful sunsets and evening skies. The sky behind is sometimes pale blue or green in which orange streaks run like wet paints. The little clouds above are small and blown and have rosy soft edges. The sky seems high and round like a great protecting roof... The shadows of the trees make ghostly shapes on the smooth white snow in the paddock...

Nonetheless, Sibford provided a different experience for different people.

Regarding the twin taboos of boarding school, sex and bullying, Eddington speculates that '[s]ex must have been a hideous and ever-present worry for the staff but so far as I know, they had little to worry about'.[25] He remembers 'the usual smutty talk and tentative experimentation in the dormitories' but that 'it was all very innocent'. He assumes that '[b]y the law of averages we must have had our quotas of homosexuals', but was unaware of such friendships, instead focusing his romantic interest on a younger girl, a situation that was regimented by the fact that, with respect to romance, '[w]e were chivalrous to a degree, and for a boy to touch a girl's breast on the outside of her stout school uniform was considered the ultimate in abandoned libertarianism'—Eddington recalls A. J. pulling him aside and, 'with a prurient curl of the lip', lecturing him on 'purity of both mind and body'. By contrast, he was aware of bullying at Sibford: 'For several terms a group of senior boys formed a gang which roamed the school after hours, picking on smaller boys to whom they had taken a dislike. Armed with cricket stumps they would then march their victims to a small dark storeroom at the end of one of the corridors, where some beating and other unpleasantness took place'.[26] And he recalls that a classmate vividly remembered such bullying many years later.

That student was James K. Baxter who had been deposited with his brother Terence at Sibford by his New Zealand pacifist-activist father, who then travelled in Scotland and Europe with his wife.[27] Baxter, who published his first book of poetry at eighteen and is still regarded by many as New Zealand's greatest poet, went on to become a man of extremes in belief and action, ranging at different times from bacchic excesses to puritanical privations. His biographer W. H. Oliver notes that at Sibford he 'was deeply shocked by the physical violence and sexual vigour of the dormitory', and illustrates the point with lines from one of Baxter's poems:

> O from sugared childhood came
> On to the watershed of tears
> With those small angular companions,
> Handler of the penis and the pen.
>   Hard to forgive them even now,
> Precursors of the adult nightmare . . .

Baxter goes on to speak in the poem of his tormentors, describing one as 'Nero of the dormitory' and another 'with the habits of a jaguar'. Oliver says that elsewhere Baxter 'refers rather cagily to "undesired sexual enlightenment", "barbarities of the dormitory", and "amateur sadists and sodomites"'.[28]

Knight, unlike Eddington, did not have any love interest of consequence. She seems to have had a boyfriend, or to have wished that some particular young man would be her boyfriend, but no one, including her sister, can remember his name. Naturally she had the sexual preoccupations to be expected in a post-pubertal young woman whose self-consciousness is heightened by being at boarding school. She was conscious of how some of the other girls were developing more quickly or abundantly—a feeling exacerbated by the fact that, as she unpacked for Spring Term 1940, one of her teachers chastised her for not including a brassiere among her other items of clothing. At the same time, she was also naive about sexual goings-on and did not know the meaning of 'bugger' until a student called 'Poig' enlightened her. And it was not until she was an adult that she remembered one of her teachers had a framed photograph in her room of another woman which later led her to wonder if the two women had a Sapphic relationship.[29]

However, Knight was aware of bullying, remembering that 'the other boys and girls were inclined to tease, which I found impossible. I couldn't bear being what they called "ragged"'.[30] And in her fiction she suggests that such ragging could involve sexual harassment. In *My Father's Moon* the narrator Vera and some junior students are coerced by older girls to go to Harper's Hill, which is out of bounds. After making their way there through a thicket which scratches and tears their clothes, they come into the open where the older girls spring on them, tie them up, push them down the steep slope of a quarry, and then pull off Bulge's knickers—'Her lumpy white thighs show about the tops of her brown woollen stockings'. The older girls run off with warnings not to tell, Bulge weeps silently, and Vera thinks 'the real hurt is something we cannot speak about' (34-5). When Amy declares she will report the incident, Vera cautions her: '"That's a bit too daring", I say, hoping she will do as she says' (36).

Whether or not actual Sibford experience informs the draft or the published version of the ragging scene, the point is that the fiction is fundamentally concerned about 'the real hurt . . . we cannot speak about'. At the end of *My Father's Moon*, Vera lies in bed after lights-out, 'longing for the cherishing words familiar in childhood' (38). That is, what she hopes for is not what she has—cherishing—for the pain continues. It is arguable that what she hopes for is always already lost, because such cherishing is more what we desire to have than anything we truly ever had.

> Plan for—
> —VICTORIOUS LIVING
> 1. I am SURE that there is a GOD.
> 2. He is not lacking in knowledge, wisdom and POWER for He made (and still operates) the whole universe, from the smallest electron to the most distant nebula.
> 3. As Jesus taught, this God calls Himself MY father, and cares for ME moment by moment—Nothing that interests me is too small for Him.
> 4. By using suitable <u>means</u> we can make UNLIMITED use of the POWER of God.
> 5. These means are:—
>   A. Total surrender of the WILL and the SELF.
>   B. CONSTANT prayer about the need of the moment whether for more faith (trust, confidence, reliance, dependence) that God is ACTIVE, or for more love to Him (and to His nature of <u>absolute</u> honesty, absolute love +c [etc.] +c) or for more love to those around us.

C. Expectation of God's <u>miraculous</u> dealings with us and through us.

D. The definite 'quiet time' in which God's guidance for the day is sought and DEFINITELY OBTAINED.

Letter from Wilfrid Knight to Monica Knight, c. 1938[31]

Monica Knight's religious habit of mind was formed at home under the influence of the Wilfrid Knight who identified with the Society of Friends during his post-imprisonment period, when he tended to be dour, melancholy, and even quick to anger. At that time, she admired him for his sober, sometimes sad, demeanour which suggested a long-suffering man. Her core beliefs were few and simple and, whether or not she knew it, related to several of the Ten Commandments: she believed in a benevolent anthropomorphic deity, but not a nicely-defined one; she loved and honoured her parents; and she believed killing was wrong and therefore all war was evil. The words and deeds of her parents, particularly her father, would have led her naturally to know that stealing, lying, and coveting your neighbour's goods were wrong. Slander would not have been a problem, her mother's jealous or elitist put-downs of others (like Aunt Daisy) making it unattractive. As for adultery or coveting a neighbour's spouse, it probably did not even become a concept for her until she was more precisely aware of how Kenneth Berrington had altered the family dynamics.

The 'Plan for VICTORIOUS LIVING' Wilfrid Knight sent to his daughter at Sibford suggests a man who in some significant way 'changed his mind' under the influence of the Oxford Group. His 'Plan' is clear and definite, optimistic and fervent, as well as pragmatic. It was compatible with Monica's being an outgoing, positive and confident young woman who, although frequently worried, would not let worry lead her to despair but would instead seek practical solutions.

Certainly her concerns and experiences while at Sibford never led to the religious fervour that characterised fellow student James Baxter's life. Her prayers, if devout, focused hopefully on her studies, her teachers and friends, and prudently on the weather and her health, three of them concluding with an urgent invocation for God to curb her warts. Likewise, she had a relaxed attitude about the Meetings at Sibford Gower that were more meditative than hortatory and, of course, at times boring. Rather than distract herself by attending to what those around her were doing, as Eddington did, she sometimes brought a novel instead of her hymn book to read. Something like John Buchan's popular novel *Huntingtower* allowed her to lose herself in the adventures of its street urchins in Glasgow.

There were also less formal occasions for the students to develop ethically and morally. For Monica, one of those occasions was a visit to the school by the famous pacifist and feminist Vera Brittain who had abandoned her studies at Oxford to train as a nursing auxiliary. The wartime deaths of her fiancé and her brother, along with her work with war-wounded soldiers in England, Malta and France—including German prisoners of war—led her to start a popular and controversial 'peace crusade' that became so effective the government blacklisted her and restricted her travel. In addition to attending her talks, she read Brittain's *Testament of Youth* (1933) and *Testament of Friendship* (1940) and was much impressed by them.

A comparable learning experience had some parallels with the situation in *Pride and Prejudice* (Chapter VII) where Mr Bennet makes clear that he does not want his daughters to socialise with the officers billeted in homes around Meryton at the time of the Napoleonic Wars. When a group of soldiers camped overnight outside the school in the late 1930s, A. J. forbade his Sibford girls to visit them. Bennet's concern ostensibly had a social basis, for he did not want his daughters to marry beneath their status, whereas Johnstone's prohibition claimed to have a moral one. But the concern of both, one a father and the other a symbolic father, did not speak directly to the prevailing interests of those girls whose youthful romantic inclinations were stirred by young men in uniforms and given an added frisson by the prospect of war:

> *Once during the mobilisation some soldiers camped by the pump immediately outside our school. Though told not to, we could not resist going out after dark into the freezing evening to stand by their fire and to exchange stories and trophies with these handsome men in their new uniforms. We took our supper, slices of dry bread, out to them. They accepted the offering with well-mannered gratefulness though it was clear they had plenty of nice things, like baked beans, which we did not have. They wrote, in their best writing, in our autograph books:* it's a grand life if you don't weaken and fight the good fight but don't fight too hard. *One of them gave me a button off his coat which I still have.*

'My First Editor' (29)

Elsewhere she tells of Johnstone's reaction:

> *We were all told we were not to go out and talk to the soldiers because we were brought up as pacifists in the school and war was wrong . . . But of course we did, all of us . . . The next day, of course, we were all put on what was called the 'all-day punishment' which was three freezing cold strip washes, not allowed to speak to each other, and go to bed straight after prep, that kind of punishment.*[32]

The thoroughness of the all-day punishment indicates how seriously Johnstone regarded the transgression, and the cold-water strip-washes suggest that in addition to encouraging a pacifist disposition he also wanted to dampen temptation.

The reader of *Pride and Prejudice* never finds out if Lydia Bennet learned anything from her father's concern, before or even after she married Wickham. Monica did not realise anything about Johnstone's either until after she left Sibford.

> *I hated the Quaker boarding school the first year, but I grew to love it very much.*
> Elizabeth Jolley (Headon 42)

The transition to formal schooling was something of a shock. In her first year her marks for effort/enthusiasm were half As and half Bs while those for achievement were mainly Bs, with four Cs and a D. But across her six years at Sibford she went from being a middle-C student to a solid-B student, although there was a conspicuous slump in her second-last year. During her eighteen terms at Sibford she excelled in Esperanto in her first year and Anatomy in her final year, receiving all A's. In the subjects she took over several years, she did best in Art, Biology, English, French, Geography, German, History and Science, poorly in Mathematics and worse in Woodwork—working on a tray in Spring term 1940 and producing a stool in Summer Term. In all she received three F's (in Domestic Science, History and Mathematics), thirty-two C's, ninety B's and twenty-one A's.

During that time she grew an inch and a half to 5' 7¾" and gained nearly a stone, to 143 pounds. And she had the usual health problems, like eye trouble in Spring 1935, and illnesses that confined her to The Ark or San (for Sanatorium) for a fortnight in Spring 1937, for a month in the Spring of 1938, and for ten days in the Autumn of 1938; and she was at home with German measles and then an inner-ear infection in the Spring of 1940. But nothing stopped her from engaging in sport, at first somewhat diffidently. She learned to swim, became proficient at cricket and tennis, and was considered very promising as a forward in hockey, being chosen as Vice Captain. Later, in 'My First Editor' she recalls the ups and downs of her hockey career: 'We played matches at country schools and against Village Ladies. Once, in order to avoid showing gaps, we sewed our brown woollen stockings to our knickers. As we ran about the field the result was disastrous' (29).

Her General Reports praise constant progress and achievement that correlate with her effort and enthusiasm, although they clearly imply that she would not do well to pursue a career in Mathematics or Woodwork. Both her sport and general reports also note that she would do better if she would talk less. Increasingly they use approving terms and phrases like 'helpful, courteous and unselfish' (Spring 1935), 'meets difficulty with cheerfulness and courage' (Autumn 1937), and 'a valuable influence in school life' (all three 1938–1939 terms). She was a Prefect in her last year, her final report, written by Johnstone and signed by him and Burgess, saying, 'She has been an excellent Prefect' and 'We are very sorry to lose her' (Summer 1940). In all, she seems to have been a student greatly cherished for being high-spirited and good-hearted.

> *I wrote stories, mainly about rabbits which were rather like people I knew, and sent them home to my sister. I made up stories to tell in the dormitory at night. I made for myself a picture of a longed-for cosy home life which never existed but which, in thought, comforted.*
>
> 'Self-Portrait: A Child Went Forth' (305)

The whole time Monica Knight was at Sibford she was an enthusiastic reader and that, coupled with Burgess' encouragement and advice, led to her writing. Outside of class, she read on average a book a fortnight—Trollope, More's *Utopia*, much of Dickens (*Oliver Twist*, *Great Expectations*, *Dombey and Son*) and all of George Eliot's novels, along with Dostoevsky's *Crime and Punishment* ('jolly good') and Ibsen's *Peer Gynt*. She read youth writers like Anne Hepple and Francis Brett Young ('marvellous'), popular writers like Daudet and Chesterton. She watched the film *Man about Town* and listened to recordings of Beethoven concertos and Dvořák's *New World Symphony*. As well, she attended the Banbury and District Musical Society's ninety-ninth concert in October 1939, where Elisabeth Schumann sang Brahms,

Mozart, Schubert and Strauss; and its one-hundredth concert the year later, performed by the London Philharmonic.

From Spring through Summer Term of 1939, at 'Age 15', she carefully created her own anthology by copying thirteen poems by nine writers into a red notebook, printing 'POEMS' on the cover and writing 'Monica Knight' above a flourish in the lower right-hand corner of the cover. They were Arnold's 'Scholar Gipsy', Brontë's 'No Coward Soul is Mine' and 'The Old Stoic', Brooke's 'The Soldier', Dixon's 'November', Goethe's 'Erlkönig', Hardy's 'Darkling Thrush', Owen's 'Anthem for Doomed Youth', Stevenson's 'Requiem', and Tennyson's 'Farewell', 'Break, Break, Break', 'Crossing the Bar', and 'Lady of Shallot [I-IV]'. Most Sibford students knew Rupert Brooke's and others' pacifist/anti-war poems, and still other poems were taught in class, like 'The Scholar Gipsy' on which she wrote a brief essay in January 1938. But the rest seem to be of her own choosing and were clearly favourites since she took the trouble to copy out thirty-seven pages of them. They are poems likely to appeal to a young girl, for they are romantic by inclination, most obviously in Tennyson's Arthurian 'Shallot' with its famous lovers and the suggestive 'indefiniteness of meaning' so admired by Edgar Allen Poe. Or they are Romantic by convention, with pastoral and autumnal images, self-devised epitaphs and Brontë's Stoic's imploring to have 'In life and death a chainless soul, / With courage to endure'. Some of the authors had a lifelong influence on her and were later quoted in her writing, including Hardy, whose complete works she reread in her seventies.

The inclusion of Brontë relates to the fact that she studied the women poets included in Binyon's *Golden Treasury* in Burgess' class, writing an essay on 'Some 19th Century Poems by Women Writers' for which she received A minus, one of her highest-ever marks from Burgess. She emphasised Brontë's 'great courage and faith', Elizabeth Barrett Browning's love for Robert Browning and also her 'hopeless despair', along with Mary Coleridge's observation that 'lovers must face the truth about each other'. If the essay begins naively ('It was in the early part of the 19th Century when women were recognised as being able to write poems and books'), it nonetheless shows her ability to focus on key features of those women's work, features that would also figure in her own.

She enjoyed writing essays and published her first piece at sixteen in Sibford's *The Owl*, on vitamins, to be followed by another on the elements needed for plant growth.[33] Those articles show her capacity to apply herself to scientific topics, and testify also to Darlington's strength in science, for the word 'vitamin' was only coined in 1911, and the other article is as much about hydroponics as photosynthesis. In Burgess' English class she also enjoyed the opportunity to go beyond standard précis-writing ('Strikes', 'The Attack on Newdegate'), topical essays (shopping, on motor tours), and the lit crit essay ('Cassius', 'Brutus') to something more like 'creative writing'. For example, in Sixth Form, when told to write on a set topic, she could not help but segue into her own fancies. Thereby an essay putatively on 'Friendship between Animals and Mankind' goes from analysis of boys trading animals, to old ladies curing a cat, to the faithfulness of the shepherd's dog and thence to the observation that 'nothing is more comforting than to whisper your sorrows into the soft pointed ears of a heavy farm-yard horse and then to feel him rubbing his head gently on your shoulder. As if he is saying—"I know how you feel and I'm very sorry for you"'.[34]

One of her free exercises for Burgess, 'Her First Minuet', written in June of 1939, has autobiographical elements in it, most obviously the fact that she makes the girl in the story her own age, sixteen. A more subtle touch is naming the girl Kemmeter after Marie Kemmeter, the German girl who worked as an au pair in Birmingham in the 1920s, sometimes looking after Monica and Madelaine as infants. She visited Kemmeter the year before she wrote the story, while in Germany at a youth camp for girls, where she discovered that Kemmeter had named one of her two boys after her father Wilfrid Knight. In the story, Anne Kemmeter wears a special dress to the dance her father has planned, her hair piled in ringlets and powdered—'A more beautiful sight can hardly be imagined'. Burgess thought it was 'Much too short but good' and gave it seven out of ten, the mark she gave Knight most of the time.

Years later she said that a number of experiences at Sibford helped her to become a writer of fiction, in addition to reading the assigned classics and magazines she found in the library, like *Punch*. She credits doing translations from French and German and having teachers read aloud to the students in class and before bedtime as being helpful. She even good-naturedly thanks the village postmistress for being her first editor because, when she drafted a Golden Jubilee telegram to her father, including words like 'congratulations, venerable, half a century, jubilee, beloved', the postmistress took the pencil and reduced it to *'loving birthday wishes'* followed by 'Monica' ('My First Editor' 29-30). And she often remarked in interviews that she thanked Arthur Johnstone for her lifelong habit of making the 'quick note' which she used as a writer and would recommend to her creative-writing students: every morning Johnstone would tell students to make a quick note for their weekly letters home to be written during a Sunday morning letter-writing session that he supervised.[35]

In her own time Monica let her imagination run on at greater length. For instance, when she was fifteen she wrote three untitled stories featuring Fluff, Jerry and Inky and collectively called 'Bunny School'.[36] Whether meant as children's stories or adult fables, they have both childish and mature elements in them. Regarding the former, Fluffy and his/her pals are of indeterminate gender (whereas the older characters are specifically mother figures), and there is a great preoccupation with having a warm place in which to sleep and getting enough to eat, the latter elements perhaps reflecting anxiety about room and board at Sibford; and there are also sinister elements appropriate to horror tales, like the widow's son-in-law, Douglas, an ominous green lizard who wears a 'nearly white' top hat and pink socks which in the third story, he says, catch on the stairs and prevent him from helping a dying widow.

But the mature elements are quite striking, the triptych skilfully mixing sameness and difference: each of the pieces is an adventure story that begins in daylight when the bunnies enter into a dark wood and cross a stream to some remote place where actual or metaphorical danger threatens. Most striking of all is the description in the final story where, 'As they mounted the hill, Fluff looked back over the Journey they had come' and, the narrator notes, 'The moon looked like a half sucked acid drop—not like an old man's face'. It is the most 'writerly' element in the three stories, as she likely knew, for she used the same image in her 100-word encomium about Sibford, saying, '... and to the east an almost full moon rises like a half sucked acid drop behind the bare black branches of the trees'.

Otherwise, she was not considered 'arty', nor did she present herself as such—she could not dance, sing, nor, despite lessons at home, play the piano. At Sibford she was not particularly good at art or craft or drama, and she seemed unaware that any of her fellow scholars took such work seriously. She did not know that James Baxter handed Barrie Naylor a poem a month for Naylor's encouragement and advice, but could recall that he had twelve toes and would wiggle them at the girls to make them scream. And she later wondered how Paul Eddington could have gone on to become such a talented actor, for she only remembered that 'he had such a little pointy head'.[37] Nonetheless, she was very serious about her writing, weaving into it elements of her reading and daily life, and accessing her own innermost thoughts while composing them. When she sent the Bunny School stories home to Madelaine, she said they were written while 'wishing to be out of the San and walking about in the woods and fields. The part about the Widdow [sic] was a bit like a dream I had'. The first and third Bunny stories feature '"Widder" Ward', a woman with a miserable and worry-filled life.

Her father's estimation of the stories was typical of him: 'splendid descriptions and choice of language'.[38]

What needs to be explained is why her studies went off the rails in her September 1938–June 1939 school year: her marks averaged C for all three terms, whereas they averaged B in all her other years.

In the autumn of 1938, she spent ten days in The Ark, losing five pounds while she was there, but Burgess' comment in her General Report does not cite that or anything else as the reason why, as she wrote, 'Monica is finding the work of this form difficult'. Next, in Spring Term, she lightened her load by dropping Geography, but her marks fell even further, to three Bs (Art, Science and Domestic Science) and three Cs (English, Geography and French). She had no health problems, and Burgess wrote that in English she was '[a] steady, conscientious worker' and that generally 'Monica has worked steadily and cheerfully and made progress. Her conduct is very good'. Then in Summer Term her marks improved slightly when she added German for another C, and her C in English returned to B. Her health remained good, and no one was otherwise fussed: Pat Kenning said she made good progress in tennis, and Burgess said she was 'a good influence in school life and is always willing to be helpful'.

The probable causal experience was the 'long golden summer in 1938' immediately preceding the start of the 1938–39 school year—described in 'Of Butchers and Bilberries'.[39] Then fifteen, Monica and her mother went to the continent with Mr Berrington for the month of June. Earlier in the year she and her mother, accompanied by Berrington, saw two films at the Odeon cinema in Wolverhampton, *Sisters* with Errol Flynn and *Algiers* ('Come with me to the Casbah') with Charles Boyer—Monica Knight fell in love with both of them, later writing that it was fortunate that the two men never met on screen, since thereby 'Fidelity was easy' (42). The 1938 trip to Germany challenged the Hollywood view of love and fidelity.

When in Lindau am Bodensee, Margarete Knight bought her daughter a dozen little dolls in sailor suits, which she played with as looked out of the hotel window at butchers in a shop across the street:

> *They wore flat blue hats and dark blue and white aprons. Their belts were strong and broad, leather, I thought. And their knives were worn on the hip, pushed neatly into wooden scabbards and drawn with gestures of fearlessness. The butchers pushed against each other with their bodies and they shoved the hanging carcases, slicing and boning with deft practised movements. Shoving and jostling shouldering meat from one place to another they sometimes paused to look up to my window. They waved and called out. I knew they were calling something friendly but I could not hear their voices. I waved to them and watched them and in my hands the little dolls, forgetting they were sailors, were dancing the butchers' dance. (43–4)*

Pouting, angry at Berrington's usurping her father's position, when her mother asked that she join her and Berrington for a trip to Bregenz, she responded, 'Why are we with him! I never said I wanted to be with him!' Turning to the window, and waving to the butchers, she said, 'I want *them*'. The while, staring out the window, not seeing the butchers, she was wishing her father would come, 'in his cloth cap and cycle clips, all the way up the long hills and through the mountain passes on his bicycle'.

She willed that Wilfrid Knight be a Shining Knight come to her rescue: 'It was a possibility', she thought (44).[40] Then Kenneth Berrington knocked on her door and asked if she would consider going with them, in order to make her mother happy. When she asked if it really mattered that much, he said, 'I think... that her happiness matters very much' (45). Within days, she resolved to try to be like him ('Mr Berrington' 37).

> *If she can swim, it does not matter how deep the water is.*
> Passer-by on seeing Monica at the Schwimmbad, Frankfurt 1937[41]

During Monica Knight's second long golden summer, that of 1939, she stayed in Hamburg with penfriends of her mother, journalists Hans and Frau Denie Lund (called the Beckers in 'Of Butchers'). Through them, Margarete

Knight had arranged for her to attend a 6–16 August *BDM* camp or *Bund Deutscher Mädel* (League of German Girls), a camp primarily concerned with forming friendships, socialising the young women and teaching them to work and play together.[42] At the beginning of August she and her mother took the train from Birmingham to Hull where Margarete Knight saw her daughter off aboard the *MS Caribia* on the thirty-three hour trip to Hamburg.

Conditions in Germany were even more severe than at Sibford. The Lunds had to live frugally, and Knight recalled how bad the food was at the camp: she managed to trade her inedible black bread for Lenchen Haake's barely edible grey bread, but she had to eat an improbable daily stew of green beans with unripe pears and little green apples. 'The Führer', she was told by the camp Führerin, 'eats green apples every day' (41). Nonetheless, she greatly enjoyed the various singing, dramatic and sporting activities—particularly the high jump—as her photographs show.[43]

She improved her German, and she expanded her friendship circle. The postcard she sent her parents and her sister on her first day at the camp said:

> It is very nice here at the Jugendherberge [youth hostel] and I am learning such a lot of German. I have two good friends, they are Magdalene Haake and Lisa Farms. Magdalene has two dark plaits but Lisa is very fair. Magdalena is 15 years old and Lisa 14 or 15, I don't know. Today we went to watch horse jumping and a sort of military parade with cannons . . .[44]

And she returned home from the camp with her notebook filled with the names, addresses, and birthdates of new-found German friends she vowed to stay in touch with. An alphabetical list of some of those young women opens her essay 'Of Butchers and Bilberry Baskets': Annelotte Biefeld, Gerda Böttcher, Inge Edelmann, Magdalene Haake, Rose Marie Haccius, and Renate Tybussek. She corresponded with a Lenchen Haake for a time, but their letters petered out after Monica failed to respond to hints about sending a food parcel.

Although Renate Tybussek did not write at all, Monica Knight could not forget her as the girl who followed her mother's firm instructions not to take off her black knickers the whole time she was there, even keeping them on under her nightgown (39). Today it is difficult to decide what was more remarkable, Renate's mother's anxiety or the daughter's unquestioning compliance. And it is impossible not to speculate about what happened to her and the other girls, although that is difficult to determine since some will have died and others become difficult to find on account of changing their names by marriage.

One of them went on to become a *Jungmädelführerin*, a leader of the *Deutsche Jungmädel*, an organisation ten- to fourteen-year-old Hamburg girls were required to join. Another strong-minded young woman married a man who was a disappointment and so divorced him, reverting to her maiden name. And a third, whose mother became a respected mayor in post-war Germany, became a university professor of child psychology. One said she had never been at the camp but was in Saxony the whole time, sent there by her parents who were fearful for her safety; and another said she was there, but after the time period Monica Knight was there. In 1999, shown Knight's notebook from 1939, those intelligent, sharp-minded women would not deny, but could not explain, the fact that their names, addresses and birth dates appear in it in their own handwriting.

Nearly fifty years later she wrote, '[t]he summer in Germany ended suddenly when I was rushed in an unreliable car to the docks and pushed on to a small ship, a cargo boat bound for Hull. Herr Becker, after incomprehensible discussion with the captain, threw my rucksack across to me' ('Of Butchers' 42). When she arrived aboard *Der Schwan* on Monday 21 August, there was no one to meet her, and so she used her return ticket to take the train to Wolverhampton by herself.

As planned, Wilfrid Knight took Monica and Madelaine on his motorcycle and sidecar for a trip they had planned to north Wales. When Hitler's troops invaded Poland while they were away, in the early morning of Sunday 4 September, they hurried home.[45] Back in Wolverhampton, with Berrington visiting as usual, Knight fell to his knees to pray, insisting, 'No, nothing so evil would happen again'.[46] A comparable scene appears in 'Clever and Pretty' where the chronology is changed to have both the invasion and the declaration of war take place while the father and his daughters are in Wales, serving as the climax to a narrative about a young army deserter who returns home where he sexually assaults the sister referred to as 'Pretty'.

'Mr Berrington' and 'Of Butchers and Bilberry Baskets', companion-piece meditations on the remarkable summers of 1938 and 1939, conclude with the complex realisation that 'it was then that I began to understand that all war is wrong and that both my father and Mr Berrington loved my mother very much' ('Of Butchers' 45).[47]

Monica Knight failed to meet Charly Mews in Berlin for Christmas 1939—the last she heard was from his 8 August 1938 postcard while she was at the camp in Hamburg, 'Wish best wishes to you', he wrote. In March 1940 she received and answered the letter from Steffi Bauer. In June, after seeing *She Stoops to Conquer* in Stratford, she left Sibford School, having finished her studies. Steffi Bauer, who never replied, turned out not to be a Jew in a concentration camp but a Jewish Austrian freedom fighter fleeing Franco with her medico-husband who was later killed in action. She died in 1992 in Vienna, having fought to prevent situations where people were forced to lead miserable and worry-filled lives.[48]

3

Pyrford—A nurse should be unable to make a mistake . . .

> *My mother felt that being a nurse was a bit vulgar but my father declared on several occasions that it was God's work. My mother said the material for my uniform, when it arrived, was simply pillow ticking. She said she had better things in mind for me, travelling on the continent, Europe, she said, studying art and ancient buildings and music.*
>
> 'But there's a war on', I said.
'Oh well, after the war'.
'Only Connect! (Part 1)' (26)

At the beginning of November 1939, Margarete Knight asked her daughter what she wanted to do when she left Sibford. They ought to think about it, she said.

It was a reasonable question. At Sibford, Monica Knight's best subject was English but she never spoke of becoming an English teacher, and the idea of writing for a living like Monica Ewer (after whom her father said she was named) was probably unthinkable even to herself. She did next best in Biology and displayed concern for the wellbeing of others, but other than that there was nothing until her last year at Sibford to suggest that she would want to pursue a career in the health profession as a curer or carer.

Her limited ability in Maths was counterbalanced by her success in Biology at Sibford, but on the externally administered Oxford School Certificate

Examination her overall performance was quite average. She wisely avoided Mathematics in that examination, and for the rest of her life she was unable to form more than a rough idea of what fractions and decimals were or what their purpose was. For her, budget-balancing remained an exercise of pocketing any windfalls or, more likely, making up shortfalls from her own pocket. Thus, her lifelong claim that she would have gone on to study medicine had Sibford offered more appropriate subjects—she gave Latin as an example—seems wishful thinking; that problem could have been solved by completing her secondary schooling at another Quaker institution, as fellow scholar Jean Sinclair did when she went on to The Mount in York in order to become a Biology teacher.[1] As for Monica Knight's wish to become a medical doctor, Mathematics itself would have remained an insoluble problem.

Her mother's questions might have focused her mind on the question of what she would do when she left Sibford in six months or so, and perhaps she discussed it with her parents over the Christmas holidays. Her father addressed the topic at the beginning of 1940, sending her a list of muscles along with a diagram of facial muscles from a Bilston school book. Then at the end of January, when she was confined to The Ark, she became an under-nurse for Ma Johnstone in Braithewaite, a girls' dormitory. Still another possible impetus for choosing nursing as her next step might have been the fact that she was ill from mid-March and then diagnosed with measles in April, a condition followed by otitis media. That experience led her to thank God for saving her from death, or at least deafness, in those pre-penicillin days.

She inquired of the St Thomas Hospital in London about admission to study in their general nursing course, only to discover that, at sixteen, she was too young for entry, although she was old enough to study orthopaedic nursing. Today, a male surgeon of the day says sixteen-year-old girls were not admitted to general nursing because it was thought they were too young to be exposed to death, a less likely occurrence in an orthopaedic hospital. A nurse of the day insists that younger women could not study regular nursing because it was feared that in a general hospital they would have to deal with men's genitals. In orthopaedic hospitals, both surgeon and nurse recall, male patients wore a diaper-like garment called a slip tied at the corners, but neither was forthcoming about how men without the use of arms washed or how those in full body casts relieved themselves.[2]

St Thomas sent an application form for their orthopaedic nursing course. When she started to fill it out, she encountered an unspoken tradition of

Nightingale hospitals, namely that they favoured young women from the upper end of the social spectrum: the form asked, 'How many servants does your family keep?' She was perplexed but, sensing that 'None' was unacceptable and not knowing what was more appropriate, she cautiously wrote 'Two'.[3] The question might have improved Margarete Knight's dim view of nursing as a profession, for she thought of nurses as being hard-hearted, although it is anyone's guess what she would have thought of her daughter's answer to the question. Completing the admission form, Monica Knight wrote 'Society of Friends' as her religion.

Apparently two servants would do, because she was accepted to study at the St Nicholas and St Martin's Hospitals in Pyrford, some twenty-five miles southwest of London, where St Thomas had relocated its orthopaedic ward on account of bombing taking place over London. Amy Sturge, the Quaker philanthropist who funded Monica Knight's study at Sibford, wrote to say she had provided a reference for her. She later said her sister Winifred Sturge, Headmistress of the Mount, had praised Monica's work during the epidemic at Sibford, when volunteers were wanted to assist in the nursing.

> *[A nurse] should be unable to make a mistake.*
> Evelyn Pearce, Preface to the 1937 *General Textbook of Nursing*.[4]

Built by the Church of England in the early 1900s, St Nicholas (for boys) and, 600 yards away, St Martin's (for girls) had begun as hospitals for Waifs and Strays, most of them suffering from surgical tuberculosis or the effects of poliomyelitis. By 1940, training at Pyrford was an education for women largely conducted by women, one that introduced trainee nurses to situations and responsibilities that home and dormitory life deferred. It did not presume to provide a liberal education to the extent that Sibford did, in that it did not encourage exploration or self-directed growth. Nurses were expected to learn without questioning and to act without thinking.

In that respect, Pyrford suited Knight—by convention in nursing, she was called by her last name—because she was, she wrote, 'completely naive' and thus, 'it was lucky that I went into the rather sheltered life of being looked after as what was called a "probationer nurse" because we were very much looked after'.[5] Pyrford prided itself on its heads-down, hands-on, disciplined approach, regarding some other hospitals (for example the Queen Elizabeth in Birmingham) as 'marriage factories'. But, like any intelligent, curious and imaginative young woman, Knight did not allow her education to get in the way of her learning.

The first her mother heard about Pyrford was when she received the package with the material for her daughter's uniforms.

Before traveling to Pyrford, Knight spent several days at the London home of her Sibford friend Peggy Yeoman who also had been accepted for study at St Nicholas and St Martin's. Delayed by an air raid in London, the two girls missed their train to Byfleet and then, on a later train, miscounted the stations to Byfleet and got off at Woking by mistake, having to take a bus back toward Pyrford. Arriving about 5:30 pm on Saturday 31 August 1940, Knight was given a cup of tea and a uniform and sent straight onto duty on the big boys' ward. At the end of her hectic, noisy shift she was exhausted and happy.

There was no training as such at Pyrford, and probationers simply learned by doing, that is, by doing what they were told to do. The hospital was well equipped, and the experienced staff well trained:

> *It had been made partly into a military hospital and the crippled children were crowded together so that in a ward for say, 25 to 30 children, there were about 65 . . . They were all crowded together and part of the hospital was taken over and equipped for soldiers. Then the emergencies . . . we were really not equipped for that in that people like me and the other girl that went from school had just arrived there and we were pushed into uniforms and sent on to the wards. I had not the faintest idea of what to do. It's true staff nurses and other nurses were there telling us.*[6]

Her study at home and Sibford could not have prepared her even to imagine some of the things she was to encounter during her time at Pyrford. Her further and higher education commenced immediately because overnight the nearby Vickers airplane factory was bombed by the Germans. The next day—Sunday—she learned a new type of fear, the sort caused by not finding a man's pulse, being told by the staff nurse, 'He's dying and you'll only find the heartbeat'. She also saw 'a body that's been steam-burned [which] is really very frightening'.[7]

That education involved her emotions as much as her intellect, and it continued even when she was transferred after a few days to the ward for crippled children. 'That was pretty rough too, because the children had been crippled and hidden away for many years and then brought to hospital. You don't see crippled children like this any longer because children aren't neglected. Well they were hidden because people were ashamed of them... the parents'. In fact, the learning curve was so steep that, she said, she would have left but for the fact that 'I didn't know how to so I stayed'.[8]

Patients on the adult orthopaedic ward fell into two categories, war-injured and regular medical. Those with war-related injuries included civilians, like an eighty-year-old woman who, during the night of the attack on the Vickers factory, fell onto an electric heater and burned herself badly. The soldiers comprised men with injuries acquired at home or abroad. Some of them had self-inflicted wounds which were among the worst because of their inept choice of the knee, for 'that is the worst joint to shoot'.[9] The regular medical patients included younger and older male and female orthopaedic patients with breaks and other injuries, with deformities needing repair, and with various joint ills, tubercular ones prominent among them.

Patients with long stays entertained themselves and socialised in various ways, reading, writing or studying, taking photographs or playing chess. Ambulatory patients or those in wheelchairs could play billiards or walk the two miles to Byfleet for a smoke and a drink at The Anchor. Long-term patients remained solitary or made friends, or formed themselves into groups—like Breakspeare, Connor and Dunn (they never used Christian names) who sat around discussing life and women, mainly women. Dunn, confined to a plaster 'boat' for years before Knight arrived, was there for years after she left.

Another long-term patient was a twenty-six-year-old pacifist, at first thought to have a tubercular hip but finally diagnosed as having rheumatoid arthritis. He had entered the Hackney Hospital in northeast London in April 1940 but, because of air raids on London, had been evacuated to Pyrford in June, where he would remain until October 1941.

From a poor family in Bromley-by-Bow where his father was a London City Missionary, he had received bursaries to the Coopers' Company School in Bow and then to University College London (UCL) where he received an MA in English and a Diploma in Librarianship. During his time at UCL he was a student radical who contemplated becoming a member of the Communist Party but instead joined the Society of Friends in March 1938 because of his strong pacifist beliefs. However, his pacifism might have been motivated as much by a fear of war as an objection to it: after hearing a visiting doctor lecture on Freud and 'A New Attitude to Illness', he speculated on the possibility that his illness was psychosomatic and provoked by the onset of World War II. Thus he analysed the various stages of his illness for their correspondence with the historical events leading to the war—for instance, *Kristallnacht* occurred the day before his hip pain started. His concern about being conscripted was so great that in May 1940 he applied to be registered as a conscientious objector, although it was hardly likely that he would be called up for military service since he could neither stand nor walk. Further, when a surgeon proposed (and later performed) a tenotomy, severing the tendons of toes 3–5 of the foot, he asked if the foot could be amputated instead.

In a plaster boat, like Dunn and the others, he hovered on the edge of the Breakspeare clique but felt intellectually superior to its members and diffident about discussing with them his stance as a conscientious objector. And not without reason, for another patient who heard of his pacifism said he ought to be shot. The only way he got away from them was when he was put outside with the tubercular patients who, according to the regime of the day, were treated like potted plants and left out of doors year round, brought inside only at night and in rough weather. As an alternative, he tried chatting with the better-educated chaplain Father Edward Rudolf about religion and politics, but was critical of the priest for smiling too much and having 'something of the forced manner all parsons have'. He also faulted him for not discussing controversial topics in his sermons, like pacifism.

He was the sort of person likely to be attractive to Knight for being an older, intelligent, educated, Quaker pacifist who, improbably, had a good collection of classical records and a wind-up gramophone (on loan from the otherwise despised Father Rudolf). However, he also had a fiancée who regularly visited, a young woman from Kent who had been at UCL with him where she was transformed from a member of the Plymouth Brethren to a liberal doubter like himself. He was also self-absorbed, with a tendency to blame others for his problems and to resent not being taken as seriously as he thought he should be. And he was a serial flirt, making it impossible to know what nurse he would next choose and why.

His journal describes one nurse as 'all of a piece throughout: physically + mentally + spiritually *integer vitae*'; another was 'the only one for whom I might possibly fall'; a third 'the only one to whom I could express anything of what I feel'; and still another 'full of life and . . . always smiling without affectation'. Since a patient's privacy was limited to an unlockable bedside table, his record of infatuations was sometimes recorded in transliterated Greek—'flirtation', for example, became ζλιϱτατιον. Nurses he favored received letters he carefully composed, boxes of chocolates he ordered in, and scarves he learned to make in occupational therapy. Such one-sided affairs lasted an average of three weeks and most often terminated when a nurse was transferred to another ward or left the hospital.

His first journal entry describing Knight remarks that she was 'the only person in the ward who understands me in the least'.[10] Two days later, she was 'very sweet, very young, girlish', but their exchanges remained firmly platonic.[11] They often discussed pacifism, the Society of Friends, and Christianity, including the significance of the Sermon on the Mount (a favourite of her father's). They also talked about music—she loaned him recordings of Beethoven's *Violin Concerto* and Mozart's *Eine Kleine Nachtmusik*, which pleased him, but he was angry when she gave him a bag of records and one of the disks was broken. Despite their common interests, he neglected to share his impression of her, and so she remained more a soul mate than a heart throb.

As for romance, although all the nurses were single (and had to resign if they married), some already had love interests nearby or farther off or even away with the forces overseas. Those who did not would hardly regard an orthopaedic hospital as the best place to find a man: many of the male patients were married; many were long-term patients; the shorter-term ones, on discharge, would be returning to where they had come from; and many would remain permanent invalids. Besides, the nurses worked long as well as hard. Day nurses worked from seven in the morning until nine at night with three hours off during the shift, and a day off per week, possibly having had to work the night before; and night nurses had only two nights off after nine days of work. If a nurse had a day *and* night off together, she needed permission to stay out overnight, as Knight sometimes did when she visited her Sibford school friend Libby Holden in Epsom.

Knight and Yeoman played hockey, tried unsuccessfully to keep a vegetable garden, and went to the cinema or took walks in the countryside.

> *We tried to be out of doors as much as possible because that's what you need when you're nursing, is fresh air. But otherwise you're in the ward atmosphere, or the theatre, or on night duty and then you're sleeping in the day, you know, you just would go out for fresh air.*

When she looked back at her Pyrford time, her view was that opportunities for boyfriends were 'absolutely hopeless', and that she had a very innocent youth.[12]

Knight was in awe of one of the senior nurses, Jean Sapcote, but feared Sapcote despised her.[13] That clearly was not the case, since Sapcote invited her home to meet her husband, and they remained friends until Sapcote died. Similarly, Knight was attracted to a high-spirited nurse named Joyce Broom from a strict Baptist background. She wrote in her recycled Sibford Form V Biology notebook, 'I wish I could see her again, I mean Broom, hair like spun gold and a throat as lovely as she is marvellous'. And for a year or two she kept a poem Broom wrote, beginning 'Spring's too fast— / So live in the present...'

Closeness between nurses is suggested in *My Father's Moon* when Vera wakes to hear singing, laughing and shrieking in the bathroom next door. Peering through a hole in the wall she sees tipsy X-ray technicians Snorter and Diamond dancing, bodies touching, and then bathing together. Vera says, '[t]he little dance, the bathroom dance, gives me an entirely new outlook'. Later Snorter enters the anaesthetic room with only one Wellington boot, her hair uncombed. She opens the old cricket bag containing her equipment, saying *'And on the beach undid his corded bales'*, the last line of Arnold's 'Scholar Gypsy', a poem Monica studied at Sibford. Vera surprises herself by responding *'Minuet du Salle de la Bain'* in reference to the 'bathroom dance'. Snorter rebuffs Vera's shy invitation to intimacy by correcting her pronunciation, and Vera responds, 'Oh yes, of course', muttered hastily: 'An apology' (*My Father's Moon* 57–9).

As for the senior nurses, Knight thought many of the older nurses were 'battle axes' who 'really took quite a pleasure in being cruel to you'. She said that such treatment, along with the strangeness of the new work and the long hours with few days off, 'was really very hard in that you felt such a fool all the time and, of course, you did get very tired, and sometimes the patients were not very pleasant because many of the patients were from a very rough background. The soldiers were better'.[14]

An exception to the norm was Matron Daisy Zunz, a quaint carryover from a previous tradition. A Belgian woman with her own maid, Annie, Zunz was remote but kind, leading Knight to realise later that 'when you are young you don't understand the kindness that's being shown to you and the care... that's being taken of you'.[15] Others—the battle axes—seemed to parody the control and efficiency that Florence Nightingale espoused, like the elderly but fearsome Sister Dawson who had a little dog and rode a bicycle between the two different hospital buildings. Called Madame Zopla by the men in the wards for using a surgical adhesive of that name as the medical equivalent of duct tape, she would strap a man to his boat in such a way that he could not fall out of it when the bed was tilted on its axis. Later she would remove the tape in one quick, agonising rip. Her farewell to the Quaker pacifist, heading for a commune on his discharge, was to tell him as he was leaving the hospital that he was lazy.[16]

Knight and Yeoman managed to modulate the hospital's structure of dominance by senior women over the junior ones to a small but significant extent. Given their commitment to equality as preached and practised at Sibford, they were offended by the tradition of new probationers serving the other nurses in the dining room: 'you sat at the very end of the dining table and before you could eat anything or have a cup of tea, porridge, whatever they were having, you had to serve all the other nurses; and if you were lucky you managed to gobble something to eat before the meal finished'.[17] After enduring the Pyrford system for a time, Knight and Yeoman told newly arrived probationers that they would not ask them to serve them as the nurses 'moved up the table'. She and Yeoman continued to serve meals, with the result that 'as we all moved up the table and round the dining room by the time we had finished there we had wiped out that custom'. Non-compliance, like compliance, was also stressful: 'It was really an ordeal that'.

The seventeen-year-old Sibford girls did not take on the doctors even though they could be as bad to the trainees, and even to patients, as the some of the nurses were. Knight's bête noire was Mr (later Sir) Rowley Bristow who had been with the Royal Army Medical Corps at Gallipoli and who played a Bad Doc role to Good Doc Ronald Furlong. In his late fifties, Bristow combined old-school arrogance with new-school talent: a pioneer in hip-replacement therapy, when his first patient had the bad grace to die of pneumonia some time after successful surgery, Bristow operated on the corpse and retrieved the prosthesis to display proudly in a cabinet in the hospital foyer. Although he was, according to her, an irascible surgeon, nonetheless she said 'every nurse should have one so that her knees will quake and her hands will shake'.[18]

She was speaking from a position of thrice-removed subservience in the hospital hierarchy that was a patriarchal system, as indicated by its gendered terms: the doctor was superior to the matron, who in turn was superior to sisters, who were above nurses. And nurses in the 1940s, especially probationer nurses, were required to perform in a wider zone than today: 'if you were a probationer or nurse you did EVERYTHING'.[19] They polished the brass faucets, doorknobs and window hardware in the wards, sometimes chided by the cleaners for not doing a good job; and they made beds, fed, bathed and toiletted the patients, and wheeled them off for X-ray or for therapy. Later in the course they also took temperatures, changed dressings and, initially under supervision, gave injections and drew blood. They were required to serve morning and afternoon drinks to the patients, take them their meals, and to make meals for other nurses on the wards.

Nurses were also expected to be more attentive to a patient's personal wants than today—the Quaker conscientious objector, for example, managed to get his nurses to run errands and do favours for him, buying his phonograph records, knitting wool and camera film in the village, and ironing his scarves at home. Nurses were even expected to kneel by a patient's bed and pray for his soul if they believed he was on the threshold of death, a ministration intended to evoke divine intervention, but one that imaginably might just as easily cause the patient to expire of fright or despair. At one end of the spectrum she was more like a maid than today's nurse, and at the other, more like an interceding angel.

Then as now, nurses or sisters were overworked, especially in this wartime period when there were fifty patients on the men's wards at St Nicholas and St Martin's. Too much time devoted by a nurse to one patient meant too little time available for another equally or more needy patient. Any possible friendship with patients had to be transacted on the run while bathing or toileting or conducting other procedures, with or without screens. And in any case nurses had their own homely domestic lives and attendant hopes and worries to preoccupy them when they left the hospital after their long day or night shifts.

There is a connection between nursing and writing. Both require a gaze which is searching and undisturbedly compassionate and yet detached.

'Little Herb of Self-Heal' (51)

One of Knight's particular preoccupations was her writing, as exemplified by 'Lehmann Sieber', a story she wrote out of homesickness soon after she started nurse training. Her reference to home is significant, for the story explores the nature of the family and discovers tension within it that suggests broader societal dysfunction. Allusion to home is signaled by five things: the mother's name Emmi could refer to her mother's friend Emmy[20]; the daughter's name is Anne, like the Anne Kemmeter in Monica Knight's 'Her First Minuet' (written at Sibford) who was named after the Marie Stapf Kemmeter of her childhood; Kemmeter came from Magdeburg, one of the two cities named in the story; one of Kemmeter's sons was named Hans, a character in the tale; and the title of the story is an amalgam of the names of two of the girls from the Hamburg *Bund Deutscher Mädel* (Ingeborg Lehmann and Ilse Siebert), Knight's summer-camp friends in Germany the previous summer.

Like her earlier efforts, 'Lehmann Sieber' exhibits Knight's focus on family or family-like groups. It also uses dialect and is attentive to detail, employing nature imagery for symbolic purposes, in this case using 'Father Tree' and 'Mother Tree' to tell everyone when it is time to go to bed—she has nature model what family behaviour should be. With description reminiscent of the 'Bunny School', the story depicts an idyllic scene near Dresden:

> *A large red sun was setting behind the pine trees when little Max climbed over the fallen tree trunks to join the bearded Father. Over one shoulder he carried his axe and on the other shoulder sat Max grasping the curly head for safety. In this way the pair descended the mountain side on their way home to the wooden painted house. The woods were dark and a gathering wind rustled in the tree tops . . .*
>
> *A small path led them through the trees till they [father and son] came to a clearing through which a small mountain stream danced and tumbled, to the right was the house, the heavy wooden door stood open [and] a friendly patch of light lay on the ground.*

Inside, there is an idealised family: Hans the woodcutter husband, the young son Max, and the three women whose lives are centred on the hearth—the housekeeping mother Emmi, and the two older daughters, Anna and Karinchen.

The family is structurally like the Knight household except for the added son. Max is the centre of focus and the major discordant element in the drama. Presumably innocent and pure of heart, he nonetheless displays exuberant behaviour that threatens to become something else as he drives his sister/horse about the house with a whip. Such a scene recalls literary counterparts, like Vronsky beating his horse in wartime *Anna Karenina* or Gerald doing the same in peacetime *Women in Love*, or even Freud's essay 'A Child Is Being Beaten', and so might suggest the sexual undertones of such paradigmatic works. But one need not look so far, because comparable scenes occur in her other writings. For instance, in a short descriptive essay she wrote in a Sibford notebook when she was thirteen, a drunken greengrocer comes out of a pub and whips his fallen cart-pony until it cannot rise. And there is the much-ashamed character in her adult story 'The Jarrah Thieves' who confesses to having whipped his bread-cart horse in a comparable way (81).

It is only in the last paragraph—after the evening meal, sleepy Max in bed, the girls sewing, and Emmi knitting as Hans starts to doze—that the other discordant element is introduced, when Emmi tells of a letter she received from her sister in Magdeburg saying that she and their mother are moving to Dresden. The story closes with Emmi's remark, 'This of course means that they are considerably nearer now and we shall be able to see them more often. I am extremely excited'. No one responds to her announcement, perhaps because its choice of 'nearer' rather than 'near' triggers the reader's sense of Emmi's apparent ambivalence about her sibling and/or mother—something that is underscored when the reader is told in the last line that Emmi '<u>almost</u> got up and danced around the kitchen' (emphasis added).

Whatever its merits, 'Lehmann Sieber' exhibits her promise as a writer of fiction, and it is of interest for reading like an early meditation on the Knight household and her own experience within it. It is more like a fable than an allegory, one embodying floating anxiety about the potential for family harmony to be disrupted from within or without. The anxiety could be explained by the events leading her to being sent to Sibford, her ambivalence about her mother's relationship with Kenneth Berrington, and her recent trip to Germany where she met the girls at the camp in Hamburg and where Marie Kemmeter visited her.

If the Hamburg summer camp introduced Knight to further socialisation in the company of young women, something she obviously enjoyed, it was socialisation more in the service of state than of God, and it was implicitly at odds with Sibford's Quaker pacifist ideals. As she makes clear in 'Of Butchers and Bilberry Baskets', the experience, suffused with Hitler's aura, was equivocally inspiring at the beginning but then ominously so when Hans Becker/Lund hurried her onto the steamer back to England. Finally, when she was back with her family in Wolverhampton, the undercurrent of the experience surfaced when Germany invaded Poland and, as her father fell sobbing to his knees, Great Britain and France declared war on Germany.

> *A shape with lion body and the head of a man,*
> *A gaze blank and pitiless as the sun,*
> *Is moving its slow thighs, while all about it*
> *Reel shadows of the indignant desert birds.*
> William Butler Yeats, 'The Second Coming', lines 14-17.

'Lehmann Sieber' was written at a time when Knight's own sense of how things fall apart was emphatically confirmed by the sound of frequent air raids overhead. On fifty-seven consecutive nights the month after Knight arrived, German planes tried to bomb the Vickers aircraft factory three miles from Pyrford where defensive Hurricane fighters and offensive Wellington bombers were made. If the Germans hit the Vickers plant, they would kill the factory workers or injure them, in which case they would be brought to the hospital; if they hit the hospital, then innocent hospital staff and patients would be killed or injured, including the pacifist who, feet or no feet, had no way of escaping the war.

At Pyrford, looking back on Sibford, Knight remembered the excitement of mingling with the blush of handsome, cheeky soldiers gathered outside the school. Predictably, Johnstone's all-day punishment reinforced her memory of them but not his point about them. It was the experience of Pyrford that initiated the process of her internalising the lesson she would eventually have learned even without Johnstone, that despite the soldiers' looking handsome and cheerful, 'somehow though I knew war was quite wrong'.[21] Those young men were not unlike the young men in the dark blue hats and aprons she saw from the window of her hotel in Lindau am Bodensee in the summer of 1938, their knives 'pushed neatly into wooden scabbards and drawn with gestures of fearlessness' ('Of Butchers' 43). Defiantly, she had told her mother, 'I want *them*' (44). In the context of her first experience of love and war she was learning what it was she really wanted.

4

Birmingham—The most powerful thing in this life . . .

One of the most complete and satisfying moments in my life was when Trent, a rather large girl with very dark hair said to me 'What do you think is the most powerful thing in this life Wright' (we always used surnames). We were lying sprawled across her bed half dressed in untidy comfort and I replied almost without thinking 'Sex I suppose' and thereupon we embraced each other in a very close and intimate embrace which lasted for some seconds with the thrill of passion and satisfaction so warm and dear and so safe and final that for a while neither of us spoke and then we kissed tenderly and I went off to my own room which until then I had shared with some one else of whom I was very fond and of whom I shall be writing.
Vera, narrator of *A Feast of Life*

Monica Knight—still called Knight from Pyrford—passed her final orthopaedic examination at the St Nicholas and St Martin's Hospitals in Pyrford. Then she applied to be a trainee nurse in the three-year course at the Queen Elizabeth Hospital in Edgbaston, four miles south of central Birmingham and twelve miles from her home in Wolverhampton. On 150 acres of land donated by the Cadbury family, it was an impressive new 540-bed hospital designed to house nearly 600 students and staff, including 300 nurses (60 for every 100 patients, according to the formula of the day), 230 student nurses and 42 sisters, along with the Matron, Assistant Matron and their Charge Sisters.[1] Opened by the Queen Mother in 1938 and run in accord with Florence Nightingale's principles and practices, its motto was 'To heal; to teach; to learn'.

She was one of the 117 young women accepted into the 1943 Preliminary Training Scheme the QEH had been running since October 1938. In the first of three annual intakes for 1943, she entered on 5 January and so was identified with the 14th PTS. Trainees were provided with room and board and laundry, were paid about £40 per year (a figure increasing about ten percent per year throughout the course)[2], and were given a day off per week and a month's leave per year, usually taken in two fortnightly moieties. They worked 7 am–9 pm day shifts with four hours off during that time, or 9 pm–8 am night shifts for twelve nights, followed by three nights off; the first- and second-year trainees wore yellow uniforms, the third-years blue. They were instructed on personal hygiene (shave the axillae, use deodorant) and given advice and exhortations about their public behaviour (don't talk about patients on buses), but there was not a word on birth control. Unless they had a sleep-out pass, they were always on duty and had to be in their rooms in Nuffield House by 11 pm and present at breakfast for roll call by 6:40 am. When the nurses had seated themselves in their assigned areas, senior nurses closer to the servery and junior ones closer to the door, the dining-room door was locked.[3] Like the nurses, the trainees had to be single or resign if they wanted to marry. A trainee nurse's life was more regimented than a soldier's.

They were often hungry and usually tired, but generally they remained high-spirited. They relaxed and socialised in their rooms with their gramophones and radiogrammes, reading, or letter-writing to friends and family; they played tennis or cycled, walked to Five Ways for tea at Kunzles, for a treacle tart at Barrow's, or took a tram into Birmingham to shop at Marshall and Snellgroves or to eat in the Burlington Arcade. They went to theatres, cinemas and concert halls, and followed romantic interests as well as they could, given the strict dormitory rules.

Matron Catherine Smaldon, only thirty-five when she was appointed in 1940, was respected and revered as 'rather like Queen Elizabeth the Queen Mother, an educated intelligent and beautifully spoken lady'—Miss Snowdon, Matron of the Queen Hospital in *Miss Peabody's Inheritance* probably is based on Catherine Smaldon.[4] But the senior nurses were often feared and resented for their authoritarian and exacting ways.

Sometimes the probationers even hated particular nurses, as Knight did when Christmas Day of 1944 went wrong and she got into a contretemps with Senior Nurse Linday over Linday's patient. Linday told her off, bringing Knight to tears, causing her to work herself into a 'mental frenzy'. And sometimes they even hated a patient, but they had fun with them as well; and they played practical jokes on each other, Knight once hanging an effigy of a mother and baby from a beam with a note attached saying "'E done me wrong'.[5] Of the forty probationers in the 14th PTS, twenty-three of them went on to qualify as State Registered Nurses, but Knight was not among them.

If her previous training stood her in good stead, nonetheless at the QEH she was expected to learn and to do more than at Pyrford, an expectation that kept increasing because of the war. That expectation was supported by an impressive nurse-training innovation introduced by Matron Smaldon in 1943 to replace the traditional learn-as-you-go system, a method that inherently had a hit-or-miss quality about it. Called the Block Training System, Smaldon's original version was described by the 1944 *Nursing Times*:

> *12 weeks Preliminary Training School; 6 week's study each year with 1 week's revisions block to both the Preliminary examination and State Finals. Post-registration nurses did one week's introduction then followed the pattern from the second year.*[6]

So confident was she in the concept of theory-driven practice that she maintained the program throughout the war, despite its requiring the periodic withdrawal of the nurses from the wards. According to Clifford, 'she felt the advantages outweighed the disadvantages for all concerned'.[7]

Smaldon's confidence would have been rigorously tested as the hospital's load increased exponentially. By 1940 QEH beds had doubled to more than a thousand, and bed occupancies had increased from 3,000 in 1939 to more than 12,000 by 1943. In the four years from the evacuation of Dunkirk in June 1940 through to the end of 1944, nearly 14,000 civilians and soldiers passed through the operating theatre of the QEH.[8]

In early May 1944, without explanation, all civilian patients were transferred out of the hospital. The mystery was explained by Operation Overlord, which commenced on D-Day, Tuesday 6 June 1944, landing more than 150,000 allied soldiers in northern France. Two hundred and sixteen patients on stretchers arrived by train at the nearby Selly Oak station on

1: Fehr family home, Florianigasse 2, Vienna, VIII, late 19th century (water colour by 'Riffler').

2: Wilfrid Knight in his late twenties. 　　3: Margarete Fehr in her early twenties.

4: 'Flowermead', the Knights' first home of their own, c. 1925-1928.

5: Monica holding Madelaine at 'Flowermead'.

6: Madelaine and Monica and their father's Ariel, July 1931.

7: Margarete Fehr Knight, 1932.

8: Wilfrid Knight, 1932.

9: Kenneth Berrington.

10: "The Hill", Sibford School, 1939.

11: *Drei Führerinnen*, Inge Edelmann, Monica Knight and Lenchen Haake, August 1939.

12: Sibford scholars, Libby Holden, Ishbel Whittaker and Monica 'Beaky' Knight, 1939.

13: 'Waldhof' youth hostel, Wingst, Germany.

14: Monica Knight, c. 1939—'Soon that smile will be wiped from my face'.

15: St Nicholas and St Martin's orthopaedic and tubercular patients in courtyard, Pyrford, c. 1940-1942.

16: Father Rudolph listening to music with Leonard Jolley.

18: Monica Knight with child, Summer 1940.

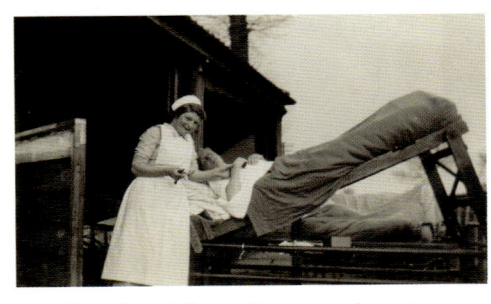

17: Close friend Joyce Broom with patient.

19: (Left) Monica Knight, trainee nurse, c. 1943.
20: (Bottom left) Gertrude Whele (1904-1957), Monica Knight's friend and mentor.
21: (Bottom right) Eleanor Ann Ellwood, 1940, a senior QEH nurse Knight much admired.

22: Fleetwood-Walker Home, 91 Hagley Rd, Edgbaston, Birmingham.

23: Guy Walker and Colin Fleetwood, in the late 1940s.

24: Peggy Frazer.

25: Edna Kenyatta (1910–1995), Monica Knight/Fielding's friend and confidante, early 1950s.

26: Elizabeth 'Strix' Strachan (1890–1962), late 1930s, proprietor of Pinewood from the early 1940s.

27: (Top) 48 Paisley Crescent, Edinburgh, the Jolleys' home, 1950-1956
28: (Left) John Broom, friend of the Jolleys, before a painting based on Robert Burns' poem 'The Deil's Awa Wi' The Exciseman'.
29: (Bottom) The Jolleys' home at 62 Abbey Drive, Glasgow, 1956-1959.

Wednesday evening, to be unloaded at the rate of two per minute and taken by ambulance to the QEH where doctors and nurses were on standby. They were patients who had been displaced from the Portsmouth hospital that received the first of more than 17,000 injured soldiers returned to England from the D-Day beaches.

Between Saturday and Monday 10–12 June 1944, convoys brought in another 500 wounded soldiers, some as young as fifteen: the equivalent of another full-hospital complement of patients arrived in less than a fortnight. Between June 1944 and March 1945 fifty-three convoys brought in more than 4,000 casualties. The second convoy had enemy combatants as well as allied ones, Knight finding Canadian, Finnish, French, German and Norwegian soldiers among them. Later she befriended a wounded Polish soldier named Elert, and was appalled to be told that his family had been shot because he deserted the German army to join the English one. Sympathetic to such a man who was despised by her nursing colleagues because he had been in the German army, she queried a patriotism that could not imagine that others might legitimately hold a different point of view; and she could not respect colleagues who hated Germans just because they did what they were told, for that was precisely what English soldiers did. For their part, some of those German prisoner-soldiers, especially the young ones, were so frightened that they feared their food was poisoned and would not eat until a nurse tried some of it first. And some of them were arrogant and defiant, especially the officers, like the Oxford-educated SS prisoner with badly damaged legs who alienated himself by telling his nurse what would happen to England when Germany defeated it: two armed guards were placed outside his door, as if he might escape, one amputated limb at a time.[9]

The twelve-hour QEH shifts were immediately changed to a rolling roster of eight hours on, eight hours off, eight hours on, seven days a week, with days off and sleeping-out passes cancelled. When some of her colleagues complained about the new regime, Knight was outraged that they would not make extraordinary efforts to help the extra number of foreign soldiers because they had been trying to maim and kill British ones. Similarly, she was angry at nurses who smugly regarded the large number of wounded enemy patients as an index of British success in combat. She could only think of what she regarded as the murder of hundreds and thousands of men and wish that their deaths could have been avoided. Worst, in her opinion, were nurses who made a less-than-wholehearted effort, like the blues (the senior nurses) who did not affix the German prisoners' bandages tightly enough, meaning she had to redo them. They so filled her with anger that it tested her pacificism.

Knight's nurse training and nursing work in Pyrford and Birmingham consolidated one of the intuitions she developed from her 'golden summers' of 1938 and 1939 in Germany, namely 'that all war is wrong'. If her correspondence with Charly Mews and her summer in Hamburg had humanised her image of would-be members of 'the enemy', including Marie Kemmeter, Hans and Denie Lund, and the young women she lived with at the youth camp, her work at St Nicholas and St Martin's and at the QEH incontrovertibly demonstrated the senseless harm war wrought on innocent civilians and on soldiers who were pawns in others' grand plans. In particular, her QEH experience showed, to her surprise and disgust, how even nursing friends could treat foreign soldiers as unworthy of the same sympathy and care they would normally give to their own. The conclusion was inevitable, that war was equally dehumanising to the opponents on all sides of the conflict.

Although the QEH was committed to the best practices of the day, some of the work of the nurses was like many of the menial tasks of their colleagues in Pyrford. For example, junior nurses washed cups and dishes, counted cutlery, served morning and evening cold and hot beverages to the patients, made beds, and cleaned basins, lockers and cupboards—one nurse was advised always to have a cloth in her hand so that she would look busy. Operating-theatre nurses had to cut and fold the gauze dressings, make the bandages, wash, patch and sterilise the rubber gloves and even recycle dull hypodermic needles for resharpening. An added touch was the requirement that they dismantle and oil the trolley wheels. Senior nurses had the dubious distinction of being the only ones trusted to test urine, a form of alchemy involving a Bunsen burner, test tubes, chemicals and a *'very small room'*.[10]

By contrast, some of the treatments were new and even revolutionary. CTAB (cetyl trimethyl ammonium bromide), a liquid detergent, was introduced, obviating the need for operating-theatre staff to wash their hands with a bar of soap for twenty minutes. And penicillin replaced the sulphonamide 'wonder drugs' from the late 1930s. Grown in jam jars at nearby Hollymoor Hospital, such small quantities were produced that the patients' urine was collected in order that the poorly metabolised drug in it could be recovered and reused. It was in such short supply that it could only be administered to soldiers, not even to hospital staff. A nurse whose thumb was so badly infected that amputation was contemplated was not treated with it and had to spend seven weeks in sick bay recovering.[11]

The week after Knight's twenty-first birthday, although she was technically not qualified to do so, she administered her first painful 5-cc injection of penicillin into the thigh of a soldier with gas gangrene, an often fatal subcutaneous infection that produces gas from the necrotising tissue. And an experimental technique for suturing nerves with human hair was successfully trialled by Dr Higham: a nurse would volunteer strands of her hair which were sterilised in an autoclave and used in place of the traditional surgical thread. Despite being so fine, it was strong, formed tight knots that did not slip or come undone, and ultimately was resorbed by the body.

Techniques new to her included perineal, bladder and stomach irrigations, along with an on-the-spot lesson conducted by one patient on how to insert and remove his glass eye. She was also fascinated by the intrigue surrounding thyroidectomies, operations whose success rate improved the more the patient was relaxed: the first day the patient would be prepped by shaving the neck area, painting it with iodine and then sedating him, but no more. When he awoke, the nurse would explain that the doctor had been called away or the operating theatre was unavailable. Called 'stealing the purse', it was a process that was repeated for several days until the patient, by then sure the operation would not take place, awoke without a thyroid gland. Another treatment new to her was actually an older one still in use by the QEH: instead of administering saline infusions and like treatments intravenously, they were given rectally, with mixed results. Still another treatment new to her was also old, although it was not in the textbooks, namely the use of maggots to cleanse wounds—an unsuspecting soldier named Arrison was frightened into a terrible state when he saw them crawl out of his bandages.

Knight enjoyed January and November 1944 stints on the babies' ward but nearly fainted when she watched ear, nose and throat dressings being done. A keen and confident learner, her skills continually improved to the point where she once performed a rectal washout when the sirens came on and the lights went off: only being alone in the dark was frightening for her. Ultimately she preferred being a casualty nurse, and she could play the 'fool nurse' when sent elsewhere, knowing that, if she pretended not to know anything she would be left in peace. But she was no fool, for Sister Hammond thought she was the best nurse on the ward and introduced Knight as her orthopaedic nurse to Hammond's visiting mother. Others praised her similarly.

Along the way she encountered situations for which there are no right names: relatives fainting at the sight of their loved ones, legless amputees, lying in half-length beds designed to facilitate attending to their stumps[12]; finding Mr Collett's tube blocked, Mrs Staycey's tube out and Mrs Thompson choked; never again hearing from her longest-term patient after he was transferred to Coventry—Knighty, a quiet brave man she bonded with, had had a tobacco tin blown into his hip; empathising with a patient who could not speak and could hardly breathe, wishing Mrs Thompson would die rather than suffer. She inadvertently fed Mr Sargent who should not have had a meal because he was scheduled for an operation and could be asphyxiated if he vomited under the anaesthesia, but she was too afraid to own up to having done so. Sometimes, to borrow from Dryden, the priest continued what the nurse began.[13]

Her opportunity to share such experiences and thoughts with her sister Madelaine was limited for she was preoccupied by her new role and Madelaine, who started a dispensing course after Sibford, met and then married Patrick Kennedy in April 1944, and drove a milk truck after that, filling in for men away at war. As she had done at Sibford and Pyrford, Knight made friends with those around her, some of them occasional roommates, probationer nurses including Pat Goode, Mary 'Dickie' Doyle, Norah 'Sticker' Harvey and Alix Macswiney—Harvey the source of the long blonde hair used as sutures in Highham's nerve surgery, and Macswiney a classmate from Sibford. They partied in their rooms, exchanged books and records, went for walks nearby and on shopping expeditions for toiletries and stockings, to do their banking or to have their shoes repaired. Sometimes Knight also cycled with Macswiney or Doyle or both to visit Jolley's grandmother in Shirley, or Gertrude Whele, her mother's friend in Seisdon. Or they would stay overnight with Knight's family in Wolverhampton where they were fed by her mother, entertained by Margarete Knight's record collection, and allowed to sleep in late the next day. Alix Macswiney became a Knight family favourite and would sometimes visit Wolverhampton on her own.

Knight's interest in the arts continued. She went to a ballet with her mother and her sister and Madelaine's fiancé to see *Les Sylphides* and *Twelfth Night* and to a concert to hear Smetana's *The Kiss* and the waltz from

Tchaikovsky's *Sleeping Beauty*. Her favorite music included Beethoven's *Third Piano Concerto*, *Seventh Symphony* and *Moonlight Sonata*, Mozart's *Eine kleine Nachtmusik*, and Mendelssohn's *Violin Concerto*. Her light reading included books like Daisy Ashford's *The Young Visitor*, Monica Dickens' *One Pair of Feet*, and Albert Schweitzer's *At the Edge of the Primeval Forest*. Her more serious reading was considerable, a book or two a month of classics that ran from Austen to Zweig.[14]

Early in her QEH career she complained about her inability to write and expressed the hope that she would one day become famous. In the first week of February 1944 she worried that she had not written anything for weeks and so a week later she started a story about teapots, milk jugs and cruets in the cupboard. By June she was working on the 'Kitchen Knife', by November on 'The Man Who Was Poor', 'Rodney Cheebes [later Stone]', and 'The Bath'; and, by December, on 'The Square Peg'.

She had high hopes for 'The Bath', sending it off to *Lilliput* magazine in London, having read a copy of the magazine in late November 1944. In early December she received a formal but cordial rejection slip, her response to it juggling strong passion with good judgement: she wanted to make the editor feel sorry but at the same time conceded that the piece was probably no good. None of the pieces was ever published, but she continued to work on them and they remain in a neatly typed pile of manuscripts in the Mitchell Library in Sydney.

> [T]here are many relationships that really cannot stand the intruder. And this could be on any level, just the ordinary superficial level, or the family level, or a close relationship. A relationship between two people that cannot take any kind of other person coming in is a distorted one, really, and many people live in a sort of distortion, but they don't know it.
>
> Elizabeth Jolley (Willbanks 115)

While at the Queen Elizabeth, nineteen-year-old Knight also developed love interests that became increasingly overlapping and complicated, distracting and distressing, and above all time-consuming. Her affairs of the heart while at the QEH eventually formed the basis of the second conclusion of 'Of Butchers and Bilberries', namely, about the meanings and implications of two people romantically loving a third, as Wilfrid Knight and Kenneth Berrington loved Margarete Knight.

The year she entered the QEH she developed an infatuation with Mary 'Dickie' Doyle who was also in the 14th PTS and with whom she roomed for a time in 1943 and then again in 1944. It began in a tentative way, and by the end of December 1943 it seems to have reached and passed a critical point. She worried that Mary had become indifferent to her but did not break off the relationship for fear of hurting her feelings. For her part, Monica still felt the same toward Mary as she had before.

The relationship continued throughout the year, though never smoothly. On the first Friday of November 1944, when Knight wanted to stay at the hospital in order to write and Mary planned to go out by herself, she lost control. She shouted and threw things about until, filled with remorse when her temper subsided, she saw the diminutive Mary standing by the door in her civilian clothes waiting to go out.

That interest was not Knight's only one during 1944. In the middle of the year she was kissed in the dark by Edward Raven, a man who flattered her and advised her to listen to Brahms' *First Symphony*. Kissing him back, she thought she would not mind if it happened again, but he was 65 years old and nothing seems to have come of it. And, on the eve of her twenty-first birthday, she thought fondly of a Reggie and how she had 'loved him'. Then, toward the end of the year, she was startled by a man named Towner who told her he believed in free love and easy sex with a willing partner. She told him, she was mortified that he had such a low opinion of the trainees. As she did so, she realised how much she hoped someone would marry her out of her turmoil.

While waiting for her QEH course to start on 5 January 1943, Knight worked at St Nicholas and St Martin's in Pyrford from September through December 1942 where her friend Nurse Jean Sapcote had offered her a job in the babies' ward. While she was there, Nurse Marjory Scott informed her that the Quaker conscientious objector Knight had met at Pyrford in 1940 was now living and working in Birmingham—he had kept in touch with Scott, one of the several nurses he had flirted with in Pyrford.

He was Leonard Jolley who, on discharge from Pyrford in October 1941, had joined the Kingston Community, a pacifist commune at Rectory Farm in Charney Bassett, near Oxford. Then, in March 1942, he became a part-time librarian for the Selly Oak Colleges Library, a collection of some

60,000 volumes for the dozen theological colleges on the Cadbury estate that were devoted to preparing people for missionary work. In August 1942 he had married Joyce Ellen Hancock in the Friends Hall in Bethnal Green, London. Hancock was a young woman from, Deal, Kent who had visited him with her family in Pyrford and who, after the marriage, found a job teaching in Birmingham.

Knight contacted the newly married couple soon after she started at the QEH and began visiting them at their flat in a grand Georgian home at 37 Calthorpe Road, Edgbaston, near the Five Ways intersection. It was less than a mile from central Birmingham to the northeast, just over a mile from the QEH to the southwest, and less than four miles from the Selly Oak Colleges Library to the southwest, all easily accessible by the Bristol Road tram.

Leonard and Joyce were intelligent and articulate, he twenty-nine and she thirty when they took up with Knight in Birmingham. Each was from a very conservative religious background, his father a London City Missionary lay evangelist. Henry and Bertha Jolley and their three children, Harry, Laura and Leonard, lived in poverty in Bow, the children only able to attend university because of bursaries they received for their success as day students, Henry and Leonard at the Coopers' Company Boys' School, also in Bow, and Laura at the Coborn School. Joyce Hancock's family were strict Plymouth Brethren, her father a packer in an underwear factory when she was born and a salesman by the time she married. They had met at University College London where each took a degree in English (his with Honours), and he went on to an MA as well as a Diploma in Librarianship. They spoke and read several languages, were interested in psychology, were widely read in literature, and had strong views on politics and current affairs. They had flirted with Socialism and Communism in the 1930s, marching in various protests: a February 1933 newspaper photograph showed him demonstrating with others against the means test in tertiary education, and in March he was in a large procession of students who visited Marx's grave on the fiftieth anniversary of his death. Then in 1940 he had become a Quaker, applying for an exemption from military service on the grounds of conscientious objection, although he was an unlikely candidate for the military on account of recurring and debilitating flare-ups of rheumatoid arthritis he had had from childhood.

To Knight, Joyce and Leonard were an ideal couple—modern, educated, cultured, socially committed. She was overwhelmed by the Jolleys' responding so positively toward her, to the point where eventually they seemed to orient their own lives around her and her visits. Soon she was dismissing things that did not measure up to her new-found standards as not being, in their phrase, comme il faut. At first her visits consisted of brief hours she could barely spare from her hectic life at the QEH, hours when she met Leonard and Joyce at their home for a quick chat or perhaps a meal. But by the beginning of 1944 she would occasionally see Leonard on his own at the Selly Oak Colleges Library. She met with Leonard, or Leonard and Joyce both, every week or two, occasionally bringing Mary with her. That was at least twice as often as she visited her parents, and the frequency of her visits increased from mid-year.

Soon she was spending parts of her weekend helping in their garden, the Jolleys suggesting that she consider staying overnight with them. That led to her lying to her parents about not being able to spend all or part of the 3–4 June weekend in Wolverhampton for her twenty-first birthday and her mother's forty-eighth, although she was free on the Saturday, having to go on duty at 1 pm Sunday. She went to Calthorpe Road on Friday evening for supper, and Knight spent the Friday night there, all of them sleeping in late, after which they took the train to Stratford where they spent the day rowing and picnicking on the Spam-and-lettuce sandwiches Joyce had prepared. They also went skinny dipping at Leonard Jolley's insistence, something that made her uncomfortable, a scene recalled in the chapter 'River Shack' in *My Father's Moon* (123-35).

In that novel Veronica goes to her parents' home after the trip to the river shack, to be told that she must return to the hospital at once; in the event, Knight went straight back to the QEH, arriving at 10:45 pm. The next morning, her birthday, she returned to the Jolleys' at noon to collect her pyjamas, had lunch with them and rushed back to the hospital for her shift that started at 1 pm. Leonard and Joyce were marvellous, she concluded.

She visited them twice more in July and then went to see her old friend Gertrude Whele, who had been selling black-market eggs and poultry to her parents since rationing commenced at the beginning of 1940. A forty-year-old friend-cum-mother figure, she was a kind woman of good sense and good will who would listen patiently to Knight's long and urgent outpourings before responding, a process she called 'pulling out the old stocking to patch'. During that visit Knight talked with Gertrude and her daughter Marion about inconsequential things, for some reason not asking for any eggs—perhaps she was afraid to allow the conversation to wander off of chatty matters with Marion present. When she got home her mother berated her, and then spoke seriously to her about her daughter's friends, a conversation premised on her belief that Monica was unhappy—Gertrude had confided in Margarete Knight.

Knight was pulled too many ways at once. She could not integrate her eight-hour on/off shifts with her duties as a student-nurse, an impulse to socialise with people of her own age, an obligation to see her parents and sometimes her grandmother, and a desire to be with the Jolleys, particularly Leonard, not to mention her wish to get on with her writing. In a desperately hopeful gambit, she invited the Jolleys to visit Wolverhampton for the weekend of 16–17 September, staying overnight. If her motives were naively mixed—presumably to interest Leonard and Joyce in her parents and to persuade the parents that Leonard was focused on Joyce and not herself—she thought that she succeeded with the latter. However, to her dismay, the Jolleys seemed unimpressed by her parents, her mother's music collection and, especially, a volatile, belligerent German refugee who dropped by one evening. By the time the weekend was over, Knight realised that chez moi was not comme il faut and, likely as not, Margarete Knight had divined the true situation.

When she met with Gertrude Whele later in September, they decided upon a friendship nothing could break, Knight thinking of Gertrude as a perfect friend to whom she could tell anything. Around this time Whele was very concerned about Knight's friendship with the Jolleys, whom she called 'the Jolley boys', encouraging her to break it off. But from then until Christmas the pattern became crazier: Knight worried about Mary and about being a nuisance to Joyce and Leonard, sat a medicine exam she feared she did not pass, received a nice letter from Joyce and a worried one from Gertrude, and completed a short story, 'The Man Who Was Poor'. At the beginning of December she declined an invitation from the Jolleys, thinking she ought to spend more time with Mary and not bother the Jolleys so much. But the visits continued until Christmas.

On Christmas Eve she saw her name toward the bottom of the results list and was forced to admit how her strong start as a trainee nurse had lost its direction and momentum.

Run slowly, slowly, horses of the night.

Ovid, *The Art of Love*, Book I, Elegy XIII

Monica Knight was lying to her sister and her parents, Gertrude Whele, her QEH staff and student colleagues, Leonard and Joyce, as well as to herself. She worked too hard and wrote too little, worried too much, entertained romantic images of her own death, and she frequently begged for help from God. But her prayer was like Saint Augustine's supplication, 'Lord, make me chaste—but not yet!'

In February, during a suspension of her resolve not to visit, Leonard told her that she was repressed, they both said she had been brought up too strictly, and Joyce explained to her how some friendships end but in others the interest increases and surprises and so the friendship continues. After that, Knight prayed the Jolleys would never reach the end of her. Inevitably, Joyce invited her to visit, inevitably Knight accepted, and predictably Leonard again raised the subject of her being repressed. Worried, she hoped they would never come to the end of one another, and later she wondered why they were so kind to her, fearing that they felt sorry for her. By the end of the March, she and Leonard were making semi-public declarations and displays of affection. She was certain Joyce knew, because QEH colleagues had guessed, remarking on seeing Leonard and her walk off hand in hand from the hospital. She could imagine no alternative to loving intensely and happily through any sorrow and difficulty she encountered.

By Christmas she was pregnant. Margarete Knight's consolations would be two. She had been right about Leonard, and her daughter would not become a vulgar nurse.

I have always been on the edge—something of an exile ...
'What Sins to Me Unknown Dipped Me in Ink?' (1)

Monica Knight left the Queen Elizabeth Hospital 23 October 1945, Catherine Smaldon noting in her report that she was a 'good girl who would have done extremely well had she continued'.[15] Three months later, Leonard Jolley's position also changed, for at the beginning of 1946 he was elevated from part-time to full-time employment. He had become Librarian of the Selly Oak Colleges Library, replacing Joanna Franks who had resigned to join the Ministry of Aircraft Production. His salary suddenly doubled to £400 per year.

After she left the QEH, she went to work for the Raynor family at 76 Witherford Way, Selly Oak. They were an educated, motivated and upwardly mobile couple. Emily Jean Brockliss Raynor held an MA and DPhil in Chemistry from Oxford and taught science in a secondary school. Geoffrey Raynor had an MA and a DPhil from Oxford and was an ICI Research Fellow at the University of Birmingham, ultimately becoming a Professor and Dean there, and a Fellow of the Royal Society.[16] They had a year-old boy, and Jean had a sister who often visited.

When she arrived at the Raynors', circumstances were not propitious for a happy stay, in part because she brought a great deal of emotional baggage with her. Her secret had been exposed, and so she had been humiliated in the eyes of her QEH colleagues.[17] Her mother made her feel guilty for her shamelessness and then shamed her by taking pity on her, being solicitous about her health. Both parents encouraged her to come home. But Knight wanted to remain close to Leonard and distant from her mother. As a result, she was recognised while shopping by a woman from the QEH, and risked being recognised by a fellow student who had been kind to her at Sibford and who lived in the very next house in Witherford Way. As for the work itself, despite being paid £6 per week, she felt overburdened by duties that included babysitting in addition to housekeeping, tasks that emphasised her own predicament.

Living with the Raynors was unlike anything she had experienced before. It was not like home or school, where adults focused their attention on her wellbeing and education, nor was it like a hospital where older women modelled professional behaviour and mentored younger women who aspired to their roles. Living with the Raynors was a job, one in which she felt that her efforts were more taken for granted than appreciated, one where Jean Raynor was more a boss than a parent or older sister. Thereby small inconveniences became large, like being limited to bathing once a week when she was used to doing so daily. And large ones became great, like Raynor's apparent scrutiny of her movements that would have felt like her mother's suspicious gaze. And Knight was always conflicted about whether to visit her parents on the weekends or to be with the father of her unborn child whom she had not named to either Raynor or her mother. Like Vera Wright in *My Father's Moon* telling her mother that the father of her daughter Helen is dead (1), she told her mother that the father was a patient at the QEH who had died of TB. Margarete Knight did not believe her.

Jean Raynor's brusque authoritarian ways reminded her of her mother's, and possibly Knight was envious of Raynor's sister who was the same age and studying physical education at a teachers college, which predicted a more certain future than Knight's. Living with the Raynors and looking after their young son would have forced her to contemplate her own prospects and to see how their son had been born into a more comfortable situation than she and her child would find any time soon. She took some reassurance in the fact that Leonard had said that if anything happened to her, he would look after the baby. The Raynors' household is perhaps reflected in Daddy Doctor's and Mummy Doctor's regimented Wellington household in *Cabin Fever*.

After Leonard was promoted, he and Joyce decided to buy their own home, settling on 15 Chadwick Avenue, Rednal, a semi-detached house, about four miles southwest of the Selly Oak Colleges Library. They were pleasantly surprised when Edward Cadbury, Managing Director of Cadbury and a bibliophile who served on Jolley's Library Board, bought the house for the company and allowed them to rent there from March 1946. And they also were pleased to have a place of their own, with no landlady to monitor their comings and goings, as Mrs Hall had done in Calthorpe Road. Leonard was now his own boss, so he and Knight were better positioned for meeting during the day for a walk or to visit the dentist and the doctor or such.

On one such visit, while eating at Kunzles, he saw someone who knew him and told Knight he imagined the woman would think he was with a common prostitute. That remark crushed her and she went to bed miserable. The misery of her life became more extreme closer to the birth which was scheduled to be in a nursing home under the supervision of Doctor Peggy Frazer. One cause of her distress was Jean Raynor's suggesting that Knight ask her mother whether or not she should continue to visit Wolverhampton on the weekends or remain with the Raynors. Even if it were a well-meant concern for the baby, to her it must have felt like a pincer movement by the two 'bad mothers' in her life. In the event, she interpreted it as Raynor's wanting to get still more work out of her during the last two months of her pregnancy. Defiantly, she continued to visit her parents but refused to accept her pay for the month of April so that she would not feel she should have to work so hard during that time.

On the night of 29 April 1946, she went to bed reading Samuel Richardson's *Clarissa: or, The History of a Young Lady*, a book about Clarissa Harlowe, 'virtuous, noble, wise, pious, unhappily ensnared by the vows and oaths of a vile rake, whom she believed to be a man of honour'.[18] Sensing the impending birth of Andrew Leonard or Sarah Tamar (the names she had chosen for her baby), she had tidied her room and cupboard, washed her hair and taken a bath before going to bed. When the contractions started before dawn, she attempted to wake Jean Raynor at 4 am but was unable to do so, trying again an hour later. The Raynors got up, reassured and assisted her, Jean Raynor calling an ambulance and riding with her as it lost its way to the Ashleigh Nursing Home in Wentworth Road, Harborne. On Tuesday afternoon, 30 April 1946, assisted by Sisters Russ and Robbins and the aptly named Dr Gathergood (attending for Dr Frazer who was unavailable), she delivered her daughter.

When Leonard and Joyce visited, Joyce helpfully advised her on how to avoid having to return to the Raynor household, pointing out that employers and employees only had to give a month's notice before employment ceased. During that conversation, Leonard became so angry with the Raynors that Knight feared Joyce would understand why—his knowing that Jean Raynor had written to Dr Frazer asking whether or not Knight should have some form of holiday before returning to work for her. Unbeknownst to Leonard, Knight had already written a 'nasty' three-page letter, saying that she was not coming back and objecting to Raynor's having approached Peggy Frazer. Sister Robbins had telephoned Frazer for advice, a call that resulted in Frazer's visiting Knight and offering her a position in her own household in Edgbaston.

She stayed on at the Ashleigh Nursing Home for a month, helping Mrs Robbins with the other mothers and babies. In mid-June she and her baby left the Ashleigh Nursing Home to stay with the Jolleys in Rednal where Leonard and Joyce also had a new baby girl, born at the beginning of June. Then from the second week in July mother and daughter spent a fortnight with the Wynn family—so-called Uncle Will and Aunt Elsie and their daughter Margaret, the same people who had welcomed Margarete Knight and Madelaine from The Norlands some twenty years before.

> *In spite of social changes the isolation and loneliness of the hidden relationship still exists.*
>
> 'Mr Berrington' (36)

At the beginning of August 1946 Monica Knight joined Peggy Levi Frazer and her husband Bernard Fleetwood-Walker in their large home at 91 Hagley

Road, Edgbaston, a fifteen-minute walk from central Birmingham. One of the few women to qualify as a doctor at the University of Birmingham in the 1920s, Peggy Levi had originally married another doctor, Paul Frazer, who died young—it was said that between them they had delivered half the babies in Kensington. The grandson of Cornelius Varley, an early nineteenth-century watercolourist, Fleetwood-Walker was a painter who studied in Paris and Birmingham, becoming an inspiring teacher and well-known portrait artist.[19] It was a second marriage for each, and their household included his two sons, Colin and his year-younger brother Guy who was precisely the same age as Monica. Both boys were raised as Roman Catholics (Fleetwood-Walker was an Anglican, and Peggy Frazer, born Jewish, became a Roman Catholic).[20]

Living with them was similar to living with the Raynors in two respects. Since Knight was an unmarried mother without means, she sometimes felt as if the Walkers were taking pity on her, which to an extent they were. Further, since it was employment with ill-defined hours and tasks, she sometimes felt that they were taking advantage of her, as when she complained that Peggy Frazer expected or allowed her to do jobs that were Frazer's, knowing that Knight had too much conscience not to work harder than anyone else. Its live-in aspect compounded both of those issues, for she felt that her comings and goings were sometimes under scrutiny and subject to criticism, either for avoiding work, which she was not, or for surreptitiously meeting a married man, which she was. For those and other reasons, she sometimes referred to Fleetwood-Walker as Flitters, to Peggy Frazer as Piggy, and to the family as the Piggies. And she complained of the children that the sons of gentlemen never said thank you.

However, living with the Fleetwood-Walkers was also different in a number of ways, the main one being that she had her daughter with her in rooms of their own and they lived among people who actually cared for both of them. Peggy Frazer, despite always being busy and tired after work, liked Knight and was solicitous of her, enabling her to take unscheduled time off and making specialist doctor appointments for her. And Frazer loved the baby, playing with her in the yard and taking her for rides in her car, giving her vaccinations and looking after her when she had measles. She even intervened on her behalf when a nursery school threatened not to accept her against the fear that she might have tuberculosis. Fleetwood-Walker was also attentive to the baby, patiently getting her to pose so that he could make a chalk portrait of her which he gave to her mother. His attention to a young child in the household was the more remarkable for his being famously distracted and self-absorbed, once helplessly phoning Peggy to say he had taken the wrong train to an unfamiliar station and did not know what to do next. Knight also got on well with the two sons who sometimes helped with the washing up after dinner, and Guy was particularly fond of the baby—Colin and Guy appear as Toby and Arthur in a novel she started a decade later.

In time, she came to feel a bond with Peggy Frazer, responding sympathetically when she needed help, as when Frazer came in shaken and bruised from a bad fall after a very tiring day in London; Knight helped her into bed with the hot-water bottle. She was overcome with how pathetic Fraser seemed, becoming, if not fond, at least having feeling for her.

Peggy Frazer was ambiguously placed vis-à-vis Knight who often sought an older woman to serve as a mother figure to her, like Gladys Burgess at Sibford, Jean Sapcote at Pyrford, and Gertrude Whele in Birmingham. Such women were sympathetic listeners who could even give hard advice if it were delivered in a way that was neither condemning nor shaming. If Frazer were like Jean Raynor for being a boss, she was unlike Raynor for being non-judgemental and for welcoming Knight and her daughter into the household as if they were part of it. The fact that Frazer was a medical doctor made a difference too, given Knight's lifelong fantasy of being a doctor. Although Frazer never became a confidante to the same degree as the other three women, nonetheless Knight felt safe in her home and had special affection and admiration for Peggy Frazer, remaining in contact with her until Frazer's death.

She continued to meet Leonard regularly. She visited him and Joyce in Rednal, met him at the library when they would go to a park, or in Hagley Road when they would go out for a walk. Sometimes she would go with him to his Monday-night adult education class on 'Birmingham through the Ages', to be with him, but also to increase the size of the group to three or four and then later assure him that the poor attendance had nothing to do with his knowledge or teaching skill. By April 1947 they were experimenting with joint writing projects, producing a draft of a children's story begun by Knight, 'Waterloo Mouse'; and around the same time she had four stories politely rejected by Collins. Then, after years of trying, she had a nine-minute story she wrote in 1944 read on the BBC's 'Children's Hour' program on 23 August 1946.[21]

'The Adventures of George Henry the Caterpillar' is about a stay-at-home but plucky caterpillar who knows his mind and speaks it clearly. His routine is inadvertently upset when a benevolent cabbage, picked by the gardener and packed in a string bag, says goodbye to his mother and happily sets off to see the world, along with George who happens to be dining on him at the time. George has a number of adventures in the wider world, all of them improving ones, before he returns. 'It was not long before he settled down with a Mrs Henry—they lived on Brussells sprout [sic]—but that, of course, is another story'. It is a story perhaps better heard by children than read by adults.

'Waterloo Mouse' is more interesting, perhaps because Leonard Jolley had much of a hand in writing it. The story is suggestive of a pantomime in the way that it speaks simultaneously to both children and adults. For the children, there is non-stop adventure with a lively cast of a dozen types of animal—frogs, mice and rats, moles and squirrels and such—including a vain, officious lizard wearing a black silk tie reminiscent of Douglas from the Sibford Bunny stories, a landlubber bull called an admiral, and an angry man called Angry Voice. For both, there are disguises, intrigues and discoveries. And for adults, there are allusions (to Napoleon's aphorism that an army marches on its stomach), political references (the bad-father mouse is named Kitchener, after Britain's Secretary of State for War during World War I who was an advocate of conscription), and considerable generic inventiveness.

The fervour of their relationship remained undiminished. If Joyce did not realise, Leonard Jolley's workmates must have known. If Monica Knight's frequent visits to Jolley's library did not attract their attention, then the two or three letters a week she sent him would have done so, since they were posted in recycled envelopes he gave her after they had been received by the Selly Oak Colleges Library: colleagues would not imagine that Jolley was writing letters to himself, especially since his handwriting was tiny and hardly decipherable while hers was large and easier to read. A contemporary library colleague said that his fellow staff members were protective and not prone to gossip.[22]

When Jolley's mother Bertha visited to see her new granddaughter, she told her son that he must sort out his life before his wife discovered what was going on. Knight made comments that might have stirred another man to action, such as writing to say she could not tell their daughter the story about Father Christmas because she did not know the meaning of the word 'father'—the name they used was 'Timmy'. But nothing happened.

The whole time Monica Knight was with the Fleetwood-Walkers she experienced a different kind of loneliness from when she was with the Raynors, one that had to do with being an unmarried mother, even though she had both a family-of-origin and extended-family network that was supportive. She was pleased when Elsie Wynn visited her at the beginning of 1949, and also pleased to be able to reciprocate the visit, although she was shocked to find how much she had aged. Similarly, Mary Sheldon visited and talked hopefully and intelligently, if not expertly, about Knight's stories. Neither woman was judgemental about her behaviour. On the contrary, Mary Sheldon confided that she (the aunt) had an unhappy sex life, opening the way for Knight to tell her that she had a lover. About the same time, she was visited by her Aunt Daisy who had come to tell Monica face-to-face that she was disinheriting her on account of her being an unwed mother. And she was visited at the Fleetwood-Walker home by her seventy-year-old 'uncle' Acheson Sheldon of nudism fame from the Flowermead days who—presumably clothed—made advances to her. That, coupled with Leonard's inaction, began to make her feel such despair in addition to loneliness that by 1949 she had developed an irritable bowel complaint that neither Peggy Frazer nor her colleague Dr Hardy could control.

Leonard Jolley received a bursary from the Selly Oak Colleges Library for a study-leave tour of theological libraries in North America, leaving Southampton on the *RMS Queen Elizabeth* in early April. He proposed to bring back information about the holdings of a dozen prominent institutions. His study leave no doubt enhanced his standing as a librarian, his newly acquired knowledge of overseas philosophy and practices complementing his highly regarded University College London diploma in librarianship. While he was away, one evening Knight talked so much with Guy that it seemed as if she were being unfaithful. The next week she and her daughter spent a week in Bournemouth, visiting her Sibford school friend Edith Worrall who lived with her mother. Knight found Edith delightful company but wrote to Leonard that she seemed an old maid already, although only twenty-six. As for Bournemouth; there were only well dressed women and nurses and their well bred charges, the nurses with children perhaps reminding her of herself.

When Leonard returned to Birmingham from North America in early May 1949, he presented both Susan and Sarah with identical red cotton dresses. Neither Joyce nor Knight protested, that gesture, and their compliance, showing that the three of them were able to tolerate an enormous amount of ambiguity in their individual and collective lives in a manner akin to that of Wilfrid and Margarete Knight with Kenneth Berrington.

Three weeks after Leonard's return from New York, Knight began a novel about a nursing home, one she would work at for decades and later call *Eleanor Page*. It frustrated her every effort but at the same time kept her stable as things continued to fall apart. The day after she began to write, she imagined that it would feature Vincent, loveable and dreamy, and Katherine, satisfied in her love, who live with their three children, a grandmother and a Welsh nursemaid in an old house which has a nursing home upstairs.

She had found her topics, the home and the family, that would occupy her for the rest of her life.

5

Pinewood—Herts requires Staff: Matron, Teacher, Handyman/gardener . . .

From London to Amwell Berry in Hartfordshire thence to Bishops Starford in Essex which is a pretty neat Market town a good Church and a delicate Spring of Water . . .

Celia Fiennes, May 1697[1]

Monica Knight changed her surname from Knight to Fielding by deed poll on 14 March 1949 while at the Fleetwood-Walkers. It enabled her to sidestep her mother's criticism about having an unmarried mother for a daughter. Changing her name was something she had contemplated doing before the baby was born, but she had allowed Leonard Jolley to talk her out of it then. Fielding was a name with unavoidable irony, as he must have known: the novelist Henry Fielding wed his maid after his wife died, but Jolley made no move to marry maid Monica. Besides, she admired Fielding's novels.

The family and romantic complications of Fielding's situation were evident at the time of her twenty-sixth birthday in 1949: Leonard asked her to a Beethoven concert on Saturday 4 June; she fought with her mother over a date to celebrate their common birthdays in Wolverhampton, settling on Sunday; and for Monday she accepted an invitation from Guy Walker to celebrate *their* common birthdates by going to dinner and to a modern religious play.[2] Peggy Frazer gave her the chalk drawing of her daughter that Fleetwood-Walker had done. Leonard told her to buy what she wanted for herself from a sale at Rhodes. She bought initialled linen handkerchiefs for

Guy and some red leather for an anthology of prose she was making Leonard for his birthday in August.

In September, while Leonard was away in Scotland, Guy took her to see the new musical comedy by Herbert and Ellis, *Bless the Bride*, and the next Sunday, as they picnicked together, asked her to marry him; she clumsily declined.[3] She liked Guy, and his offer was a serious and attractive one, but she believed it was based on a bourgeois concept of honour and driven by Roman Catholic guilt. More to the point, she did not love him, and did love Leonard.

Leonard was upset when she told him about Guy. He still did nothing; and then he wondered why she flirted. It was, of course, to be admired. In her usual way, she worried that Leonard and Guy were both wretched, thought that she could help them both, and knew they both wished to help her. At the same time, she thought they were selfish and demanding, and she could barely stand the situation.

She decided to remove herself from it. In addition to her immediate problem with Guy, from the beginning she felt trapped with the Fleetwood-Walkers. Although living and working at Hagley Road had many pleasant aspects, including her private living quarters, it only provided room and board and £3 per week. Returning to Wolverhampton to live with her parents was an option she refused. Beyond the control issue and the blame game, living with the Knights might even enable Margarete to drive a wedge between Fielding and her daughter. Her decision was more to get away from Guy than to force Leonard's hand. At the same time, Fielding was leaving a situation where two suitable men were vying for her approval. Thus she was explicitly declining the possibility of a romantic situation structured along the lines of her mother's with Wilfrid Knight and Kenneth Berrington.

So she set off for Amwellbury where four months would feel more like four years.

> *Pinewood, Amwellbury, Herts requires Staff: Matron, teacher, Handyman/gardener. Elizabeth Strachan, Ware 52*
>
> New Statesman and Nation, 8 April 1950 (414)

To escape the hothouse atmosphere at the Walker residence, from 8 March 1950 Fielding spent a fortnight in Banbury, near Sibford, with her old Quaker friend Mrs Edith Lamb. While there, she asked Leonard to send her the address of the *New Statesman and Nation*. She wanted to change her job, and in that connection she visited Miss Burgess, inquiring into the possibility of work at Sibford. Leonard suggested she stay on in Banbury, feigning illness, but she could not do so because Mrs Lamb's home would be filled the next week with boarders come to Banbury for Sibford's Old Scholars' weekend. And she would not do so, telling him she would not walk out on Peggy Frazer without giving proper notice. While in Banbury she told Mrs Lamb all about the 'Tim' whose frequent letters and packages had impressed Lamb—the packages were books Leonard sent, including Parson Woodforde's *Diary of a Country Parson*, Virginia Woolf's *The Voyage Out*, and Somerville's and Ross's *Experiences of an Irish R. M.*

In mid-April 1950 she and Leonard visited the first institution that responded positively to an application from her. When they arrived in Betchworth, some twenty miles southwest of London, they found the school to be a muddle. Monica did not feel at ease with the Director—big, vulgar, wealthy—and was put off by her masculine colleague, despite her being a handsome woman with deep brown eyes. Nor did she approve of the monkey and dogs in the kitchen. Thus, when offered the position there, she delayed her response to it.

The following Friday, 21 April 1950, she left Hagley Road, to stay temporarily with her parents in Wells Road. Fleetwood-Walker gave her £5 as a present and Peggy Frazer wished her well. Colin sent a kiss to her daughter, and Guy Walker was greatly upset, vowing to find her on her birthday which was in seven weeks' time. Then on Sunday she and Leonard visited Pinewood, a progressive school in Amwellbury. It occupied Amwellbury House, Great Amwell, near Ware, three miles northeast of Hertford—the name refers to Emma's Well dating from antiquity, the original estate of Great Amwell being mentioned in the Doomsday Book. Celia Fiennes, the most famous of the eighteenth-century female English domestic tourists, commenced her first (1697) journey from her uncle's Amwellbury House which predated the Reformation, its history including tales of being haunted, with chanting monks appearing the evening before snow fell.[4] By the 1940s it was much diminished, large portions of it having been pulled down to save on heating costs, but it still showed signs of elegance, with remnants of Gilpin wallpaper in some upstairs rooms. Amwellbury House was large enough to accommodate about a dozen live-in staff members and thirty or forty students.

There Fielding discovered the proprietor, sixty-year-old Elizabeth 'Strix' Strachan (rhymes with 'strawn') sitting on her bed in a large untidy study with wallpaper featuring roses and leaves, wearing a red cord costume with a yellow scarf and thick brown stockings. Fielding liked her firm mouth and long thin nose but most of all she liked the expression in the clear grey eyes. She found Pinewood itself to be big and untidy and was surprised to see someone painting pictures on the wall of a decapitated harlequin with clowns playing football with his head.

Leonard Jolley too had been looking for a new position since returning from his study tour. His trip to North America had confirmed his disinterest in administering a theological library, and his Selly Oak position had no promotional prospects. So he had applied for positions in Harpenden, Leeds, and Liverpool. Thus the day after they visited Pinewood, Leonard went for an interview at the nearby agricultural research school, Harpenden. The interview went well (by chance he had read the deputy's book on soil erosion), but he did not receive an immediate offer. Since he had nothing definite except his position in the Selly Oak Colleges library, and Fielding liked Strachan better than the Betchworth woman, she accepted the Pinewood offer.

As she continued her stay in Wolverhampton before taking up the position, her parents doted on their granddaughter, but Fielding quarrelled heartily with her mother, throwing a milk bottle across the kitchen the last night she was there.[5] She wanted no more to do with them, wondering why her mother always found fault with her and never accepted what she thought and did. Two of the things they argued about were her working as a domestic and her continuing refusal to tell her mother who was the father of her child. She left Wells Road to start work at Pinewood on Wednesday 10 May 1950.

Strachan's advertisement for Pinewood in the *New Statesman* said it was a school, 'for children 4-14—where diet, environment, psychology, and teaching methods maintain health and happiness'. Her teaching methods were based on Friedrich Froebel's model that focused on very young children and emphasised the importance of play as a learning activity. Strachan also fancied herself a kind of A. S. Neill whom she often visited, Pinewood her version of his Summerhill School in Suffolk. Neill's notions of participatory governance gave everyone, staff and students alike, an equal say in the management of the school where attendance at lessons was not compulsory.[6]

She feared she did not go far enough to meet with Neill's approval. But critics might say that she went too far or that she misunderstood the distinction Neill insisted on when he advocated freedom, not licence. They would argue that at Pinewood genial tyranny alternated with anarchy by default, and that the children did not benefit from care from people in need of it themselves. Still others would insist that Strix was a charismatic, well-meaning woman, and that Pinewood was a magic place where students blossomed. Those differences of opinion would reflect the variety of backgrounds of the staff and students, for the heterogeneity of Pinewood was the antithesis of (say) Sibford's hierarchic structure, Christian ethic, and Quaker staff and students who pursued a vocational curriculum.

No one would disagree that Strix was flamboyant and eccentric and that, like Tufty Johnstone at Sibford, presented as a bit of a mystery. The school's mythology had it that she had a tragic love affair, that Pinewood had seen illegitimate births, a suicide, a double murder. In fact, Strachan was the third-oldest of the nine children of a well-off Scottish couple, all of those surviving into adulthood being strong 'characters'.[7] She founded Pinewood school in Crowborough, Sussex, in the 1930s, moved it to Newquay in Cornwall when war broke out, settled in Ware, Amwellbury, in the early 1940s, and then moved on to The Manor House, Bradninch, Devon, in the mid-1950s, closing it in the late 1950s.

A colleague said she drank stout in the morning and whiskey at night, and smoked all day. She lay abed a great deal, amidst heaps of toys, broken furniture, beautiful lace, and portraits of herself by a German artist, with masses of sweet-smelling flowers trailing out of vases in summer. She dressed oddly, elegantly, or both, sometimes wearing a lime-green costume for days on end, or a moth-eaten fur jerkin she carefully placed on the trunk in her study. Her unusual clothes intrigued the students who would lift her skirts to marvel at her bloomers, Strix roaring with laughter. She encouraged them to ransack the toy chest and invited staff to listen to classical music with her in her room. She once asked Fielding to do so with her on the bed, offering her a whiskey, but Fielding declined both offers, for she found the atmosphere oppressive and the portraits to be suggestive of something elusive and not quite desirable. Strachan even invited the mother of one of the students to stay the night with her. An adoring ex-student likened her to

Isadora Duncan, a more bemused one to Margaret Rutherford playing the bicycling medium in Noel Coward's *Blithe Spirit*.

She was motivated by idealism and generosity, not profit, resulting in the school always being in financial difficulty, her sister Edith sometimes visiting to bail her out. That same generosity could easily be conflated with disingenuous self-interest in some of her gestures, such as freely accepting children from local council schools who perhaps should have been sent instead to special-education institutions because of their learning and/or behavioural difficulties. They were possibly the only ones who provided the school with a regular income stream.

She had an offsider, Edna Kenyatta, who monitored such impulses, the two forming a complementary pair. Fielding later portrayed such women in her novels as zany, sometimes larcenous, women who flouted convention if not the law: Dr Arabella Thorne and Miss Edgley at Pine Heights in *Miss Peabody's Inheritance*; Hyacinth Price and Heather Hailey of St Christopher and St Jude's in *Mr Scobie's Riddle*; and Josephine Peycroft and Miss Paisley of Trinity College (Cheathem East) in *Foxybaby*. Most directly, Strix Strachan and Edna Kenyatta are reflected in Patch Palmer, Principal of Fairfields, and Miles, her Deputy, in the opening chapter of *My Father's Moon*.

Many of the staff at Pinewood were unwed or divorced or widowed mothers, or women abandoned by their husbands. Each had a 'story' that was sometimes tragic and always sad in its own way. Few stories were as colourful as Edna Kenyatta's, the wife of Jomo Kenyatta. Born in 1894, he became a left-wing Kenyan political leader who studied in Moscow and London and in the 1930s was an outspoken and controversial African nationalist. Charged and convicted for leading the bloody Mau Mau rebellion in 1952, in 1960 he was elected President in absentia; and, after Kenya's independence in 1963, was elected its first President, serving until his death in 1978. When he returned to Kenya in 1946, he left Edna behind with their three-year-old son Peter Magana Kenyatta.[8] She joined Pinewood in 1948.

Many of the men were like characters from a Balzac or Dickens novel, such as the artist Melville Hardiment who married six times (twice to the woman he seduced when she was sixteen). Or like the men from Fairfields in *My Father's Moon*, some with the same names as the men at Pinewood, such as Rudi Pohl, a Czech, whose overnighting with his French-speaking Swiss fiancée Rosemary is tolerated by Patch and Miles because they do not even pretend to pay him any salary for his work as the gardener. Another was Olive Morris' husband who suddenly appears at Fairfields with chickens and ducks, honey and jam, fruit and vegetables, the meat relieving the vegetarian diet that Vera Wright says prevailed, 'because the local butchers, unpaid, no longer supply the school' (16).

Strix charmed or cajoled her staff to work for little and rarely paid the live-in staff their thirty shillings per week, an inconvenience she might not have appreciated since she seemed not to worry about money—her novel way of dealing with one woman was to pay her 30 shillings per week and then charge her 30 shillings for her truck-driving husband to stay at Pinewood on weekends. The live-in mothers knew they might be homeless if it were not for Pinewood, a fear she might not have known either, being childless. She even reneged on paying Fielding the £2 per week originally offered for her to be Matron, saying that her qualifications were not what she claimed. Fielding was reduced to a nominal 30 shillings per week too.

To be sure, the title of Matron was inflated, for Fielding was a Jill of all trades working with others who were doing the same. She was responsible for one of the bathrooms (Edna Kenyatta for the second and Rosemary Pohl for the third), cooked much of the time, washed the children's clothes, ironed them, made and supervised the meals, and during the day was in charge of what was called 'the nursery'—she complained about having to spend long hours with nursery children.[9] Once, having promised but having failed to pay her before going on holiday, Strachan posted her £7/7—for a month's work, a sum not divisible by any number relevant to a lunar or calendar month.

The parents of some of the children chose Pinewood because they preferred a progressive boarding school in the country, its proximity to London being another attraction. Some of the children were survivors of marital minefields, some daughters and sons of unwed mothers, a whole string of them said to have been sired by the famous painter Augustus John. Or they were the children of parents too distracted, too distressed, or otherwise too busy to care for them; or business or consular people who could not do so because they lived abroad. Or the children of artistic couples, like the three children of photographer Michael Wickham and his wife Tanya—she had painted the murals on the wall during one of her periodic stays at Pinewood—and Angela Pleasence, daughter of actors Donald Pleasence and his wife Miriam Raymond, who never paid fees the whole decade she was there. Others came from North America, Australia,

China, France and Persia, some remaining at Pinewood during the summer, some not returning home for years.

Strachan was convinced that eating raw vegetables had cured her of breast cancer after she had a mastectomy years before. As a result, she was a strong believer in the importance of diet, resulting in shredded cabbage serving as the basis of Pinewood's food pyramid, taking some pressure off the school's parlous financial situation. The fare also included homemade yoghurt, rusks, porridge and such, all supplemented with cod liver oil, rose hips, Vitamin B_{12} and malt extract, sweets being served only on Saturday. Unsurprisingly, it was 'awful' for some and 'wonderful' for others but, as at Sibford, carnivores and vegetarians alike agreed there was not enough of it. One student, whose parents sent chocolates and tins of tongue that never reached her, collected chestnuts on the school grounds and sold them in order to buy ice cream.

Likewise, the curriculum was variously criticised or praised. While some of the ex-students remember happy art and music lessons, others do not remember any classes at all, but rather long sessions spent gardening. One student's report from Strachan said, 'A term of ups and downs but unless consistency is the prime virtue she did well and satisfactorily'. Out of class, Strix's philosophy of self-paced learning led her to instruct Fielding never to tell the students what to do, once leaving a distressed boy who had climbed to the top of the school's totemic fir tree to make his own way down. When older children encouraged a newer student to climb higher than was prudent, Fielding, perhaps imagining the rib cages of stranded children bleaching on the branches, got Rudi to fetch him down, unable to do so herself because she was not wearing knickers.

Students from time to time were encouraged to frolic naked. When Arthur and Edna sprayed them with garden hoses on the school grounds, Fielding thought it was innocent enough and that the boys and girls looked nymph-like, as from another world. But Strix also took them to swim in the pond of a country house where the elderly owner would only let them do so unclothed, and some of the girls were uncomfortable with that. Moreover, she did not police or discourage traffic between the boys' and girls' upstairs dormitory rooms at night, even though some staff and students were concerned about that too. One student told of a young girl being restrained, stripped, and sexually humiliated by a mixed group of other students, and several other women said that they were sexually abused by adults at Pinewood during the 1950s, in some versions by a man on the grounds, in others by a man in the building itself. Such danger is suggested in the 'Fairfield' chapter of *My Father's Moon*: Vera, returning to the school during an evening thunderstorm, sees 'someone standing, half hidden, quite near, in the same place where a man was standing on that first afternoon . . . I feel afraid. I have never felt or experienced fear like this before. Real terror, because of his stillness, makes my legs weak' (11–12).

Nonetheless, Pinewood was a nurturing and improving place to many, especially those who had no alternatives, or no better ones. Angela Pleasence, sent to Pinewood when she was two, believed that her life depended on Strix and Pinewood, and embraced them both. When she left at eleven to attend a secondary school in Ware, she went to live with Pinewood's housekeeper Mrs Spence, calling her 'Nan' and her daughter 'Aunty', and thus the school seemed to extend its protection to her. While Pleasence cannot remember attending any classes the whole time she was there, and most other students cannot remember learning much mathematics at Pinewood, she says Strix taught her arithmetic so well that even now she is brilliant at it. Strix was her nourishing mother, Pinewood her alma mater.

Certainly Pinewood produced students who went on to significant achievements. Those from Fielding's time include Christopher Barker, prize-winning photographer, Sebastian Barker, poet and Editor of the *London Magazine*, Peter Kenyatta, Director of New Channel Developments for BBC TV, Angela Pleasence, an accomplished actor (Catherine Howard in the 1970s television series on *The Six Wives of Henry VIII*), and Julyan Wickham, a well-known architect with offices in London and Amsterdam.

Fielding herself was like some of the mothers at Pinewood for being unwed, but at the same time she was unlike most of them for being there by choice and having a clearer idea of how long she would stay, when she would leave, and what she would do next. Looking back on the experience, she could say, 'though I was in a mixed-up state in the eyes of society, I was looking forward and I was perfectly happy'.[10] She approved of Kenyatta's firm hand and admired her good judgement, such as sending her son Peter to St John the Baptist Anglican school in Great Amwell. Kenyatta liked Fielding as well, hoping she might change her mind and stay on longer than the May–August period she had originally committed to, and replace a Mrs Scott who was scheduled to arrive at the end of August. But Fielding could not do so, for Leonard had been offered a local post and one in Scotland as well.

The attraction of Harpenden was its proximity to Pinewood, but Fielding regarded her Pinewood job solely as a summer one, and knew if she stayed on while Leonard was at Harpenden they would only have limited time together. She also believed he would prefer the Scotland job because it was more prestigious, and moving there would constitute a cleaner break. In the event, he accepted the offer to be Librarian for the Royal College of Physicians in Edinburgh, leaving the Selly Oak Colleges Library on 15 July 1950. He had finally told his wife about his relationship with Monica Knight.

Her desire to follow Leonard was passionate, but he sometimes seemed diffident about that prospect. Any misgivings she had were over such details as when she could come to Edinburgh, whether they would live together or separately, and if she should work to help him acquire the money to buy a house—they needed £200 as a down payment and a loan for a further £2,000. His responses were prompt, if sometimes peevish: he said he wanted her in Edinburgh, but he did not clarify the question of who would live where. As Fielding made preparations to join him in September, Kenyatta asked if 'Tim' had asked her to marry him yet and cautioned against giving all of her money to anyone, including him. It was Edna Kenyatta, fifteen years older than Monica, whom she always remembered as another of the older women she turned to for encouragement and caring advice.

As for Elizabeth Strachan, despite Fielding's initial favourable impression of her, she came not to admire her, but rather felt sorry for her. Under other circumstances Strachan might have served as one of her mother-figures, offering warmth and dispensing advice like Gertrude Whele. But, despite their differences—Strix with her devil-may-care attitude and Margarete Knight with her controlling ways—from Fielding's point of view each of them neglected the children in her care, including metaphorical children like Fielding herself.

The cosiness of family life had never existed in reality for me.
                                         'The Changing Family–Who cares' (81)

Monica Fielding did not have much success in finding the time and space to write at Pinewood, not even to work on the novel she had just started at Hagley Road. However, that novel—about the young woman who wanted to look after her own family on the ground floor of her house while running a nursing home upstairs—incorporated the fantasy implicit in everything she did from the time she left Sibford: she was always concerned to attend to the health and wellbeing of the 'family' which, in addition to herself and her daughter, had included her patients and colleagues in Pyrford and Birmingham as well as the parents and children in the Raynor and Frazer/Fleetwood-Walker households. At Pinewood she was once more in a 'family', but one where she was able to observe those around her in a more detached, more writerly, way then ever before.

What writing she managed to do was largely in her diary and letters where she made her 'quick note'. She documented the people and the place in notes varying in tone and topic, from jeremiads to character sketches to lyric descriptions of her surroundings. She told Leonard that the hay-mowing reminded her of Levin cutting his grass in *Anna Karenina*. Ranging from the ecstatic to the despairing, the writing Fielding managed to do at Pinewood shows that she had some perspective on her situation. After a fortnight there, tired after having washed up after supper, she wrote a little meditation for Leonard on the strange shabby house, the green leafiness and the sleeping children. In it she celebrated evening solitude, appreciating being alone, fearful of having her 'aloneness' taken from her.

Writing letters and confiding in her diary also helped her to reframe the picture of her family of birth. When her Aunt Daisy wrote to her, complaining as usual, this time that Fielding had left Birmingham without visiting her, she just thought she was an old fool. When her father visited for several days not long before she left Pinewood, staying at the Station Hotel, he was shocked by some of the people he met and some of the things he saw, but was pleased to talk with the children while his daughter worked. Before he left, he said that she should make sure she was doing the right thing in marrying Leonard, that real love only came from God. When the response to his visit by some of her colleagues implied that Wilfrid Knight was ineffectual or even risible, she was able to see how he appeared to them. She did not comment on the fact that her mother never came to Pinewood, although she visited Gottfried Leiser in Germany during the time. Those events and non-events helped her to gain some perspective on her parents, their relationship with each other and with her.

Fielding's writing, and the reflection associated with it, also helped her to evaluate her own resources and test her own capacity for resolve. Thus, when gastroenteritis became particularly bad in the school, she could overcome her fear and dislike of her mother in order to send her daughter to stay with her grandparents in Wolverhampton from the second week of August until she left Pinewood.[11] That decision was not without cost, for it gave Margarete Knight an opportunity to telephone Pinewood and remind her daughter that she was a fallen woman and a bad mother, as she held the mouthpiece so that she could hear the child crying.

She also held her resolve regarding Guy Walker. Although she had not told him where she was, he found out and on the day before her birthday showed up unexpectedly in a fancy automobile with an expensive gift, embarrassing her in front of her colleagues. They went boating on the river at Broxbourne where he begged her to leave. During the next month he sent her three letters and telephoned to ask if he could see her again. She wrote back to say that he must accept the fact that she did not love him and would not marry him. He telephoned again anyway.

As usual, what buoyed her spirits most were Leonard's frequent letters, his occasional visits, and their excursions to London. She met him there in May and June where they went to the zoo, picnicked in Hyde Park, bussed to Greenwich, or relaxed in Regent's Park. She expressed sympathy for Joyce and a concern that neither Joyce nor Leonard suffer on account of her; and she worried about his procrastination, saying the break needed to be complete and not one where he was torn between them.

From July his letters became more businesslike. By then he was in Edinburgh, settling into his new position and looking for a place for them to live. He set her tasks she was not good at, like liquidating her savings account and cashing in war loans. And he pressed for help with raising the money, at least in part because some of the places he looked at seemed far out of their reach. One, in a Georgian building in New Town where the Royal College of Physicians was located, cost £3,000. He also urged her to ask her parents for an interim loan; she worked up the courage to do so, but they said no. At the same time she declined to make a similar request of Berrington, knowing that, independent of her mother's feelings, he would be suspicious of Leonard and against her marrying him, for he cared for her very much. Then Leonard insisted that she, still unwed, change her name on her identity card and food coupons from Fielding to Jolley by declaration, something that was particularly confronting for her: she felt that women always had to do the nasty, degrading things.

Leonard seemed to be placing too much of the responsibility for raising the establishment finance on her: she was lucky if she earned £10 per month, and had no friends of means from Sibford, Pyrford or Birmingham she could approach given her compromised situation. If he had no money because of his divorce, and if his parents were not people of means, he had at least as many friends as she, and better-off ones at that. In the end, she was able to send him more than three quarters of the £200 he eventually needed as a down payment for the not 'really wonderful' house he found for them in Edinburgh.

Love is my double or nothing.
                                  Elizabeth Smart, *By Grand Central Station* (113)

Several examples show how Monica Fielding was able to regard her Pinewood co-workers in a writerly way. In June, she wrote to Leonard to say she had flirted in the kitchen with a man who for some reason was given to firing off a children's cap gun. Edna Kenyatta told her a story about his having had an affair with a woman who previously worked there—just as they were about to consummate the relationship, he shouted he wished his mother could see him in action, leaving an alarmed Armarella unsatisfied. The story finds its way into *My Father's Moon* when Vera hears shooting somewhere on Fairfields' grounds and Tanya (the name in fact and fiction of the woman who painted murals on the wall) tells her, '"That's . . . Frederick the Great, literature and drama . . . Got a mother . . . Shoots off gun for sex. The only trouble is darling", Tanya drawls, "the orgasm isn't shared". She disappears into the bathroom saying she's taken an overdose and so must have her bath quickly' (13–14).

And there was Mrs Norris, a good woman with a bad husband. She had two girls in a church school in Clevenden and a month-old baby and four-year-old child with her at Pinewood where her husband, a drunken, thieving, conman, would show up and cause trouble. Norris, a music teacher yet assigned the most menial tasks, was kind to Fielding from the beginning, showing her how to do things and explaining the politics of the place. In return, Fielding gave Norris a dress that Miss Prior of Sibford had given to her and offered to lend her money. Norris' husband would come and go unpredictably, usually after midnight, sometimes stealing whiskey and food from the local hotel, The George IV Inn, an escapade attributed to a

Mr Morris in *My Father's Moon* (15-17). Norris received a letter from him in Paddington one day, saying that by the time she read it he would be dead. Later that night the police called to tell her that he had been arrested and Fielding thought that 'in a way' it would have been better for Mrs Norris if he had killed himself. Wanting to cry over the situation, she felt that someone like Norris could shake people's faith in others.

Two further colleagues occupied Fielding's imagination. Of those two, one held her imagination directly. She was an unkempt, sometimes 'unwashed, back-to-nature vegetarian, who, despite a neck and chest burn resulting from her hair catching fire on a lamp two years earlier, was nonetheless quite attractive; Ann Prestcott was estranged from a two-year marriage to an 'idealistic' husband who lived in a hut in a forest while she worked and boarded with her two children at Pinewood. Some chemistry caused her and Fielding to argue when they first met, Prestcott bossing her about the kitchen, leading her to tell Leonard and Edna that she would not be treated like an imbecile and that she would leave the next time it happened. Prestcott wrote poetry and claimed to have produced 7,000 words of a novel (anticipating Hailey in *Mr Scobie's Riddle*), but when Fielding said she too was a fiction writer, she showed no interest. Still, Prescott continued to attract her as a wayward child might do, coming and going unannounced, leaving her children for days at a time, when Fielding would look after them unasked. And she astonished Fielding by having two men stay overnight in her room, the next night going out with her husband and again leaving her children unattended. Whatever her talent, Prestcott eschewed middle-class values and threw herself into her own version of a true artist's life.

When Prestcott left Pinewood in June, two men came to collect her. The one called Pluto entered Fielding's room, sat on her bed and told her how impressed he was with her, but that introduction served only a pretext for his telling her all about himself. She thought he was a poseur, telling him that she had four children and that he should get out. Though both fascinated and repelled by Prescott, her ways and her companions, Fielding's preferred paradigm of an artist's life was modelled more on Bloomsbury than Bohemia, one that combined passion, commitment, intellectual and creative exploration, and personal intimacy; and so she held on to her dream of life with Leonard in Edinburgh.

The person who occupied her imagination indirectly was the mother of some of the children in her charge. Those children were Georgina, Christopher, Sebastian and Rose Emma Barker, Georgina the oldest at eight when they were sent to Pinewood in 1950, and Rose Emma the youngest, not yet three. Fielding felt that they were difficult children but was especially attentive to them. She rescued Sebastian Barker when he got his knees wedged in the banister and no one else noticed and, when Georgina Barker had a bad nettle rash, she tracked her temperature until it was back to normal. Some of the Barker children may be recalled under slightly different names in *A Feast of Life* as Georgina, Samson and Rose.

Rose Emma, brought to Pinewood when she was two, captured Fielding's attention more than any other child at Pinewood. A tough, sturdy, resilient child with great blue eyes and full pink cheeks, she was precociously self-contained. Fielding attended to her before the others, taking her to the swings in the park, giving her one of her daughter's frocks because she had none that was not torn. Perhaps she feared for Rose's well-being in a crazy place that seemed a metonym for a crazy world. Whatever the reason, after Fielding left Pinewood she sometimes used Rose Emma as a pseudonym when she wrote. She did so without knowing that the girl had gone on to become a mother with an eating disorder and a history of alcohol and drug abuse who died in Cambridge at thirty-five.

The mother of the four Barker children, the Features Editor of the prestigious *House and Garden* magazine, lived in London during the week, after work frequenting Muriel Belcher's club in Soho where she learned to drink and to flirt from experts like Francis Bacon and Lucien Freud. On weekends she lived with her children in Tilty Manor House in Duton Hill, Essex, some twenty-five miles northeast of Great Amwell. On Friday afternoons, she would arrive with a Swiss au pair to collect her children after Fielding had washed and dressed them, polishing their shoes and combing their hair before presenting them to her at the front door. Fielding knew that their father George Barker was a second-rate poet (in Leonard's opinion), but she did not know that the intelligent, attractive, stylish thirty-seven-year-old professional woman was not Barker's wife or ex-wife. She was the wealthy Canadian novelist Elizabeth Smart who five years before, in 1945, published the poetic novel *By Grand Central Station I Sat Down and Wept*. A tour de force, it was considered 'one of the best achievements in Canadian literature to date' or, alternatively, 'one of the few successful pieces of sustained lyricism to be produced in our time or any'.[12]

Much later she would meet her again, and later still she would review *Necessary Secret: The Journals of Elizabeth Smart*. But at the time she knew nothing of the book nor of its being based on Smart's ménage à trois with George Barker and his wife Jessica Woodward, or that Barker, a self-absorbed misogynist, protested love for both his wife and Smart but practiced fidelity to neither, producing fifteen children with various women. And she did not know that, before George Barker, Smart was involved in a ménage à trois with surrealist German painter Wolfgang Paalen and his French wife Alice Rohan.[13] And not, of course, that Smart and Michael Wickham, Tanya Wickham's husband, had been living together since 1948.[14]

All Fielding knew was that, as a single parent, Smart's success as a writer and editor came at the cost and worry of having to leave her children at Pinewood. However much she envied Smart's wealth, glamour and independence, she worried about her and her children.[15]

> *I met my husband, Leonard, when I was seventeen and I'm still with him . . . He was very poetic and very fond of music . . . I kept up a friendship with him and then we married later on . . . I get letters from people who have never had anything like that. They've not had anyone that they can completely trust or who sustains them.*
>
> Elizabeth Jolley (Willbanks 115)

At the end of August she set off from Amwellberry to London and thence to Edinburgh, to begin her life with Leonard Jolley. When she stopped in Wolverhampton to collect her daughter, Margarete Knight's first question was whether or not she was married—Margarete Knight was holding a letter from Leonard Jolley addressed to Monica Jolley in care of Wells Road. When she answered, Yes, that that they were married in London on Saturday, her mother asked how a letter postmarked 'Saturday' in Edinburgh could arrive in Wolverhampton on the same day. She said Leonard travelled to London Friday night and must have posted the letter from Edinburgh before he left.

The period after Fielding left the Queen Elizabeth was the last stage in a journey that began for her in Wells Road and led from Sibford and Pyrford, from Birmingham and Amwelberry, to her being with Leonard Jolley for the next forty years. During that last stage she claimed a new identity by changing her name and declaring her independence through seeking employment outside of a household. But what began auspiciously ended doubtfully. She was still lying to her parents about the father of her child, still maintaining it was a TB patient from the Queen Elizabeth who subsequently died. And she was lying about her relationship with Leonard Jolley whom she had not yet married.

6

Scotland—The horror of marriage lies in its 'dailiness' . . .

Your purpose in life must not be the the joy of wedlock, but by your life to bring more love and truth into the world.
Leo Tolstoy to his son Ilia, letter 3 (1882–86)

Monica Fielding left Pinewood as planned, on Monday 28 August 1950, when Elizabeth Strachan returned from leave. She and her daughter went to Glasgow to stay with her sister Madelaine while waiting to move into their new home with Leonard in Edinburgh when it became available in a month. Madelaine had been living there for a year, dispensing drugs in a pharmacy during the day and studying the Margaret Morris Method of dance and movement in her own time. She had a boyfriend whom she considered artistic—Hugo looked like Beethoven, furnished his basement room with pictures and a big wall mirror, had jugs and Minton tiles above the fireplace, an aquarium, cacti, books of poetry and a record collection that was à la mode if not comme il faut. Later Madelaine found Monica a furnished flat with a Mrs Affleck at 224 Great Western Road.

In early September she and their daughter met Leonard Jolley in Edinburgh when he showed them their home-to-be at 48 Paisley Crescent. Modest but conveniently located, it was an easy bus ride to central Edinburgh just over a mile to the west and had a view of the Firth of Forth to the east about the same distance away. Then the three of them travelled back to Glasgow where they went on a wet but pleasant bus trip into the countryside with Madelaine and her boyfriend Hugo. They spent the next day enjoying their reunion, Leonard taking the train back to Edinburgh for work on Monday in the library of the Royal College of Physicians.

He returned to Glasgow the next weekend as well, when they were all to go to the beach at Dunoon for the day. If he did not know beforehand that Madelaine's boyfriend was a cross-dresser, he learned it on the day and was so put off that he misled them about Hugo's being at the station, and they all boarded the trains, leaving him on the platform. Thus, before the outing began, the day was ruined, for Madelaine was wretched, the child irritable, and Monica sick with the anxiety of having to soothe everyone without revealing Leonard's lie. Afterwards, she felt his behaviour was indicative of his attitude toward others and their feelings.

Leonard's behaviour that day suggests what many people before and after said, that he did not suffer fools gladly, his sister even adding, 'and in his opinion everyone was a fool'.[1] Such arrogance could be understood as resulting from his disappointments, doubts, and fears which provoked his hurt, angry responses—something perhaps encompassed by Monica's affirmation.

Edinburgh was called the Athens of the North for its intellectual and cultural life. The Royal College of Physicians served as a symbol of this, with its illustrious history of having received a Royal Charter from Charles II in 1682, its fine location, and its handsome buildings, the Victorian one at 9 Queen Street designed by Thomas Hamilton and the Georgian one at Number 8 designed by Robert Adam. Their oak-panelled rooms were spacious and grandly furnished, the Great Hall featuring a lawn of Persian rug.

Despite the elegance of Queen Street and the ambience of the RCP, Leonard Jolley was disappointed in his new appointment, believing that some elements of his job were beneath his dignity. He objected to the fact that, as well as looking after the library, he had to handle some of the college's official correspondence, effectively serving as an administrator to the Secretary and Treasurer of the College; he complained that he was expected to invigilate examinations and to translate foreign words and phrases for students who otherwise could not address the questions; and he resented having to arrange exhibitions and lectures, sometimes at short notice. When he voiced such disappointments, he disregarded two important facts. He had the standing of neither the Librarian of the British Library nor that of the National Library of Scotland, and he was lucky to have the RCP job at all: if his academic degrees were excellent, from 1939 to 1950 his practical experience was modest, limited to three months of cataloguing and press marking in the Library of the Institute for Civil Engineers in London ('I was the messiest labeller in the history of libraries in the British Isles') and four years as a part-time employee in the Selly Oak Colleges Library, followed by four years as its Head Librarian. Moreover, his new library held far fewer monographs than the Selly Oak Colleges Library[2], and any claims for being overworked would be hard to substantiate—it went unremarked, if not unnoticed, when he took off a morning or afternoon to work on his allotment.

His general doubts related to his ambivalence about being a medical librarian. He appreciated many of the RCP's holdings, like its early editions of the Roman Celsus' *De Medicina* and William Harvey's 1628 book on the circulation of blood, along with the manuscripts of William Cullen and Archibald Pitcairn. But he worried about illness and was afraid of doctors, and so wondered if he had made a mistake taking a job related to medicine.

More particular doubts pertained to the fact that his approach as a librarian was at odds with the RCP's idea of what a medical library should be and do. He took both a historical and curatorial approach to acquisitions, whereas his employers were more concerned about the utility of the holdings for practising physicians. The tensions were accentuated by the fact that he was intimidated by the RCP medicos who had none of the respect for librarians that trainee missionaries in Selly Oak had displayed. Not open to being persuaded otherwise, most of the doctors wanted their books to be practical and, new or old, elegant or not, able to answer their questions correctly and quickly. At such times, his inclination was to act disrespectfully, apparently oblivious to the fact that such behaviour could make his position less secure.

His major fear during his first two years in Edinburgh was a variant of the one he had in Birmingham involving his secrecy about his domestic arrangements. Though his divorce was not finalised, he had represented himself to the RCP as a married man with a young child, and desperately did not want to jeopardise that. Thus he renewed his earlier pressure on Monica to change the name on her ration books and identity card to Jolley when she was in Glasgow before she joined him at Paisley Crescent. As well, he demanded that Joyce tell no one, including her Plymouth Brethren family, about their marital break-up. Similarly, he never told his parents or siblings about it.[3]

In Glasgow, still trying to change her name to Jolley, Monica worried about Joyce, paradoxically wanting her to have whatever she wanted, and concerned to hear that she was contemplating taking a teaching job, one that might have the same drawbacks that she had found at Pinewood. She worried, too, about being excluded from Leonard Jolley's correspondence with his wife.

Monica and Leonard Jolley moved into their new home in Edinburgh on Monday 25 September 1950. The previous week they had looked at it and wondered if they really wanted it. Never having owned a house and never having lived together, they found those prospects perplexing. In that same week before taking possession, removalists from Wolverhampton had come and gone, Monica noting with disappointment that her mother had sent too many toys and too little furniture, mainly her bed from Wells Road, some books in tea chests and wedding presents from her sister Madelaine's failed marriage. Leonard Jolley was coming out of a failed marriage of ten years, Monica having contributed to that. Beyond the trial of her first decade of home life at 'Flowermead' and in Wells Road, she had lived for nearly twenty years in institutions—Sibford, Pyrford, the QEH, the Ashleigh Nursing Home and Pinewood—or with someone else's family—the Raynors, the Jolleys and the Fleetwood-Walkers. Like her mother before her, she had partnered with an attractive, intelligent, older, talented man, bringing to the relationship mainly romantic notions underpinned by goodwill and hope. She seems to have had no idea that Joyce might have found Leonard Jolley hard to live with.

Immediately it was a fraught time for both, and Leonard took his frustrations out on her within a week. That elicited a response peculiarly her own: she confessed to having provoked him and, by a logic natural to her, resolved never to do so to her daughter. Listening to Beethoven's *Fifth Symphony* and sensing the Slough of Despond all about her after a decade of following Leonard Jolley, she contemplated retracing her steps.

For the month of October she saw no one. She said she did not mind the seclusion, yet in the middle of November she called the police when a woman knocked at the door—or maybe she did not do that, for she wondered if the incident might have been a dream. During the same time, feeling unwell, she wrote about the suffering of being apart even while with Leonard. By December, she was writing, he was marking papers, and they were very close. As they listened to Gluck's opera *Orpheo ed Euridice*, they thought how their life was like that of those inseparable lovers—sad. In thinking so, they knew they were discussing how ordinary they had become.

'Ordinary' in their case meant a de facto relationship new to both of them in significant ways. He was as if married for a second time, but minus the lover who was now his partner; and Monica was as if married for the first time, to the man who had been her lover: their ménage à trois had been dismantled and they were like Knights before and after Kenneth Berrington. If nothing else, their sudden full-time physical and personal closeness would be an issue, and at first there was much more tension than before.

From early 1951 he undertook to help her impose order on what he called her new-found freedom. What appeared to be his solicitousness in Birmingham began to appear as control in Edinburgh. When he lectured her on not having trust, it fed into her inclination to be accommodating. When he chided her for talking too loudly about the price of plants or for eating thick gravy on a piece of bread, she was nearly brought to tears, but said nothing. When he discouraged her from corresponding with friends from her past or from inviting friends to their home, she was distressed. And when he advised her on what she should and should not read, she was both grateful and constrained. His regime for 'improvement' seems common to many domestic situations where one partner has greater power, in his case both rhetorical and social, and it fed into her inclination to be placatory.

For his part, Leonard worked 9 am to 6 pm during the week, told her little about his work, and invited her to few RCP functions.[4] It did not help, either, when he would describe to her the grand rooms and sumptuous fare at some of the RCP events, nor when he sometimes returned tipsy from a function. He was always anxious about getting all of his holiday and sometimes went on leave by himself, something that distressed her. Likewise, he applied for a position at the University of Hull without telling her, later saying that he believed she would not have given it another thought if he had told her.

Leonard Jolley's inflexibility about visitors could be hurtful. In 1952 he several times required Monica to postpone a visit by Edna Kenyatta and her son Peter, and in 1954 he said Madelaine could not come if she brought Hugo with her, and so she had to withdraw the invitation—something that caused confusion and disappointment that persisted until the two sisters died. Of course, he could make exceptions, as when he approved of Monica's asking Alix Macswiney Blakelock, her friend from Sibford and the Queen Elizabeth Hospital, to come to Edinburgh in 1954. She arrived for a week with her sons Adrian and Nigel but stayed for a month because Nigel came down with summer pneumonia. What assisted Leonard Jolley's tolerance, despite the four Jolleys and the three Blakelocks having to live together in a two-bedroom house, was that Alix was a very pretty woman. Moreover, Leonard imagined that Monica might have had a 'past' with her at the QEH—he was always hopeful for a confession, but when she had told him that she and Mary were like Swann and Odette in Marcel Proust's *À la Recherche du temps perdu*, he did not see what she meant.[5]

> *Jan. 1. The year opened with a strong gale: snow lay on the second: it grew milder to the end of the week. Jan. 25–28. More heavy snow. Jan. 27. 22 degrees of frost, the coldest in Edinburgh for several years.*
>
> Leonard Jolley, *Gardening Diary*, 1952

Leonard imposed a more congenial kind of order on the relationship through a favourite hobby, gardening. It was one they had shared before, in Calthorpe Road in Birmingham, where they met for a second time and where their love first flourished. Monica thrilled to be part of it, as shown by entries they made in a diary Leonard Jolley maintained from January 1952 through May 1954. In her 'Preface' to it, 'M. Fish' wrote, 'I did just want to say "How deeply grateful" we are to Mr L. Jolley for attempting a work of this kind, an arduous task no doubt, and for one of somewhat sluggish literary activity—a doubly arduous task. His style is easy to read if a little monotonous . . . But monotony of this kind can hardly go on for weather changes and snow lying will automatically give way to "rain falling" "wet" "rain falling"'.

A hundred-page record, the *Gardening Diary* shows that both Leonard and Monica revelled in the small front and back gardens they established in Paisley Crescent and in their allotment at Salisbury Green outside the wall of King's Park, at the foot of Arthur's Seat, and it gives a perspective on their relationship. His entries tend to be objective, in a tiny economical script, relying on unqualified nouns and verbs and colons rather than connectives, though his comments betray his allotment shed as untidy and his planted rows crooked. Her entries, in larger looser script, tend to be personal, more concerned with communicating with him than with documenting their activities—and revealing that she was the one who picked up the thorny rose clippings he left on the footpaths.[6] He planted in Latin (brassicas) or proper nouns (Michaelmas White and Perfection broccoli), and she harvested in English—spring and autumn Broccolli [sic], Brussel sprouts [sic], cabbage and kale. He loved his roses, she wallflowers. What stands out most is that the hundred-and-fifty entries (five of his to each of hers) are never edgy or critical but mutually supportive. Even criticism takes on that tone: when he writes below her sketch of a plot of roses that 'Fish is muddle headed', she responds, 'I don't like Stxe! Not much'.

The *Diary* collects clippings of letters they wrote to the editor of *Amateur Gardening*, sometimes under pseudonyms: 'T. Oates' of Edinburgh advocated burning clay soils in order to increase their productivity; and M. Knight, of Wolverhampton, made a case for older roses over hybrids, concluding, 'the cabbage and single roses have an uncorseted charm and grace which the hybrid tea lacks'. If the clippings show their exuberance for their gardening experiences, the *Diary* shows how well Leonard and Monica interacted when they did so in support of some activity with complementary benefits for each. They shared the work and pleasures of imagining and designing the plots, ordering the seeds, bulbs and plants, purchasing tools and sprays and the like, preparing the soil, sowing, tending and finally harvesting their vegetables and collecting their flowers. From January through December, they worked hard at their gardening, building borders, digging in posts, stringing wires, and then planting and tending to an enormous variety and number of flowers, fruits and vegetables.

Reminiscent of Virgil's *Georgics*, the *Diary* presents an image of gardening as an ideal domesticity: the man and woman working together, he more the builder, she more the harvester, both providing food and flowers for the table. There is not so much *otium*, leisure, as represented in Virgil's *Idylls*, but rather a *dignitas* enabling a homely harmony that generates respect and affection.[7]

Their ordinary family was, according to Tolstoy's formulation, unhappy in its own way. Yet the *Gardening Diary* shows there were periods in Edinburgh when Leonard and Monica appeared to be very much in love. What Monica contributed to it must at times have been hopeful to the point of despair.

Late in the first year of the *Garden Diary*, Joyce divorced Leonard, the decree nisi being issued in late September 1952. Two months later Monica travelled by train to Wolverhampton, to visit her parents for three weeks. Whether or not Monica knew she was two months pregnant with their second child, Margarete Knight would know soon enough if only because her daughter sought medical attention for a minor pregnancy-related problem while in Birmingham. Still not believing she was married to Leonard and unhappy at the prospect of a second child out of wedlock, Margarete Knight showered attention on her granddaughter, constantly feeding her and buying her new clothes, blaming Monica for a lack of self-control, and predicting a wretched life for her granddaughter. When Wilfrid Knight told Monica to be kind to her out-of-control mother, she called him an old fool. Leonard Jolley remarked that her mother was crazy and that her parents' relationship with Kenneth Berrington was sado-masochistic.

Unknown to her parents, Monica had gone to Wolverhampton in order to meet and marry Leonard Jolley in the Registry Office on Saturday morning, 6 December 1952. He joined Monica and Madelaine there, Madelaine being one of the witnesses, the other a Miss Gladys Mamer, commandeered off the street by Monica—a man she first approached said doing so would make him late for work. Finally Monica Elizabeth Knight Fielding Jolley de facto was Monica Elizabeth Jolley de jure. He had the marriage certificate to prove it, and she had the sterling silver wedding ring she paid six pence for at Woolworth's in Birmingham. And they had Richard Charles Henry Jolley on 16 June 1953.

The month before, Monica wished they need not get married, but the dailiness of living had already taken over.

> *The truth is more like this: life—say 4 days out of 7—becomes automatic; but on the 5th day a bead of sensation between husband and wife forms which is all the fuller and more sensitive because of the automatic customary unconscious days on either side. That is to say the year is marked by moments of great intensity, Hardy's 'moments of vision'.*
>
> Virginia Woolf's *Diaries*[8]

The Jolleys were pleased with their new home, each in her or his own way. Costing £2,250, it was in a late-1920s housing development unique for being highly 'paisleyed', with Paisley Avenue, Crescent, Drive, Gardens, Grove, and Terrace, all named after the first Baron Paisley, the sixteenth/seventeenth-century owner of the original estate. To Monica, its best features were its magnificent view of the Firth of Forth and easy access to King's Park. Leonard quipped that he liked it because its two bedrooms meant there was no room for visitors. The area attracted people starting careers and families, like Leo Blair, a young law lecturer with political ambitions, who lived with his wife at number 84 with their sons Bill and Tony, the former going on to become a Queens Council, the latter becoming British Prime Minister.

Soon after they arrived in Edinburgh, they resumed the types of writing projects they had in Birmingham. Late in 1950 she had an idea for a short story, early in 1951 he had drafted an article called 'Who Should Write the History of Medicine?' and by April he was writing something for the Scottish 'Children's Hour'. They jointly submitted two stories for the *Observer's* December 1953 competition, 'The Comforter' and 'The Spruce Tree', without success. At the same time, she continued the writing that was so important to her in Birmingham. She tried to revive their 'Waterloo Mouse', and in February of 1951 she sent three stories to the 'Children's Hour'. The following February, she attended a class on 'The Art of Writing' at the University of Edinburgh that she found 'quite interesting'. By the end of 1952 she was preoccupied with publishing a novel, in November submitting the manuscript of *Eleanor Page* to publisher Rupert Hart Davis and then to Heinemann. Fantasising about its being well received, she imagined being praised in the *Observer* and people asking Leonard what it was like being married to a novelist. Her fantasy extended to hoping her success would enable her to buy Leonard some Coopers marmalade and a pair of binoculars and to have the kitchen painted. By Christmas the manuscript had been returned with a rejection slip. In February the next year, 1953, A. P. Watt, the oldest literary agency in England, also returned it, saying they could not think of a publisher who might be interested in it. A month later Victor Gollancz, founder of the Left Book Club and publisher of Ford Maddox Ford and George Orwell, confirmed that opinion with his own rejection slip.

She comforted herself with chocolate and, a few days later, made one of her hopeless resolves to put away her writing and devote herself to housekeeping. It was a commitment that lasted overnight, for in the morning she once more had hope for what she had come to call *Elephant Page*.

> [W]e had a dear little garden... we were isolated... but I made one or two very good friends. One was a woman who was fifteen years older than I was... [s]he became the most valuable friend... a most valuable and loved friend. I think a few friends are more important than a whole lot.
>
> Elizabeth Jolley (Reid 42)

The Jolleys' new home in Paisley Crescent also pleased her for the opportunity it provided for visitors, to the extent that Leonard allowed them, something she never had before. Their main visitors were neighbours Bill and Nora Bland who lived with their nine- and sixteen-year-old sons, at 11 Paisley Terrace, up the hill from the Jolleys. Bill Bland, five years older than Leonard, held a First-class Honours degree in Electrical Engineering from London University. He was an administrator with the Post Office in Edinburgh, his intellectual interests wide and generally compatible with Leonard Jolley's, except that he was not interested in classical music. Nora Bland, sixteen years her senior, had a University of London degree, was a secondary-school teacher of History, and had little interest in literature. She was also sympathetic and loving and, as a result, became Monica's Gertrude-figure in Edinburgh.

From September of 1953, Monica began to see Nora more and more often. She became concerned with dressing correctly and with offering the correct food and drink to the Blands, hoping her new £5 Indian rug would persuade Nora that she had taste. After one visit, when she told Nora she copied her, she could not sleep for fear that she had talked too much; if she expressed an opinion different from the Blands', she would worry they might think her juvenile. Then, if Nora did not visit, she wondered if she had offended her. Leonard also socialised with the Blands, going with them to *Macbeth* and to *Le Bourgeois gentilhomme* during the 1954 Edinburgh Festival. In July 1956 she took an automobile trip with them to Berwick-on-Tweed in England when Leonard was at a library conference in London.

The only other visitor Leonard fully welcomed was John Broom, from Bathgate, roughly equidistant from Edinburgh and Glasgow. A poet, librarian, bookseller and Unitarian minister eleven years younger than Leonard, he was someone they met through their contributions to *Amateur Gardening*. With his quick mind and strong theological and political opinions, he was just the sort of person Leonard would engage in a test of wit and will, using his position and seniority to advantage. Broom was also a man at the start of a slide from being a social drinker to being an alcoholic.[9] From mid-1951, he would visit most Sundays, their talks sometimes continuing through the night. Around this same time Leonard and Monica, who had never drunk before, started to do so regularly.

Leonard and John Broom had lively discussions, with Jolley forced to defend the more conservative position. At a time when Scottish nationalists were blowing up letter boxes marked 'Queen Elizabeth II', Broom took their side, saying that when Elizabeth became Queen Elizabeth II of England in 1952, she should have been Elizabeth I in Scotland for she had no royal namesake there. If Monica were somewhat out of her depth in such conversations, she refused to be excluded from them. So, when Broom and Leonard were trading examples of arcane knowledge in support of their positions, she interjected with a tale of being amazed when an egg frying in the pan flipped over, unaided, before her eyes. Such quirky contributions on her part would deflect her husband's claim to be superior and allow her to ingratiate herself with people like Broom.

The three of them talked about pornography in literature and theatre, and at one point even managed to combine the topics of sexuality and theology. They also discussed the Scottish 'convertion' from Scottish Presbyterianism to English Anglicanism in King James' time. As they did so, Broom, two years younger than Monica and having just broken up with his girlfriend Mary, looked fondly at her and said that falling in love was better than convertion.[10]

Their ongoing problems with the Knights in Wolverhampton were the sort that Tolstoy had in mind when he wrote of unhappy families. Monica could not disentangle herself from the melodrama that was her parents' life, and Leonard, who had cut off contact with his own family, made missiles that he insisted she fire at them. In 1953, when Monica was trapped in the second week of a reluctant cold war with her mother, Leonard offered to call it off, but he did not: Margarete Knight was a target he could not resist.

He had become a target for her too and, as a result of Kenneth Berrington's death, she had by far the greater financial resources. One of her stratagems was a a subtle double bind with a sting in the tail, apparently offering help while criticising her daughter's inadequacies: when Ruth Marian Jolley was born 9 September 1955 and Monica had difficulty breastfeeding her, Margarete Knight hired Ilse Gaugusch, her Austrian friend who had said of Wilfrid Knight that '[s]aints are very nice in heaven', to assist the Jolleys for an indefinite period. The never-married ship's steward who spoke half a dozen languages and had worked for several different shipping lines, was a model of efficiency if not tact, believing honesty was more important than kindness. With a grim cheerfulness, she took their new £5 rug outside to the clothesline and nearly beat it to shreds, next taking the radio apart to dust the inside. Alarmed, Monica thought having Leonard's meals on time might fall victim to Ilse's take-no-prisoners regime. For her part, Gaugusch thought Monica was a good mother but too much under Leonard's influence, such that her confidence was undermined. Her example was of Richard once being of two minds about going out into the cold to play. Monica went off to consult her book on child psychology while Gaugusch pushed him through the door and slammed it behind him: when Jolley returned to say the book endorsed the parent's making up the child's mind in such cases, she found Richard happily playing outside. Of Leonard Jolley, Gaugusch said he either liked you or he did not and, if he did not like you, he would tell you.

After being with the Jolleys for six weeks from the beginning of September 1955, Ilse Gaugusch suddenly had to return to Austria to help her grandmother who had had a stroke. That was perhaps just as well for both Frau Gaugusch and the Jolleys because it looked like she was in it for the long haul, and it was inevitable she would turn her attention to improving Leonard Jolley. He might have found her more formidable to deal with than the more histrionic Margarete Knight.

Another time, when Margarete Knight brought her granddaughter home from Wolverhampton to Edinburgh by train, she did not get out of the taxi, but returned immediately to the station for the trip back to Birmingham. After the event, Monica wished she had more forcefully pressed her mother to come in for a cup of tea, seeming to have some sense that the shaming/blaming caused each of the players to withhold what she most wanted, mother-daughter intimacy: it was a lose-lose game. Possibly she was constrained because of Leonard's involvement but, whatever the reason, she rationalised playing the game by reasoning that her mother felt guilty about Berrington's money and thus there was no reason for her not to accept it.

The move from Birmingham to Edinburgh had been a good one for Leonard Jolley's career. He had some important successes, like winning funding to consult with the British Museum about the deterioration of the Cullen manuscripts, permission to fill gaps in the holdings of the medical books, to buy photocopying equipment, to refurbish the library, and to use space in the basement and on the ground floor of 8 Queen Street. The lecture he gave on Pitcairn in his second year at the RCP was impressive enough to make the College think they had been well rewarded for the 50 guineas they gave as an honorarium. It also made the College concerned that Jolley might take a position advertised at Leeds, and so it resolved to increase his salary to £900 from 1 January 1953, to rise by £100 per year until it would reach £1,400 in 1957, if Jolley stayed that long. The £900 was a considerable improvement on the £400 he received from the Selly Oak Colleges in 1946 and, at forty percent of the value of their house, not a small salary.

But the College's expression of support for him could do nothing to relieve Jolley's anxiety amongst doctors, and he was right to imagine that the RCP was a dead-end job in the same way as the Selly Oak position. Each was a specialist library with no growth prospects to enable the Librarian to improve his situation. Besides, Jolley thought his employers and colleagues were Pharisees since they did not share his approach to acquisitions, an attitude he displayed in a variety of ways. One of them was to use his Annual Reports to advertise his successes and to frighten his superiors about serious problems that would result if he were not given an ever-larger budget. In one instance, he stated that 'it was essential to decide whether the aim was to maintain the library as an outstanding research library or merely to purchase text-books', and the Convener flatly responded that it was impossible for the Library to maintain its former status. Like Sir Humphrey Appleby in *Yes Minister*, Jolley was learning that is unwise to ask a question if you might not like the answer and that it is sometimes inconvenient to have a policy on every matter.

He started to look around for another job. After his failed interview at Hull, he spoke with the successful applicant, poet Philip Larkin from Belfast. The two men jokingly agreed that in future Jolley would apply for jobs in the north of England and Larkin for jobs in the south. As it turned out, the next job Jolley applied for was in Scotland: on 6 August 1956 he interviewed for and was offered the position of Deputy Librarian at the University of Glasgow. When she first became aware of his application, Monica was disappointed at the thought of having to leave her home and garden, despite the inconveniences.

> When I read Proust's <u>Remembrance of Things Past</u>, it seems to me he surely wrote in ink of a rich violet and inscribed such names as Gilbote and Monsieur de Charlus or Guermantes with flourishes and embellishments of his pen with great enjoyment and delicately painted his steeples and clouds and his hedges of wild roses with the same leisure and ease, I know that really such writing only comes with great labour. But my ink is not violet and I have no flourishing names to inscribe on the pages and if I confess to having a little of Madame Verdurin in myself, I do not like making this confession as it is not the most attractive side of her I find in myself, I am not going to be able to describe such dinners such conversations such evenings as she, Madame Verdurin, drew about herself and her little circle.
>
> Opening paragraph of *A Feast of Life*, 15 March 1956

Six months before Leonard Jolley's interview in Glasgow, Monica started writing a novel that remained unnamed for a time. Her preliminary thoughts on the task recall her reading of Marcel Proust's turn-of-the-twentieth-century, seven-volume *À la Recherche du temps perdu* two years before. In *Du Côté de chez Swann*, the first volume, Madame Verdurin is an odious woman of dubious taste and no tact who bullies weak people into faithful attendance at her soirées. There, the conversation consists of gossip about fashion and the arts, the highlight of the event being, in Verdurin's opinion, her own 'discovery', the composer Vinteuil who plays for her on command.

Of the only three habitués at the Jolleys' soirées, two were Bland, Nora not a fan of literature and Bill not a fancier of music. The Vinteuil in her life was John Broom, the poet with whom she enjoyed a flirtatious literary relationship. When Broom was with the Jolleys, the conversation was intelligent and lively, witty, catty and risqué. He prefigured a world she could create around her, if only Leonard Jolley were more considerate of her hopes and needs. Knowing which derrières to kiss and which to kick, Mme Verdurin instructed her husband to tell their most important guest, Monsieur Swann, that she 'writes quite delightfully' (283). Those three little words—*writes quite delightfully*—were an early move in a chess game that later saw the widowed Madame Verdurin become the third wife of Prince de Guermantes, completing her ascent from the middle class to the aristocracy.

Monica knew that Leonard would never promote his wife as Verdurin did his. Besides, the Madame Verdurin she recognised in herself was obsessed with becoming a writer rather than a princess.

As she prepared to leave Edinburgh, she realised that she would have to achieve that success on her own.

> *I think [Leonard] preferred for us to listen to music or be together in the evenings. You see the trouble of writing is you have to be on your own. I did write a bit during the day. I did write a whole novel in Edinburgh. . . Then I started another one, starting in Glasgow. . .*
>
> Elizabeth Jolley (Reid 129)

Leonard and Elizabeth Jolley arrived in Glasgow in November 1956, his having persuaded her to use Elizabeth rather than Monica as her name. She did so for the rest of her life.

If she had described 62 Abbey Drive in Glasgow, she might have said the main difference between it and 48 Paisley Crescent in Edinburgh was that it was much larger. It had four bedrooms as well as what the Jolleys called the Blue Room, Billiard Room, and Book Room. Nonetheless, personal space was still in short supply because they had joined the East-West Friendship Society, renting rooms to mostly male students—African, Chinese and Indian along with British ones. Elizabeth and Leonard shared one bedroom, Richard and Ruth shared another, Sally had one to herself, and a boarder had the fourth. The situation was made somewhat more congenial for the fact that each bedroom had its own hand basin, thanks to the previous owner who was a plumber.

As Deputy Librarian at the University of Glasgow, Jolley received an annual salary of £1,400, nearly ten percent more than he would have been earning in Edinburgh. But the project was a much larger one: in Edinburgh a small handful of librarians worked with 50,000 volumes, but in Glasgow there were some fifty staff working with nearly half a million volumes and a budget of over £30,000 per annum, more than ten times the RCP's library budget. There were 6,000-7,000 students and some 700 teaching staff at the university to be served.

Jolley's knowledge as a medical librarian was at least tangentially apropos of his new job, since the University of Glasgow had an impressive medical school that was being threatened by feuding between its Western Infirmary and its Royal Infirmary. But his biggest challenge came when the Head Librarian, R. O. MacKenna, made him responsible for reclassifying the entire library, reorganising its holdings on the shelves so as to group together books on the same subject. Physically, it was a huge job, one for which his more routine responsibilities at Selly Oak and Edinburgh did not fully prepare him. But he was suited for the job since the scheme to be used was based on the one at his own University College London and had proved satisfactory to the University of Leeds for thirty years.

At the same time, he was coming to be known as a capable and improving scholar, and was eager to develop in that direction. So he devoted as much time as possible to two publishing projects. One of them was founding and editing *The Bibliotheck: A Journal of Bibliographical Notes and Queries Mainly of Scottish Interest*.[11] The other was fulfilling a publisher's contract to write a book on cataloguing, research and writing that, in theory at least, would assist with his re-cataloguing effort. Thus he worked long hours at the library and then continued his reading and writing at home. As in Edinburgh, in Glasgow he was not forthcoming to his wife about his work, admitting that she had no idea what he did at the RCP but not subsequently telling her anything about it.

For her part, their Glasgow house was not the home Elizabeth had dreamed of, for their passion of the 1940s did not survive the domesticity of the 1950s. The tension between them increased as she grew frantic from attending to everyone's needs, desperate that no one was attending to hers, all the while trying to work on her new novel. Leonard had been overwhelmed by the details of finalising the sale of their old house and buying their new one. She comforted and dispelled his fears, accommodating them but refusing to be disabled by them herself. She resolved to continue working on the novel she started a year ago in Edinburgh, a book she considered a sermon from her heart, one she associated either with documenting the family's current happiness or with forestalling its impending unhappiness.

Then, on 8 July 1957, she entered the Western Infirmary for six weeks, diagnosed with ulcerative colitis, her long-standing problems from Birmingham and Edinburgh having worsened. The prognosis was that she would not be a permanent invalid but that she would have to live within some limitations which would not excessively restrain her once she and Leonard had accepted them—a colostomy was contemplated. Thus Leonard suddenly had to look after the children for much longer than he had ever done before. They declined Margarete Knight's offer to come for the duration, although in August they accepted her assistance to the extent of sending Sally and Richard to visit their grandparents. Leonard Jolley was much helped by eleven-year-old Sally, and both were assisted by three women who cleaned house, fixed the children's meals, and sometimes babysat.

The two younger children could drive Leonard to distraction. He wrote to Elizabeth in hospital about how Ruth's displays of affection ended with her raiding his pockets and of how his pleasure at her rubbing her head against his knee was followed by alarm when her purring turned to squeals of demand. Her cracking him over the head with a stick when he was bent over was followed by Richard's nearly sending him over the edge when he leaned over his father's shoulder while drinking tea and breathed on him milkily. Leonard Jolley was not, he admitted, a natural child-lover.

Their separation and his caretaking the children prompted him to recall their time together before, regretting that they had not got together when they first met again in Birmingham. However, his wish for a return to the joyful time before their marriage was an expression of hope unaccompanied by a method.

When Elizabeth returned from the hospital, she predictably found things worse than before she left. The house had become very damp, the boarder's chimney badly affected by it. Leonard required attention too, and she immediately had to deal with his disappointment that his friend Les Wheeler failed to make a promised visit to Glasgow for Leonard's forty-third birthday on 12 August. Wheeler might have re-evaluated their friendship, for on 20 April he and his wife Louie had served as witnesses to Joyce Hancock's marriage to fellow technical-college teacher Raymond Mitchell in Exeter. Jolley's sister Laura was also part of their wedding party, having sided with Joyce during the marriage break-up. Since the Jolleys did not see the Wheelers or the Lams, nor the Blands either, their friendship circle in Glasgow had virtually shrunk to a point, John Broom.

There was nothing she could do to restore Leonard's friendship with people he knew from the time before he met her. Besides, she was full of determination to get on with her book and had made a few notes for it, although she was fearful that it would take so long to draft that she would never have time to rewrite it. It was during her first week home that she wondered if *A Feast of Life* might be a good title. It was a breathtaking display of optimism.

Gertrude Whele died 18 March 1957, and Elizabeth started her second book in early 1958, hoping to finish it by September. It was to be about a woman overcome by desire for a younger man, with her husband's knowledge. In early February the Jolleys talked about sexual love outside of marriage. Whoever raised the idea, Leonard was against it because of the deception it would inevitably entail, and Elizabeth praised his wisdom for making that point. Two days later, he suggested that she visit Nora Bland in their new home in Hermitage Gardens in Edinburgh. She did so, but she could not unburden herself, for Nora did not encourage intimacies to the extent of her previous mother-substitutes—Jean Sapcote in Pyrford, Peggy Frazer in Birmingham, Edna Kenyatta in Amwellbury, and—until recently—Gertrude Whele.

When she returned from Edinburgh, John Broom had to cancel his scheduled Sunday 9 February visit because of a heavy snowfall. The day turned into a domestic storm as well when Leonard complained about lights being left on, the hot water heater not being turned off, and the number of eggs consumed for breakfast—fingering their new boarder as the culprit. When she went sledging with the boarder in the afternoon, Leonard declared that it was adultery to go out sledging with another man. The last misfortune for the day, from her point of view at least, was when Leonard made her write an unkind letter to her parents in connection with a loan she was paying back to her father at the rate of £4 per month. She regretted letting him dictate what she did, just as she resented having to drop friends if he did not like them. She saw the point in his anger about sledging with the boarder, but blithely countered it by saying she was happy to be in the fresh air.

The next Sunday, following his custom of reading her diary and then writing in it himself, he added an entry, as if it were hers, slating his selfishness, petty mindedness and bullying, but also evoking a memory of their recently being out alone on a walk together, the first time for a year or more: he described it in lyric terms, suggesting the interlude released all tension between them. Elizabeth declined the gambit, resolutely describing the same walk in a matter-of-fact way.

In March both of them socialised separately. She went to the cinema with international students to see three films in the middle of the month.[12] As she returned from the first film—called, ironically, *Freedom*—she feared that Leonard might be angry with her for going out with a young student. Instead she found him having a wonderful time at home with Anne Thomas and Margaret Sprott, two young nurses from the Western Infirmary who would sometimes overnight with the Jolleys.[13] A week later Leonard went to the ballet with Mary Wilson, a pretty, young nurse who, like Thomas, had looked after Elizabeth in the Western Infirmary. And in May she went with the current boarder to see a Sadler's Wells production of *The Marriage of Figaro* at the King's Theatre.

All along, she had remained an epistolary friend and literary confidante of John Broom. When Broom made his first Glasgow appearance, in April 1958, she gave him part of *A Feast of Life* to read. She did not completely trust him, she said provocatively but told him they had respect and sympathy for each other despite never having been intimate. That confusing message might have derived from feeling guilty about giving the manuscript to Broom without Leonard's knowing, while at the same time she was angry with Leonard over his response to a draft she had shown him. He had disapproved of the actions of the main character in 'The Return', taking that character to stand for Elizabeth herself. She rationalised the act of giving part of *A Feast* to Broom by saying Leonard had a bad attitude whereas she was well intentioned.

Broom's response was enthusiastic. He praised the work's vitality, especially the love scenes between the characters Vera and Lois, and he was also concerned to know if the Gertrude figure, Hannah, was meant to be a sympathetic character when she disapproved of Vera's sexual behaviour. He urged her to press on, for her own satisfaction and because he wanted to know what happened next.

> *I could inform the dullest author how he might write an interesting book. Let him relate the events of his own life with honesty, not disguising the feelings that accompanied them.*
> Samuel Taylor Coleridge to Thomas Poole, 17 February 1797[14]

Elizabeth Jolley interleaved chapters of *The Feast of Life* (soon called *A Feast of Life*), the first manuscript she drafted, with chapters of the second one she wrote, *George's Wife*, the original title coming to stand for both, the pair filling eight notebooks.[15] In the *Feast* component, begun in Edinburgh in March 1956, Vera tells the story of her early life, starting with when she was a girl living in the Black Country around Birmingham. *George's Wife*, begun in November 1957, is also narrated by Vera, now married to businessman George Forsyth. The time is 'the present', perhaps in Glasgow—there is a reference to the funnels of ships, cranes and ship-building yards such as would be seen on Glasgow's Firth of Clyde. The two texts are interlinked by means of flashbacks in *George's Wife* to people, places and events from Vera's earlier life represented in *A Feast*.

A Feast describes 'Flowermead' (called by that name) and then a house in the Black Country, with governesses and other visitors from Vienna; boarding school and the Harper's Hill incident; nurse training at St Cuthbert's where Vera observes the naked frolicking of Snorter and Diamond; general training at the Queen Alexandra where she is attracted to Lois and where Trent asks what is the most important thing in the world ('Sex I suppose'); and Hannah (modelled on Gertrude) who offers advice on love and life.

In *George's Wife*, the Forsyths live in a house larger than their previous one. Vera, who had changed her name from Monica when she was eleven years old, has three children, Elizabeth who is nine, Tristan almost three, and Rose who is only a few months—the same age differences and gender distribution as Jolley's children. As the draft goes along, Jolley changes the names of the first two children to Georgina and Samson, thus giving the three children in the book names that recall Georgina, Sebastian and Rose Emma Barker at Pinewood (called Fairfield in the draft). Georgina behaves like Elizabeth Jolley did with her mother and Mr Berrington in Europe: she refuses to go to the theatre her mother attends with a man who is not her husband, and then the man returns to find Georgina and successfully talks her around to joining them. And George acts like Leonard when he complains to Vera about too many eggs being eaten at breakfast.

In the fifth notebook, written a year after Jolley's hospitalisation in the Western Infirmary, Vera, unwell and confined to her bed at home for some weeks, recalls a previous relationship with Joanna and her husband Jonathan Metcalf when she was a trainee nurse and he was a doctor at the Queen Alexandra Hospital. She concludes by remembering Hannah, who related her chain-making childhood, and who invited Vera to come and stay with her to protect her from the Metcalfs whom Hannah feared were taking advantage of her. In the denouement of Part One of *A Feast*, the day after Vera and Jonathan kiss for the first time, he sends her a letter saying, 'I cannot give you all the love you ought to have . . .'

The discussion between the Jolleys on extramarital affairs were consonant with ideas Elizabeth would have been introduced to when she was a class of one being tutored by Leonard and Joyce Jolley who were imbued with the Bloomsbury ethos while at University College London in the 1930s. A collection of men and women prominent in the arts, humanities and social sciences, Bloomsbury members were also distinguished for their commitment to open sexual relations between and among them, and for its indifference to societal norms in regard to gay, lesbian and bisexual sexuality. In his *Principia Ethica* Bertrand Russell celebrated the pleasures of human intercourse and the enjoyment of beautiful objects, Russell being able, Leonard Jolley noted enviously, to have frequent sex without the reward of paternity.

Elizabeth Jolley read and liked Woolf's work in the 1930s when she wrote a Sibford essay on 'The Duchess of Newcastle'. It was a liking refined and extended by her steady reading of Woolf's novels and essays, like *Orlando* in the mid-1940s and *To the Lighthouse* in 1949. In 1944 Leonard and Joyce gave her *A Haunted House and Other Stories* and, when she was at Pinewood, he gave her *The Captain's Death Bed and Other Essays*, and *Orlando: A Biography*, published in 1928 and known by the 1940s to be based on the life of Vita Sackville-West, Virginia Woolf's bisexual lover. Defined by Woolf as truthful because fictional, *Orlando* depicts the sexual and other adventures of a man from Elizabethan times who lives until World War I, along the way becoming a woman and giving birth at the end of the book: the book, among other things, *Orlando* is an implicit history of the evolution of modern sexuality. The fantasy of the novel is Orlando's gender switch (and improbable longevity) and its 'truthful' aspect is the psycho-social counterpart of that, namely Woolf's belief that 'sexually defined selves or roles are merely costumes and thus readily interchangeable'.[16] It is a concept Jolley might have resonated with, just as she might have been fascinated by a novel 'in which a meditation on the configurations of the family as it is structured around the stereotypical heterosexual couple does not in some sense dominate the plot'.[17]

> *I am one of those devoted wives who would go wherever her husband goes. And I suppose because we had a very difficult time at the beginning, not being together, I didn't want to stop him from doing something he wanted to do.*
>
> Elizabeth Jolley (Headon 43)

From the beginning of 1958, only fifteen months after they arrived in Glasgow, Leonard Jolley made plans to move again. The same month he complained about her sledging with their boarder, he asked his boss R. O. MacKenna to write him a letter of recommendation for the University Librarian's position at Nottingham. MacKenna did so, praising Jolley's character, intellect and knowledge of cataloguing, but the application was not successful.

Though Jolley had moved up to a more impressive library in Glasgow, he had moved down a rung of the hierarchy, and his prospects for advancement were bleak. His immediate predecessors in Edinburgh and Glasgow had one hundred years of service between them before they retired, and MacKenna, a year older than Jolley, showed no prospect of retiring. He stayed on another twenty years, meaning that Jolley would not have become Head Librarian in Glasgow until he was sixty-four-years old.

He knew that Glasgow had served an important function for him, his work in a large academic library complementing his time in smaller but important specialist libraries. In addition, the book he was working on, *The Principles of Cataloguing*, would be an important addition to the conference papers and journal articles already on his curriculum vitae. Thus he persisted, asking MacKenna for another recommendation in December.

Writing to the University of Western Australia, MacKenna recalled that when Jolley interviewed in Glasgow, he 'appeared before the committee with a hang-dog look and a solemn face, and no optimistic resolution was in sight: the first question, produced by the Chairman, elicited a typical Jolley humorous response with his delightful smile, and then the committee warmed to him'. He refrained from adding that Jolley did not suffer fools gladly, although that was his opinion.[18] The application was successful, and Jolley accepted the offer from the University of Western Australia, despite Wilfrid Knight's warning that at Jolley's age—almost forty-five—the equator constituted a point of no return. Similarly, Elizabeth Jolley, at the time unresponsive to him and with no heart for working on her book, wondered why he had applied for a job in Australia: did he know things would be better there, or was it once more a hope without a method?

On 21 October 1959 the Jolleys moved out of 62 Abbey Drive, the children having spent the previous ten days with the Knights in Wolverhampton. Then they went to Hull where Leonard Jolley discussed the university library with Philip Larkin and Elizabeth wrote farewell letters. Next they went to London, staying overnight with Les and Louise Wheeler who were running a bookshop in Slough. It was a disappointment for them, Leonard sensing that the Wheelers still disapproved of his leaving Joyce, Elizabeth feeling that they resented her for being the one who broke up the marriage.

In London they stayed at a Quaker hotel. On the morning of Sunday 25 October Elizabeth visited Dr Peggy Frazer who was living in London. In the afternoon Aunty Mary Wynn came all the way from Birmingham to say goodbye, Elizabeth taking her to the National Book League for tea. And in the evening she met with Alix Macswiney who, fifteen years ago, had asked her what was the most important thing in life. Around noon on Monday Wilfrid and Grete Knight delivered the children, visiting for only a few minutes before they caught the 2:10 train back to Birmingham. At last, on Tuesday 27 October 1959, the Jolley family sailed from Tilbury on the *RMS Orion*. They stopped at Gibraltar, Naples, Port Said, and Colombo before arriving in Australia a month later.

Leonard Jolley had his new book with him, and Elizabeth Jolley had a trunk of manuscripts. Everyone was full of his or her own excitement and anxiety, Leonard and Elizabeth no doubt concerned with an ambiguous pronouncement Leonard Jolley had written in her diary, to the effect that family life is the same the world over and so would be no different in Perth. Not so sure, from before the time they left Glasgow Ruth wondered if there would be loos in Australia, and Richard wondered if his grandmother would be there. Only if she flew by broomstick, Elizabeth thought.

7

1960s—After the flight of the cockatoos...

The bright light I think was the first thing and that all our clothes seemed very shabby. The second—or perhaps even before the bright light—was the extreme friendliness of everyone. Everyone looked after us.

Elizabeth Jolley (Reid 50)

A few days after they disembarked in Fremantle on Monday 23 November 1959, *The West Australian* newspaper reported that 'New University librarian Leonard Jolley arrived in Perth this week with his wife and their three young children. English-born Mr and Mrs Jolley have been living for some time in Scotland where Mr Jolley was deputy librarian at the Glasgow University'. Though the *West Australian* reported the University of Western Australia's press release on its 'Page for Women', the significance of the Jolleys' arrival pertained to Leonard, not to his unnamed wife or children.[1] That was also reflected in the group who meet them at the Port of Fremantle passenger dock, UWA Professor of Modern History, Fred Alexander[2] and his wife, along with Jolley's UWA predecessor and official welcomer, Miss Emmy Wood[3], and Ali Sharr, Western Australian State Librarian.

Fred Alexander had visited Glasgow to recruit Leonard Jolley, arranging for him to visit several British libraries before departing for Australia. Although surely kindly meant by Alexander, the reception was somewhat tense. He had worked with Wood for a decade and thought highly of her, but Jolley, always wary, would have assumed that Wood was disadvantaged on account of being a woman. She was the 1927 appointee of unpopular and long-serving UWA Chancellor, J. S. Battye[4], and for more than three decades had been in charge of a library that was in a parlous state. From the beginning, Jolley figuratively kept his distance from her.

Alexander had been Chair of the State Library Board since 1952, and so had been involved in Ali Sharr's appointment in 1953. If he knew that Jolley and Sharr had been classmates in the librarianship program at University College London in the 1930s, he might not have known that Jolley disliked Sharr. The animosity was ostensibly based on the fact that Jolley held the honours degree required for entry to the UCL's Diploma in Librarianship, but Sharr did not, something that led Jolley to wonder how Sharr had managed to gain entry to the course without it. As a result, he belittled Sharr as being more like a country librarian who dispensed books aimed at the lowest common denominator than a scholar-librarian, like himself, serving scholarly readers.[5]

It is hard to imagine Jolley and Sharr getting on together. Twenty years before, not long after leaving UCL, Jolley declared himself a pacifist whereas Sharr went on to become a Captain who served at the front with the Royal Artillery during World War II. Jolley was slight and presented as shy, but Sharr, a pipe-smoking man of athletic bearing, was a frank autocrat who nonetheless was greatly admired by his colleagues. Perhaps most importantly, Jolley was not a team player, certainly not one who tolerated a subordinate position, and Sharr was already a man of considerable achievement. While the UWA library's collection held fewer than 200,000 books, Sharr's 500,000-volume library served the needs of some 700,000 Western Australians. In fact, geographically it was the largest library system in the world, covering more than 1,000,000 square miles—Sharr's vision was to see that there was at least one branch library in every local authority and a book in the system for every citizen in the state. It was not surprising that, during their dockside meeting, Sharr asked Jolley to consider the possibility of an alliance between the university and the state library so that the two institutions could make their combined resources available on a state-wide basis, an idea both Fred Alexander and Emmy Wood supported. Nor was it surprising that, without hesitating, Jolley replied that he had not come all the way from Scotland to share his job with anyone.

Elizabeth Jolley was also on the alert when she was introduced to half-English/half-Danish Mrs Alexander who was about Jolley's mother's age and had the same forename and nickname, Margaret and Gretha—pronounced 'Gree-ta' in Margaret Alexander's case and 'Gray-tuh' in Margarete Fehr's.[6] From their having met in Glasgow, Elizabeth Jolley knew that Fred Alexander regarded himself as *primum inter pares*—appointed to the university thirty-five years before, he had seen a convocation of Vice Chancellors come and go and had many significant achievements to his credit. She intuited that Gretha Alexander also regarded herself as the first among her own equals, the UWA faculty wives, and considered herself responsible for modelling and guiding their conduct. As a result, Jolley wondered if she would have agreed to come to Australia if she had met Gretha Alexander in Glasgow. Whatever the tensions during this welcome, Alexander maintained control of the situation, especially when he calmed titillated customs officials who proposed going through all of the Jolleys' bags and cases after finding *What Katy Did* in one of them. He was able to persuade them that the book was not pornography but an American children's classic, and that its wholesome nature characterised the rest of the things the Jolleys had with them.

On board the *Orion* Elizabeth Jolley wondered whether or not, at thirty-six, passion was over, concluding that she had had all she wanted. Her thoughts on such matters might have been given an added fillip by a letter from John Broom that awaited her arrival. He said he had had a dream about her—not a Freudian one, he said, the reference to Freud declaiming what was disclaimed.

The Jolleys were one of a number of academic families joining the UWA in the 1950s and 1960s, for the university doubled in size in a decade from some 1,700 students and fewer than 100 academic staff in 1953 to nearly 4,000 students and 250 staff in 1963, appointing two dozen new professors during the period.[7] Like others before them, the Jolleys were put up for a few days at the Captain Stirling Hotel on Stirling Highway, about a mile west of the bell tower of the university. Then they were allocated a rental house at 10 Parkway, on the western edge of the campus. It was in one of two precincts where the university owned houses reserved for newly appointed and visiting staff members, the other being in Monash Avenue, a half mile north. Their settling-in was somewhat eased by Ali Sharr's loaning Leonard Jolley lawn furniture and garden hoses for the hot summer months, a gesture Jolley did not thank him for and a loan he did not return.

For a woman who did not leave the house for six weeks when she first went to Edinburgh and who might have called the police if anyone came to the door, Elizabeth Jolley was overwhelmed by the friendliness she encountered in Perth. 'Everyone looked after us', she said.[8] Friendships flourished within and between the Parkway and Monash communities, young families borrowing and loaning various items, driving each other to dentists and doctors, and sharing in the care of their children. There were friendly rivalries, too, such as the card-playing one maintained by the Jolleys and their library colleagues against Maths/Engineering people like Monash-Street Alan (Electrical Engineering) and Joyce (Mathematics) Billings. Elizabeth liked the card game *Racing Patience*, but Leonard's preference was for the word game *Nebuchadnezzar*. Additionally, the men played cricket and the women hockey—there is a videotape of Elizabeth showing that she maintained much of her Sibford sporting skill. She also played squash with a colleague from the library who played like a man and, unlike most other faculty wives, she rode her bicycle everywhere. And there was frequent horseplay between families who, however, took care that Leonard Jolley not get wet when spraying each other with the garden hose. His personal space was not to be violated.

The same friends were also on hand when their disciplinary skills were needed. A Professor of Medicine went to the aid of a colleague who suffered a fatal heart attack; a colleague in Law advised another colleague on what to do when that man was accused of murder; and a colleague in Educational Psychology, unasked, routinely told Elizabeth what she was doing wrong in raising her children. They were all so much in each other's pockets that Elizabeth and Ruth, hearing their cat Sam was run over and killed outside the Seddons' residence in Victoria Avenue, went there with a shovel only to discover the Seddons had already buried Sam with appropriate mourning and weeping—the Seddons thought he was their own cat. So, because the Jolleys had buried the Seddons' cat Hester years ago under the hibiscus in their back garden, Elizabeth concluded that they were 'kit for kat'.

Both Leonard and Elizabeth were closer with other couples than ever before, perhaps because such relationships were not burdened by their past, because the children were older and the Jolleys freer to socialise, or because the community about them offered wider and more varied opportunities. Elizabeth was struck by the relative informality of Australian social life. They were closest with Professor Harry (Mathematics) and Hannah Levey who had arrived from Melbourne the year before. The Jolleys' friendship with the Leveys paralleled that with the Blands in Edinburgh but was more intimate for the Jolleys. One important difference was that, unlike the Blands who had two boys, the Leveys had two girls, Ruth, a year older than the Jolleys' Ruth with whom she was a close friend, and Amanda, her year-younger sister who often tagged along with them.[9]

In addition to being a good mathematician, Harry Levey was a welcoming man with a broad sense of humour who did not take himself too seriously. He liked things that Jolley disliked, such as organised sport, but was also interested in the arts whereas science was a mystery to Jolley who referred to physics and mathematics as 'the exact sciences'. When Tom Lehrer, Harvard's popular musical satirist-cum-mathematician was performing in Perth in May 1960, Levey invited him to lunch with the department. Despite Lehrer's satirical song 'New Math' which famously trivialised the new-math fad of the time ('the important thing is to understand what you're doing, rather than to get the right answer'), Lehrer himself turned out to be famously dull and the lunch was a flop. But Levey was unfazed.

In the Leonard–Harry relationship, the intimacy was embedded in mock heroic behaviour which enabled each to disguise his affection for the other while simultaneously expressing criticism of him: when the ebullient Levey persuaded the dour Jolley to attend a cricket match at the WA Cricket Ground, Jolley spent the whole day interrupting Levey, who was rapt in the intricacies of the game, to ask how soon it would be over; and, after Levey dropped him off, Jolley entered his house declaring Levey was an idiot he would never talk to again, his new mate entering his own house with the announcement that Jolley was an ingrate he wanted no more to do with.

In her relationship with Hannah, Elizabeth continually wished that they could spend more time together and share thoughts and feelings that went beyond the details of their children's schooling, their husbands' work, and the comparable discussions of the other faculty wives. At the same time, she was committed to a need for restraint: she valued feelings between women as having a kind of depth that does not exist between women and men, feelings better left unprobed if the friendship were to last; some degree of restraint helped avoid any subtle feelings that might lead to misunderstanding and anger.

Leonard had little to do with Hannah, but Harry was impressed with Elizabeth, saying 'She's like a long drink of cool water', and he was sympathetic with her on account of the effort her devotion to Leonard entailed. As a result, on the stipulation that she take driving lessons, he offered the Jolleys the use of his automobile while the Leveys were on study leave for a year from August 1961. Fifteen harrowing lessons later, the Jolleys were mobile, Elizabeth appreciating the freedom it gave her and the convenience it afforded, and Leonard enjoying being chauffeured, particularly appreciating the opportunity to travel to Geraldton to the north and throughout the southwest of Western Australia. Being mobile also facilitated their looking about for a home to purchase, settling on 28 Agett Road, Claremont, which they bought for £4,000, moving into it on 16 February 1962. A three/four-bedroom Federation home, it was in an excellent position, less than ten minutes by car to the university to the east, a ten-minute walk to Claremont shops to the west, a five-minute walk to the Swan River to the south, and diagonally across the street from the handsome turn-of-the-twentieth-century Claremont Teachers College and its impressive grounds.

Shortly before Harry and Hannah returned, Elizabeth nervously practised parking the Leveys' Holden in their driveway against their return. When Harry drove his car for the first time, the engine performed alarmingly, causing him to return to the Jolleys and accuse Elizabeth of having blown the head gasket on the engine. 'Impossible', she said, 'I never even used it'. Leonard nodded agreement with her, and they both turned their backs and went inside. Dumbfounded, Harry drove off. When he took the car to be repaired, he scratched the passenger-side door on a newly installed driveway gate latch and told the garage mechanic to fix that too, the man replying that 'Mrs Jolley had that panel fixed in the same spot only last week'. Harry then realised it would not be productive to discuss the car's misadventures while in the care of the Jolleys and useless to worry about what would go wrong next.

Parties and other social gatherings also figured large in the lives of the UWA community. The Jolleys' tolerance for them differed, perhaps because Leonard was not so much constrained by the thought of getting home so that the babysitter could leave, perhaps because he could tolerate small talk so long as a good share of it focused on him. Thus, at their first New Year's Eve party, Elizabeth went home early, surprised that Leonard stayed behind with a brassy blonde a little the worse for drink. Leonard hosted and Elizabeth catered the 1960 Library Christmas function for some sixty colleagues. And they also held more than their own share of parties, Elizabeth once being surprised when she was passionately kissed under the mistletoe by someone from the English Department. From the beginning, both of them were recognised as 'characters', he for his needle-sharp and dead-accurate verbal barbs and she for her unconventional dress, her bicycle, and her general non-compliance with conduct considered comme il faut for a UWA wife.

The situation was entirely new to them. Parkway, virtually on campus, and nearby Agett Road had many advantages beyond proximity to the university's public lectures and its musical and dramatic performances, as well as to local shopping and various bus routes. Leonard was in his element socially, his acerbic misanthropy tolerated, even approved, as the badge of an eccentric scholar. His antics with Elizabeth were valued as entertaining, although it was not always clear when they were behaving naturally or play-acting, as when they dumbfounded colleagues and friends with their spontaneous rendition of the pheasant-plucker song ('I'm not a pheasant plucker, I'm a pheasant-plucker's son / I'm only plucking pheasants till the pheasant-plucker comes . . . '). But Elizabeth Jolley, although she was grateful for the many social and cultural opportunities the UWA and Perth provided, was nonetheless anxious about some aspects of her new environment.

In the first instance, her anxieties related to professional and class issues. In Scotland, her world was the home, her status that of a spouse and parent. In Perth, the distinctions between the private and the public spheres, home and university, were more porous. Though Leonard Jolley was sensitive about the fact that he was paid the same as a professor but did not hold the title, and he was ambivalent about the MA ad eundum gradum the university conferred on him, his position made a difference it had never made before.[10] Elizabeth Jolley soon realised how contingent her own situation was: not only was she a wife, but the Librarian's wife; their children went to school with the children of other university families; their older daughter would soon be a UWA student herself, taught by colleagues and friends.

In addition to levels of academic appointment, class also was an issue, as was ethnicity and country of origin. For example, there had been a number of eastern Europeans appointed to the staff in the 1950s, some of them refugees, and of the two dozen professorial appointments made between 1954 and 1963, British men outnumbered Australian men by four to one. Elizabeth initially preferred the non-British appointees, like the Braybrookes (Law) from New Zealand and the Leveys from Melbourne. Moreover, levels of accomplishment were important, including the accomplishments of faculty wives. Some were artists, like the sculptor Margaret Priest, and some were tutors, like the poet Fay Zwicky. Still another was a children's novelist, Dorothy Sanders, wife of Professor Col Sanders (Education), who wrote under the pseudonym 'Lucy Walker'. Sanders, who kindly gave Jolley advice on publishing opportunities, did not have an inflated opinion of the literary quality of her own work, nor did Jolley have a high opinion of it.[11]

Leonard Jolley immersed himself in his various tasks which included reclassifying the staff, reorganising their services, securing and managing a substantial increase of expenditure on periodicals and books, creating specialist libraries in departments across the campus or in a special area of the library, and controversially creating an Open Reserve section. Undoubtedly his greatest achievement was overseeing the planning and construction of the Reid Library, approved in 1958 and opened in 1965. Complimenting Jolley on his accomplishments, Fred Alexander wrote that '[p]erhaps the most striking feature of the last few years of the university's half century was the development of the Library'.[12]

In the process, he made as many enemies as friends, a professional liability, for librarians are always in an awkward position vis-à-vis administrative superiors who become deaf to their constant demands for ever-larger budgets—'wisdom crieth in the streets and no man regardeth her', as Jolley put it.[13] Similarly, librarians are often offside with academic colleagues who cannot understand why their departmental budgets should be reduced so that the library's can be increased. Nor did he bend over backwards to be gracious to his main clientele, the students. When his decree appeared on a noticeboard that there were to be no dogs or small children in the library, as if it had recently been overrun with them, a woman wrote to complain against his coupling 'dogs' with 'small children'. 'Madam', the notice in his miniscule hand replied, she had completely misunderstood him, for he certainly did not advocate coupling dogs with small children. And when a young man complained about the unfairness of women being allowed to take bags into the library whereas men had to leave theirs in the lobby, Jolley responded via a note on the board saying that as the young man went through life he had the right to expect a good many things but that he would be greatly disappointed if he expected fairness to be one of them. Whether his unpleasantness was more constitutional or more the result of his worsening rheumatoid arthritis—his mobility problems were immediately apparent on his arrival in Western Australia—it did not take long for the students to dub him 'Hopalong Acidly'.

> *I must say it was painless in many ways. But you know looking back it took me two years to pick a flower and arrange a flower in the house . . .*
> Elizabeth Jolley (Reid 50)

If the transition was liberating for Leonard, it was unsettling for Elizabeth Jolley. Her father's reference to having passed the point of no return was salutary in the sense that it encouraged her to review her situation and determine what could best be made of it, the first step of which was to contemplate the nature and extent of her unhappiness. In the first instance, her response was involuntary and somatic, for by the middle of January 1960, just six weeks after their arrival, symptoms of her ulcerative colitis returned, a condition she self-medicated with phenobarbital.

The first task of her 'going on' was to find schools for teenage Sarah, six-year-old Richard, and three-year-old Ruth to enter when the 1960 school year started in February. Sarah went to Methodist Ladies' College. For Ruth it was the UWA Kindergarten and Nedlands Primary School and, when they moved to Agett Road, East Claremont Primary. Richard went to Nedlands Primary School. Then he went to Christ Church Grammar School and Ruth to MLC, Ruth later studying nursing at Royal Perth Hospital and the Sir Charles Gairdener Hospital. Sarah was a capable scholar, Ruth a willing one, Richard less willing, often running away from Christ Church, arriving home before Elizabeth who had just dropped him off. Both Ruth and Richard completed their studies by correspondence school, Sarah going on to her BA from the UWA.

Elizabeth Jolley's worries increased from February 1960 after Leonard went east to attend his first meeting of the University Librarians' Committee in Melbourne. When he returned, having met the University of Sydney's Andrew Osborn[14], the only other Australian university librarian he considered to be his peer, he repeatedly and lengthily spoke about Osborn's Associate Librarian, Jean Whyte, whom he thought virtually worshipped Osborn. For her part, Whyte much later told of Osborn's proposing that they picnic at the Warragamba Dam which was then under construction west of Sydney. A particularly unpromising idea in her opinion, it required them to climb innumerable stairs that eventually became more like ladders. The less-than-six-foot frail Jolley and the more-than-six-foot robust Osborn dramatically flagged at the same point, the former with his typically mournful look, the latter with a panic-stricken one: Jolley's arthritis would not allow him to climb higher, and Osborn's acrophobia prevented him from doing so. Whyte had to lead them both down like little boys.

If Leonard's desire was to be considered 'a great man' like Osborn, Elizabeth read it as his desire for the great man's Deputy Librarian, and so she worried about other women he might meet on his interstate trips or even in the UWA library. That worry increased in the first few years with the perception among some people that the library's post-1960 female appointees consisted of those chosen by the female Deputy Librarian and those who were 'Leonard's girls'. When he travelled to Melbourne, Auckland, Hobart, and Canberra for a fortnight in August 1960 to interview prospective senior staff, her colitis flared once more.

In March 1960, she read and liked local author Bert Vickers' book *Though Poppies Grow*.[15] That prompted her to think she should return to her own book, a thought that vied with her desire to write to Nora Bland in Edinburgh instead. Then, in April, she thought of writing about the love of one woman for another, but there were several obstacles. At the time, Leonard required a great deal of attention, having become discontented with the university and the library, developing foot problems, and, in her opinion, generally letting himself go with respect to his hygiene and bearing. She was oppressed by the fact that he was always saying that life had given him nothing and left him behind. At the same time, she was also overwhelmed with dental appointments, hers and Sarah's, as well as by a suddenly busy social life, including too many coffee mornings and, once, a fear that the people she invited to dinner would forget to come. In the midst of it all, in the first week of March her luck changed—like an egg turning itself over in the frying pan. Never having won anything before in her life, she took first prize for an egg recipe she had submitted to a radio station. When four dozen eggs arrived from the Egg Marketing Board, she hopefully set about writing more recipes.

Throughout the 1960s Elizabeth Jolley's workload was enormous but unacknowledged and largely unappreciated—Leonard Jolley alone was virtually a cottage industry. She felt as though she had four children whose comings and goings she had to coordinate, as well as doing the shopping, cooking, clothing, washing, gardening, and looking after the dog and (later) the poultry in their back garden. Moreover, she had to perform general police and crowd-patrol duties, particularly between Leonard and Richard who were chronically alienated from one another.

It was more than six months after their arrival in Australia that she contemplated writing in earnest. By July 1960, she had returned to *A Feast* again, continuing to work on it for the rest of the year, along the way imagining that it might become a trilogy. Her response to being overloaded with the household and her writing seemed paradoxical at the time: she took on more work. During the 1960s she serially devoted herself to three outside activities that absorbed a great deal of her attention. The first was the UWA's Tuart Club for faculty wives, which she joined in 1960, she and Hannah Levey helping at its Christmas function, a party Leonard did not enjoy.[16] By April 1961 she was its Secretary, complaining about petty conventions that exasperated her, like the white gloves and intergenerational tensions among older members who were aghast when young heretics proposed that between luncheon courses a few women from each table exchange places with the same number from other tables. The President wrote to her confidentially asking that she oppose the outrageous idea.

Quick to perceive that she could turn her poor entertaining liabilities into an asset, Jolley only had to host a few dinners where the roast was burned and Leonard was on his worst behaviour to convince her Tuart Club colleagues that she should not be relied on in that role. She also resented the wardrobe makeover a colleague attempted when she escorted Elizabeth into Perth for a perm, new shoes, a dress, and a de riguer but superfluous brassiere; on her return home Leonard said she looked like a superannuated prostitute. She continued to dress as she wished, not out of defiance, but because ever since school at Sibford she had been largely disinterested in fashion conventions, from the time her mother tried to get her to subscribe to certain standards early on Madelaine had claimed the 'pretty' position and Elizabeth the 'clever' one'.[17]

Her motives for joining the Tuart Club in 1960 might have involved some quiet expectation for the wives of more senior university men to be seen contributing in their own way to university life. More importantly from Jolley's point of view, although it was the sort of thing she found hard to do, she joined because members of the Club had been kind to her, particularly members of the Committee.[18] They met the wives of arriving families, helped them to settle in and introduced them to the ways of Perth and the university. Her aim to achieve community and enjoy the friendship of the other faculty wives included establishing an independent identity, and meeting people more widely across the university than her husband's friendship circle made available. Her motives did not include finding 'material' for her writing, although that inevitably happened: the attempted wardrobe makeover immediately led to her starting a short story called 'The New Clothes'. An unexpected bonus of joining the Club was that her membership led to her first book, albeit a modest, self-published, editing job. With the help of three colleagues, Jolley edited *Cooking by Degrees*, a forty-page pamphlet of 140 recipes by sixty-five of her Tuart Club colleagues, the proceeds of its sale going to the UWA branch of the Save the Children Fund.[19] Jolley's pièce de résistance was onion soup.

Her first paid extramural job began in April 1963 when she started work at the Victoria Nursing Home, a C-Class hospital on the north-east corner of Victoria Avenue and Bay Road, just around the corner from the Jolleys' home in Agett Road.[20] She said she took up the work to gain some independence of family routines she had become trapped in: Leonard would go to work at 10 am, expecting to be fetched for lunch and returned again before being brought home at the end of the day, the children meanwhile having returned home at 3 pm. The result was that she had no time for herself. Thus she disciplined them into changing their expectations if not their routines. A bonus was the money she earned which helped pay for having her manuscripts typed and posted.[21]

She accepted the work despite believing that the Home, owned by a church organisation, was concerned more about corporate profit than Christian care—she felt underpaid because her Pyrford qualification was not acknowledged, and she resented being bullied into working during a strike. Leonard Jolley observed that such work made her a scab, and he otherwise disapproved of her working there, probably because her plan was succeeding and he felt the inconvenience of her absence. Nursing filled a need in her almost as much, she imagined, as being a doctor would—not long after she arrived at the UWA, she had investigated the possibility of studying medicine, just as she had earlier done at the University of Glasgow.

Once more her new environment inspired her writing. She imagined a separated woman who worked at the hospital going home to bake pies after work—and suddenly there was Julia the cook: 'I'm not baking apples today for anyone!' she announced in Jolley's new story, 'The Sick Vote' (45). 'If they want apples they can stuff them . . . ' (45). Julia went on to become Mrs Rawlings who declares in *Mr Scobie's Riddle*, 'They can stuff themselves . . . and bake their own fuckin' apples' (118).

Jolley also talked with a patient who inspired her. A bachelor her father's age, Andrew Dungey, retired from the Titles Office, was a piano teacher-*cum*-tuner who told of his small cottage overhung by pine trees in the hills east of Perth, of riding up and down those hills with his dog on his motorcycle, and of being devastated when the dog was injured and had to be shot. An ambulatory patient, he would walk the quarter mile to 28 Agett Road for a cup of tea and a chat with Jolley, at the beginning of March 1965 confiding that he thought he would not go on much longer.[22]

On another visit he told of teaching piano to two young girls in a Jewish household when one of them asked if he had holy pictures. When he offered to bring some from home for her to look at, she took him upstairs to show him pictures hidden under her mother's mattress. But, as they started to look at them, the housekeeper interrupted them, demanding to know what he was doing there. Dungey felt awful because what the woman said sounded so true. Presumably she was reading the appearances as facts.

Dungey's traumatic experience of having his intention misunderstood, his Christian impulse denied, is the profound regret of Martin Scobie who is represented as having precisely Andrew Dungey's experience—the girl's name, holy pictures, housekeeper and all—in *Mr Scobie's Riddle* (95–8), Jolley's award-winning novel in which the bachelor ex-music teacher Martin Scobie is a patient in a nursing home.

Eventually Dungey's interruptions became too frequent and too long, Jolley having to turn him away at the door or ask him to leave after only a perfunctory visit, as she did early in March 1965, the week after he predicted his death. The following week, as she backed out of the drive, she saw him entering the back gate and drove off so that he would not see her leaving. That night he died in his sleep of a heart attack, his death effectively providing the answer to Martin Scobie's riddle: What is it we all know is going to happen but we don't know when or how? (120).

She was appalled at having failed Andrew Dungey by disappointing him in a cowardly way. As she worked on 'The Talking Bricks' from the beginning of August, she regarded it as a kind of atonement to Dungey that was written with the hope that it might be a comfort to others as well.

Elizabeth Jolley's work at the Victoria Nursing Home ended in the second half of 1965 because of preparations for Leonard's 1966 sabbatical. He was to spend a year studying the library as a teaching instrument, with six months in the School of Postgraduate Librarianship at the University of Sheffield, then three months lecturing during the northern-hemisphere summer in the Graduate School of Library Science at the University of Illinois, and three months in France and Germany looking at the 'new-campus' universities. Elizabeth had to make most of the arrangements. Finding Sibford too expensive as a boarding school for Richard, she also turned down accommodation her sister Madelaine had worked hard to find for them in Birmingham. She did not want to be too close to her parents, even though her father had sent £400 to help with expenses.[23] She also feared that Madelaine was jealous of her literary aspirations and fearful that she had designs on the family estate, thoughts prompted by paternal Aunt Daisy's death in February 1965. Because her friend Alix Macswiney, now married, lived in Tunbridge Wells, Elizabeth chose to live there while Leonard travelled. At university expense, they sailed first-class on the SS *Flavia* on 30 January 1966.

Homecoming was no idyll for Elizabeth. At first, her mother was 'awful' about their visit, and then she wanted to make all the arrangements for it. Leonard had provoked her by suggesting that her parents probably would be unwell during the sabbatical and she would be conflicted about having to leave them in that state. Instead, while they were there, Margarete Knight's brother Walter Fehr died, leaving Jolley's mother, at seventy, the last of her line with her brother Walter's unmarried daughter Ilse who had osteomyelitis of the cranium.[24] The pull came from the opposite direction: right in the middle of their trip, in June, Harry Levey died in Perth at forty-three years of age, leaving Elizabeth powerless to provide the consolation and practical help she would have liked to give her beloved Hannah. Then, by the time they returned, Hannah had moved with her two girls back to Melbourne where she returned to her profession as a pharmacist. While in England Jolley worked on a story called 'Night Runner', a piece related to *A Feast*.[25] She might also have started thinking about and working on a draft later called *The Leila Story*. And as they sailed back on the SS *Oronsay* in early January 1967, she started and finished a draft of a story called 'A New World'.

> *The only thing it was good for were people buying cosmetics who would never have gone to buy cosmetics because they felt they were too ugly... I learnt a bit about human nature [selling Watkins products], and there were people who obviously missed their mothers and wanted to buy the products because their mothers had bought them. That was an interesting revelation as well.*
>
> Elizabeth Jolley (Reid 54)

Elizabeth Jolley's third job in Western Australia was the door-to-door selling of Watkins products she started in November 1968 and continued through July 1969. Watkins products featured essences, herbs, spices, condiments and various powders, lotions and potions—wares that fit into a case which could be carried from her automobile into someone's home.[26] She took the job, misleadingly called work from home, to fit in with the children's school hours.

Some people said the Watkins products were overpriced, but that was not always so. The mark-up was 40–100%, some items priced the same as in stores and some less, like the shampoo Jolley sold at $1.00 which was on sale at $1.30–$1.35 in stores. Her concern was more about some of the products themselves, for she feared they were not always what they claimed to be. She suspected, for example, the Superbe Hand Lotion she sold for 37¢, the moisturising cream (75¢) and the furniture polish ($1.50) all came from the same vat and were only differentiated during bottling by adding the scents of lavender, rosewater or beeswax.[27]

Even though she kept detailed records, a third of the time her columns did not add up. Using her figures nonetheless, her records show that in November 1968 she sold $103.40 worth of products for a profit of $41.22. However, she was also her own best customer, purchasing nearly a quarter of what she sold, which she bought at the wholesale rate ('the house is full of Watkins products'). So her profit might only have been about $30 for the thirteen days she worked, only $2.30 a day, less than the wholesale price she would have paid for one of her own bottles of Simply Elegant Coconut Oil Shampoo. But it got worse: by 1969 the amount was down to an average of $5.76 per month, none of the figures taking into account her fuel (eight gallons of petrol in November 1968) or wear and tear on her automobile (the grease/oil change and brake relining needed in July 1969).

Whatever she grossed or netted, she soon learned that such work could be as soul-destroying as Willy Loman found it to be in Miller's *Death of a Salesman*. On her first excursion, to Swanbourne, she did not get invited through even one door because the residents, remembering the woman who worked the route before her, were emphatic in refusing her entry. A fortnight later she drove straight home as soon as she reached Swanbourne because she could not summon the strength to get out of her car: what was worse than the prospect of being turned away was being invited inside where she was made so aware of the sad lives of so many of the women confined to apartments and houses. At one of the houses she visited weekly she helped the elderly lady there give her bedridden husband a blanket bath ('Only Connect [Part 2]' 78).

The work went much better when she displayed her wares to her astonished UWA colleagues. It is impossible to know who was more embarrassed at the incongruity of the situation, but the women of the Tuart Club were easy marks when Jolley, on her knees before them, spread out her wares, giving them change in the form of packets of jelly crystals and/or liquid manure ('Only Connect [Part 2]' 77).[28] Business was brisk as people bought things just to get her out the door again, and she was particularly fond of the Ellises, who seemed to eat Watkins mustard with everything.

Jolley felt that, whether selling to the ladies of the Tuart Club or to the women in Swanbourne, Watkins work was essentially awful, but she knew how such work brought her in contact with the sort of people and the kind of experiences she wrote about best. If it was not worth the effort in terms of the extra income it generated, in terms of the number of characters and incidents it inspired for her work, it was a goldmine. It immediately led to two stories whose names suggest their indebtedness to Watkins products, 'May I Rest My Case on Your Table?' and 'The Travelling Entertainer'.

> [I] made an attempt to join the two landscapes in the very first story I wrote here . . . I went for a walk in Nedlands where we were living to post a letter the first night we were in the University cottage. When I came back I wrote a little description of the

warm evening and the way everything looked oriental . . . I give those impressions to the old man in 'The Hedge of Rosemary', then I use his childhood to join those impressions with the part where he grew up.

Elizabeth Jolley (Kavanagh 442)

How can I be the same person after the flight of the cockatoos?

'A Sort of Gift' (75)

By 1961, in addition to *The Feast*, Elizabeth Jolley was also writing short stories, revising old novels, and starting new ones. The novels she was working on were *The Cardboard Diary* in 1962, *Mr Scobie's Riddle* in 1965, *The Leila Family* and *The Prince of a Fellow* in 1968.[29] In all, her commitment for the decade was five draft novels—seven if *The Feast* is counted as a trilogy—and more than two dozen short stories.[30] However, her critical and publishing success at first did not keep pace with the rate of her production. One early disappointment was *Westerly's* rejecting 'Poppy Seed and Sesame Rings', the editor, short-story writer Peter Cowan, urging that the end be reconsidered and a change in point of view be resolved. Jolley's frustrated response suggests that Cowan's thoughts were right-headed: she did not know where the beginning ended, and the ending began, and was she certain the story did not have a point of view. Another disappointment was her story 'The Pelican' being beaten in a newspaper competition. She was sensitive regarding direct criticism and intolerant of the condemnation implied when someone else's work was accepted over her own. By contrast, she was pleased to receive a letter from Beatrice Davis, Angus and Robertson's highly regarded editor, who apologised for being slow in considering two manuscripts. Jolley lived in hope, and she was even tolerant a week later when she received another 'nice' letter from her, rejecting *The Leila Family* and *Mr Scobie's Riddle*.

At the same time there was some success. In 1965 Kylie Tennant chose her story 'The Talking Bricks' for inclusion in her *Summer's Tales 2* anthology, and in the same year 'A Hedge of Rosemary' won the Victorian Fellowship of Australian Writers' State of Victoria Short Story award. That was followed when either Jolley raised her standards or Cowan lowered his, *Westerly* accepting 'A Hedge of Rosemary' in 1967 and 'The Rhyme' in 1967. Another eastern-states success matching that of *Summer's Tales* came when *Quadrant* editor James McCauley accepted 'The Sick Vote' in 1968. Those journal publications placed her work in good company, then-prominent Western Australians Gerry Glaskin, Tom Hungerford, Henrietta Drake-Brockman, John K. Ewers and Bert Vickers also appearing in that issue of *Westerly*, and eastern-staters Vincent Buckley, Alec Hope, Geoffrey Lehman, and Grace Perry in *Quadrant*. The BBC World Service broadcast 'Bill Sprockett's Land' in 1968 and 'A New World' in 1969, although Richard Attenborough—a long shot, she knew—did not take her screenplay treatment of 'A Travelling Entertainer'. At the end of the decade, the BBC also accepted 'May I Rest My Case on Your Table?' for broadcast in 1970, after it had been previously rejected by various publishers.

Elizabeth Jolley's first published stories show how much she wrote from her experience, contemplating various aspects of it from different angles, such that her stories sometimes overlapped or contained echoes of each other. For example, 'The Rhyme' seems like a parodic script for a B-grade movie featuring members of the Tuart Club. It opens with a Mrs Urchangeal, 'returned from far away cities of obscure gaiety and a life in hotels of doubtful repute', but not, apparently, 'having strayed from the narrow paths of duty and devotion to responsibility'. (46). Urchangeal resumes the Presidential chair of the Ladies of the Auxiliary who meet in Mrs McQueen's Pickling Shed where some of them peel onions and others knit while everyone discusses the current scandal: it centres around who 'Sarah K.' might be, that name signed as the author of a possibly obscene poem, 'Loneliness in a Lavatory', written on the wall of that convenience. Mrs Sympson repeatedly wonders if the culprit could be Sarah Keddie, a reasonable guess but for the fact that the Keddie girl is named Sandra. The inconsequential conversation segues to an inconsequential conclusion featuring Anti Mote, Aunt Maud of Jolley's youth.

Two of her first pieces also feature characters who might be auditioning for appearances in later stories. 'The Talking Bricks' has a distracting echo with 'The Rhyme' via Mrs Keddie's daughter Sarah in the latter and Mr Hughes' sister-in-law Keppie in the former, as well as Mr Hughes's dead wife Sarah. More a sketch than a story, 'The Talking Bricks' is a lyric meditation that includes music-teacher Martin Scobie along with Mr David Hughes, a Welsh migrant, both of them in a nursing home. Jolley later incorporated it, verbatim in parts and altered in parts, in *Mr Scobie's Riddle*.[31]

'The Sick Vote' prefigures some of the characters and intrigues in *Mr Scobie's Riddle*. At this early stage Mrs Hailey is not yet Matron's lover

Miss Hailey, and Matron is Matron Rees, not Hyacinth ('Hya') Price, but its central scene anticipates the one in *Scobie* where Matron Price tries to get Scobie to give her his power of attorney or to sign over his estate to her (193): in 'The Sick Vote' Matron plots to have Mrs Murphy vote for Matron's brother so that she can then use him to oppose Town Council resolutions. When the Justice of the Peace arrives to witness Mrs Murphy's signature, Hailey squirts him with fly spray and Matron looks for castor oil to soothe his eyes while Murphy marks her ballot. Predictably, she places her X beside 'Hodge', because she always liked the name (46).

'A Hedge of Rosemary' most completely anticipates how Jolley integrates materials from her own life with her typical techniques, topics and themes. The old man has moved with his wife to Australia from the Black Country in England, the rosemary matches Margarete Knight's in Wells Road, and 'Thank you kindly' and 'Much obliged' (see 69 and 75) are phrases belonging to her father, just as contemplating the bottoms of his boots was one of his habits, for her was conscious of the sole/soul trope. The old man also claims a background which includes chain shops and chain-making (74–5), as Gertrude Whele did, and as Jolley mimicked in one of her biographical blurbs.

The story neatly foreshadows Jolley's typical topics, migrants, elderly/institutionalised people, widows/widowers; and her themes focus on the family, loneliness and the possibilities of love. The father in 'Hedge of Rosemary' is in a neither-here-nor-there condition: he is no longer British, but not Australian either, unlike his son and grandsons; no longer a husband and father but a widowed and barely tolerated live-in grandad. Initially 'terrified by the silence and loneliness' of the Australian bush, he could not stand 'the still quiet nights in the bush when he was alone with the silence'. He is left with his memories of England, the 'chiming of city clocks through the comforting roar of the city and the friendly screech of the trams as they turned out of the High Street into Hill Street' (74). The task in front of Jolley was to decide whether or not she wanted to construct more Australian-oriented characters and, if so, how to go about that.

Beside the prize for 'A Hedge of Rosemary', she won $50 in 1967 in an *Australian* contest for the best letter from a mother to her fifteen-year-old son. Addressed to 'Dear Theodore' (the name meaning 'gift from God'), the mother exhibits the quirkiness displayed in some of Jolley's later work, like writing to someone who is in the next room. In that letter the mother asks him to be polite to visitors ('some people in their lives have hard experiences which makes them seem odd or stupid or narrow-minded'), not to be scornful with his live-in aunt (she has nowhere else to go, he should not hurt anyone's feelings, nor try to be clever at someone else's expense) and to avoid being empty and vulgar. Her key message is that 'real friendship needs love and thoughtfulness, kindness and responsibility to others'. A professional writer at last, as well as the mother of a fifteen-year-old son, her response to the success of her submission was to wish that raising a child was as easy as writing a letter.

The 1969 President of what she had come to call The Treachery Club, Jolley relinquished the Presidency of the Tuart Club and concluded her work on the executive the same year; her mid-December farewell speech was, she thought, awful. She felt tired and ached all over.[32] On Christmas Day she fretted that Leonard's library colleagues disliked him because he always fulminated against people in authority. On Boxing Day she hoped that Sarah, who three days before had married Brian Nelson (a recent UWA Honours graduate in English), would be happy at Cambridge where Nelson's Hackett Scholarship would take him for further study.

At the end of the year, reflecting on the end of the decade, Jolley concluded—presumably in relation to writing—*C'est un triste métier*. She attributed the sentiment to Emile Zola, but it is more likely from Voltaire: *C'est un triste métier que celui d'homme de lettres; mais il y a quelque chose de plus dangereux, c'est d'aimer la vérité*—'Being a writer is a melancholy task, but there is one that is more dangerous, which is loving the truth'. Over the years, while 'doing life', Elizabeth Jolley would several more times feel that writing was *un triste métier*.

8

1970s—I was sort of on the market...

Exile seels your eyes, allowing you to see only what your longings and your sense of loss will permit.
Andrew Riemer (80)

I didn't really want to join a tennis club. I suppose really I wanted to be my own and create, though I didn't . . . I couldn't explain that. It's only since I got old that I can explain that possibly the writing of fiction was the life I really wanted and then I set about starting to work towards that.
Elizabeth Jolley (Reid 56)

'After all', Elizabeth Jolley told Jennifer Ellison in September 1985, 'publishing is a business'.[1] By that time, she had learned that there is a difference between writing and being a writer and that being a writer is an activity that usually benefits from knowing at least the basics of the publication business. In England and Scotland she had written assiduously for two or three decades, submitting work willy-nilly, with virtually no publication success. At that time, she seemed to think that success was a matter of hard work and good luck: you came up with an idea, typed it up, and sent it off to an editor who, if you were lucky, selected it for publication, or who, if you were unlucky, rejected it, in which case you blamed the editor's insensitivity, poor taste or obvious prejudice.

During the 1970s Jolley continued her Australian education in becoming a writer, an education that had started soon after she arrived. She learned by observation, advice, and experience that 'luck' was a loser's term for circumstances that often could be understood and sometimes consciously turned to advantage. As a result, during the 1970s she began to figure in Australia's cultural conversation as she learned how to access what Robert Dessaix calls its 'intellectual infrastructure'.[2]

The process of gaining that access was not a simple one. On arrival, recalling Ruth having wondered if there would be lavatories in Australia, Jolley realised that question translated into others, the main question being whether or not they would be welcome in Australia. She understood that the biggest challenge for migrants was to give up one set of values for another.[3] Although the term 'migrant' is not usually used for Australian writers who have come from English-speaking countries, especially England, nonetheless Jolley was a migrant writer. That might account for her admiring *Alien Son*, the autobiography of Judah Waten, the Russian-born, Jewish-Australian, communist writer and cultural activist in Melbourne whose family had immigrated to Western Australia when he was an infant.[4] The dislocation of Jolley's migration to Australia was amplified by her earlier British experiences of displacement, and her writings can be read as a species of migrant literature that articulates a longing for belonging and negotiates a resolution in writing to the experience of exile.

Jolley's themes have roots in her life in England, which involved two overlapping cycles related to longing and belonging, the first cycle producing more a feeling of homelessness, and the second producing more a feeling of lovelessness. Wilfrid and Margarete Knight also struggled with issues related to location/dislocation and longing/belonging: his derived from imprisonment followed by ejection by his parents from their home; hers from rejection by her parents and exile from her homeland—'Because of her marriage my mother was an exile.' ('"What Sins"' 4). Jolley even had a sense of being an exile in her own street ('Self-Portrait' 304). And she felt the same within her own home when her mother formed a relationship with Kenneth Berrington. That internal exile concluded when she was sent to Sibford where she was always aware of being (to invoke a recurrent phrase from her writing) 'on the edge' because of not being a birthright Quaker, although Sibford ultimately came to feel like home to her. Jolley wrote that 'Perhaps my vicarious experience of homesickness and exile starts, without any knowledge or understanding, from the early memories of incomprehensible unhappiness' ('Self-Portrait' 303).

The decade of the 1940s had been transitional. It led to a kind of homelessness and lovelessness at the St Nicholas and St Martin's Hospitals which seemed cold and industrial and where the staff seemed to be uncaring toward the trainee nurses. At the Queen Elizabeth Hospital she found friendship with several of her fellow trainees, particularly Mary Doyle, and, outside the hospital, with Leonard and Joyce Jolley, a friendship that became a reprise of her parents' relationship with Berrington. From that point, her pattern of exile escalated when she had to resign from the QEH to have her baby, followed by finding work in two households she had to leave, and then living and working at Pinewood, an institution that presented an image of Home as Hell.[5]

After Pinewood she joined Leonard Jolley in Scotland—another migration, another hopeful anticipation of family, community and belonging. In Edinburgh their relationship became more companionate than passionate, and then in Glasgow it became more companionate than loving. When Leonard decided that they would move to Western Australia, she wrote, 'I trailed along like an obedient squaw. The desire for space was irresistible...' ('Tricked or Treated?' 67).

For Sale five acres virgin bush partly cleared and fenced with round poles for horses one acre lucerne abundant water power available tin shed for tools septic system possible pig licence suitable stone fruit goats and almonds G.P.O. thirty-six miles.
'Country Towns and Properties' (11)

—I thought you'd like to know
about the woman who had your place
before you she was there till she had
to be taken away they said her heart wasn't in it
then she lost the use of her legs and
they reckon she turned vegetable—
'Interruption from the Fencing Wire...' (69)

The early 1970s seemed to reiterate, mutatis mutandis, some of the features of the Jolleys' life in the previous decade. In late 1970 they again resolved to purchase land, this time a bush block. Although the enthusiasm to do so was more Leonard's than Elizabeth's, she too was optimistic about the pleasures it could provide, if more aware of how the work to maintain it would fall to her rather than to him. Heartened by advice from their accountant that, if they committed themselves to losing money by growing vegetables (he recommended tomatoes as reliable failures), they could call themselves primary producers and take their expenses as tax deductions. The Great Land Hunt commenced by Elizabeth noting that buying land was like a marriage in that there is only a certain amount you can do beforehand.

Predictably, the process proceeded somewhat haphazardly, places they liked being sold before they could act or withdrawn from sale just when the Jolleys got interested. One drama revolved around seven acres south of Jarrahdale, near the Medulla Brook off the South Western Highway. Leonard and Dr Phillip Goatcher (who owned the property with his wife Dr Phyllis Goatcher) each thought his desires had been fulfilled when they shook hands over the deal, until Goatcher realised that Jolley had misunderstood the down payment to be the purchase price. Jolley was so excited and anxious about what they called Goatcher's Valley, choosing the trees they would plant as they drove back from inspecting it, that Elizabeth said she would do anything in the world to get it for him. His predicament reminded her of the wealthy landowner in Tolstoy's story who accepts the offer of all the land whose perimeter he can walk between sunrise and sunset—he dies as the sun goes down, having striven for more than he could reach. The answer to the question posed in 'How Much Land Does a Man Need?' is the six-foot-by-two-foot plot the Bashkirs buried him in after he died of exhaustion.[6]

Eventually the Jolleys acquired a charming, parkland-cleared rural block of five acres with a small three-room-plus-veranda weatherboard cottage and a winter creek in Green Street, Wooroloo, off the Great Eastern Highway, some forty miles east of Perth. It cost $7,500, an amount Leonard Jolley did not hesitate to borrow from his Deputy librarian. 'Matron's Cottage', so called because it had belonged to the Matron of the district hospital on the grounds of the nearby Wooroloo Prison, was, Elizabeth thought, like a cottage out of Patrick White facing a hay field out of Tolstoy country. It was not the land Leonard had lusted after at Jarrahdale, but they still could personalise it with their own mythologies. Leonard's relied on the fact that in the Matron's bedroom there was a man's wooden leg leaning against the corner wall, still wearing its sock and shoe—his fantasy might have related to the celebrated escape of a one-legged prisoner from the Albany Prison some years earlier.[7] Elizabeth's imagination reworked the image of the Kadova Arab horse stud on the hillside opposite as settings in her first two novels, *Palomino* and *The Newspaper of Claremont Street*, and as the locales of the majority of the stories in her first collection of short stories, most obviously its title story 'Five Acre Virgin'.

At first a joy to the whole family, the Wooroloo property soon became a retreat mainly for Leonard and Elizabeth. They bought a chainsaw and a rotary hoe and enjoyed planting flowers, vegetables and fruit trees—150 trees in November 1971. Ultimately, however, Leonard's point-and-plant method became too much for Elizabeth, for he would sit in his chaise longue in the shade pointing to various sunny spots—'*here*' and '*there*'—where he expected her to dig holes, plant trees, add topsoil and then water.

Next, Wooroloo served mainly as a retreat for just one of them, usually Leonard, who might spend a weekend or even a week or more there by himself. He sometimes found the strength to walk to the air-conditioned employees' pub on the prison property where he spent the afternoon drinking cold beer, but sometimes had to make do at the cottage with the bottle of whiskey and the loaf of rye bread he brought with him.[8] He enjoyed his solitude, studying nature as he had done since he was a boy—a fine poem he wrote while there begins, 'The fruit picked the screams / of the parrots no longer disturb. / The fowl shower black dust / over my page'.[9] At other times, he might invite some of the young UWA women librarians to drive him to Wooroloo for a country lunch, events that annoyed Elizabeth, especially if he expected her to be there in the kitchen preparing their picnic. She only rarely would overnight there by herself. Although she too found it a peaceful place to write, she did not like being there alone in the dark.

Sometimes, however, Wooroloo fulfilled its promise as a place where Leonard and Elizabeth regained their original closeness through conversation, alone together or when entertaining others. That often happened when they hosted lunches, or dinners on the veranda at sunset. At one such event, with the Finlay-Joneses (psychiatrist and microbiologist) and their daughter, along with the Joels (both painters) and their daughter, Jolley suddenly came up with the idea for her short story 'Grasshoppers'. The children's presence suggested something sinister—the evil in people

—although she insisted her impression had nothing to do with those particular children. Thus her initial name for the story was 'The Devils'.[10]

The Jolleys' neighbours to the south were not evil either. They were feckless, in Elizabeth's terms—they could not or would not help themselves—but their effect was as if diabolical.[11] Called Mrs Dreery by Ruth and Elizabeth to distinguish her from her Claremont counterpart, a neighbour they called Neckless, each was suspicious, self-centred and smug. The first weekend the Jolleys visited after taking possession of their new property at the beginning of November, she climbed the fence three times, unbidden, cheerfully to deliver forewarnings of bushfires, snakes, drought, prison escapes, poisonous weeds and salinity. The husband reminded her of Wilfrid Knight in his mild manner, being very quiet in all he did.[12] However, after a lifetime of farming, he was feckless because he could no longer make a living from his ten acres and he would not apply for the dole. He was too proud for that, and yet not proud enough to stop his place from looking like a rubbish tip. Even his tractor crawled from the shed 'like a sick animal'.[13]

They were a plague on the Jolleys, she by her dire predictions which were the more offensive for being likely, since they made them realise how ill-prepared they were when they purchased their Wooroloo block, how with more thought and planning they might have bought a better one for the same price. Mr Dreery was irritating too, in his passivity before his wife, and in the slow decline of his own property which increasingly contrasted badly with the improvements the Jolleys were trying to make on their own. Their fecklessness threatened to overcome Elizabeth as she became complicit in their lives: she raced the husband to hospital when he got a splinter in his eye, she nursed the wife when she fell and hurt herself, and she sold their eggs and fruit for them all the while.

Her dilemma was an acute one: the woman had been diagnosed with cancer before the Jolleys went to Wooroloo, but her bad behaviour appeared to predate her illness, even if it was aggravated by it. Having such a person as a neighbour was not something Jolley had been seeking when she worked so hard to find Leonard a place where they could relax, enjoy themselves, and perhaps even recover more of the happiness from their early days together. After the woman died, Jolley wrote:

> *As she became more seriously ill her face, normally gaunt, looked round. This roundness made me see something of the child she must have been. To be reminded*

that there was once a child, with all the shy hopes of childhood, and who is still a part of the adult, is sad.

And after her death, for the rest of his life her husband, unbidden, would step over the fence and come across for a visit and a glass of port.

> *Sometimes now, after all this time, he speaks about his wife and the tears well up in his innocent elderly eyes and it is as if she has just died all over again and left him alone in his paddocks here at the edge of the bush for ever. Because of this it is possible to know that love exists where the idea of it may be overlooked . . .*
>
> ('No date required' 89–90).

As she meditated on Mr and Mrs Dreery, Jolley was in the middle of the process of internalising the three verities she discovered when she read Tolstoy's 'What Men Live By'. She had to learn what dwells in people, that it was not given to people to know their own needs, and that people live not by the care of themselves but by love.[14]

At times Wooroloo, an additional burden on their finances, was not a place of relaxation but one of never-finished work on the land, work for entertaining, and unwanted worry about her neighbours. There seemed to be nowhere Jolley could rest and recover, no one who tended to her emotional and material needs, and certainly no one who was concerned to facilitate her writing.

From the late 1960s to the early 1970s two women in Perth also competed for her time and attention. The first was Edith Lamb, a Sibford woman who had been kind to her in idyllic times, when Jolley and her Sibford fellow-Prefect Edith Worrall had visited her cottage in the 1930s. She was again comforting in troubled times, more than a decade later when Jolley—as Monica Fielding—and her four-year-old daughter stayed with the Lambs during the hiatus between leaving the Fleetwood-Walkers and going to Pinewood. Edith Lamb and her husband Joseph, a Quaker whose lineage reached back to the Quakers' 'Lambs' War' in the seventeenth century, had followed their daughter from Sibford to Australia when Jenny migrated in 1958. After they became frail and unwell in the late 1960s, the positions of dependency were reversed, with Jolley feeling some imperative to be a caretaker. She would visit Joseph at home, bathing him, cleaning his mouth and teeth, and otherwise looking after him until he died in 1969. She thought how he looked so old and frail in a knitted cap in bed, just like something in a nineteenth-century Russian novel. And she visited and bathed Mrs Lamb at home as well, and then attended to her in hospital when she broke her hip, until she died in hospital at ninety-three. All the while Elizabeth worried about having so little time in which to do so much, uncharacteristically bowing to Leonard's insistence that she resist the Lambs' urging to babysit the daughter's twins so that Jenny could work as a teacher.

If Mrs Lamb's condition was something Jolley's Florence Nightingale training had prepared her for, her encounter with the second woman was more like that of Flaubert's St Julian the Hospitaller who struggled with the needy leper who turned out to be Christ. Ludmila Blotnicki was a counterpart to Andrew Dungey, but one with whom Jolley became much more deeply involved.[15] The Blotnickis were Polish refugees who had lived stateless for a decade before reaching Perth in 1950 where she descended deeper into her schizophrenia. Jolley met her in 1965 when their husbands introduced them to each other as writers. Both Blotnickis needed medical attention, and so Jolley soon was making appointments and driving Ludmila to the doctor. During that time she became aware of the extent of the woman's instability when she wrote a hateful letter to Hannah Levey telling lies about Jolley.

Ludmila's dependency became so oppressive to the Jolleys that Leonard hung up when she telephoned. But Elizabeth would take her calls, especially the frantic late-night ones when Ludmila might plead to be picked up immediately in some suburb, hanging up without naming the street. After the death of Wladysław Blotnicki two years after Jolley first met him, Ludmila's behaviour became even more extreme and unpredictable. She so alienated her doctors that some were reluctant to continue seeing her, and Elizabeth even feared she might interfere with the Jolley children. During the 1970s she was placed into various homes and hostels, including the Graylands Mental Hospital, when she was unable to care for herself after open-heart surgery.

When she escaped from Graylands in February 1971, she phoned Jolley who found her sleeping on the floor surrounded by her own vomit in her abandoned Wandana apartment near King's Park where the electricity had been cut off. Jolley pretended she had come because she loved Ludmila who, touched, agreed to return to Graylands if Jolley would secure her permanent release, a promise Jolley made but did not intend to keep. Soon after, wearing a beret, smoking a cigarette through a cigarette holder and dressed in loose slacks like a 1920s vamp, Ludmila displayed a new lease on life. She took taxis everywhere, gave her jewellery away, and once was found reclining on the verge at the intersection of Thomas Street and Kings Park Road, handing out the remainder of her savings to passers-by. She also started to plan a party for all her doctors, nurses and presumed friends, a plan Jolley knew was hopeless. Aware of the coolness between them, sixty-four-year-old Ludmila told forty-eight-year-old Elizabeth that she loved her and that Jolley ought to be glad that she was loved. Jolley knew it was true, but at the same time she had to acknowledge that, along with pity for Ludmila, she also felt irritation and distaste.

She continued to visit until it became impossible for her to do so. But Ludmila Blotnicki's effect on her, like Andrew Dungey's, became evident in her subsequent writing. During the early 1970s she was working on two pieces, both called 'Pear Tree Dance'. One of them, a poem begun in June 1973, had a central image that can be read as a woman like a tree in an orchard or an orchard tree like a woman:

> In a shower of promised leaf and flower
> Will stand a bride blossomed in living lace.
> And from the tinfoil label
> Comes a fragile music
> 'The Pear Tree Dance' (51)

The other version was a 3,000-word piece in prose. Begun in August 1973, it featured a woman referred to as Weekly or the Newspaper of Claremont Street because of the fact that she cleaned local houses weekly and thereby knew everything that went on in the neighbourhood. The day Weekly took possession of five acres of bushland she had bought, she planted a pear tree. The last paragraph describes the event unambiguously:

> *For the first time in her life the Newspaper of Claremont Street, or Weekly as she was called, was dancing. Stepping round and round the little tree she imagined herself to be like a bride dancing with lacy white blossom cascading on all sides. Round and round the tree, dancing, firming the softly yielding earth with her new boots. And from the little foil label blowing in the restlessness of the evening came a fragile music for the pear tree dance.*

Doing Life: The Australian Years

Jolley referred to her early prose version of 'Pear Tree Dance' as a benign offering to the BBC.

Having finished and sent it off to London, she imagined another version, one with a grim ending. That version appeared a decade later, toward the end of her novel *The Newspaper of Claremont Street*, in the scene where Weekly is at her recently acquired bush block. The hysterical Russian widow Nastasya Torben bullies Weekly about the correct way to plant a pear tree. As Weekly does so, in a scene basically identical to that in the prose above, Nastasya stands nearby watching. Then, as Weekly starts to leave, she implores:

> *'Veekly! help me!' Nastasya's voice broke into the dream dance. Nastasya was stuck fast in the wet clay, the new boots were now quite covered by the mud and Nastasya was unable to pull her large swollen feet out of them.*
>
> *'Veekly you have to get me out from here! It's so cold now and tonight it will freeze!' Nastasya's voice rose to a pathetic scream as she called after Weekly. 'Veekly!', the voice followed Weekly up the slope.*
>
> *'Veekly help me! You cannot leave me. Tonight it will freeze. It is so lonely here no one can hear me except you. Help me!'* (114)

> *[T]hey would go out and be an hour late coming back and if they left a child in the house you couldn't leave, you see. They thought I was stupid but I wasn't. Then they resented paying extra for that extra hour. I wasn't stupid.*
>
> Elizabeth Jolley (Reid 59)

Another repeat of the 1960s was Jolley's once again taking a job. In addition to performing her own housework at Agett Road and devoting time to the bush block at Wooroloo, from March 1970 until mid-1972 she worked as a Flying Domestic, sometimes taking her daughter Ruth with her. Her first assignment was in a residence at 3 The Coombe, Mosman Park, overlooking the Swan River. Along with a few others closer to her home, she had jobs at Windsor Towers, at 9 Parker Street, in South Perth, where the UWA's retired Vice Chancellor and his wife lived. Having previously been introduced to Elizabeth Jolley as President of the Tuart Club, when Sir Stanley Prestcott saw her entering the building, he exclaimed, 'Mrs Jolley!' Unfazed, she replied, 'I'm the cleaning lady'.

Flying Domestically, as she called it, was worth more to her than the dollar an hour she earned to pay to have her manuscripts typed and to use for postage.[16] Like selling Watkins products or working in the Victoria Nursing Home, it too gave her material for her writing. She preferred occupants not to be at home when she cleaned, for that gave her the occasional opportunity to write in the comfort—even elegance—of someone else's home. Making her quick little note in the iconic residence in Mosman Park designed and built in 1960 by Perth architect Geoffrey Summerhayes and his wife Joslyn, or in one of the apartments with panoramic high-rise views from the twenty-one-storey slip-form concrete structure Alan Bond built in South Perth in 1969, was a far cry from the pre-dawn writing she did in her room in Agett Road.

Joslyn Summerhayes, occasionally home when Jolley cleaned, remembers her always arriving with her notebook. At morning tea she would sit at the table writing down things she had heard on the radio. And at lunch time they would have a chat while eating sandwiches of mashed avocados which Summerhayes introduced her to, Jolley telling her of scripts she had rejected by the BBC or the ABC. The design of the Summerhayes house made it a generally low-maintenance place that required little cleaning of the heavy-duty sort portrayed in *The Newspaper of Claremont Street* where Weekly would dismantle the stoves before cleaning them.

Details of the Summerhayes' home appear in 'Another Holiday for the Prince', the first story from Jolley's book *Five Acre Virgin*. The mother and daughter clean for a Mrs Lady whose house, 'all vinyl and bathrooms', was so clean 'you could do an operation in any room'. There is 'the wide river below shining so peaceful with the far bank dark with trees and all the lovely homes piled up on this side of the hill' (12), and the mother surprises the daughter by giving her an avocado at lunch—'It's an acquired taste', she says (13). Likewise, the setting of 'One Bite for Christmas' could suggest 3 The Coombe, where the daughter Mary cleans, her mother having retired to the country. The owner Missis Butterworth has gone horse riding, and there are avocados available for Mary's visiting brother Donald and his friend, aptly called Fingertips, who is angry that the built-in TV defies being stolen (34).

As before, Jolley borrowed themes as well as characters and settings. An important example occurred while she was working in the home of the Belbins who lived in the Claremont area. Jolley would discuss with Jill Belbin the younger woman's experience of writing to her mother in Tasmania, reciprocating by telling her how she wrote to her daughter in Cambridge as well as to her own mother in Wolverhampton. The initial result was a draft story about how the mother–daughter relationship is inevitably altered by the birth of the daughter's first child. Originally called 'The Nature of Love', by the 1980s the draft evolved into her story 'Paper Children'.

> *You will go to things [at the FAC] and I won't necessarily come with you.*
> Leonard to Elizabeth Jolley in 1974 (Reid 57)

In retrospect Jolley's original decision in the 1960s to seek experiences outside her immediate family was a crucial one. They turned out to be a re-run of her English experiences, and she could be more reflective and analytical about them the second time around. Her Victoria Nursing Home work shared similarities with that at St Nicholas and St Martin's Hospitals in Pyrford and the Queen Elizabeth Hospital in Birmingham, as did her Flying Domestic work with live-in-work at the Raynors and the Fleetwood-Walkers. The Tuart Club, like Sibford, was a community of senior women who sought to provide a family for people whose homes were elsewhere, and her sales of Watkins products mainly took place in the homes of Tuart Club women. The second time around, she strove even harder to be the sort of person Henry James admired, someone 'on whom nothing is lost'.

Jolley's strategy of getting out of the house for regular work of one kind or another continued to bear fruit into the 1970s. She published half a dozen short stories by 1973, four of them indebted to Wooroloo for their settings and one of them indebted to her Victoria Nursing Home experience for its characters.[17] However, if her apprenticeship was a necessary step in the development of her career, it was not a sufficient one. She needed more than the Fellowship of Australian Writers for support and the UWA's *Westerly* as an outlet. She was convinced, with good reason, that t'othersider publishers and editors were not keen on writing from the west.[18] But Jolley would not have made the transition from a local, or even regional, writer simply by continuing with her current tactics or others that she tried unsuccessfully, like writing for the Education Department's school newsletter or writing for TV Channel 9.[19]

Australia's short-lived 1972–75 Whitlam Labor government was the 'luck' she needed. During the 1970s the impact of global diasporas and consequent ideological shifts were shaped in several ways, including a new multicultural framework for its immigration policy and a new emphasis on Australia's cultural independence from Britain. That latter emphasis produced both a film renaissance and support for local literature in the forms of art-access programs and regional publishing houses. Nationally, the Australia Council replaced the Australian Council for the Arts, its Literature Board disbursing grants to individuals, publishers and writers' organisations. And locally there was the miracle of the new Fremantle Arts Centre (FAC) begun in October 1972 to foster the work of Western Australian artists, craftspeople and writers.

The FAC was the brainchild of artist and poet Ian Templeman, Executive Officer of the Festival of Perth and a member of the Fellowship of Australian Writers (FAW). He founded the Centre to exhibit arts and crafts by Western Australian practitioners and also to publish the work of Australian writers that would be illustrated by those artists. One of the FAC's core activities was an Arts Access program which ran leisure courses in, among other things, Appreciating Literature and Creative Writing, an initial problem being to find and keep good teachers. Templeman's choice of Jolley was an inspired one, if serendipitous. He had met her in the late 1960s when he first read his poetry at the FAW, so that when they ran into each other years later on the corner of Broadway and Stirling Highway in Claremont and she greeted him as 'The Caretaker', the job was hers—'The Caretaker' was the name of a poem he had read at the FAW and had published in *Westerly*.[20]

As Elizabeth Jolley drove to her first meeting with the nine people enrolled in her February 1974 FAC class held in the Fremantle Arts Centre's grand, cavernous building which had served as Western Australia's Insane Asylum until 1915, a bus rear-ended her car on the Causeway roundabout. When she finally met her students, she found that they came from a broad spectrum of backgrounds and had varying expectations. There were teenagers and septuagenarians, people whose therapists thought creative writing might help them and people desperate for others to hear their life stories; there were hopeful aspirants who could find no other opportunity for practical advice and assistance; and there were a number of UWA colleagues, some of them genuinely interested in literature and writing, some of them friends Jolley had cajoled into attending in order to make up the numbers. The latter outnumbered the others at some of her early classes, Jolley becoming miffed when they did not formally enrol. She rued the fact that she was being paid so little for teaching so many, but she was in fact a victim of her own success.

That success partly involved the rigorous application of her belief that western literature was a continuum in which basic human hopes and fears, longings and desires, were progressively examined from different points of view. At first her students might be taken aback when she handed out a Roneographed scene from Euripides' *Medea* for them to study as a treatment of a wife/mother's predicament—for her, 'relevance' was not a synonym for 'contemporary'. They were also surprised by the musical interlude at the midpoint of each class when she put her little cassette player on the desk and played anything from German Lieder, as her mother had done in her Adult Education Class, to Gluck's aria of Orpheus' grief over the death of Eurydice[21], to 'I Am, I Said' from Neil Diamond's recent *Stones* album (contemporary and popular work was relevant too).[22] She would invite the students just to relax while they listened to it, or to enjoy some scene it portrayed to them, or to use it as a prompt for something to write about.

Each of the 7–9 pm thirteen-week-long courses had a theme, such as 'Battleaxes and Sex Kittens', and Jolley would distribute handouts to guide discussion of the theme.[23] One handout was a list of quotations from Shakespeare involving references to girdles and belts, images which happened to be a preoccupation in something Jolley was writing at the time.[24] Often the classes featured a local or visiting writer who spoke in the last half of the session, like Barry Oakley in the third term of 1975. And often the sessions ran over the scheduled time, many staying on to continue the discussion, or Jolley and perhaps the visiting speaker adjourning with them to a nearby pub or a café for a chat and a glass of wine. In the course of those discussions, the students came to realise that Jolley was what today is called an 'emerging' writer with publications to her name—if nothing else, they would have seen *Pinup*, a tabloid-size 'literary poster' on the FAC bulletin boards featuring her story 'Mr Parker's Valentine'. In that way her teaching not only furthered her goal of establishing a life apart from Leonard and her children, but it did two other things as well. It created her first audience, and it gave her an opportunity to develop the persona she would use as a writer. As the husband in her story 'The Performance' says of his wife, she put a lot into her performance and it took a lot out of her (29).

Another of the FAC's innovations was to offer summer schools in country centres where writers, painters, potters and jewellers would run intensive day or week-long programs for people eager for such tuition. And so Jolley sometimes found herself driving more than 400-miles round-trip to Geraldton or Albany to meet with country people interested in writing. From the late 1970s the FAC also established and maintained book clubs with its 'Travelling Notebook' program, commissioning Jolley to research and write the first three *Travelling Notebooks*. They were sensible and helpful study guides for the general reader interested in texts that were primarily American, British and European, although each guide gestured toward Australian literature. At thirty-to-fifty pages long, they were her first 'lit crit' publications.

She also tutored in country towns like Dalwallinu, Hyden, Kojonup and Wongan Hills. As before, she found material for her writing in such places, particularly in her images of the landscape ('the wheat', as she called the wheatbelt) and in her vignettes of sad individuals and bad marriages (for instance, in 'The Long Distant Lecture'), and, if she understood him correctly, she even managed to attract an offer of marriage from one of the shire presidents (she did not inquire closely). As in Fremantle, she was a success with her audiences which were largely comprised of women who appreciated the interest she took in their lives and the advice and help she gave them about telling their stories. Jolley's FAC country tours were another occasion she used to create a community of dedicated supporters. Country women were readers she greatly valued, people who remained faithful for her entire career.

A natural extension of Templeman's vision was his founding the Fremantle Arts Centre Press (FACP) in 1975, a regional press with a charter 'to promote, encourage and give wider publication to Western Australian writers and artists'.[25] In doing so, he enlisted the support of the Western Australian Literary Fund (later the Western Australian Arts Council) which provided an annual grant, the Literature Board of the Australia Council to subsidise selected FACP titles, and the Council of the City of Fremantle with whom it had a symbiotic relationship. The Fremantle Arts Centre Press made an instant impact on the Western Australian arts scene, maintaining its pre-eminence long after Templeman left it in 1988.

Having read her published stories and having talked with her about how many others she was writing simultaneously, Templeman asked if she had enough work to fill a small book of short stories. She assured him that she did, not bothering to specify that she filled a drawer under the bed and a cupboard in another room with her stories. He scheduled Jolley's stories as the FACP's first book of fiction in its new single-author series.[26] Auspiciously, before it appeared her draft novel *Palomino* shared first prize in the 1975 Victorian Fellowship of Australian Writers' Con Weickhardt competition for an unpublished novel.

Templeman launched Jolley's *Five Acre Virgin and Other Stories* on Saturday 30 November 1976 before an unexpectedly large audience of 400. After he spoke, she responded appreciatively and then, dressed in her caftan and carrying a large bag as usual, she proceeded into the audience to thank people for coming. She handed out gifts as she did so, including small tins of beetroot for students who had done particularly well in her classes.

Beetroot and all, that was Jolley's way of conducting the business side of writing at her first launch. And it seemed to work, for in the first two-and-a-half weeks the print run of 750 sold out from the UWA Bookshop, the Grove Bookshop in Claremont, and the Terrace Arcade Bookshop in Perth, the only places the FACP had the ability to supply. So did the second print run of 750, in the same three bookshops and in the same time frame. It received four reviews, one local and three interstate ones, all of them positive, Jean Bedford, a leading novelist, identifying it as part of 'the new wave Australian writing'. *Five Acre Virgin* became a mainstay for the press which republished it time and again with different covers, and later published it together with its successor, *The Travelling Entertainer*, as *Stories*. On its own, *The Travelling Entertainer*, first published in 1979 with a print run of 2,000, also quickly sold out. And so did her first novel, *The Newspaper of Claremont Street*, with 500 hardcover signed and numbered copies and 3,000 in paperback format. It is still in print more than a quarter of a century later.[27]

Jolley had learned the difference between writing and being a writer.

> *People are all exiles, without choice, from childhood. Because of this, each person is the sole custodian of certain experiences and memories which no one else possesses. These experiences and memories deeply enrich Australian literature.*
>
> 'The Pill, the Condom and the Syringe' (226)

During the 1970s Jolley wrote out of the knowledge of the migrant experience she brought with her to Australia: her confused sense of it in her family home; her encounters with it through continental refugees she met both at Sibford and in her parents' home; her acquaintance with it through the foreign soldiers she nursed at the Queen Elizabeth Hospital; and—above all—her personal experience of it as a kind of displaced person from the time she first left home for Sibford. All this informed her sense of what it was to be a privileged English-speaking, white, middle-class 'new Australian' in post-war Western Australia, although being middle class was not something she foregrounded in her own behaviour nor the status she used for most of her early characters.

Her first two books of short stories and her 1981 novel *The Newspaper of Claremont Street* enact the migrant experience of exile. Migrants are the main characters in most of the stories in *Five Acre Virgin* and ten of the eleven stories in *The Travelling Entertainer* of 1979. Even in her 1983 book of stories, *Woman in a Lampshade*, they feature in eleven of seventeen stories. Similarly, the protagonist of *The Newspaper of Claremont Street* is the daughter of Mrs Morris, the migrant cleaning lady in the first book of stories, her antagonist Nastasya Torben an immigrant whose dislocation is the greater for the fact of the language shift from Russian and the cultural differences she encounters in Australia. Focused on community, communion and connectedness with the past and the present, the three books present characters who exhibit a longing for belonging, and they also prefigure Jolley's interest in sexuality and her concern about lovelessness.

In her early work she often recycled plots, techniques, imagery, quotations and other words and phrases. She also recycled characters, some of them reappearing with the same names as major or minor figures in her other works, just as Balzac did in his *Comédie humaine*. Mrs Morgan, her children and her husband (once) appear in the first six stories of *Five Acre Virgin*; in the second, *The Travelling Entertainer*, she morphs into Mabel Doris Morgan who writes letters to her boarder-son ('Wednesdays and Fridays'); and then she again appears as Mabel Morgan, the novelist in Jolley's radio play 'The Well-bred Thief'. Her daughter Mary, as Margie Morris, becomes the protagonist cleaning lady in *The Newspaper of Claremont Street*. And Mr and Mrs Morgan reappear in Jolley's 1983 novel *Mr Scobie's Riddle*, Night Sister Shady being her daughter. Sometimes even differently-named characters recall other ones, like the Dutch land swindlers Uncle Bernard ('Outink to Uncle's Place', et al.) and Uncle Otto (in 'The Agent in Travelling' and in *Milk and Honey*). Thus at the beginning of her career Jolley treated many of her characters as if they were a community, jokingly telling Templeman that some of them would live forever, meaning that, if she killed a character in an earlier story, s/he might reappear in a later one.[28]

In *Five Acre Virgin* that community is more dystopic than utopic except for the parodic one represented by the Morgan family. The mother's borrowing of the home-owner's car and cash for a weekend trip in 'Another Holiday for the Prince' (2) and inviting less-well-off people to hold wedding receptions and parties in the penthouse or elderly people to soak their feet and to bathe while she cleans in 'A Gentleman's Agreement' (13) are victimless crimes that 'gave a lot of pleasure to people without doing anybody any harm': they exhibit communion. By contrast, 'The Shepherd on the Roof' is a sober satire on marriage and domesticity, where the husband says, '[m]utual contempts' when the wife asks what keeps them together and, when one elderly pink-washed spouse says, 'Tootsey Wootsie Wootsie?', the other replies, 'Lovey Dovey Dovey!' [49]). However, 'Shepherd' invokes communion through the protagonist, Mrs Grant, who wants to give shelter to a young unmarried couple after they have had a car accident. When her husband forbids her doing so, she pleads, 'It's a responsibility', and he snaps, 'Whose! Not ours' (52)—one of many examples in Jolley's work of men excluding and women including, like Leonard's rejecting Ludmila Blotnicki's telephone calls when Elizabeth accepted them.

The Travelling Entertainer also has echoes of Jolley's reliance on her Australian experience, with its faculty spouses, country landowners, nursing homes, hospitals, door-to-door selling, and lecturing in country towns.[29] It focuses especially on love and its various possible manifestations, 'Mr Parker's Valentine' imagining but not realising a more promising outcome than 'The Shepherd on the Roof'. After the Pages buy a house from an old widower, the husband only reluctantly acceding to the wife's request for the widower to live on in the shed at the back, the man invites them on Valentine's Day to a meal he has prepared in the shed, to share communion with him, as it were.[30] After dinner the man shows them a valentine he kept hidden, unopened, in the rafters of the shed for fifty years, the point of which is lost on Pearson Page—they should get rid of him, he declares. When his wife says the man is ill, he replies, 'That's his lookout' (90). The valentine is Mr Parker's warrant for believing in the possibility of love.[31]

'The Agent in Travelling' is more expansive for how it actualises love against the odds and achieves connectedness with both the past and the present. Bernard Oons, a 'new Australian', works hard in order to bring out his wife and daughter from the old country, but one decade becomes three before he finally returns to the Netherlands to collect her, by then effectively a migrant to his own country of origin. His wife, who has been remarried for twenty years, resolves their dilemma by redesignating him her 'brozzer' and giving him a room in the attic where he lives comfortably and happily until he dies. She tells him he is to say he has come back from Africa—when he protests 'Australia Mitzi!' she responds, 'Oh Ja! India. Who here will know the difference?' (54). Reminiscent of Mrs Morris, Mitzi does not regard either imposture or bigamy as legitimate impediments to enacting family.

Two other stories in *The Travelling Entertainer* anticipate a darker theme, the possibility of evil in people. This was the idea that occurred to Jolley after watching the two young girls at Wooroloo, something she said she only went on to investigate in 'Grasshoppers' and 'The Fellow Passenger'. 'Grasshoppers' is a sophisticated story about Peg and her fifteen-year-younger lover Bettina, whose sexual relationship at first is not much remarked on, any more than is that of Peg's ex-partner and his new relationship with a man. Instead, Jolley first focuses on Peg's and Bettina's young daughters, Kerry and Miranda. They do not seem so much evil as self-regarding and heedless of the needs of others, Bettina's daughter Miranda especially so: they bully the grandmother into making paper hats that they cruelly reject as inadequate; Miranda finagles Kerry's sweets, and ultimately Kerry drowns in the dam by means unknown. That behaviour is replicated when Bettina appropriates Peg's clothing and bullies money from her; and Kerry might well have lived if Peg and Miranda had not peremptorily parked the girls with Peg's mother and flown off to India.[32]

Since Jolley said that in her first draft Bettina was thoroughly evil but in the final one more foolish than wise, it is possible that she also revised her initial thesis about an innate evil in some children to something more like a concept of Original Sin which affects children and adults alike.[33] Certainly, when Miranda says she is Bettina and Kerry is Peg and that '[i]n a minute we're going to have a cuddle' (141), the suggestion is that the children are mimicking adult behaviour rather than conversely. This notion (the fragile border between evil and foolishness/carelessness) and this situation (three generations of a grandmother, needy children and wild grandchildren) reappears years later in Jolley's *Orchard Thieves* (1995) in a fashion that more clearly affirms the power of love in the face of needless/needy 'evil' of self-interestedness.

If Peg and Bettina are middle-class by origin but oppositional hippies in their lifestyles, the Abrahams family in 'The Fellow Passenger' is solidly bourgeois. Dr Abrahams, his wife and their daughter Rachel are passengers on a luxury liner to Australia. It is a remedial voyage, 'as if he were ill because of his sympathetic nature', although there are 'conflicting reasons and feelings which were all perhaps a part of being unwell, perhaps even a part of the cause' (72). En route, he is accosted by an ill-kempt, overly familiar and sinister stowaway with a limp, a man who greets him with 'All you have to do is to treat me like a fellow passenger' (71). After Abrahams buys the stranger a drink and food, he feels a gladness which might have made him sing, but 'men like Abrahams simply would never burst into song' (73). Perhaps; but he did so once many years before (73). It was when, lost on his way to find a patient, he asked a man for directions and, because of how the man's eyes shone as the man patted his horse, 'Abrahams felt as if the intimate caress . . . was meant for him' (74). When the stowaway demands money, Abrahams notices his beautiful young hands and 'a suggestion of caress in the man's eyes' (75). And when he demands clothing—shirts, socks, underwear, a bag for them, and even a passport—Abrahams suddenly finds himself treating him in his cramped cabin.

The intimacy involved in touching the man's thigh wound brings laughter and gladness to both of them, but the intimacy is too confronting for Abrahams—the stowaway's demand was 'a pleading and a promise', it was a 'command' (79). He quickly becomes revolted by his fellow passenger, turning him in to the stewards who take him away, perhaps an echo of Jolley's betrayal of Ludmila. In the meantime, Abrahams' young daughter has affected a limp and wants to dress as a stowaway for the ship's fancy-dress party, the child's behaviour once more mimicking that of the adults, once more articulating Jolley's recurrent theme of innocence complicated by experience.

In 'Grasshoppers', Peg does not obsessively analyse how her affair with Bettina ends but instead holds Bettina between her naked thighs in the image invoked by one of the story's epigraphs, Rilke's poem 'Pietà' that begins 'Now my misery, complete, fills me up' (135). She regards the ending of the relationship as the end of passionate love.[34] It is an image that relates to innocence complicated by experience, and so to the event of her daughter's drowning. Conversely, Dr Abrahams, the man whose timid love is chronicled, finds ending his momentary affair to be 'life-returning', for he prefers the life that Peg dreads. 'He stood relaxed letting life return as he watched the grotesque game [deck tennis] and, with some reservations belonging to his own experience, he found the sight of the Worcester Sauce Queens [two elderly widows] charming' (83).

In the novel *The Newspaper of Claremont Street* Jolley defines a 'third way' of achieving community/communion/connectedness and negotiating sexuality and lovelessness. Cleaning-lady Mrs Morgan's daughter Mary, transformed into elderly Margarite 'Margie' Morris, is sexless and loveless. She lives rent-free in a single room in return for cleaning the toilets and sweeping the halls and verandas; her main pastime and pleasure is darning, patching worn-out materials with a herringbone stitch; she has no company and no fellow-feeling for any particular person beyond her larcenous but charming brother Victor. When Crazy, the itinerant neighbourhood cat, chooses to have her seven kittens in Weekly's room, she forces them on willing children in the homes where she cleans and drowns those she cannot place.

Weekly does, however, have one passion: 'There was something she wanted to do more than anything else, and for this she needed money' (8): she wants land in the bush above the escarpment she sees as she walks to work every morning, land where she can plant the fruit trees she remembered from her childhood. Her grandmother had told her, 'People and trees is special' (6), and Weekly wants a pear tree of her own. Put differently, being unlike Peg for never having known passion, and unlike Abrahams who opts for civility, she chooses the land. She is like the farmer in 'The Performance' in *The Travelling Entertainer*, or like characters in *Five Acre Virgin* who own land and are obsessive about it, nurturing it as they might a loved one. Even those who are rough on the land are capable of writing lyric poetry about it, as in Uncle Bernard's poem of the grapes ('Tokay, Shiraz, Grenache . . .' [59]) or in Martha Dorsoba's catalogue of [a]pricots, plomms, nectarines, peaches, almonds, apples' (78).

What stands between Weekly and the object of her desire is Nastasya 'Narsty' Torben, a Russian émigrée whose apartment Weekly cleans, a woman who hijacks Weekly's life. When Nastasya's husband falls ill, she sends Weekly off at midnight to find a doctor—a doctor who thinks Weekly is as crazy as Nastasya for taking on Nastasya's irrational dependence on her husband; and, when the husband dies, Weekly takes her in 'for just one night' (58).

It is an arrangement that seems likely to become permanent, despite Weekly's wishes to the contrary. Nastasya's behaviour becomes increasingly erratic, as she devises exotic costumes, planning parties, taking taxis, giving away her jewels and money—everything Jolley had experienced with Ludmila Blotnicki. There is the reproach—'You ought to be pleased and grateful you are so much loved' (68). There is even a moment when Weekly holds Nastasya in a non-erotic echo of Peg's holding Bettina: unlike Peg she is thinking about the five acres and how 'More than anything she wanted to be there alone' (96). Later Weekly's attempt to put her into the mental hospital by subterfuge fails. Sensing it, Nastasya asks if Weekly wants her to stay with her, and Weekly lies, 'Why yes o' course I do' (107).

Regretting not having taken Nastasya to the hospital, overjoyed at the rain that will make her new land productive, Weekly dances—dances for the first time in her life—imagining 'a veil of lacy white blossom falling all around her... And from the little foil label, blowing in the restlessness of the evening, came a fragile music for the pear tree dance' (113). Then, in the most sinister moment in all of Jolley's fiction, as Nastasya, stuck firmly in the mud in gumboots borrowed from Weekly, continues to bully her about the correct way to plant a tree, Weekly dances away, ignoring Nastasya's plans of 'Help me!' It is as if the bizarre marriage-like ritual includes enacting the till-death-do-us-part clause.

Writing is an art and a craft, but it's like everything else if you want to sell it. You've got to go into the business world.

Elizabeth Jolley (Williams 282)

During the 1970s Elizabeth Jolley continued to maintain roles outside of the home. In the 1960s they were ones that involved working in the margins of other people's lives, with the Tuart Club, Watkins, Victoria Nursing Home and, in the early 1970s, Flying Domestics. In the 1970s she also started to work within what is now called the 'culture industry', the turning point being the 1973–1974 period.

Leonard Jolley continued to require attention. He took a second study leave on his own, travelling to the University of Sheffield School of

Librarianship for the first half of 1973, spending some of the time travelling in Europe, but then an operation on his feet in May in Sheffield required him to cancel a trip to Italy and come home as planned.[35] On his return he had a follow-up operation in October and then, during his recuperation, expressed his thoughts and feelings in what he no doubt believed was a principled and witty way. When John Dawkins, a mature-age UWA student and also Secretary to the Hospital Employees' Federation[36] organised a November 1973 strike of nursing aides and hospital assistants at the Hollywood Repatriation General Hospital, Jolley wrote a letter to the Editor of the *West Australian*.[37] Although a unionist, he regarded compulsory unionism with distaste and, having been hospitalised nine times for seven operations in the past decade, said (among other things) that Dawkins would not know a bedpan if he were hit over the head with one, prudently adding, 'Far be it from me to suggest illegal violence . . .' Dawkins sued Jolley along with West Australian Newspapers Ltd, leading to a year-long case, which left Leonard in a panic and Elizabeth fearing that they might lose their house. In the event, it took the jury of two women and four men some twenty-three minutes to find in favour of Jolley and West Australian Newspapers Ltd on 5 November 1974, but once more his heedlessness and self-centredness had made life difficult for her.

In the midst of those concerns, Jolley had wound down her Flying Domestic work by 1974 as the prospect of FAC work emerged.[38] Her writing had been noticed to the extent that she was invited to speak to local teacher college students and also to address an English-teacher's association. Following the success of *The Five Acre Virgin*, such requests continued, becoming increasingly substantive. She was invited to address the First Australian Conference on the Family and Health held at the UWA by the Royal Australian College of General Practitioners in August 1977. Her talk, called 'Where Do I Look for Help', led to her first academic article when it was published in the *Proceedings* of the conference.[39] Similarly, in August 1978 she gave a paper on death and dying at a Chaplains' Conference at the Royal Perth Hospital. On the day, she was irritated at the hypocrisy of a pink-and-white-faced speaker who talked about the happiness of the aged being cared for 'in God's loving goodness'. Whether or not that provided extra motivation, her talk was so moving that she received a standing ovation, many of the men and women in the audience openly in tears.[40] In 1978 she was also offered part-time teaching in the Western Australian Institute of

Technology's newly established three-year course in creative writing, work she carried in addition to her teaching at the FAC.[41]

For Jolley, the biggest event of the decade occurred when Ian Templeman, in the hope of attracting attention to his newly established press, brought a contingent from the FACP to Writers' Week which was held during the prestigious 1978 Adelaide Festival. In addition to Templeman, there was the FACP's Manager Terry Owen, Jolley and Alan Alexander along with Tom Hungerford, the third author in their single-author series.[42] Hungerford, a seasoned traveller who realised it was Jolley's first aeroplane flight, reported to Owen that on arrival she had gone straight to her hotel room because, he thought, she was not holding up very well. It is true that Jolley was worried about the fact that it was the first time she had left Leonard alone in order to indulge herself. It is also true that she was luxuriating in her large room on the fourth floor of the Grosvenor Hotel, overlooking the park and the River Torrens, appreciating the writing table, five lamps, and brass taps in the loo. It was the first time a porter had carried her bags to a hotel room since she was a girl travelling with her mother in Germany.

In the morning, as Hungerford led her to the Festival tent where she was to read as part of Writers' Week, they discovered that her reputation had preceded her, for broadside sheets of *Tabloid Story* featuring her story 'The Owner of Grief' were blowing about the Festival grounds. She read from her humorous story 'Mark F', about a mother's disastrous attempt to help her daughter with correspondence-school assignments. That was a major public step in constructing her public persona as a wife/mother/writer in her mid-fifties. And she was successful in the role, for she held the audience's attention while ΠO, a young Melbourne poet was ringing a bell to disrupt the readings of 'writerly' writers.[43] Writing at the time of the 1978 Adelaide Festival, R. F. Brissenden remarked:

> *To the casual observer Writers' Week may sometimes look like nothing more than a seven-day booze-up punctuated by poetry readings and literary brawls... In fact, it has developed into a remarkably significant cultural and education event, which affects not only the production, dissemination and reception of Australian writing within Australia but also the whole relationship of local writers and their work with the world at large... Nobody questions the uniquely important role that Writers' Week now plays in literary life of Australia.*[44]

Neither a boozer nor a brawler, by the end of the festival Jolley was disenchanted with writers who read too long, 'ego-type' writers and their hangers-on. She thought she might never again attend a writers' conference. But then she decided she was as much an egoist as any of the other writers and resolved to keep on with her work.

> Thou thy wordly task hath done.
> Home art gone and ta'en thy wages.
> Shakespeare, *Cymbeline*, act 4, scene 2, lines 260-61

In the first half of the decade Elizabeth had to deal with thyroid and gall-bladder problems that threatened operations, with no likelihood of someone 'stealing the purse' without her knowledge; with a traumatic visit from Irma Roitman, her mother's nemesis whose speech and mannerisms bore a distressing resemblance to Margarete Knight's; with the deaths of Mrs Lamb, and Joyce Broom, her Pyrford friend and perhaps a model for Snorter and/or Diamond in *My Father's Moon*; and with Leonard's six-month absence and the year-long drama resulting from his letter to the *West Australian* about John Dawkins.[45]

In the second half of the decade her traumas were more intractable. There was the death of her much-loved father in October 1977 and that of her mother in August of 1979. Her father's friend Bill Cotterell, who quoted *Cymbeline*, wrote to say that Wilfrid Knight 'never lost [his] fresh spirit at the centre + yet his life was almost a continual battle with feelings of guilt + persecution'.[46] Elizabeth continued her long conversation with him in her mind, often appropriating a sentence or two from him in her writing or expanding on some thought or feeling he expressed. It was an 'intellectual bereavement' for her, 'a bereavement of not writing letters'. She did not weep for her mother but was thankful for her death and hopeful that Margarete Knight, after her 'terrible loneliness and unhappiness', was now talking in heaven to Wilfrid Knight. She said she would not miss her; she had her Dad—she wrote to him in her mind but never wrote to her mother, 'because she did not want my letters'.[47]

Finally, there was Leonard's Jolley's retirement, at sixty-five, from the UWA at the end of 1979. An ominous, if not overwhelming, prospect for what it meant in terms of the increased care and attention he would need, was the celebration of the event in early December. He did not tell her about it, claiming after the fact that he did not know spouses were welcome, something that left her speechless with anger and humiliation. If his behaviour had not become intolerable, she had become intolerant of his behaviour.

When Ludmila Blotnicki told Elizabeth Jolley in 1971 that she loved her and that Jolley should be glad, she was confounded to find herself in the position of St Julian the Hospitaller: she once referred to Blotnicki as Jesus waiting in the rain in Mt Lawley. She knew what Blotnicki said was true, and she knew she could have continued the relationship as Blotnicki wished, and that perhaps she should have. But she was stopped by a growing revulsion and by a sense that the capacity to love could be overwhelmed by the demands of others. Simultaneously pushed and pulled by equal forces, she was driven to continue in a relationship she was complicit in. Yet she was stayed by a feeling that others might disdain her, even as she understood that for her affection, love, and the experience of exploring friendship were essential to her life. That is the position she found herself in during the early 1970s.

As if previewing the developments represented in *Five Acre Virgin*, *The Travelling Entertainer* and *The Newspaper of Claremont Street*, Jolley began to adopt the discipline of restraint in relation to friendships like that with Blotnicki, something she felt as a loss because she feared it precluded finding relationships that might be enriching and rewarding—but something that also reassured because it precluded the distaste of others. Thus in fiction and life she explored the limits of friendship, investigating how she might try to find a way of being in the world, not only as a wife and mother but also a person and writer.

In Jolley's gathering catalogue of consolations, reference to her melancholy task—*C'est un triste métier*—came more hopefully to be countered by a favourite proverb *Die mit Träven säen, werden mit Freuden ernten*—'They that sow in tears shall reap in joy'.

9

1980-84—The inside of people's survival...

I suppose I am interested to explore the inside of people's survival.
Elizabeth Jolley (Ellison 176)

Elizabeth Jolley's commitment to writing and publishing produced twelve books from the middle of the 1970s to the end of the 1980s, nearly one a year. Her achievement is the greater when one considers that, except for one, all of those books were subsequently published in the United States and the United Kingdom during the 1980s and that translations of five of them into half a dozen other languages began in 1988 with *Miss Peabody's Inheritance*.[1]

Jolley's institutional publishing history is instructive. *Palomino*, her first novel, appeared under the imprint of the new Outback Press in Melbourne, *The Newspaper of Claremont Street* from the five-year-old regional Fremantle Arts Centre Press, and *Miss Peabody's Inheritance* from an established academic press, University of Queensland Press. Then Jolley achieved a lifetime ambition, to be published by Penguin, when Penguin brought out *Mr Scobie's Riddle* and *Woman in a Lampshade* in 1983. Penguin Australia, begun in 1946 largely as a distributor for its English parent company, was adapting to a globalising world when it began publishing Australian work in 1963. Jolley started to publish exclusively with Penguin in 1986, with *The Well*, when Penguin was on its way to becoming one of the three largest English-language publishers in the world.[2] Thus, by the second half of the 1980s she had, in her modest phrase, reached some measure of success.

Success came only through trial and error. Jolley submitted the novels written in the 1960s or before (*The Feast, The Leila Family, Palomino* and *The Newspaper of Claremont Street*) as well as five variant collections of short stories to thirteen different publishers in Australia and England before her first big break, *Palomino*, which was also her first big bust. Outback Press accepted *Palomino* by telephone in mid-1977 and, when she met with its representative at the Adelaide Festival in 1978, she felt it was the happiest day of her life. The next day he had forgotten to bring the contract with him, after which anxious months became angry years, with an incomplete print run materialising in 1980 (the date on the copyright page), but no royalty cheques ever appearing.[3] Four more years passed, including a court action to regain the rights, before the UQP reissued it.

Likewise, she endlessly sent stories to newspapers, popular magazines, local and overseas journals, and competitions—in one year alone she received thirty-nine rejection slips.[4] But canny persistence paid off. Thus, for example, in 1968 she unsuccessfully sent 'Hilda's Wedding' to the ABC and after that to four anthologies, five competitions and six magazines/journals in Australia, the UK and the US. Then she sent it to the ABC once more and they accepted it for broadcast in 1976. Like Crazy the cat in *The Newspaper of Claremont Street* (59), nobody could wait like Jolley.

She had to become thick-skinned too in order to survive some of the editors' comments. One editor asked her to excuse the ABC's long delay over 'The Disciple', likening their indecision to 'a child with a complicated toy: we don't know what to do with it but we don't want to give it up'.[5] And other comments ran the gamut from unhopeful to unhelpful. One rejection slip said, 'Unfortunately we don't have any money', without saying whether or not they would have accepted the piece if they did. More explicitly, James McAuley of *Quadrant* said she used too many capital letters; Richard Walsh of *Pol* that her work was too menopausal; *Westerly* that 'This is not US'; and the ABC that 'Nowhere in Australia is there a market for anything like this or an audience for anything like this'. Beatrice Davis of Angus and Robertson thought that *The Newspaper of Claremont Street* was good but sentimental and twee. And another rejection slip said that the author was obviously disturbed and should seek professional help immediately.[6]

Throughout the 1980s she was supported by her agent Caroline Lurie of newly formed Australian Literary Management. They met for the first time at the 1980 Festival of Adelaide where Jolley's second book of short stories, *Travelling Entertainer*, was launched. Lurie remembers Jolley was 'flirting outrageously' with the FACP person who was to launch the book and was 'surrounded by people who knew and liked her work, and she was clearly very excited by it'.[7] Jolley's enthusiasm was matched by Lurie's knowledge of the publishing world, something which relieved Jolley of much anxiety. They also became great friends and close confidantes, remaining so until Jolley died.[8] One of Lurie's first jobs was to pressure Outback Press over *Palomino* in order to salvage as much as she could for Jolley.

> Abstinence sows sand all over
> The ruddy limbs and flaming hair,
> But Desire gratified
> Plants fruits of life and beauty there.
> William Blake, *Gnomic Verses* (195), epigraph to *Milk and Honey*

In the first week of January of 1975 Jolley participated in her first Fremantle Arts Centre Albany Arts and Crafts Summer School, ten days on the south-west coast, where she realised that teaching creative writing was an 'act'[9]. In March of 1975 she started a radio play, 'The Performance', which turned into a short story. She was thrilled by its double point of view, resulting from its dual first-person narration—two men in a psychiatric ward talk to one another, one relaying to the reader the story his postman-roommate tells him.

The postman's life has came undone partly by an estrangement from his wife, a teacher of creative writing for whom each class was a performance which drained her, and partly through a disaster he believes he has caused. During his mail rounds he had become aware of an elderly reclusive woman always at her gate awaiting a letter. Unkempt, dressed in rags, her house neglected and tumbledown, she was the sort of woman children call witch as they hurry by. Each time he arrived there, the old woman told him about her son and four grandchildren in England, and each time he pedalled away, having no letter for her; he could hardly bear seeing hope 'die away at my reply' (22). When her long-awaited letter arrived at Christmas, he struggled with his load to bring it to her quickly. Surprised not to find her at the gate and fearing she might have died, he let himself into the house and saw her sitting amongst piles of discarded clothes engaged in a performance, picking up one and then another rag, sometimes scolding, sometimes cajoling, as she taught it to recite poetry. She waved him away, telling him to come back in an hour and, as he left, he saw her hold one cloth to her breast, rocking it, 'as if to console forever the upset, hysterical rag' (24).

She did not come out again, and he did not stop again. In April he opened the letter from her son, thinking reading it to her might bring her back to reality. Finding it a duplicated, form letter, with 'Grandma' handwritten after typewritten 'Dear', he resolved not to deliver it. The next morning, seeing her standing on the pavement with arms filled with packages, he pedalled by without looking toward her, and then, hearing a screeching of brakes, turned to see she had been hit and killed by a car. The breakdown for which he is hospitalised is a consequence of his concluding he could have saved her had he stopped, and that the groceries strewn across the road showed how 'she had intended to go on living' (29). He is anxious to be released from hospital because his wife had boldly come to his farm during their estrangement and, when he invited her to stay for a rest and cup of tea, kissed him and told him her stories. He realises now that '[s]he needs to talk, and now if I'm not there because I have to be in here, because of this, it's the same thing as I've done to the old woman by not looking at her' (29).

The time of writing 'The Performance' was fraught for Jolley. She was concerned about her children, as well as about her relationship with Leonard, realising it was his arthritis she could not stand, not him. She worried about the starvation of family life, even as she began to develop her writing career through teaching for the FAC and submitting manuscripts for publication.[10] *The Newspaper of Claremont Street* was making the rounds of publishers, and she was in the middle of reworking the novel that became *Palomino*. Having told Ludmila Blotnicki four years earlier that she loved her in order to entice her back to Graylands Mental Hospital, Jolley had dropped her—but the fate of Nastasya in *Newspaper* when Weekly chooses the land over Nastasya's love is evidence that she had not forgotten Blotnicki and the conundrum she represented.

'The Performance' is not only a story about the starvation of family life, but also, like *Newspaper*, a story about love in all its myriad forms and in all its betrayals—the central theme of Jolley's novels from the 1980s onwards. For, just as she conceived the *donnée* for 'The Performance' while in Albany, she also discovered her novels' central motive: the desire to be with a chosen companion, which in *Palomino* is described as a 'step[ping] off into friendship which would go deeper into discovery every time we were together'.

> *There is not a man of them who when he heard the proposal would not deny or would not acknowledge that this meeting and melting into one another, this becoming one instead of two, was the very expression of his ancient need.*
> Plato's response to Aristophanes' description of love in the *Symposium* (192d)

Jolley's novels across the 1980s are *romans à thèse*, didactic thesis-novels whereby the narrative serves some political, philosophical or other point, and thus they demand close attention to their assumptions and arguments. They present what might be called her unified field theory on love. One of her theses is Socrates' argument in Plato's *Symposium*, that it is better to be the lover than the beloved. Another is her contemporary version of the myth of love Aristophanes tells in the *Symposium*, a myth about the origin of heterosexual and male- and female-homosexual love, and their equivalent natures. And, most importantly, there is Jolley's version of Aristophanes' argument that everyone is trying to find the prelapsarian complementary half s/he was separated from: everyone is wishing to be with a chosen companion, stepping deeper into friendship.[11] Her novels develop these theses and their corollaries: love is a gift and cannot be willed; to be chosen is to be blessed; loneliness is a near-irredeemable anguish; cherishing another is a consummate virtue; the need to be loved or cherished can lead to desperate dependencies and dire acts; quite ordinary, needy people are capable of redeeming acts of generosity; and—always—there are the consolations of delight in the land (a place to be known and cherished) and in the creative rapport that flows between writer and reader, musician and audience.

Such theses derive from the moral code that Jolley's father advocated and practised and Jolley's schooling and nursing training reinforced. But her disposition was not Methodist or Quaker or professional. Rather, Jolley's novels are informed by a profound attention to the suffering of lovelessness—of being, to use her recurrent phrase, 'on the edge' socially and emotionally—and by a deep hopefulness in the redemptive power of love in all its forms. In Jolley's vocabulary, both she and her work are simultaneously pessimistic and optimistic.[12] Put differently, the stepping-off place for Jolley's fiction is suffering. Her writing always recognises the suffering that comes from being without material and social supports, but it is the suffering of loneliness that drives the quest for perfect friendship in her fiction.

As much as anything else, Jolley's passion to explore this dual focus—loneliness/lovelessness and the redemptive power of love—accounts for the remarkable structural innovation of the novels during this decade, novels that, even as they recycled characters, situations, settings and phrasings, at the same time progressively experimented with narrative structures, voices and modes.[13] Thus, Helen Daniel included her in *Liars*, an account of Australia's new 'anti-realist' writers of the period. But Jolley, an immigrant deeply steeped in English and European cultural heritages and lately come to acceptance within the Australian literary scene, at heart belonged to no school or persuasion of writing.[14] Her innovative writing can best be understood as a response to the understandings about life she had from her experience, the insights about writing she had from her reading and teaching (and life with Leonard), and the desire she had to understand better the question she set herself: how to encompass the possibility of love in the lives of ordinary people.

It is a novel about a very rich woman. I can't say anything more about it except that two women appear to love each other.

Report of an alarmed publisher's reader[15]

If you read some novels simply for the story—excuse the cliché—you might as well hang yourself.

Elizabeth Jolley, (['Chocolate'] 22–3)

Awkward in places, controversial in others, Jolley's first and fifth published novels, *Palomino* (1980) and *Milk and Honey* (1984), are unlike the other novels of the 1980s for being first-person narrations which, in Jolley's words, tend to being slow-moving, even tiresome[16]—they both incline to being heavy-handed *romans à thèse*. *Palomino*, like 'The Performance', is a dual first-person narration, within which there is a complex (and not always plausible) intercalation of monologues, letters and diary entries. And it is controversial for the number and type of relationships represented: its protagonist, Laura, loves a much younger woman, Andrea, just as Laura had loved Andrea's mother long before and, some time after that, formed an intense attachment through letters to a much older woman, Esmé Gollanberg; and Andrea comes to love (and be lover of) Laura, even as she tries to stop loving her married brother, Christopher, by whom she is pregnant at the time she goes to stay with Laura. Similarly, *Milk and Honey* is structurally complex, 'for it is a retrospective tale told by its hero, Jacob, a kind of bizarre whodunit, complete with gothic trappings (whispers, mirrors, fires, attics, asylums) and deaths indeterminately accidental or intentional, caused by a person or persons who remain unknown. Here too, as in *Palomino*, there are unconventional relationships: love across age gaps, for Jacob is husband to one older woman (Louise Heimbach) and lover of another (Madge); infidelity, for Madge is cheating on her husband Norm; and sibling incest, for Louise and her brother Waldemar have a child named Elise.

> *[T]he secret delicious knowledge that I could . . . step off into friendship which would go deeper into discovery every time we were together.*
> Laura, thinking of Andrea, *Palomino* (26)

> *It's not the immediate thing one misses but something from before . . .*
> Laura, in an unsent letter to Andrea, *Palomino* (257)

Laura encapsulates *Palomino*'s subject (and Jolley's writerly focus) when, during their interlude together on her farm, she tells Andrea that '[i]nstead of wars and politics we are concerned with a friendship between two women, with the harvest from the land and with the birth of a baby'; their friendship, she says, is 'so delicate . . . it's the ideal of an Idyll' (219). Such an ideal friendship is tightly tied to loss—to missing 'something from before', to the loneliness that Laura describes as 'the worst of all the other suffering' (192; also 222), and Andrea feels 'drives me mad' (11). Remediation of such anguish through the discovery of someone whom one can love and who, ideally, can love in return is the highest good in Jolley's world, a good that trumps any normative morality's imperative to heterosexual love. As Laura tells Andrea, when speaking of Andrea's incestuous love for her brother, 'wrong' is a 'strange, unprofitable word' (240; see also 193).

Still, the very strength of the governing imperative in Jolley's fiction—to escape the anguish of loneliness by loving/being loved, and so recover something from before—is dangerous both to oneself and to others unless accompanied by a key virtue: restraint. *Palomino* invokes the principle of restraint as it relates to the friendship that is love when Laura describes herself as 'her own wardress' (19, 136), and Andrea both recognises her 'discipline' and fears Laura's loss of 'control because she is hurt or angry' (127). Indeed, the novel turns on Laura's learning the moral significance of restraint as it relates to the longing to be what elsewhere Jolley calls being 'the giver and the recipient of the whole' (*Georges' Wife* 93).

First, there is the lesson of Laura's humiliation when she was used by Andrea's mother, Eva, in ways that compromised her dignity and taught her that 'now that I have given up this restraint, I have nothing' (152). Then there is the lesson learned when she restrains herself from succumbing to the cherishing of Dora, the young girl who keeps house for her after the disastrous time with Eva. Laura, having resisted her loneliness one night, wakes in the morning 'grateful things were not changed . . . [grateful] I was forced to understand my loneliness more' (29). And, most tellingly, there is the back-story of the lesson learned through Esmé Gollanberg, the medical colleague of her long-time epistolary, even adulatory, friendship, whose announced visit Laura had so passionately anticipated. When Esmé arrives—old, unlike Laura's imagination of her, and with a newly acquired husband—Laura is bereft; and when Esmé suffers a heart attack, she administers an injection that kills her. Though not clearly an act of murder, Laura accepts that her failure to be careful in selecting the right injection was born of anger and jealousy, and so accepts imprisonment. Still later she recognises the narcissism of her love for both Eva and Esmé, saying of Eva that 'I look[ed] for myself in her and never saw her' (220) and of Esmé that 'I created for myself your perfection' (180). She comes to understand in regard to Esmé that 'I should have loved you for the pleasure you had in living' (180) and that '[i]f only I could have wrapped you round in love, nothing of what happened, could have happened' (182).

Thus Laura comes to know the virtue of allowing others to love where they need and where they wish, despite one's own need. She comes to know that anguished loneliness can lead to dependency and predation, to murder and mayhem; and that love is a gift that cannot be willed, that to be chosen is to be blessed, and that the surest anchor in life is to love in despite of loneliness.

> *[Jacob] is quite warped. He can only manage when he is rescued from outside by something. And then at the end he is still in a structure but he has discovered that life really depends on service. It's a bit of a golden dawn at the end.*
>
> Elizabeth Jolley (Ellison 183)

> *... it was not [Norm's] fault that Madge did not love him, only his misfortune.*
>
> Jacob in *Milk and Honey* (8)

If *Palomino* affirms the hopeful capacity to love despite the anguished loneliness that motivates love, *Milk and Honey* (1984) more fully explores the murder and mayhem that shadows the need to be loved. Indeed, *Milk and Honey* had a mixed reception, hailed by some critics, but described as dark, eerie and disturbing by others.[17]

The novel's protagonist, Jacob, arrives to study music and live with the Heimbachs, Austrian immigrants to Australia. Early in the novel, when ordered to do so by the father Leopold, Jacob thumps the idiot son of the household on the chest and he collapses. Jacob is then led by his foster family to believe that he has killed Waldemar, not realising that he has been taken away to live in the attic. When Jacob finds out and remonstrates with Aunt Heloise, she tells him that the situation they contrived allowed them to keep Waldemar at home rather than institutionalise him, as they had to do to his mother. 'Waldemar did not ask to be born' (119), she whispers; Leopold could not place his son, who was innocent of everything, she continues, in an asylum as if he were punishing him, for Waldemar is incapable of understanding any explanation; and then, eyes filling with tears, she says, 'You were given all our love and care ... You will never understand enough Leopold's love for you' (120).

The Heimbachs are a step above feckless for having, like Weekly, a plan for survival and a step below felonious for their manipulation of the sort not uncommonly practised within families. When Jacob is thirteen, Leopold's seventeen-year-old daughter, Louise, coerces him into becoming her fiancé. Some years later, knowing Louise is pregnant by Waldemar, the Heimbachs stage-manage the marriage and persuade Jacob that Louise's baby is his, even though he had found himself unable to consummate the marriage. The Heimbachs then live off his earnings, their manipulation like that of his other relatives, Uncle Otto and Aunt Mitzi, who have been swindling Jacob out of his estate ever since his parents' death. The difference, however, is that the Heimbachs present Jacob with an elaborate simulacrum of love, one he is predisposed to accept as the real thing. His parents dead, his home, land and assets gone, Jacob, the child of migrants, is like a migrant who finds a new home—who finds a sound of love—with the Heimbachs, *heim* being the German for home and *bach* for stream.

This home is a treacherous world where the aunts ominously discuss someone in code during a game of Scrabble. Aunt Heloise alludes to a *Goldgräberin*, whose death was kind of *selbstmörder*, akin to a bee's jumping into honey (135). But, Tante Rosa says, it was *freidtod*, free death or suicide, the bee dying as a result of trying to get what she wants (136).[18] As Jacob listens to them, he begins to sense he has been a token in a game they are playing. And, when he goes for a walk in the garden, he discovers that Madge, the lover he has taken up with since his marriage, is dead, rolled up in a carpet with the food-encrusted wires of Waldemar's twisted dental appliance beside her (145).

There is no end in sight to this tangled web of dependency and deception in the name of love—and so, as in many *romans à thèse*, Jacob changes abruptly. When an interviewer asked who killed Madge and why, Jolley answered that she did not know and did not care.[19] Rather, the narrative resolution comes from two related actions on Jacob's part. One of them, in two movements, implies repentance for self-absorbtion (akin to Laura's understanding of the narcissism of her love for Eva and Esmé). Louise now dead, Jacob embraces both Waldemar and Elise as if they were his biological children; and together they embrace humility, Jacob consciously and they innocently, when Jacob elects to serve as a cleaner in the asylum where Waldemar is a shave-nurse and Waldemar's daughter/sister serves as a kitchen hand. Jacob's second action, one that brings closure, is his seeking forgiveness through reconciliation with Norm for alienating his wife's affections and ultimately being responsible for her death.[20] More related to theme than to plot or even character, *Milk and Honey's* narrative resolutions echo *Palomino's* ethic. Jacob says, 'I realised too late how much [Norm] had loved [Madge], how unselfishly he was able to love. And, unlike me, was able to put her happiness first or tried to, always before his own' (8).

> *Everything's there ... Birth, marriage, separation, bigamy, divorce, death—several deaths, all kinds of human effort, memories, joy, pain, excitement, transfiguration, love and acceptance.*
>
> Heather Hailey about her novel *Self Stoked Fires* (*Mr Scobie's Riddle* 23)

Mr Scobie's Riddle was published in 1983, the year before *Milk and Honey*, and the same year Jolley published *Miss Peabody's Inheritance* and *Woman in a Lampshade*, a collection that includes some of her best short stories. It was a magic year in any writer's calendar, a year that arrested the attention of literary reviewers and secured Jolley a national readership. In retrospect, the year needs to be understood as a fruition of her long years of persistently rewriting the short stories and novels she brought from England and adapted to Australian settings; of her writing from the perspective of her new country; and of her slowly learning how to access likely markets, from the BBC World Service, to ABC radio, to Australian print and book publishers.

The success of *Mr Scobie's Riddle* was the result of this long apprenticeship. Jolley began the novel twenty years earlier while working as a carer in an aged home, and she described it as at first 'a lament... too painful to read'.[21] As she characteristically revised and reworked her manuscript, she invented a narrative that transforms a lament about loneliness, aging and death into a comedy of hope that embraces the predations (the fecklessness and felony) of those seeking to buffer loneliness through striving for economic security or (erotic) friendships, or both. Like so many of Jolley's stories and novels, the setting of *Scobie's Riddle* is an institution akin to those she experienced at Sibford, when nursing as a young woman, and when working as an aged-carer. In *Scobie* the institution is St Christopher and St Jude, a nursing home governed by Matron Price where day and night staff struggle to find happiness.

Matron Price and Heather Hailey, once school friends and now sixty-something lovers, have an apartment there, Hailey being an involuntary patient with more freedom than most. She had owned a school for girls, but Price and her brother commandeered it after a scandal between her and one of her students. At the same time, Hyacinth Price is married to a Mr Rawlings, an ex-con who comes and goes irregularly, for he is now bigamously but faithfully also married to housekeeper Mrs Rawlings, another school friend of Price, who lives in a caravan on the grounds. Finally, the staff includes another lesbian or bisexual pair, Frankie and Robyn, youthful promiscuous lovers who also live somewhere in the 'home'.

These denizens have nocturnal counterparts, other couples or near-couples who struggle for love and security, and whose innocent Breughel-like excesses in the dinette are presided over by Night Nurse M. Shady. The night-time cast includes Mrs Morgan (a patient and possibly Shady's mother) and Rob Shady (possibly her husband), along with his colleague Boxer Morgan (possibly her brother)—both are on the lam from the law, both live on the grounds but Matron Price cannot figure out where.[22] Mrs Morgan, Rob Shady and Boxer Morgan materialise at night to play poker with Matron's brother Lt. Col. I. Price (retired), who brightens up considerably, however, as Night Nurse Shady writes in her report, he 'loøse lose bad' (8): he is steadily gambling away his sister's nursing home to Mrs Morgan. Iris Price has been billeted with three presumed-to-be-senile old ladies, one of whom, Mrs Tompkins, turns up at 4 am with two unknown elderly gentleman she introduces to the hospital brandy. 'Slept well', is Shady's ambiguous report (6). Her last report is 'Lt. Col. Price lose very bad but enjoy himself and Mrs Morgan' (9). It is provident that St Christopher and St Jude is named after one saint who safely carried the Christ-child across a dangerous river and another who is the patron of lost causes.

Martin Scobie is one such Christ-like child. He is pressured by Matron Price and Mrs Rawlings to sign over his money and the title to his home at Rosewood East, even as he is pressured by his niece, Joan, and separately by her brother, Hartley, to do the same in their favour. At the end of the novel the problem is neatly solved: Scobie dies before any of his economic suitors succeed, and so never loses his money; his niece and nephew jointly inherit his estate, including Rosewood East. Joan partners with a painter-boyfriend; Hartley marries Robyn, and Hartley's mate Horry Briggs marries Frankie, who has a baby, Miriam, by Hartley. Thus the novel's comedic resolution.

F. M. Cornford defined Greek Attic comedy as a narrative that begins with an impediment to a marriage, dissolves it, and ends with that marriage.[23] Jolley gives us antic comedy. Multiple and diverse liaisons lead to babies that lead to a commune at Rosewood East to which Heather Hailey—the other Christ-like figure in the book—is invited by Frankie and Robyn. Frankie/Frances asks Hailey to be godmother to baby Miriam, and says that her next baby will be by her husband. Hailey says it sounds 'a reasonable plan', noting, '[t]his baby, this is, in a sense, Mr Scobie's grandchild!' (210). After accepting the invitation, Hailey realises that the novel she has been writing (and foists on a reluctant Scobie) lacks an idyll, and then imagines such an idyll as a dance that takes place among the pines at Rosewood under a transfiguring sun, dancing as she does so. In Hailey's imagination, the Pine Tree Dance is about the house and garden, about a child being born, the joy of the new mother, and the anticipated joy of living there. Her imagining and dancing echoes Laura's description in *Palomino* of the 'ideal of an Idyll' of loving friendship, even as it also echoes *Newspaper*'s pear tree dance, with all its ambiguities of love desired, love given, love betrayed, and love surviving through connection to the land. Hailey thinks that she will dance her vision again later, write it down later; she thinks that '[h]appiness . . . is the hardest thing of all to write about' (212).

Like *Palomino* and *Milk and Honey*, *Mr Scobie's Riddle* is a *roman à thèse* structured more by theme than plot or character. But *Scobie* is richer, less insistent in its message, its fifty-or-more characters representing a panoply of positions, the people occupying them all benign. Even Hyacinth Price, although she presents as hard of heart and cunning in method, still loves her husband: 'Perhaps it was the one good thing in her life, she thought, loving a worthless husband and trying to do her best for St Christopher and St Jude' (154). Thus Price enunciates a position akin to Jacob's in *Milk and Honey*, a position that the secondary characters of the novel embody in the form of the commune they will establish at Roseville East. Through the prospect of Roseville East, Jolley finds a way to write about the 'hardest thing'—happiness.

> *It is a tremendous pleasure to initiate a person whom one believes to be innocent. To be the initiator . . .*
> Diana Hopewell to Miss Peabody, *Miss Peabody's Inheritance* (34)

> *Plato, [Hopewell] wrote, says that the poet is a light and holy winged thing, and there is no invention in him until he is inspired out of his senses . . .*[24]
> Diane Hopewell to Dorothy Peabody, *Miss Peabody's Inheritance* (130)

With the exception of *The Well*, Jolley's novels across the 1980s are characterised by a kind of stylised realism where the mimetic impulse to imagine and represent the landscape of the inner life is conveyed through heightened modes of telling—intense lyricism in *Palomino*, gothic grotesquery in *Milk and Honey*, and carnivalesque comedy in *Scobie's Riddle*.[25] Jolley experimented still again with narrative mode in *Miss Peabody's Inheritance* (1983), this time shaping her novel as a lapidary metafiction—a novel which is not only about the desires and expectations of her characters but also about writing and reading fiction, and their providing a space of communion akin to the experience of 'stepping deeper into friendship'.

Peabody's metafictional structure hinges on there being an untitled novel-in-progress embedded in the main novel. In the main novel, Dorothy Peabody writes a fan letter to Diana Hopewell after having read her romance *Angels on Horseback*. An epistolary friendship ensues, in which Hopewell treats Peabody as an innocent to be initiated into mysteries unimagined by a fifty-plus spinster who lives with and cares for an invalid mother. Hopewell establishes intimacy by asking, 'Are you in love?' (7), in response to which Peabody invents a boyfriend who was killed in the war 'before the complete blossoming of the romance' (14). Hopewell elucidates the pornographic overtones of *Angels on Horseback* that seem to have escaped Peabody; and she explains that her novella *Love at Second Sight* is 'about two utterly abject women, both post menopausal, who have a brief and unexciting love affair' (47). And all the while Hopewell tells Peabody about the novel she is currently writing and includes passages from it in her letters. Inexplicably, she includes a letter of complaint to her doctor about a diathermy burn she has received (87–8).[26]

The passages from Hopewell's current novel feature Dr/Miss Arabella Thorne, Headmistress of the Pine Heights school for girls, along with Thorne's personal secretary Miss Edgley, and her friend Betty Snowdon, Matron of Queen Hospital. The three women annually tour the continent, ostensibly for *Kultur* but more so to indulge in the pleasures of wine-women-and-song more discreetly to be had away from home. The complication this time is that Thorne has invited one of her students, sixteen-year-old Gwendaline Manners, to travel with them, something Edgley especially resists. Nonetheless, the trip goes ahead as planned by Thorne, who on arriving in Vienna disappoints Edgley by taking three rooms at their usual pension rather than the customary one large room for three people: one for Edgley and Snowdon, one for herself and one for Gwenda. In the midst of a thunderstorm which frightens her, Gwenda goes to Thorne's room, and there ensues an 'idyllic, tender, hilarious and ludicrous' night together that includes both Gwenda confiding her desire to marry and have children and the bed collapsing underneath them (61). When the party later travels to England, they encounter Mr Frome and his daughter Debbie, also a Pine Heights student. After they all attend a production of *The Importance of Being Ernest*, Ernest Frome proposes to Gwenda, and Thorne is disconcerted until she imagines inviting *both* Gwenda and Debbie to the next holiday's Wagner festival in Bayreuth.

Arabella Thorne compares to Hyacinth Price in *Scobie* for being head of an institution teetering on the edge of insolvency, and for having a dependent female lover. But she also shows the darker side of the 'tremendous pleasure' of initiating an innocent, the experience that underpins the mentee–mentor relationship that appears in so many of Jolley's novels and so often is connected to the desire to be a 'chosen companion'. Thorne is a calculating seducer who uses her position, age and experience to her own advantage as she entices students, heedless of their best interests. She cruelly badgers and belittles the exasperating Edgley—wanting to 'break every bone in Edgley's boring body' (42), and shaking her by the shoulders so violently that Snowdon remonstrates (92). And, though she is capable of restraint, unlike Laura's hers is a restraint born of self-interest rather than self-understanding. Yet, for all this, Arabella Thorne also represents Jolley's understanding of the terrors of loneliness. Thorne needs to reduce her staff, and knows it is the hapless Edgley that she should fire, but resolves instead to dismiss one of the attractive, hard-working junior mistress; not only does Edgley have nowhere to go but, 'without Edgley, she herself has no one' (59). The most sympathetic thing Jolley's narrator has to say about Thorne is that '[t]he emptiness Miss Thorne feels is alarming' (121).

Peabody reads Hopewell's letters/novel at night, after work and tending to her mother—in the evocative, allusive leitmotif of the novel, 'the nights belong to the novelist'. As she reads, her attention is riveted by the richly sensual and creative life the letters suggest Hopewell enjoys. She is deaf to the nuances of those letters (her mother calls her 'Dottie'), nuances provided by Jolley to give readers enough clues to suspect that the riches of Hopewell's life exist more in her fiction than in fact. What matters most to Peabody is that Hopewell responded to her timid overture, made her feel special, and later sent presents—instalments of her novel, jars of honey, and coloured sheepskins that Peabody proudly gives to office colleagues. She feels cherished, and she creates for herself an ideal friend.

So enthralled is Peabody that life and fiction fuse, so much so that she goes to the theatre district in London in hope of seeing Thorne and her party there when (in the embedded novel) they attend a second play, *An Ideal Husband* (124–7); and so much so that during a flight from London to

Perth she wonders if one of the Pine Heights party, who became separated from the others in London, might be on the same aeroplane.[27] Peabody's journey to Australia is made possible both by her mother's death and by her being fired after her uncharacteristically sociable behaviour makes her work colleagues uneasy. Even so, her journey is a measure of the transformation of her inner life brought about by her having a friend—through reading a novel. She travels in the opposite direction from the women in Hopewell's novel and for reasons more akin to love than lust. Her hope is to meet Hopewell, to realise their friendship, but on arrival she finds that not only was the friend she idealised as living a rich life on her country property in fact bedridden in a nursing home, but also that Hopewell has died before they could meet—a possibility obliquely signalled by Hopewell's letter to her doctor mistakenly sent to Peabody. In a bravura twist of the novel's metafictional structure, Jolley's Peabody then takes from her handbag the last pages Hopewell has sent and sits down to complete the novel: 'All she really needed to enter into her inheritance was a title' (157). As she picks up her pen, Peabody as reader is so transformed by the space of fiction that she becomes the writer.

The opening line of *Peabody*—'The nights belonged to the novelist'—would do for a title, for Peabody has learned that '[t]he evening, belonging to the novelist, was hers too' (70). Elizabeth Webby calls attention to a passage where Arabella Thorne, en route to Australia, borrows a literary journal from the young man in the next seat because it is '[j]ust my sort of reading', only to be confounded by a 'discussion . . . of structuralist reading and the exposure of the artistic process' (151).[28] The passage topically and tellingly satirises academic fixations of the time, and the joke is characteristic of the linguistic and literary play of Jolley's novels of this period. But the passage and its allusion also serve her metafictional purposes, for Jolley's literary allusions are always tightly woven into the thematic fabric of her novels. The article Peabody reads alludes to the then-current critical enthusiasm for French critic Roland Barthes' concept of the 'death of the author': in *Peabody*, an author dies and a reader becomes the writer. The reader of Jolley's *Miss Peabody's Inheritance* is left with a sense of the creative possibilities not only of love that flourishes on barren ground but also of understandings that flourish through the writing and reading of fiction.

People pursue happiness very often at the cost of somebody else. Well, take publishing for example. If you're in, somebody else is out. You know, it's all very highly competitive.

Elizabeth Jolley (Ellison 176)

You're sick, Elizabeth. You're sick.

Thea Astley, launching *Milk and Honey*

By the mid-1980s Elizabeth Jolley was well aware of Australia's 'intellectual infrastructure' and becoming more adept at manoeuvring within it. For example, following a lead Dorothy Sanders had given her, she often wrote thirty-minute radio plays for the BBC, and then, if they were rejected, rewrote them in a twenty-minute format for submission to the ABC. If they were rejected again, she turned them into short stories and sent them on their rounds of literary journals. A wrinkle on the technique was to enter ABC competitions which required the use of pseudonyms by mailing her entries to her sister Madelaine in Birmingham who would then post them to Australia where they would look like radio plays from English writers who, Jolley hoped, would have an advantage over local ones.[29]

Other things had to be learned on the battlefield, as it were, two sites of conflict being festivals and launches. At her first international conference, Toronto's prestigious Harborfront International Festival of Artists in October 1983, the largest gathering of writers in the English-speaking world, she saw literary posturing and backstabbing of international calibre among those present, like poets Ted Hughes and Lawrence Ferlinghetti, playwright Eugène Ionesco, and novelists Salman Rushdie and Angela Carter. When she left Toronto for London, en route to Australia, she sat next to Salman Rushdie on the plane and came to like him very much, not minding when his head leaned against her shoulder as he slept. But when she met him again a few months later at the 1984 Adelaide Festival, they were not close: Rushdie, Angela Carter and another British writer were a clique who made a nuisance of themselves by objecting to conditions at the Raywood Conference Centre in the Adelaide Hills, demanding to be transferred to the Townhouse in central Adelaide.[30] Jolley keyed on Carter as the prime villain of the three, the prolific feminist writer from England who, more than fifteen years younger than Jolley and married for a second time, was there with her baby. In a letter to Leonard Jolley she fulminated at length about Carter's being unprepared for the talk she was to present, so 'British' in her demeanour and so unpleasant to the Festival staff. One might suspect she protested on account of how much attention Carter attracted, although Jolley received four lines in the twelve-column-inch Writers' Week column of the *Adelaide Advertiser* ('Elizabeth Jolley found her bed full of millipedes') which was more than poet A. D. Hope got.[31]

Thus she must have been surprised at the end of the year to read in the *Guardian* that Carter chose *Woman in a Lampshade*, her third collection of short stories, as one of the three best books she read in 1984, although Jolley did not record a response to the fact. Likewise the following year when Carter's November 1985 front-page review of Jolley's *Foxybaby* in the *New York Times Review of Books* concluded that her 'fiction shines and shines and shines, like a good deed in a naughty world'.[32] Nor did Jolley explain her motives for including Carter's *Nights at the Circus* among her 1985 books-for-Christmas choices that appeared a month later in the *Sydney Morning Herald*.[33] The next year, Jolley's 'The Last Crop' was anthologised in Carter's *Wayward Girls and Wicked Women*.

Her introduction to the rough-and-tumble of launches took place when she attended the annual South Pacific and Commonwealth Languages and Literatures Society conference held in September 1984, at Macquarie University in Sydney where *Milk and Honey* was to be launched. First, she was pleasantly surprised to hear from academic Joan Kirkby that *Peabody*, published the previous year, had been set for one of Macquarie's courses and so would sell 400 copies, and then she was pleasantly perplexed to see that the Macquarie library catalogue classified *Palomino* as pornography—Leonard Jolley had observed that the reclining nude woman in the cover illustration appeared to be in the Sims position for a gynaecological examination. Next she was gobsmacked when fellow novelist Thea Astley began her *Milk and Honey* launch speech with, 'You're sick Elizabeth, you're sick . . .' seemingly attributing to her the same psychological and moral defects exhibited by the characters in her book.[34] Hurt by what she considered to be an ungracious introduction, particularly since she was concerned to establish a base of sympathy with unfortunate people like those represented in *Milk and Honey*, she nonetheless was already trooper enough to play along with Astley, responding, 'I don't mind being told I'm sick . . . I know I am'.

The greatest insult and injury occurred when Douglas Stewart and Astley attempted to introduce Jolley to Beatrice Davis, Australia's feared doyenne of book editing whom they had described as charming, attractive and vibrant: Davis turned on her heel and walked away, saying she and Jolley had already met, which they had not. Not only was Davis the judge who caused the Miles Franklin Award—the most sought-after and lucrative novel prize in Australia—to be withheld for 1983, when *Scobie* had been short listed, but it was Davis whose letter of rejection two decades earlier had said that Jolley was mentally disturbed and in need of psychological help. Her response was to characterise Davis, then seventy-five, as a disagreeable old woman with flinty blue eyes.

Through these two and other experiences, in the first half of the 1980s Jolley learned a great deal about the business of writing. From Carter she learned that overseas writers who support each other's work do so to their own advantage. From Astley she learned that having a three-time Miles Franklin Award winner launch her book, although risky, can be a good career move. (For reasons of her own, Astley asked Jolley to reciprocate the favour by launching her novel *Beachmasters* at the Canberra Word Fest in February of 1985.) Most importantly, she had learned to separate the concepts of genius and morality in her estimation of writers. As for editors, she remained wary of them all her life. When asked in 2001 if she had read Jacqueline Kent's new biography of Beatrice Davis, her Freudian slip spoke volumes when she snapped, 'Beatrice Davis was the enema of writers!'[35]

After all her successes in the first part of the 1980s, Jolley still had to determine how to proceed when she ran out of suitable draft materials in the trunk she brought with her from Scotland or wrote in the early 1960s, like the manuscripts that became *Palomino*, *Milk and Honey* and *Scobie's Riddle*. *Miss Peabody's Inheritance* marked a promising new direction, one she would have to explore for further possibilities or abandon in favour of an alternative that would enable her to remain innovative in the competitive market for literary fiction in the 1980s.

10

1985-89—Optimistic and fond...

I want, in my writing, to be optimistic and fond.
'"What Sins to Me Unknown Dipped Me in Ink"' (11)

[A]fter all publishing is a business isn't it?
Elizabeth Jolley (Baker 216)

The magnitude of the step Jolley took from the 1970s to the 1980s is nicely symbolised by the change from her draft novel *Palomino*'s sharing the Victorian Fellowship of Australian Writers' Con Weickhardt Prize for an unpublished novel in 1974 to *Palomino*'s outright winning the Weickhardt award for a published novel in 1980. The door she had been knocking on for years had finally opened and suddenly she had to deal with things she had anticipated and some she had not.

When she was a trainee nurse at the Queen Elizabeth Hospital thirty years before, she once wished she could make the editor of *Lilliput* sorry for having rejected a story she submitted. Now she had to adjust to her work being accepted and her reputation as a writer becoming widely known. She was pleased by her success but soon learned that it meant more than just submitting something, having it published, sending a copy to friends and family, and anticipating reviews. Increasing success involved dealing with the minutiae of publishing and promotion in the midst of the dynamics of her family. It involved making adjustments in order to deal with new demands in ways that suited her best.

Inevitably, becoming more of a public figure affected her relationship with her husband, especially since her career was on a rising trajectory while his had declined. When her career first began to take off in the mid-1970s Leonard Jolley told her that her FAC classes were 'something that has started for you ... and I won't be involved in it'; and when she hesitated to accept a work-related invitation that did not include him, he said to her, 'You will go there and I won't necessarily come with you. This will be something you do on your own'. That was, Elizabeth Jolley remarked, 'the beginning of a new way of living for us, and it was all right'.[1] Pragmatically, still more independence within the marriage would be necessary to her new career, and equally it would be an adjustment for them both, and especially for Leonard Jolley after a lifetime of being attended to by women at home, in hospitals and in libraries.

When he retired at the end of 1979, his being at home on a full-time basis meant that Elizabeth had to devote still more time and attention to him, the situation straitened by the deterioration in his health. Prior to his retirement, their relationship around her writing had been complex. She was frequently frustrated by his mercurial responses to her requests to read her drafts, although he was always willing to advise on syntax and the like. Sometimes he would decline to read something, or tell her that he would do so but could not fit the piece in for (say) a month or more—perhaps not unreasonable responses, given the volume of work she generated and the fact that writers sometimes prefer dishonest praise to honest criticism, and Leonard was not given to dishonest praise. Alternatively, he might take a self-regarding interest in what she had written, as he did with *Palomino*, wanting to know who the real-life models of the characters were and the details of what took place between them. Elizabeth found that inhibiting and prohibitive of her asking his advice, or at least for the time being, for inevitably she would again seek his help.

In his retirement, however, he became more expansive and helpful. He was limitlessly informed about matters biblical and theological, good at mythology, history and philosophy, capable at foreign languages and literatures—Greek, Latin, French, Italian and German—and a knowledgeable literary critic. He provided her with references and quotations, like the details of Dante's *Inferno* for her novel *Foxybaby* and information on Girolamo Cardana for *The Sugar Mother*. Crucially, he introduced her to what he called the Climactic Curve which deals with the rising/falling actions and the denouement traditional in western narratives, and he helped her see how she first successfully employed it in her story 'Dingle the Fool'.[2] In her subsequent writing and reading, she concentrated on the technique—and on pacing generally—coming to call it the Sophoclean Curve. From his own experience he also advised her on the anxieties of dealing with public appearances, bad reviews and starting new projects; on practical matters like depositing her papers with the Mitchell Library; and, something she became famous for, leaving room on her handwritten pages for further notes and keeping those separate pages in files so she could work on them individually and reorder their sequences as necessary. When they worked together harmoniously, it was almost like their early days in Birmingham when they had written stories jointly.

Despite her concern that her children might find her being a novelist an embarrassment, that did not seem to be a problem, and they sometimes made contributions to her work, if in unconventional ways. Ruth occasionally accompanied Jolley during her work at Windsor Towers, coining terms and images that Jolley appropriated and recycled in the speech of the Morgan women while they worked at 'South Heights', like 'boiled head' for a bald head, Peril Page's having two sets of collarbones and a double breastbone, and the riddle about what lies at the bottom of the ocean and shivers.[3] Ruth also provided the title for one of the novels after visiting Hedges' shop and saying of a gossip there that she should be called the local newspaper. At the same time, Jolley was never quite sure to what extent her children read her work, even though she gave them copies of her books. And so she was surprised to find that Richard had scrawled in the margin of one of her manuscripts that he would prefer the character in her story 'Dingle the Fool' to be named Dino, the Jolley family dog's name, rather than its nickname Dingle.[4] What proved to be of most concern to them—and to her—was the disruption her overnight trips caused, especially those lasting several days or more. It is telling, then, that her first published essay was from an address she gave at the First Australian Conference on Family and Health. She spoke of the fear, guilt and anxiety that family difficulties engender, and the paper was titled 'The Changing Family—Who Cares?'

> *You can't have a book club meeting without mentioning death.*
>
> Elizabeth Jolley (Reid 72)

Certainly Jolley cared, even as she persisted in another life she also wanted—'the writing of fiction'.[5] She expanded her campaign of speaking at book clubs, schools, and civic groups, addressing literary and other conferences and reading at festivals. Like many writers, she was not sanguine about the thought of another writer's book being ranked above hers; like many writers, she seemed to feel that, if someone else's book sold, hers would not. But beyond ambition there were two other motives. One was her genuine concern for her readers, mainly women, who wanted to talk about literature. If she was upset with her Tuart Club colleagues whom she felt should have known better than to obsess about lesbian women in *Peabody*, she thrilled to most responses, even when seemingly off target—like the woman who criticised 'The Shed', saying, if it were she, she would have built a shed straight away, or the woman in England who said no one ever wrote about the East Anglian countryside around there, and so wanted to thank Jolley for doing so.[6] And at academic conferences she would attend sessions on her own work. Even if the presentation were arcane, biased or otherwise inadequate, she always thanked the presenter for the time and thought devoted to her work. She was passionate about the importance of a book's capacity to speak to another person's lived experience and felt needs, however misunderstood or irrelevant the response seemed to the author. Thus in interviews she often related her technique of leaving 'sophisticated spaces'[7] to the reader's creativity. Her phrase referred to her way of writing stories through juxtaposed passages. She thought that such writing 'allows the reader to make discoveries between the spaces on the page'.[8] Her trust was that the 'reader reads very creatively', and that 'a reader can make up his own version . . . [that] I always feel if a person has something to hope for then he has something'.[9]

And, second, Jolley was respectful of would-be writers. She shared with them her own story of persistence, reassuring them that, correctly handled, anyone's experience could form the basis of successful fiction: there was no such thing as a new story, she told them, but 'nobody has ever written the exact feeling and observations that you and I have had . . . The colour that you give it is the important thing'.[10] For many students, her most important advice was that writing required observation, and so she commended making 'the quick little note'. She also insisted that stories usually needed more time spent on rewriting than writing; that knowing and using effective literary techniques was essential—and that spelling, grammar and punctuation *do* count, as does presentation. In other words, if writing is a business, it requires hard work and necessarily benefits from a professional approach. Two techniques she particularly emphasised were the Sophoclean Curve and 'the little dance', contrastive prose set into the text in order to 'lighten' the writing. Jolley's learning that writing about loneliness and need—being 'on the edge'—requires something that 'lifts' it, something optimistic, came from both her teaching and her reading. She learned from a student in one of her classes who became hysterical, then danced around the room, then sat down and said she felt marvellous. And she learned from reading Judah Waten who told of being advised by his father that a play they had seen should have had a wedding scene with a bit of music in it 'to lift what might be a grim message . . . a little dance [put] into writing'.[11]

A number of her students, including those at the FAC and in its country-school programs, went on to have work published in respectable places. Her WAIT/Curtin students from the 1970s and 1980s won the Miles Franklin (Tim Winton) and *Australian*/Vogel novel awards (Winton, Fotini Epanomitis), along with Western Australian Premier's awards (Winton, young-adult writer Glyn Parry, screen writer Sarah Rossetti, poet Tracy Ryan)[12]. Rossetti recalls Jolley presenting as a hippie-like grandmother in sandals who smiled and called each student 'dear', causing them to sigh, 'Oh, no, here we go'. As soon as they felt safe or bored or both, 'she'd reel off a few of our swear words at us, adding that there's room for a few in good prose, but not many. Her eyes glinted at moments like those'. And Parry still recalls her emphasising the importance of 'the little dance'. What Jolley's students could not know was how she regarded teaching as her own education, as she refined her ideas about the writing techniques she discussed, and how she used her students as life studies on youthful speech, dress, mannerisms and preoccupations.[13] What they did come to know, in Rossetti's words, was 'the glint of intelligence, her dry wit'. She said 'Elizabeth may have been as old as our grandmothers, but she was sharp as a tack, unshockable, one of a kind. How lucky we were to have to have been there'.

Jolley's speaking and publishing engagements became so time-consuming that, when she received a Senior Fellowship from the Australia Literature Board in 1984, she cut back on her twenty-hour-per-week teaching load, keeping only one class at the FAC and two at WAIT.[14] During the 1980s she fitted in at least one speaking engagement per week, not counting her tutoring at Bandyup Women's Prison in 1984 and the Canning Vale Prison in 1985. Those engagements included speaking at city and country schools, colleges and universities in Perth and Darwin, and attending two dozen literature conferences or literary festivals, an equal number in Perth and

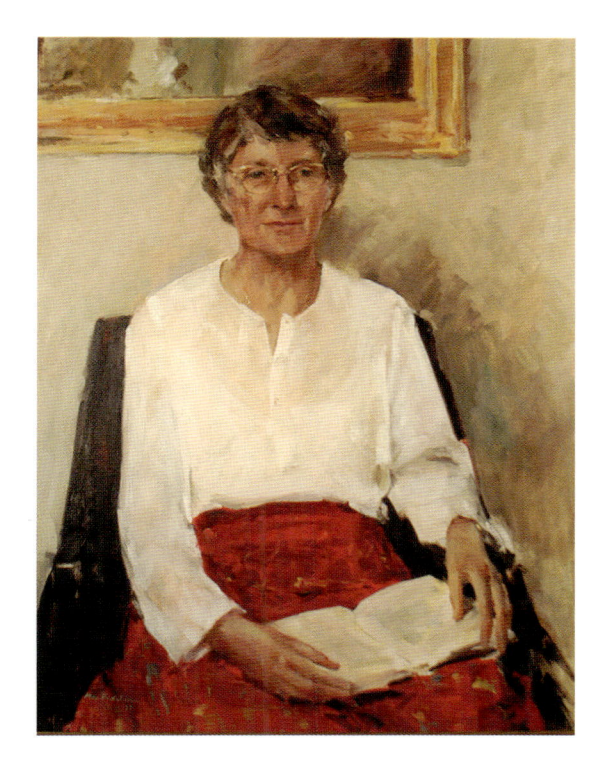

30: Jolley after publishing her first book (*Five Acre Virgin*, 1976), portrait by Meg Padgham, 1977.

31: Leonard Jolley on his retirement, portrait by Ben Joel, 1979.

32: Quilt by Lesley Fitzpatrick (1999) based on Jolley's 'Pear Tree Dance'.

33: Ludmila Blotnicki, 1948, model for Nastasya in *The Newspaper of Claremont Street* (1981).

34: Hannah Levey—'the person who showed me how to live in Australia', with the Jolleys.

35: Jolley with her 1980-1993 agent Caroline Lurie at Southbank readings where she performed with Edna O'Brien, London, 1991.

36: Elizabeth Jolley at Wooroloo, 1986.

37: Jolley at her Federation home in Claremont, 1988.

38: The Jolleys' cottage in Wooroloo.

39: Jolley at Wooroloo, 1996.

40: 'Woman in a Lampshade', Ruth Cracknell with Peter Giutronich, from Christina Wilcox's film *The Nights Belong to the Novelist* (1986).

41: Jolley with Ingle Knight, winner of a WA Premier's award for his script of the 1998 stage adaptation of *Milk and Honey* (briefly called *A Prince of the Cello*).

42: L-R, scriptwriter Laura Jones, producer Sandra Levy, actors Pamela Rabe and Miranda Otto, director Samantha Lang and cinematographer Mandy Walker, people involved with the film version of Jolley's *The Well*, Australia's only film accepted for the 1997 Cannes International Film Festival.

43: State Living Treasure (Robert Garvey©1998).

44: Barry Humphries with Jolley at his 2002 Curtin University Elizabeth Jolley Lecture, 'My Life As Me'.

45: Curtin honorary doctorate, 1987, Jolley's first of four.

46: Portrait by Ben Joel, 1995.

interstate and a handful in Canada, the US and the UK.[15] Jolley believed conferences and readings, whether overseas or Australian, were essential professional activities, where a writer could learn from the others' work, get feedback for her writing, and form useful networks.

The 1984 Adelaide Festival was important to her for being the first Australian one she was invited to as a guest of the organisers who paid all of her expenses. But it was the one from before, Harborfront in Toronto, which was of greater portent. On 18 October, Jolley unexpectedly met Elizabeth Smart in the Longhouse Book Shop, Smart being introduced to her as the author of *By Grand Central Station I Sat Down and Wept*, which Jolley had never heard of. Instead, she remembered Smart as the mother of George Barker's children at Pinewood whom, as Monica Fielding more than thirty years before, she washed and dressed and groomed before presenting them to the glamorous London editor for the weekend. Smart, ten years older than herself, in a misbuttoned cardigan, a cigarette hanging from her mouth, a woman with bad teeth, bleeding gums, had no memory of Jolley and, being self-absorbed, took no interest in her. Jolley wrote, 'I am looking across the table at a woman who seems to have been broken completely by the suffering in her life' ('By the Waters of Babylon' 160). The meeting so stunned her that she retreated to her hotel room and read Smart's *By Grand Central Station*, after which she wrote the opening line of her novel *Cabin Fever*: 'I am still here on the twenty-fourth floor and when I sit in front of my mirror I can see, in the mirror, someone on the twenty-fourth floor across the street'.

> 'One can condone incest . . .' she said, 'not condone exactly . . . [O]ne can see how it happens. Loneliness', she said, 'lack of what we understand as love, followed by opportunity—followed by habit. But first there is the giving way, the succumbing', she said . . .
>
> 'She's right!' Miles called out. 'She's apples!'
>
> Mrs Meridian Viggars to Christobel Selby, *Foxybaby* (100–1)

Foxybaby (1985) was the first book Jolley wrote while not working on at least one other. Like *Peabody*, it is metafictional, containing a novel-within-a-novel as well as a virtual anthology of autobiographers and novelists. It is about what drives people to write and to read, and so continues from where *Peabody* leaves off. What drives the protagonist Miss Alma Porch is loneliness, the cause of which is lovelessness, the basis of which is, she speculates, a spiritual homelessness.

> *She had read somewhere if you don't love yourself and your parents the chances are that you will not be able to love anyone. Perhaps she longed for the imagined comfort of the household to which she could at one time always return. She knew too that this profound despair was a part of the loneliness which accompanied writing* (116).

Reminiscent of Jolley's being rear-ended by a bus on the way to her first creative writing class at the FAC in 1974 and also of her driving to the Albany summer school with a potter in 1975, near the beginning of *Foxybaby* Porch rear-ends a bus while driving with a potter through the wheatbelt to Trinity College. After her accident, two other cars run into her VW, creating a scene like the one in *Scobie* where three ambulances collide outside St Christopher and St Jude's. In shock after the accident, Porch falls asleep on the bus that takes them to Trinity College and dreams what will happen during the January summer school.

The transition to the dream world is signalled when Porch repeats the opening lines of Dante's *Inferno*, rendering the passage as 'In the middle of the journey I came to myself in a dark wood where the straight way was lost . . . So full of sleep was I about the moment that I left the true way' (12); and it finishes as she reawakens, still on the bus, as her fellow passengers disembark in front of Trinity College (260).[16] Just as Virgil is Dante's guide through the *Inferno*, a journey commencing on Good Friday and ending on Easter Sunday, so Viggars, one of the students, serves as Porch's guide during the dream—her first name, Meridian, alluding to a geographical meridian passing through the earth's poles, dividing it into dark and light halves.

Like their counterparts in Hell, most of the characters at Trinity College flout what Dante would call the Cardinal Virtues and commit as many of the seven Deadly Sins as appeal to them. Lust takes up much of Jack-of-all-Jills-cum-bus-driver Miles' time. Gluttony is a favourite of many of the students: after a day of KFB (knees full-bend) with only the lettuce-and-lemon-juice diet to sustain them, they repair to Miles' after-hours kitchen where he overcharges them to gorge on chicken and white wine or lobster and champagne. Covetousness is the theme of the film students who seem to make nothing but blue movies. Such activities are libidinously driven, related to forbidden pleasures made more tempting by the living arrangements and the ridiculous diet at the school. Everything moots the question of what it is that people really hunger for.

Porch has brought with her two scenes from her new novel, one described by Peycroft as the scene of 'the elderly old man and the young girl and a baby holed up, as it were, in a dreary motel unit', the other a 'scene of desolate passion between the two [female] prison officers' (31). Peycroft wants Porch to conduct tableaux vivants accompanied by a dramatic reading, with the students playing the parts of the characters in Porch's texts. Viggars takes the lead, the part of the old man, Dr Walter Steadman, a scholar who works to bring his daughter Sandy back to health and happiness after she became involved with heroine addicts. His challenge is to convince the authorities that it would be better for him to care for her and her baby at home rather than her being returned to jail and what he regards as lascivious female prison officers. The situation challenges the students as they try to come to terms with the fact that Steadman, respectable and middle-class like most of them, a parent like many of them, a widower whose daughter never knew her mother, and an obviously caring man, has an incestuous relationship with his daughter, whom he calls a vixen, his Foxybaby. His incest leads to speculation on what a widower raising a young daughter should do about his sexual urge, down-to-earth Mrs Crisp saying Steadman should make 'a suitable arrangement to satisfy it' (217)—and with that Porch pretends 'to be searching for Steadman's sexual needs in her file' (218). Sandy's need for drugs and the Steadman father/daughter relationship once more question what it is that people hunger for.

The play-reading ends abruptly when Anna, who plays Sandy, has a baby in the attic and Rennett, who plays one of the prison officers, falls and breaks both legs while being hoisted down after serving as midwife (her brother used to be a vet). Rennett's action in 'real life' extends and completes the script about the prison officer who had the same compassion for the prisoner as the father does. And Viggars' capacity to internalise the character of the father, despite being a childless woman, does the same for her: she had focused on Steadman's expression of love rather than on the transgression resulting from his failure of restraint. She felt 'ennobled' playing Steadman (117), the experience gave her 'reason for being' (181) and, as a result, she announces she wants to take the girl home with her, 'the one who is and is not Sandy . . . The one who is pretending to be my daughter while I am pretending to be her father'. She says, 'I don't want to go on pretending, I want the real thing' (256).

From the beginning, Peycroft takes control of Porch's class. She and her assistant Paisley compare with Thorne and Edgley in *Peabody* for being a pair in which the dominant one is capable and the subordinate one inept. Jolley thought of figures like Thorne and Peycroft as representing a person who 'takes life with both hands', women who, though 'very ambitious and [who] try to initiate people', at the same time are attractive for their passion and for getting things done that benefit others, like running St Christopher and St Jude's, White Pines, and Trinity College, however improvidently.[17] Against these women, Jolley sets the Snowdon/Viggars type—women who represent a 'little line of balance' by 'spread[ing] some evenness where there are heightened or exotic characters'.[18] About the same time she was writing *Foxybaby*, Jolley remarked to an interviewer that she had not yet explored the Snowdon type of character, something she does through Viggars.[19] A wealthy widow whose husband would always apologise when having sex, Viggars says she knows nothing abut sexual love (184). Now, she says, she eats, sleeps, eats and shits, and 'come[s] to these Schools because I am lonely' (254). She is level-headed for being beyond passion, but she is not beyond the compassion she once directed, without result, toward fellow-student Rennett, 'so that [Rennett] should feel chosen' (255).

Similarly, she is solicitous of Alma Porch, once asking, 'is there a Mr Porch?' to which the ambiguous reply is, 'Well, there was . . . but he was my father' (184). Viggars, who plays the father in Porch's script and elects to be mother to Anna and her baby, comes to be Alma's guide and nurturer—*alma mater* refers to a cherishing mother, Alma Porch's dream-novel constituting the threshold to self-nourishment, actually for Viggars and potentially for Porch. The point of the dream-novel's play-reading is not the improvement of Viggars' life-in-process but rather the improvement of Porch's novel-in-progress, whose problem Porch thinks is insoluble. In regard to this, Porch finds her Virgil in Viggars, who says, 'a father does not give up just as a mother never gives up, though both may lose heart and both, as the child suffers, suffer' (258).

As the sun rises, Porch sees a man and a girl with a baby coming toward her, the sunlight shining on the red-gold of the girl's hair (259). In a moment possible only in a dream—or fiction—Viggars' spoken wish has the power of suggestion, conjuring the vision that can complete Porch's novel: 'Don't, whatever you do, turn away from them now. They are coming toward you. Make the most of it', Viggars says (259).

'Till Easter then', Viggars says, as the bus arrives at the school and Porch wakes up.

Perhaps today, tonight I should say, I'm going to meet my better half!
Katherine to Hester Harper in *The Well* (66)

When Hester listened to music or when she read certain books she was able to forget that she was elderly and ugly and lame.
The Well (108)

In January 1984 Jolley had the idea for a play called *The Well*, the title becoming *Shepherd's Well* by mid-year, and the play becoming the novel called *The Well* by April 1985, when she sent the manuscript to the typist.[20] By the time she finished *The Well*, she had refined a plot structure which served her purposes perfectly: an older character forms an 'ideal' relationship with a younger one, a relationship that is distorted by neediness and possessiveness; the distortion is made apparent by the arrival of an 'intruder', the intrusion forcing a clarification of the relationship and a resolution of the situation; and, after the resolution, the characters go their own ways to a new beginning.

Thus Jolley reworked her presiding themes, but this time she did so without recourse to comedic or meta-fictional modes. She began by wanting the characters to be 'flat on the page', but her habitual exploration led to their being more than that. It led to a novel whose tone and mode marks a departure from the stylised realism of the comedic *romans à thèse* of the 1980s—*Scobie*, *Peabody*, *Foxybaby*—where she learned to temper the first-person confessional mode of *Palomino* and *Milk and Honey* in ways that crafted readable—she would say 'entertaining'—fictions.[21] Thus she continued to experiment stylistically, this time inventing a fiction through which her continued meditation on the suffering of lovelessness and the redeeming capacities of love and fiction are more anchored in character than concept.

The Well came to her step-wise as she employed her usual method of composition, writing down thoughts, ideas and images which she would set aside while she waited for more to occur. The first scene was of two women brushing each other's hair, which was followed by a second in which she realised there was an age difference between them, and a third where they were trying on clothes to find articles they could send to an orphanage—with that, Jolley understood that Katherine was an orphan. Those scenes were followed by two more, the first in the shop where Hester sees thin, white-faced Katherine, which leads to the *The Well*'s chilling opening lines where the father asks, 'What have you brought me Hester? What have you brought me from the shop?', and she replies, 'I've brought Katherine, but she's for me'. The final scene was the one in which Hester and Katherine confront each other over the man in the well: its first draft was, in Jolley's word, 'hopeless', for her fiction depends not upon conflict in the usual sense but upon an intersection of characters who make contact and, like vectors, take on new directions as a result.[22] She reworked the confrontation between the two women into Katherine's hysterical report to Hester about a man in the well she has been talking to, and then the novel was on its way.

The older character is Hester Harper, possibly in her sixties, the younger one Katherine, fifteen at the beginning and twenty-one at the end. The intruder is a thing or person who might or might not be down the well outside the shepherd's cottage where they have come to live out Hester's imagination of a perfect life together. The relationship is an infatuation for Hester—when she brings Katherine home to her father's house, '[s]he felt a need to initiate the girl, to show her something of their life' (10). Katherine was raised in an orphanage that she calls the Home (8, 40); by Hester's standards her taste in music and dance is incomprehensible and her aping of the speech and mannerisms of American film stars distasteful. Nevertheless, Hester is delighted by the way Katherine 'grabbed life with both hands' (39), and it gives her an 'infinite secret pleasure to watch Kathy abandon herself to her own energy' (173).

In *The Well* Jolley again explores love born of loneliness and uncontrolled by restraint. To keep Katherine close, Hester spends lavishly on shared pleasures, rents out the farm house after her father's death and retreats with Katherine to a cottage on the edge of the property, where her continued wanton spending is symbolised by tossing barely used dishes down the cottage well. This dystopic version of the 'Idyll', imagined in *Palomino*, is tested by the introduction of what a novelist appearing at the end of the story calls an 'intruder' (157). The first intrusion is the prospect of the arrival of Joanna, a friend from the orphanage Katherine persuades Hester to invite for a visit—a prospect that threatens Hester, arousing anger and jealousy.

Next there is the 'something' that Katherine runs into on a dark road, following the party celebrating the Borden's purchase of Hester's property. Hester has left the party feeling humiliated and bereft—she has felt the loss of her status as the premier landowner; has been patronised by Mrs Borden who scolds her for infantilising Katherine; and has been threatened by the suggestion that Katherine should leave the cottage to work at the Bordens. When the collision happens, Hester tells Katherine she has hit a man, and perhaps she has, since there was gossip of a robber at the Borden's place. Or perhaps Katherine hit a kangaroo and, if so, perhaps Hester knows so and lies to Katherine. Or perhaps in the dark, filled with anxiety about losing Katherine, Hester is convinced it is a man. In any case, like the dishes, Hester throws the body down the shepherd's well in an attempt to protect either Katherine or their life together, or both. She then collapses with a migraine and wakes up to two more disasters: the robbery of the large sum of ready money she has kept in the cottage against all advice; and Katherine talking to a 'man' at the bottom of the well, fantasising about marriage to him, and claiming that he has the money in the well with him.

The reader never exactly knows the truth of events. What is known is that Hester, who in one scene casually reaches out and wrings the neck of a rooster (50), is capable of violence and that in her desperation to preserve her special friendship with Katherine is capable of covering up homicide. But equally the reader knows her need—she 'never [knew] her mother' (47) and was raised by her emotionally remote father and her grandmother and, for a few years, by a governess named Fräulein Hilde Hertzfeld, after which she was sent to boarding school at fourteen for two years. Remembered fondness for her grandmother could strike her 'like a pain' (46), just as the memory of Hilde's fondness for her does: she remembers being told by Hilde what beautiful eyes she has, displacing her self-consciousness about her crippled leg (120), and she remembers being taken to Europe by Hilde one idyllic summer, a trip reminiscent of Jolley's to the continent with her mother and Mr Berrington.[23] Hester's relationship with Hilde ended when she found Hilde in the bathroom, her nightgown covered with blood, calling out to Hester to bring her father. But Hester, confronted with a scene of spontaneous or deliberate abortion, is dismayed by the apprehension that Hilde has had a special relationship with her father that rivals her own with Hilde: she flees to her bed, pulling the covers over her head, and in the morning she finds Hilde gone forever. She avoided her father in his old age, a man who lifts women's skirts with his stick (10), saying he was 'an increasingly tiresome bore' (46).

Jolley was struck by Bertrand Russell's observation in his *Autobiography* that 'The loneliness of the human soul is unendurable; nothing can penetrate it except the highest intensity of the sort of love that religious teachers have preached; . . . it follows that in human relations one should penetrate to the core of loneliness in each person and speak to that' (146).

In *The Well* Jolley speaks to the 'core of loneliness in each person' by creating in Hester a character that calls on a reader's compassion even as she exemplifies failure in regard to the importance of the lesson Laura learns in *Palomino*—the virtue of restraint, of allowing others to love where they will, and to cherish despite consuming loneliness. Thus the open-endedness of the novel, and the promise of new beginnings: Katherine plans to go to America where she and her friend Joanna will both become evangelists (161); a novelist talks about needing an 'intruder' to set her story in motion (157); and Mrs Borden invites Hester to tell the Borden children the story of how the spotlight on her roo bar was broken (170, 174). At the very end there is Hester, made insignificant by her failures, feeling comforted and 'enhanced by the indifference of the land' (170), realising—finally—that both Hilde and Mr Bird had cherished her, and that she has ability to endure (174). In the end there is Jolley's faith in survival, if not a representation of what Hailey calls 'the hardest thing of all to write about'—happiness.[24]

> *There are two types of novels . . . those which end with the characters getting married and living happily ever after and those which start with the characters married and living unhappily.*
>
> Edwin Page in *The Sugar Mother* (19)

In the second half of the 1960s Jolley was working on *The Leila Family*, a draft novel indebted to *Eleanor Page*, the novel she started in Birmingham in 1949. She declared *The Leila Family* finished in mid-March 1968 although Leonard thought it needed more work. Still, hoping to place it with a British publisher, she sent her only copy to her childhood friend Betty Sheldon, secretary to the Director of Faber and Faber in London. Sheldon lost it, sending her £10 for having done so—an event fictionalised in Jolley's short story 'The Well-Bred Thief'.[25] And so Jolley returned to the book in the 1980s when she received a bicentennial grant, not trying to rewrite it but writing it anew as *The Sugar Mother*.[26] The new version echoes *Foxybaby*, with its focus on an older man inclined to incest. It is also like *Foxybaby* for being a dream, or at least an extended fantasy.[27]

Like the dream in *Foxybaby*, the one in *Sugar Mother* is Freudian, with Dr Edwin Page cast in the role of Oedipus: his parentage is problematic (205); Mrs Bott's reading of tea leaves foresees strife between a father and son, as the Delphic oracle predicted for Oedipus (64); his neighbour Daphne steps on the back of his heel, Oedipus' tender spot (71); and, like *Foxybaby*'s Viggars, who compares herself to Tiresias who foresees danger for Oedipus, Daphne foresees danger for Edwin[28]. Driven by loneliness, Page enacts—in fantasy or in fact—the oedipal desire to redeem loneliness by finding the love of the forbidden mother.

Fifty-four-year-old Page is an erudite Renaissance specialist considered an academic relic by his younger lesbian colleagues. Cecilia Page is a thirty-eight-year-old hard-working and well-regarded obstetrician and gynaecologist in the mischievously named Mary and Joseph maternity wing of the General Hospital. They have an 'open marriage', regularly partner-swapping at university faculty parties, but the marriage has problems—she feels 'trapped with him' (115).

Cecilia has recently left for a year-long sabbatical in Canada where she gives a paper on 'The Unwanted Pregnancy' (44). In their telephone conversations, she is quite open with him about meeting and travelling with Frau Doktor Vorwickl, her friend from years ago, whom Edwin thought then to be her lover, although Vorwickl was unattractive and much older.[29] Now, thinking of them together, he imagines Vorwickl has 'the power of speech and Cecilia of laughter' (18), and recalls that, although Vorwickl has a huge appetite, she attacks her plate 'with a certain restraint' (199). When he and Cecilia were together after her long day at work, '[s]he needed, he knew, to tell him everything, especially what people had said and what she had said to them' (21). By contrast, during his year-long interlude, Edwin reveals nothing to Cecilia, avoiding her calls, unplugging the telephone, promising to write but never getting around to doing so. In that regard, he is like the son in 'The Performance' who never writes to his mother, as well as like the postman who should have listened to his wife. His problem is ambivalence: 'Accompanying the wish to be with one person was the terrifying wish and need to avoid, to not be with the other person' (88).

In his boyhood Edwin had a preference for dolls (150–1) and fairy tales about girls and women (154); at school he was unable to separate from his mother (205); and in adulthood he has a tendency to spend long periods of time watching schoolchildren—'Children's bodies were loose and free in their clothes, he thought. He liked to hear their excited voices' (35). A man wanting to be a child and to please his wife/mother, he is an easy mark for a mother–daughter pair who knock on his window at night under the pretext of being locked out of their new rental home next door. After he lets them in, they stay for the rest of the year, having proposed to provide him with a baby.

Edwin at first imagines giving Cecilia, a career woman who has had three abortions (54), a surprise present—Leila's baby whom he wants to believe is his, though it probably is not. What he cannot admit is that the present is for himself, the baby he has contracted to produce with the mother–daughter team, Leila to be a sugar mother, as Mrs Bott calls a surrogate mother. He fantasises the three of them will live as a family before Cecilia's return, and then he and Cecilia and the baby-present will form another such family (both are versions of the Holy Family in that one of the parents might or might not be the baby's biological parent).[30]

Like all Jolley's seducer/mentors, he is smitten with the girl/woman Leila, despite her being physically, socially and mentally thick—'it was unendurably pleasant to teach her' (161). But his pleasure is complicated by a fear of having to explain their presence in his home, and so, in still another skewed formulation of the family triangle, he thinks of designating the older woman as his sister and the younger one as her daughter; but he fears people would think that Leila's child is his, convicting him in their minds of incest. Ashamed like a little boy, he fabulates that Cecilia knows everything he thinks, each detail of his affair, and wonders if she thinks he is a 'perv' (198). He is trapped in the ecstasy of his dream which is threatened by Cecilia's scheduled return home.

If Edwin is hungry, he comes to realise, his hunger is 'not for food' (203); what he does not realise is that, unlike Vorwickl, he has little restraint. What is needed is 'a little line of balance' which is at hand in the person of Cecilia's school friend Daphne Hockley.[31] Daring, attractive and resourceful, she proposes their raucous sexual romp in a futile effort to drive out Leila and her mother. Caring and capable of restraint, she tries to help Edwin become aware of the gravity and impossibility of his situation and encourages him to extricate himself from it by cooperating with Leila when she finds herself unable to part with the newborn baby. In a Thorne- and Viggars-like confession, Daphne reveals her motive, that the failure of the Pages' marriage would affect her too: 'I haven't got anyone . . . [T]he person who is not part of a couple is alone' (122). Edwin affirms this further odd twist of the family configuration: 'Yes, of course Daph[,] and we need you . . . We'll be more of a—well, more of a family, more together' (122). It is only at the end of the novel Edwin realises that, in order to work their scam, Leila and her mother needed a man who was lonely (204).

Edwin's dream or interlude ends as it began, with Cecilia still overseas, but it rests on a point of balance: she is stranded in Cairo but will arrive soon with Vorwickl in tow, thus proposing still another triangular domestic configuration. As if an attempt to tip the balance the other way, Edwin, a pacifist, wills World War III so that they will be indefinitely stuck in Cairo. That Edwin still desires his sugar mother and has little insight into his own condition might not be unusual in dreams or fantasies but it is usually not satisfying in fiction. Thus *The Sugar Mother* might be regarded as one of Jolley's less successful *romans à thèse* for being heavy-handed in its oedipal framework, for having an unsympathetic protagonist who fails to command the reader's compassion, and for not convincingly representing Jolley's ethic of hope that comes from loving with restraint and despite loneliness.

The Sugar Mother's unsettled feeling might result from the fact that Jolley, writing to a deadline, based it on an earlier, lost draft that was both begun and set in England—*The Sugar Mother's* landscape is English, with prominent pines, something Jolley accounts for by representing the narrative as occurring in a dream-like state; the Pages and their university colleagues are British, and the Bott family are on their way back to England. The novel is also transitional: Jolley was focusing on marriage for the first time.[32] Those two elements came together in her last three novels where all of the protagonists are English and marriage figures significantly in the plot.

Whatever its origins and sequelia, *The Sugar Mother* can be read as revealing Jolley's continuing concern with 'the starvation of family life': she portrays a wife who creates a space for herself in which she can separately develop professionally and personally in the hope that the husband, without her constant presence and attention, will become less self-absorbed. And the novel interests for Jolley's working out her presiding theme of loneliness and its relation to the desire for the ideal person who completes one's life in terms of the dynamics of family life, something that becomes the focus of her next novels—the Vera trilogy and its coda, *The Orchard Thieves*.

In the 1980–82 period Elizabeth Jolley received three awards for her stories and one for a radio play.[33] Then, in 1983, *Mr Scobie's Riddle* won the *Age* Book of the Year Award for Imaginative Writing along with the Book of the Year Award itself, and also won the Western Australian Week Literary Award for Fiction.[34] As a result of such successes, she was given a two-and-a-half-year Australia Literature Board Senior Fellowship commencing in January 1984 and, in 1985, she was given a Bicentennial grant to write a novel by March of 1987 for publication in 1988—the novel drew on *The Leila Family* and became *The Sugar Mother*. In the second half of the 1980s *Milk and Honey* won the New South Wales Premier's Christina Stead Prize for fiction in 1985, and *The Well* won the Victorian FAW's Barbara Ramsden award in 1986. *The Well* also won the 1986 Miles Franklin Award, the prize of prizes, which must have felt even more special for Beatrice Davis' having rejected her previous entry, *Mr Scobie's Riddle*, as unworthy of consideration. When her last novel of the decade, *My Father's Moon*, won the *Age* Book of the Year Award in 1989, by her own standards she had stepped into 'the realms of distinction', an aspiration she declared twenty years earlier.[35]

A variety of professional, civic and academic honours paralleled her performance from the mid-1980s, by which time she was one of Australia's most reviewed authors, including two full-page reviews within twelve months in the *New York Times Review of Books*.[36] The Australian Society of Authors (ASA), the peak body for novelists in Australia, invited her to be its President for 1985, replacing Donald Horne who left the ASA to become Chair of the Australia Council. In 1987 she was invited to be a judge of the 1987 *Age* Book of the Year awards, and she also received a Western Australian Citizen of the Year Award for Arts, Entertainment and Culture—with her own commemorative plaque in the sidewalk opposite Government House. In 1988 she received a Canada–Australia prize for familiarising Canadians with Australia's writers, and she was made an Officer of the Order of Australia for services to Australian literature, an award presented to her by the Jolleys' friend and colleague Professor Gordon Reid, Governor of Western Australia.[37] Finally, in 1989, she received an Advance Australia Award, and the Fellowship of Australian Writers in Western Australia made her a life member. Between times, the Western Australian Institute of Technology awarded her an Honorary Doctorate of Technology, its first-ever doctorate, in 1987, the year it became Curtin University of Technology.

Jolley announced that writing was a business before she knew how big a business it might become for her. The period roughly encompassing the 1980s were surely Jolley's best time financially, one index being her signing a contract in 1988 with Harper and Row in New York for the US rights to *The Sugar Mother* and *My Father's Moon* for what was euphemistically described in the press as being 'just short of six figures'—say, A$90,000. The sum might seem large but, if regarded as $4,500 a year for each book over ten years, she would have to generate another $45,000 per year to approximate (say) the salary of a professor of the time. As chance would have it, she averaged a book a year during the 1990s—*Palomino* in 1980, *Newspaper* in 1981, *Peabody*, *Scobie* and *Woman in a Lampshade* in 1983, *Milk and Honey* in 1984, *Foxybaby* in 1985, *The Well* in 1986, *Sugar Mother* in 1988, *My Father's Moon* in 1989. But an agent would take ten percent of the gross, and no one provided what professors and many other workers receive, like sick leave, annual leave, long service leave and/or superannuation. Moreover, although she produced a book a year in that decade, she did not actually write one a year, for some of them took several years and some took decades of on-and-off work; and her supply of older manuscripts was running out. In other words, for Jolley, as for most writers, income was unpredictable on a year-to-year basis.[38] Thus she was fortunate that her husband was drawing a professorial pension so that she did not have to worry about being able to maintain that level of production and, especially, that level of success—producing a book was half the equation but getting it sold was the more important half. She was pleased to be successful but more concerned with what she would do next. Rather than speak about what she earned, she would prefer to answer a question about how long it had taken her to write a book, in which case she might well have answered, 'All my life'.

Her success in the 1980s, greatly facilitated by Caroline Lurie's skill in representing her, proved far beyond Leonard Jolley's modest arithmetical gifts, requiring him to turn over their affairs to Smith Coffey, financial advisers in Perth, in 1989. It was not a bad effort for a woman he had called a Bilston Bunny nearly forty years before, an effort her mother and Aunt Daisy might have approved of if it were not, of course, for certain lifestyle issues.[39] Whatever they or anyone else might have thought, in Elizabeth Jolley's mind her business was writing and her writing was more central to her life.

11

1990–2007—Who talks of victory . . .

[I]t does seem funny she's so popular. I guess it's the great flood of work, and of course her publishers and the publicity. But it is strange how she has succeeded.
Barbara Hanrahan, *The Diaries of Barbara Hanrahan* (292)

About ten years ago you couldn't move for Elizabeth Jolley, ABC R[adio] N[ational] interviews with Elizabeth Jolley, theses on Elizabeth Jolley, etc. Now, you hardly hear of her. I haven't read any of her novels, so for those who have—when was the last time you re-read any of her novels? . . . Maybe I haven't been paying attention.
Andrew E., blogger, 10 November 2006

Blogger Andrew E. had a point, even if he had not read Elizabeth Jolley. During the 1980s, a decade conspicuous in Australia for the prominence of its women writers, her name and image seemed to appear with greater frequency than that of other women writers who were her peers. She was the only woman of eight new novelists in Helen Daniel's *Liars* and, of the other women in Gillian Whitlock's *Eight Voices of the Eighties*, only Thea Astley or Helen Garner could challenge her ubiquity.[1] In the mid-1980s a half-hour film on Jolley, *The Nights Belong to the Novelist*, featuring Ruth Cracknell, was broadcast on the ABC, Peter Kendall painted a conceptual portrait of her rejected by the Archibald committee because she was not well enough known, and Judith Rodriguez published a poem about her in *Meanjin*, 'Elizabeth and Red Socks in Perth'.[2]

By the early 1990s interest in Jolley had developed to the point where there was an hour-long telemovie of her story 'The Last Crop' broadcast on television in the UK and Australia, and throughout the decade of the 1990s and the first few years of the 2000s Jolley published or republished some 100 short stories in print and audio form—including three stories in the *New Yorker* and her fourth collection of short stories, *Fellow Passengers* (1997). In the same period, *The Well* was made into a movie that premiered at the 1997 Cannes International Festival of Film, and six of her works were adapted to the stage, including *Newspaper*, *Milk and Honey* and *The Sugar Mother*.[3] And she continued her prodigious output of essays, memoirs and reviews, many of which Caroline Lurie collected in her valuable books that bracket the period, *Central Mischief* (1992) and *Learning to Dance* (2006).

All the while she continued to garner new honours and national recognition. Ben Joel did a major commissioned portrait of her. Curtin University commenced its Annual Elizabeth Jolley Lecture Series in 1991, which featured prominent speakers like former Western Australian Premier, and then-member of Federal Parliament Carmen Lawrence (1994), author-publisher Anne Summers (1995), Hazel Hawke (1998), actor Ruth Cracknell (1999), actor Patricia ('Hyacinth Bucket') Routledge (2000), and publisher Hilary McPhee (2001); and Barry Humphries delivered the last lecture she attended, in 2002. Curtin named its new lecture theatre after her in 1994, and in 1998 Vice Chancellor Lance Twomey, her strong supporter, appointed her Professor of Creative Writing on the occasion of her seventy-fifth birthday. She received honorary doctorates from Macquarie University (1995), the University of Queensland (1997) and the University of New South Wales (2000). And across the 1990s she was in constant demand for media interviews, with anodyne, avuncular or intellectual men like Clive Robertson, Phillip Adams and Robert Dessaix; and with key ABC presenters like Jill Kitson, Margaret Throsby and Ramona Koval. Most of them stuck to the grandmother-from-the suburbs script while avoiding the Big Question. When one of them dared to begin her program by asking, 'Elizabeth, are you a lesbian?' Jolley replied with silence which she followed with more silence until the interviewer returned to the safety of the suburbs.

Her friend and admirer Barry Humphries dedicated 'Maroan' to her in 1991, a mock celebration of suburbia with such affirmations as, 'When we bought our home in Moonee Ponds / It didn't have a phone / But it had one thing to offer: / The toilet was maroan'. His alter-ego, Dame Edna Everage, the narrator of the poem, would address Jolley in a sisterly fashion from the stage of the Regal Theatre when she performed in Perth. But the image Jolley cultivated was the inverse of Dame Edna's. Unlike the self-confessed international superstar, Jolley was modest and gracious and always defaulted to a self-deprecating humour. Her modus vivendi had its roots in home, school and hospital life in England, which conditioned her to be a placator whose role was to deal with the needs of others, even when irreconcilable, and so she felt at everyone's beck and call. Retrospectively she believed she had gone to an academically second-rate Quaker school in England, not Sidcot which her friend and Penguin Publishing Director Bob Sessions had attended, and so she did not contemplate studying medicine, defaulting to nursing. Despite having started so promisingly and so much wanting to become a nurse, she had to leave the course prematurely, her fault again. And it was her fault, in her mind, that she ended up a single mother in the Bedlam that was Pinewood, finally to be rescued by Leonard Jolley.

The wife who accompanied Leonard Jolley from Scotland, the homemaker from the suburbs, the ditsy mother-now-grandmother ended up doing the things she was not supposed to do. A Russian refugee like Judah Waten might have found Australia in the 1960s receptive to his work, but in that era, when Jolley saw *Poms Go Home* on a customs shed in Fremantle, an English woman was not expected to become a prominent Australian novelist, unless she wrote along the lines of Dorothy Sanders.[4] Delys Bird wrote, '[t]he invisible orthodoxy of the early 1970s was that Australian fiction was a masculine territory', going on to recall Thea Astley's plaint that she was 'spiritually neutered by [her sexist] society'.[5] Yet, in a profession dominated by Patrick White, Elizabeth Jolley ended up most frequently compared with White—a bemused Peter Pierce asking, 'Who elected Jolley to sit at the right hand of Patrick White?' And her name stood beside Frank Moorhouse's in the headlines when their novels were declared ineligible for the 1994 Miles Franklin Award.[6] Nor was she supposed to become a professor in an English department, for that was what Leonard Jolley had trained for and all his life dearly wanted to be. In another world, like that of *The Sugar Mother*, they might have become Professor of Literature and Doctor of Gynaecology and Obstetrics.

Jolley was neither defiant nor apologetic. She merely affirmed what the early news articles foregrounded, that she was a suburban housewife-writer, an oxymoron like Dr Johnson's woman preacher. The remarkable thing was not that she wrote prize-winning novels but that she wrote novels at all. In the world where she found herself, she chose a position frequently adopted by subversives. From observation and experience she became aware of how deference and apparent ineptness could be parlayed into strengths, particularly with men, and she came to realise they were strategies many women identified with. They gave her certain rhetorical advantages like those enjoyed by her canny women in *Miss Peabody's Inheritance*. She was Edgely at ASAL's 1993 conference when she awarded Elizabeth Webby (standing in for Elizabeth Riddell) a brooch she found on the lectern instead of the ASAL Gold Medal, or when she dropped the medal Premier Neville Wran gave her before her acceptance speech at the 1985 New South Wales Premier's Literary Awards dinner.[7] She was Arabella Thorne at the 1995 Melbourne Writers' Festival when she graciously subdued a young Irish novelist who threatened to dominate a panel discussion. And she was Matron Snowdon when she introduced 'a line of balance' into a chaplains' conference in Perth in the 1970s when she brought the audience to tears. When a foolish journalist asked if she was in therapy, she was all three women at once as she responded, 'Yes, dear. I go to a man for my shoulder—would you like his name?' In her response, Edgely misunderstood the question, Thorne raked the journo for impertinence, and Snowdon let the young woman off the hook by turning the mockery upon herself.

Till I met you there were no seasons
And now again there are none.
...
In the quiet heat of summer all life is withdrawn.
      'Dead Trees in Your Absence', *Diary of a Weekend Farmer* (39)

The persona which protected Jolley and gave her purchase in the 1970s and strength in the 1980s sustained her through the 1990s. All along, her concerns were her family, her teaching and her writing. But the passage of time meant that changes had taken place with respect to all three. Most dramatically, at the beginning of January 1991, it resulted in her deciding, in consultation with family physicians, to arrange for long-term residency for

Leonard in the Alfred Carson Lodge which was half a mile from their home at 28 Agett Road in Claremont.[8] The decision was heartbreaking for her, one that left him tearful, anxious and resentful, but she had to do something. If nothing else, with their awkward showering facilities at home, she in her late sixties and he in his late seventies, bathing him was not only difficult but dangerous for both of them.

Of course, there were difficulties at the Alfred Carson too. An unanticipated one was Leonard's finding himself in a four-bed room with Professor Fred Alexander, then in his nineties, who would unnerve the authority-shy Leonard by frequently declaiming in a loud voice, 'Jolley, the Vice-Chancellor is coming—we must get dressed at once!' But fortunately Alexander was eventually moved to another ward, and Elizabeth was otherwise able to make the transition somewhat seamless. For a time she brought Leonard home in the morning to his own books and music, returning him later for the staff to bathe and medicate him before putting him to bed. As she sometimes said, he was never happier than when entering a hospital where he had nothing to do but read, listen to music and be attended to by pretty young women. He had his half-bottles of red wine in the Alfred Carson bedside table, along with his books and music cassettes, and soon he came to enjoy the company of visitors.

They both came to regard the Alfred Carson arrangement as one where they could enjoy being together. Since the mid-eighties Elizabeth had come to feel there was more tolerance in their marriage, and she did not get so angry with him; age, she realised, distanced her from passions, negative ones included and, besides, she was learning to save her energy.[9] Although she had felt it all along, she could more readily see and say that each was to the other someone completely trusted and sustaining'.[10] She enjoyed her daily or twice-daily visits, when she would tell him her news and push his chair through their quiet neighbourhood as he rehearsed for her the names of plants and trees. Fond memories of those walks, and the last stage of their lifelong companionship, are invoked in the opening and closing passages of *The Georges' Wife* where Vera pushes Mr George's chair along green leafy streets.

When he was no longer strong enough to hold his heavy books, she would read to him at length. It was a continuation of the habit they formed in the 1980s when they read to one another as a restful interlude before she returned to writing, and of his having read to her in their early life together.

She said the only time she truly rested was when she was with him.[11] She was reading Traherne to him on Friday 22 July 1994 when she realised from his breathing that he was dying, and she was reading Wordsworth's 'Tintern Abbey' to him long after he had stopped listening. His funeral service was held at Karrakatta Cemetery on Tuesday 2 August, and she later placed his ashes under the roses at their property in Wooroloo.

All life was suddenly withdrawn. At its height in Birmingham and their early days in Edinburgh, the Jolley–Knight affair was one of great intellectual and physical passion and of conflicted and conflicting emotions and circumstances. The intellectual passion never changed, remaining the core of their relationship for fifty years. Their complex relationship seems well expressed in images from Rilke's *'Liebes-Lied'*, some verses of which Jolley used as an epigraph to her novel *Lovesong* published three years after his death[12]:

> *How shall I hold my soul so that it does not touch yours? How shall I lift it across you to other things? How gladly I would stow it away with some lost thing in the dark in a strange quiet place which does not vibrate when your depths vibrate! But everything that touches us, you and me, takes us together like one stroke of the bow which draws one voice out of two strings. On what instrument are we stretched? And what fiddler has us in his hands? O sweet melody'.*

The poem represents a man who is ambivalent—there are parallels with the Jolleys' life story, beginning with Leonard's ambivalence when choosing between Elizabeth and Joyce Hancock and including Elizabeth's lifelong hope for greater intimacy. Still, her hope was sustained by moments of intellectual and personal intimacy when they resonated like two strings stroked by the same bow. The melody, which required the lover and the beloved to surrender their freedom and independence, was sweeter than any other. In a 1997 interview she said, 'I can't get over his death . . . He was such an enriching person. I'm a person who needs to tell things, and I haven't got Leonard to tell things to. I did love him. I miss him very much'.[13]

Now she had to create her own seasons. One way she did so was through pastoral work associated with her students. An instance involved a young mother who telephoned to ask for an extension to the deadline for an assignment. Although she disliked students calling her at home, given the woman's plight—she was going through a high-profile divorce, the husband was beastly, the children were anxious—Jolley conducted a hospital-like intake: are you getting enough sleep, are you eating well, can you get someone to help with the children and, surprisingly, do you need to come here to stay? No, thank you, the woman said, she just needed an extension, which Jolley granted, asking, 'Dear, do I know you?' Another example involved a male student dying of AIDS. She became so concerned with his situation that she bought his mother an airline ticket to come from the eastern states, and visited the young man sometimes twice a day, four or five times a week, until Curtin colleagues intervened, worried she would exhaust herself. It was a commitment made unbidden, unlike her ministering to the Lambs and Ludmila Blotnicki when they importuned in the 1970s. It was more like the time in the 1980s she cared for a fellow teaching colleague who was dying, bathing him and tending to his lesions. She hoped to free his nurses from routine work and worried that his family would not be able to deal with it themselves.

> M[other] said she saw the moon, so I went to look. Yes!!! The same moon that you, though so far away, can see. My mind goes back to the time when you were a new girl at Sibford, and not yet happily settled down. I wrote to you at that time and mentioned that you, in Sibford, saw the SAME moon as we in Wells Rd saw. I am grateful for your affection. It is a very big thing in my life. I believe that God has planned the FAMILY as a <u>training ground</u> in LOVE'.
>
> Wilfred Knight to Elizabeth Jolley, 17 January 1976

> There is nothing so wrong with a child that cannot be cured by the death of both parents. The only way to kill a child is with an axe.[14]

For all of Elizabeth Jolley's extreme experiences and memories in her natal home from the time she was born until she left Scotland—as she recalled them, continual struggles with her demonic mother and loving moments with her angelic father—it is surprising that none of Jolley's early work displays the strength and range of emotion that her diaries and letters make clear she held for her parents. After all, she said her father made her a writer.[15] What accounts for the change of direction her work took at the end of the 1980s with the publication of what came to be called the Vera trilogy and its coda *The Orchard Thieves*?

Not surprisingly, the explanation relates to her development as a writer in the 1970s and 1980s. During that time her writing improved immeasurably and her style changed, such that someone who did not know of Jolley and her work might be hard-pressed to guess that (say) *Palomino*, *Mr Scobie's Riddle* and *The Well* were written by the same person. With the success of her books in the 1980s, her confidence grew and, with it, an internal sense of authority. By the time of *The Well*, she had become less dependent on humour in her work, on stock characters, on resolutions effected through secondary characters, and on metafictional techniques, all of which might be seen as deflections and disguises enabling her to speak only indirectly of what concerned her most.

From this hard-won position she found an insight that allowed her to explore more deeply her central preoccupation with homelessness, lovelessness and loneliness: what in 'Decidedly Pointing to Central Mischief' she calls 'some kind of unfathomable conflict about which it was not possible to talk or to explain' (93) and which she alludes to in the frontispiece of *Lovesong* when she cites Flaubert's pronouncement that '[f]iction is . . . the response to a deep and always hidden wound'. In order to explore that insight, she needed two more things. One was a character like Hester Harper, more complex than her usual characters, introspective and willing to acknowledge her faults and also willing to take control of her own future, even if doing so could only be done through memory and imagination. Another was a genre more suitable to her particular way of developing characters and achieving resolutions. The result allowed her to go back to the diaries and the manuscript she had brought with her from Scotland—*The Feast*—to craft four major novels that form the apex of her career.

> *Remembered people appear and disappear disconcertingly in the tiniest nutshells of memory. Order is reversed. The longing for some particular way of living or for some particular person or place or possession can come back with a sharpness unparalleled by anything happening and experienced during the present time. Furthermore, understanding the loneliness and despair of knowing it is not possible to bring back a wished for person, and knowing that one person can never replace another, is understanding that this is what bereavement is.*
>
> *Cabin Fever* (8)

> ... *past, present and future are strung together ... on the thread of the wish that runs through them.*
>
> Sigmund Freud, 'Creative Writing and Day-dreaming' (135)

A year after the appearance of the last novel of Jolley's Vera trilogy—*My Father's Moon* (1989), *Cabin Fever* (1990) and *The Georges' Wife* (1993)—Drusilla Modjeska noted that Elizabeth Webby, Helen Daniel and Peter Craven had praised the books as they appeared. Now she wanted to know why the trilogy 'has not been recommended to us ... from the cover of *Time* magazine and every colour supplement in the country? To say nothing of the literary pages of our newspapers'. The achievement of the trilogy was 'awesome', she wrote, because of how Jolley 'knits past to present into a form of writing that at once mimics and explores the twilight working of memory ... Images are not so much super-imposed as realigned and reconceived, so there is no fixed viewing point, yet every point is clearly viewed'.[16]

Jolley's Vera trilogy can be regarded as traditional for being a Bildungsroman, a novel depicting the development of the protagonist from youth to adulthood, or modern for employing a stream-of-consciousness narrative technique. But the knitting of past to present in which 'there is no fixed viewing point, yet every point is clearly viewed' equally results from each of the books acting as a species of *roman-fleuve* or 'river-novel'. Instead of simply extending the time period covered in the previous one, as in the traditional *roman-fleuve*, they work by ebbs and flows, each book reiterating previous events and introducing new ones, so that each book deepens the understanding of all of them. The narration of the trilogy is retrospective rather than prospective, its time and place is the same in all three novels, in the late 1980s in Australia where Vera Wright, in her sixties, works as a medical doctor.[17] According to Lynette Felber, the *roman-fleuve* has a connection to *écriture féminine*[18] for having an amorphous subject matter, a domestic or social focus, an avoidance of a singular narrative climax, and a lack of closure.

Jolley gives us an image for this mode of narration, and its motive, in *Cabin Fever*. Vera spends several days in a hotel in New York City, having flown there from Australia to attend a medical conference. She is alone, away from home in a room that is too hot, worrying about the paper she is to present, and distracted by an 'uncomfortable memory' evoked by service doors across the hall that have no numbers and no keyholes (15). In the American meaning of the term, 'cabin fever' refers to the anxiety that arises from being confined, as on a ship or in a snowbound cabin. Vera modulates this definition when she uses the term *Reise Fieber*, travel fever, which she describes as 'something *before* a journey' (52 [italics hers]). She says the cure for it 'is to recognize the symptoms . . . [I]t is necessary to collect all the images and the experiences as if they were treasures in a small storehouse' (236).

The necessity of collecting such images and experiences competes with her attempt to focus on the paper she is scheduled to give, 'Perspectives on Moral Insanity'. She has proposed addressing the topic in light of her thoughts about her venereal-disease patients but, by a process of association, those thoughts are displaced by memories venereal, about love, which in myth is a disorder inflicted by Venus. Moral insanity is a condition in which afflicted people conduct themselves morally quite at odds with their usual behaviour, in a manner conventionally regarded as indecent or improper.[19] Hence the retrospectivity of her *roman-fleuve*: the images and experiences she collects have to do with her earlier love affairs, all of them unconventional in one respect or another. Had she known the term, Vera's mother might well have called Vera's behaviour morally insane from the time she had an illegitimate child while a student nurse in the Midlands, for that time was followed by another illegitimate child in Scotland, and Vera's leaving both behind when she sailed for Australia. Jolley's mother and Aunt Daisy might have used it too when Monica Knight also behaved scandalously.

> *All this goes on inside me, in the vast cloisters of my memory. In it are the sky, the earth, and the sea, ready at my summons, together with everything I have ever perceived in them by my senses . . . In it I meet myself as well I remember myself . . .*
> Saint Augustine, quoted in *Cabin Fever* (235)

Alone in her hotel room, anxious, Vera journeys through her past. She ruminates on five of her affairs, the first with Lois, a fellow nursing trainee. Passionate but one-sided—Lois was a 'user' and did not intervene when her brothers made fun of Vera's looks—it was Vera's introduction to romance, one that shows her openness to same-sex love and her vulnerability to being shamed. The penultimate one, with an effete, artistic Oxford couple named Noël and Felicity, took place while Vera was studying medicine in the Midlands. They were intelligent, educated, refined and abundantly passionate people, their couplings more than Vera could have imagined in her wildest Freudian dreams. They had the power to make Vera feel 'special', particularly when they called her 'poet', blinding her, despite her training, to the fact that Noël was infectious with TB, which was his lasting legacy to her.

If the affair on the urban farm with Noel and Felicity was mock-idyllic, as their names imply, her second affair at the hospital with Doctor Metcalf and his wife was more promising. An older, wealthy, educated, fashionable couple, they were apparently caring and certainly willing to take her into their circle. In addition they were passionate: after Jonathan seduces Vera, Magda invites her to bathe with them ('"Take everything off Darling! Come on Jonty! Buckets for us both"' [*My Father's Moon* 126]). The relationship ends with Vera pregnant by Jonathan, who apparently has been killed in the war. Then she learns that the Metcalfs were not so caring, or at least not so focused on her, as she had believed: all along Jonathan had been having an affair with Smithers, a man at the hospital; and she receives a card with no return address from Magda who asks her to visit her in France. Hospital post-mortem gossip has it that Metcalf got a dozen nurses pregnant, adding to Vera's shame as she listens, wearing the wedding ring she recently bought for sixpence.

Her third affair is both similar to and different from the one with the Metcalfs. The Georges are older, intelligent, educated and so on, but Oliver George and fifteen-year-older Eleanor are brother and sister, not husband and wife, though their love for one another is intense—Eleanor is her own 'wardress' (*The Georges' Wife* 29) in that regard, and Vera realises he cannot bear the thought of his sister having no one to love. The main difference is that this time Vera acts more like the lover than the beloved: he calls her mentor and, after he makes love to her, she tells him she wants him once more (*Cabin Fever* 216). However, her power meets equal resistance when she is unable to persuade him to tell his sister that he is the father of their child, and later to get him to marry her.

The awful truth is that I like to see my mother and my father but after about half an hour I want to go away again. I am quite unable to explain why this is.

Vera Wright, in *Cabin Fever* (44)

Vera's tuberculosis, contracted during her affair with Noël and Felicity, is effectively a venereal disease. The TB, coupled with her pregnancies to Jonathan and Oliver at cost to herself and her family, implies that her pursuit of love is a kind of moral insanity, one that has its origins in her natal family, according to Wilfrid Knight's letter about the training ground of love. Certainly, her meditations reveal distortions and fault lines in her family, and the persistence of the feelings engendered there.

She has always regarded her father as powerful, knowledgeable, and endlessly loving and caring—sparks fly from the soles of his boots, he knows the arcane worlds of science and mathematics, he always accompanies her to and from busses and trains and ships, reminding her that, whenever and wherever she is, she should look to the moon to know that he is not far away (*My Father's Moon* 26). Above all, he is understanding and non-judgemental. Her earliest memories of her father's cherishing are untroubled, those of her mother's caring problematic. Over time those memories change from those of an attentive husband and a needy wife to ones of a caring husband and a wife who betrays him.

The change occurs with Mr Berrington's appearance on the scene. If Vera's ideal was her father, her mother's was Berrington, and he compared favourably by most criteria: he was older, better educated, more refined, apparently more passionate than the father, and also capable of restraint. Vera is unwittingly complicit in her mother's betrayal when she travels with Berrington and her mother to Europe, her father's 'white face, anxious and sad behind his smile... the last thing I see' (*The Georges' Wife* 19). Berrington's presence benefits the mother for his being more attentive, capable and forthcoming about fulfilling her needs and desires, something even the father seems to recognise and approve. At the same time it reorganises the family dynamic, sidelining the father, who carries his wound uncomplainingly, and revealing to Vera that his feet are made of clay—when she recalls his visit to Fairfields, she remembers Frederick the Great saying Mr Wright is a harmless old fool (*Cabin Fever* 172). Vera begins to realise that his kindness is constitutional, based in his religious principles and dispensed equally to everyone he meets; as her mother says, he only had one answer to problems, 'prayer and the certainty of reconciliation' (*The Georges' Wife* 79). Vera loves the father who is cherishing and principled, even to the point of cherishing his faithless wife and being courteous to her lover. Yet that love is imbricated by her empathy for his hurt and shame, and she is pained by how foolish his actions look in response to cuckoldry.[20]

If *My Father's Moon* pays homage to the father, *Cabin Fever* is devoted to the mother.[21] Vera's 'moral insanity', her affairs with older men and her-out-of-wedlock pregnancies, could be read as defiant gestures against her mother—her affairs would punish the status-conscious mother by bringing shame on the family, and they would mock her hypocrisy and damn her lack of restraint in her passion for Berrington. Why could not Vera do the same with men of her choice? Her transgressions would also test her mother's love for her, something she had doubted since a child. As Vera reviews her images and experiences, she sees how she loves and hates her mother in equal measure, remembering that, when visiting her mother's house, 'after about half an hour I want to go away again', yet recalling wishing another time 'all at once, to be in bed in my mother's house' (*Cabin Fever* 44, 63). Together, the first two books of the trilogy test the truth of the belief that there is nothing so wrong with a child that cannot be cured by the death of both parents.

The images and memories reviewed by Vera are her way of addressing the pain of the child caught between her divided parents and her inevitable betrayals of them. Two figures are key to her doing so. One is Staff Nurse Ramsden, an older woman Vera met while nursing at St Cuthbert's during the war. Ramsden represents an ideal friend or lover, principled like Vera's father and cultured like her mother. Vera once invited her to visit her home but turned her away at the train station without explanation, fearing Ramsden might guess she was pregnant, an act of shame that Vera later regards as a betrayal—Ramsden had sent Vera a poem delicately bespeaking love, Rilke's sonnet 'Death of the Beloved'.[22] Quoted on the last page of *My Father's Moon*, the poem is about Orpheus, who invented the lyre, and his lover Eurydice, who was taken from him without warning—when Orpheus follows her to Hades, the beauty of his music-making gains him permission to bring her up to the world of the living. Orpheus:

> *Went gliding over there to shades unknown,*
> *... [Where] he sensed that yonder, after this,*
> *Her girl's smile like a moon was theirs to own,*
> *And her way of bestowing bliss.*

The older Vera, remembering, equates with Orpheus, and so Eurydice is Ramsden, linked to the father through the moon that is Vera's to own.[23]

Another woman key to Vera's addressing her pain and remorse is Gertrude, a mother-figure Vera visits because she is good at listening and non-judgemental, often advising indirectly by proverbs and farmyard illustrations. When Gertrude, more knowing than Vera's mother, intuits the trouble she is headed for with the Metcalfs, she offers advice, and Vera, already pregnant, stops visiting and writing to her. When Gertrude falls ill and dies during Vera's pregnancy and childbirth, Vera has only her mother to speak to, which she cannot. The older Vera, like Orpheus, looks backward on experiences that evoke lost loves. Her father and Ramsden, her mother and Gertrude, may be forever lost to her in fact, but they are forever available in memory.

> *I am a shabby person. I understand, if I look back, that I have treated kind people with an unforgivable shabbiness.*
>
> Vera Wright, *The Georges' Wife* (3)

> *Like my mother's house, my widow's house stands open to the spring, to all the seasons . . .*
>
> Vera Wright, *The Georges' Wife* (164–5)

A third woman who is a key treasure in Vera's storehouse of remembered people who have cherished her and thereby given her the wherewithal to go forward is the Rice Farm Widow in *The Georges' Wife*. The partner from the fifth affair Vera reviews in memory, she is caring, like Gertrude, but outspoken, like Vera's mother. On board the ship to Australia she tells Vera 'your father can't accompany you all the way in your life' (110–111). Effectively, Mrs Ruperts, the Rice Farm Widow, instructs Vera in the psychological truth of the belief that the only way to kill a child is with an axe: she helps her to see that, whatever sins Vera's parents might or might not have visited on her, she still has the capacity and strength within herself to develop into a whole and self-sufficient person.

That is something Vera can do only if she can forgive her mother for wounding the father and for the burden she feels in carrying his wound. Gertrude's cherishing is instrumental in Vera's internal rapprochement with her mother. It is telling that all during her affair with Noël and Felicity she turns to her mother and wishes to be in her mother's house. Equally, it is telling that her 'rescue' from her two lovers' squalid, tubercular cottage and her return to her parents' home occurs through an image of her parents, her white hat and his white face, walking toward her across the muddy field outside Noël's and Felicity's cottage: as Felicity remarks, like Virgil, they come to '*guide and lead*' a lost soul '*through an eternal place*' (97).

This image, so reminiscent of *Foxybaby*'s concluding apocalyptic image of a holy family—a mother, father and daughter on the horizon—suggests how the trilogy's meditation on things venereal has its origin in the family as a training ground for love. But the wisdom of the trilogy is not so much about the salvation of ideal love as it is about the lesson in survival Vera learns: that the desire 'to be the giver and recipient of the whole' is the place of loving and imagination, but that a perfect emotional, intellectual and physical 'friendship', something always to be desired, must yield to the realities of ordinary life. This is the wisdom sparely retold in the *Orchard Thieves*, which forms a kind of coda to the Vera trilogy, and in which the narrative voice has an arresting lyricism and an astonishing moral authority.

> *My love for my children makes me realise how much my parents loved me. I didn't realise it when I was younger.*
>
> Wilfrid Knight to Elizabeth Jolley, 9 April 1967.

Written after the death of Jolley's parents in the late 1980s and during the time of Leonard Jolley's stay and death in a nursing home in the early 1990s, *The Orchard Thieves* (1995) takes the understanding of bereavement in the Vera trilogy to a different dimension, and it does so through the wisdom learned through Vera's 'ruthless self-examination' in the trilogy (*Cabin Fever* 7). It was also written after the birth of her four grandchildren in the 1980s[24], something that enabled her to reformulate her knowledge about mothers and daughters, allowing her to see how, paradigmatically, a mother is simultaneously a daughter, but a grandmother, for having no mother, can develop a more dispassionate perspective on the mother–daughter pair.

The central themes of the trilogy recur in this elegant elegiac novella: anguished loneliness in the grandmother's fear for her eldest daughter who has no special lover/friend, despite her capacity and need for love shown through cherishing her nephews; shabbiness in the grandmother's middle daughter's plan to sell the family home and its orchard so the estate can be shared before her mother dies; and innocence—the steady hope for love despite the inevitable losses of experience—represented by the wild, scatological-talking, sexually inquisitive and mischievously thieving grandsons, whose tender bodies link them to their newborn baby sister in the tale.

The climax occurs as the grandmother acts calmly rather than panicking when the middle daughter does something absolutely appalling, threatening to kill her newborn son by dropping him into a steaming bath. The grandmother suddenly recalls the myth of Ceres and her baby[25], realising that 'within the action was a metaphor for trust. That was it. Imagination and trust'. That optimistic epiphany is simultaneously challenged by the grandmother's shock that 'it was possible for the child, the grown-up daughter, to hate the mother' (*The Orchard Thieves* 121). That was something Vera's mother could never understand in the trilogy, an understanding Vera had to address through forgiveness.

In response, the grandmother wants to tell the middle daughter that 'there was only one way and that way was to take and accept all that which happens in your life and simply to push on with living in the face of accusation, misunderstanding or whatever it is with whatever subsequent unhappiness. A person is never unhappy for ever she wanted to explain . . .' (122). She wanted, in other words, to explain her ethic of hope in difficult circumstances, 'the horror of family life being the most difficult of all circumstances' (80). Whatever else begins in the family, suffering begins there, and through suffering we develop into social beings. Instead of saying that, however, the grandmother/mother says, '[y]ou must trust me', repeating it as a lullaby, despite her croaking voice, until it has the hoped-for effect: the daughter/sister leans more and more forward until the grandmother reaches with both hands and effectively saves both (123).

In Jolley's world, imagination and trust enable redemptive cherishing, and the 'possibilities of being surrounded by beauty' sustain it (69–70). These are the lessons of the 'miracle and illumination of survival' (47), that Jolley's expansive tale of 'that little art which is family life' offers its readers (133).

> *Three things emerge; one is that a mother always forgives. The second is that it is often not possible to write about events until they are over or sufficiently of the*

> *past, that they can be regarded as being in that twilight between the fact and the imagined ... And thirdly; secrets if they are revealed completely, become mere facts. Secrets, if partly kept, can be seen as relating not to some kind of imitation but to something extra to real life.*
>
> Vera Wright, in The Georges' Wife (8).

Elizabeth Jolley said, 'My fiction is not autobiographical'; 'When I write "I" in a story or a novel I do not mean I—myself'; 'I am not a *strictly* autobiographical writer'; *My Father's Moon* 'isn't an autobiographical novel by any means'; '*My Father's Moon* is probably the most autobiographical book I have written'; and 'it is very hard for me to know where truth ends and fiction begins'.[26] 'For me', she wrote, 'fiction is not a form of autobiography'[27], likely agreeing with her Melbourne Writers' Festival Irish colleague Frank Ronan, who said, '[i]f my purpose was autobiographical, I'd rather write autobiography'.[28]

So how to explain—among many such examples—Jolley's listing her grandsons Matthew, Daniel, Samuel, and their mother Ruth as newborns in the maternity hospital where Vera Wright stays on as a helper after the birth of her baby (*Cabin Fever* 148)? Or naming her own mentor Gertrude Whele as Vera's mentor, or Margarete Knight's lover Kenneth Berrington as Vera's mother's lover? Or attributing a statement by Leonard Jolley to Jonathan Metcalf ('I cannot give you all the love you deserve') and one by Joyce Jolley to Nurse Ramsden (about coming to the end of a friend or lover) in *My Father's Moon* (133, 10)? When Jolley has Vera dream that her name is Chevalier in *My Father's Moon* (54), her use of the French word for Knight recalls Jolley's birth name Monica Knight, and Monica Knight and Veronica Wright are close enough to suggest the trilogy constitutes an extended roman à clef.

She was not being coy when she said her fiction was not autobiographical, certainly not 'fictionalised autobiography', or 'confessional' or 'painful disclosure', as some critics called it.[29] She readily volunteered that some characters were based on people she knew—'Trent was modelled on a real person', she said. 'I sometimes don't know what is true about Trent and what is fiction'.[30] And she knew well what autobiographical fiction was, she said, having written a novel of that sort many years ago. The genre is too painful, she told Craven, and it can prevent an author from writing again: 'Once you let yourself be autobiographical, it's very hard to go on from that and create'.[31] Her preferred term was 'autobiographical *fiction*', one not likely to enter the critical lexicon.

What Jolley meant by autobiographical *fiction* can be illustrated by reference to a remarkable account she gave about her mother deciding to holiday for a week at the Misses Galbraith's elegant guest house in Bewdley, twenty miles south of Wolverhampton, in the summer of 1934, her father explaining that she was 'homesick'. After she leaves, Wilfrid Knight announces that he, Monica, Madelaine and her rabbit are going camping on their bicycles to a farm in Kinver, also south of Wolverhampton, where a farmer he knows will give them fresh milk and let them put up a tent in his field. The trip is predictable for his burning the potatoes in the campfire the first night, Madelaine wanting to go home and Monica wanting never to go camping again, but it is unpredictable for Knight's being in tears after a short stop along the way. And it is inexplicable for their cycling on to Bewdley the next day where Knight, dishevelled and still wearing his bicycle clips, enters the guest house to seek accommodation. As he is doing so, Margarete Knight, 'her hair loose and her cheeks flushed', enters followed by Mr Berrington in white flannels and a blue blazer. As Knight and Berrington shake hands and start to discuss the weather, Knight touches her arm but she turns away, holding Madelaine and sweeping up Monica, Madelaine saying '[w]e don't like Daddy'. When Madelaine drops her rabbit on the dining table among the vegetables and plates, and the Misses Galbraith frown, the mother laughs with tears in her eyes 'till she seemed to be laughing and crying with her whole body, but silently' (7). Jolley saw the episode with new clarity, she says, as a result of newly having spectacles.[32]

She does not include this scene in the trilogy, one that surely would figure prominently in any fictionalised autobiography. Instead, it mutates and deforms, to use Craven's words. She transmutes it into fiction that shocks in a different way: in the trilogy Vera's mother never appears to deceive her husband about a tryst, her father never surprises her and Berrington together, and the daughters are never directly drawn into their adulterous triangle. Instead, Madelaine does not appear at all, and things are suggested (when the mother goes to Berrington's house for German lessons, when the father sees the mother and daughter off on their trip to Europe) and things are implied (primarily Vera's acting-out against her mother's behaviour). In the Vera trilogy, by Jolley's not revealing such secrets, seeds of doubt are sown, suspicions become certainties, misery turns to despair, anger turns to remorse.

Jolley's point is not to document her own life—much of *Central Mischief* does that very well. Her point is to write fiction and so, as she analyses her life, she redistributes different parts of her experience of her family of origin, family of marriage and of other people she knew to different characters in different situations in her novels. She turns some truths of her experience, not just some facts of her life, into fiction. In the process she seeks to discover—as Vera does through her rigorous self-examination in her hotel room in New York—the source of Flaubert's deep and always hidden wound. For both Vera and Jolley the search involves forgiving the mother in order to re-establish the family, in the spirit of Wilfrid Knight's unshakeable belief that to know all about the other is to forgive all. For Jolley there is the further realisation that forgiving all only assuages the deep wound which the writer continues to circle, licking at it.[33]

Thus Jolley's trilogy should be a disappointment for people who read it as *autobiographical* fiction in the belief that it might be a reliable source of personal information about the author, although it no doubt will continue to titillate readers interested to know more about the players and their sexual combinations and permutations hinted at in the books. Those who read the trilogy and its coda as autobiographical *fiction* must find it an impressive tour de force for its sustained and kaleidoscopic narrative brilliance, for its scope and the depth of its vision. Perhaps no other author in Australian literature has so completely anatomised and restored a character as Jolley has Vera Wright—from *The Feast of Life* through her Vera Trilogy—in order that readers have a better perspective on life and the love that can inform it. But as for Jolley, she follows Vera's wisdom about the fact that 'secrets, if partly kept, can be seen as relating not to some kind of limitation but something extra to real life'.

> *In short, the gum tree is back. It's all very nostaglic and it would be hilarious, were it not so alarmingly insular, outmoded and dictatorial.*
>
> Helen Daniel, 'Double Cover' (8)

Elizabeth Jolley's accomplishments during the 1980s were impressive, with three major overall awards—two *Age* Book of the Year Awards and the Miles Franklin—along with significant state fiction awards, from New South Wales, Victoria and Western Australia, and academic and civic honours as well: an honorary doctorate from Curtin and an Order of Australia. She might have been disconcerted at the decision not to name any Miles Franklin winner the year *Scobie* was entered, a feeling countered by its being named the *Age* Book of the Year. But she might have been able to rationalise the ignominy of not being worthy of consideration as something that said more about Beatrice Davis as a judge than of her as a writer.

During the first half of the 1990s Jolley's literary awards were as impressive as those of the entire previous decade. In 1989 *My Father's Moon* won the *Age* Award for Imaginative Writing and its Book of the Year Award, along with the 3M Book of the Year Award. *Cabin Fever* won the ANA Gold Medal in 1990, ASAL's Gold Medal in 1991 and, on the strength of those awards, in 1992 the Society of Women Writers conferred their Biennial Award on her for a distinguished and long-term contribution to Australian literature. *The Sugar Mother* received a prize for its French translation in 1993. In the same year *Central Mischief* won the WA Premier's Historical and Critical Studies Prize and the Premier's Prize, *The Georges' Wife* won the *Age* fiction prize and shared its Book of the Year Award, as well taking out the National Book Council's Banjo Award for Fiction. Then, in 1995, *The Orchard Thieves* won the National Book Council's Banjo Award for Fiction.

In other words, the Vera trilogy and *The Orchard Thieves* won about everything in sight except, of course, the 1994 $25,000 Miles Franklin Award from which three novels were disqualified, Maurilia Meehan's *Fury*, Frank Moorhouse's *Grand Days* and Jolley's *The Georges' Wife*. The judges cringed, saying their hands were tied by the conditions of Franklin's will that required the plays and novels submitted be about Australian life 'in any of its phases'; Jill Kitson implied that anything post-modern would not get a look-in. And the critics had a field day, Daniel saying, 'On the eve of the new millennium, on the eve of the republic, in the cosmopolitan Australia of the 1990s, who would have thought combatants replaying an old war would dictate our cultural definitions? . . . In the past 30 years, from the mid-1960s to the present, there have been vast changes in our collective sense of what constitutes not only Australian writing but Australian-ness'.

Jolley had contributed to those changes in Australia's sense of itself, and she continued to do so. She continued to publish, *Diary of a Weekend Farmer* appearing in 1993 and *Fellow Passengers* in 1997, and other publications focused still more attention on her, like the 1990 Festival of Perth production of *The Newspaper of Claremont Street* and the 1996 production of *Another Holiday for the Prince*—a young-adult publication of the short story from *Five Acre Virgin*—and Delys Bird's *Off the Air*, a collection of nine of Jolley's radio plays.

From the publication of *My Father's Moon* in 1989 onward, Jolley published an average of a book every other year for the rest of her career. In the last half of the decade there were three more, *Lovesong* (1997), *An Accommodating Spouse* (1999), and *An Innocent Gentleman* (2001). Delys Bird has spoken about them (and *The Orchard Thieves*) by way of Edward Said's posthumous essay 'Timeliness and Lateness' which says that 'later work which may have been seen as chaotic, lacking structure and control and so on, actually displays a radical refusal to lessen thematic or structural tensions. Late style thus may be marked by intransigence, difficulty and unresolved contradiction'.[34]

Although Jolley was seventy-two when *Lovesong* was published, she was neither unwell nor focused on thoughts of death, nor were the characters in her last three books. To the contrary, they seem preoccupied with life and living, however difficult, improbable or complicated their circumstances. While some readers might disregard Jolley's last three books as chaotic, lacking structure and control and more, what is most remarkable about them is how they recapitulate Jolley's entire oeuvre from three different points of view, the first book focusing on the sexual outsider and the other two on the family, according to Bird one of them in a low-comic way and the other in a high-comic one.

Dalton Foster in *Lovesong* is one of Jolley's 'sexual outsiders', someone who lives outside the norms of heterosexual monogamy because his needs are not congruent with it—or, as Jolley said, is someone 'with leanings towards what would be affection in the wrong way according to a good deal of society'.[35] He has a pronounced interest in a young girl in the park, and before his arrival in Australia there was a provocative encounter between a soprano choir boy and Dalton, a counter-tenor, in Kings College Chapel. That was followed by Dalton's spending half his life institutionalised while undergoing a 'cure'—Jill Kitson says he was in a prison hospital and that the cure was for paedophilia.[36]

Each of Jolley's previous novels had at least one sexual outsider, from Andrea in *Palomino*, through Louise in *Milk and Honey*, Martin Scobie in *Scobie's Riddle*, Diane Hopewell in *Peabody*, Dr Steadman in *Foxybaby*, and, Edwin Page in *The Sugar Mother*. Of course, Vera Wright is a sexual outsider in the Vera trilogy, especially so when she participates in the ménage à trois with the phthisic brother–sister pair Noël and Felicity. Likewise, Jolley was a sexual outsider for more than a decade. Whatever *Lovesong* is about, Dalton Foster suffers from Jolley's characters' common condition, one characterised by homelessness, lovelessness and loneliness.

An Accommodating Spouse is a parody of domesticity. Once more there is a comparison with *The Sugar Mother*, the protagonist, like Edwin Page, an English migrant who lectures on literature in an Australian university. If Jolley critiques society's institutionalising marriage as normative and valorises heterosexual pairing as preferred over triangular relationships, this novel is like a ship of fools whose passenger list is entirely comprised of love-seekers like the ones Aristophanes imagined: Jolley has redrawn marital boundaries and compartmentalised them to accommodate Delaware Carpenter, a twin, who marries Hazel, a twin, whose sister Chloë seems part of the bargain, for she is sometimes a stand-in (as it were) for Hazel, perhaps as respite for Hazel to produce triplet daughters; and, in a distorted echo of *The Sugar Mother*, Delaware is encouraged by Hazel to serve as a sperm donor-in-vivo to half of a lesbian pair who want to have a child. Thus he will be their Sugar Daddy as Leila was Edwin's Sugar Mother. In its revision of the concept of the ideal family, *An Accommodating Spouse* substitutes the ménage à trois as something beyond comme il faut and approaching de rigueur. This is the low comedy Delys Bird speaks of, one tending toward farce.

Finally, *An Innocent Gentleman* is what Jolley avoided for the whole of her career, a roman à clef. Set during World War II in the English Midlands, it features Henry Bell (a maths teacher at the Central School), his wife Muriel Bell (an Austrian woman who teaches German at night school) and family friend Mr. H. (for Hawthorne, KC)[37], a wealthy barrister who sits on a conscientious-objectors' tribunal and studies German with Mrs Bell, who dines with the Bells every Sunday, and who meets her in London where they attend the opera *Fidelio* and stay together in a hotel. In addition, there are the Bells' two unnamed young daughters who are at risk of sexual predation by an odd young man, Victor, who seems to live under bridges—an experience not unlike the predation depicted in Jolley's story 'Clever and Pretty'. It is no wonder that Jolley's sister Madelaine did not like the book for the bad memories it invoked of her bad Knight family-of-origin experiences.

What Jolley adds to the mix is a mother for Mrs Bell and an extramarital sex life for Mr Bell—perhaps poetic justice at last for both. And what she takes to a logical conclusion is the import of her own line from 'Of Butchers and Bilberry Baskets' which this time she puts in the mouth of Mr Bell, at first said reproachfully and then wonderingly, when he thinks/speaks of '[a] woman loved by two men and neither of them can give up their love for her' (93).[38] Jolley has Muriel conceive and deliver a baby sired by Hawthorne but named by Henry, as Leopold. Despite many odd elements, including a pseudo-medieval joust with headlocks and headbutts between Hawthorne, 'the Cad', and Bell, 'the Accessory' (237–8), a stasis is reached and the ménage à trois becomes the permanent geometrical configuration of the family. When Mrs Tonkinson, a seer, leans over the baby as Henry is out pushing the pram, she says that the next baby will be a boy and will be his (252). The scene recalls Heather Hailey saying, after being told by Frances in *Scobie* that her first baby is by Hartley but her next one will be by her husband Horry, 'it seems a reasonable plan' (210). This is the high comedy, tending toward romance.

The comedy of *An Innocent Gentleman* deflects attention from the seriousness of the book to Jolley herself: the simplistic conventions of the roman à clef facilitate her effectively speaking directly about what she had previously symbolised through her use of family-like structures or implied through her redistributing autobiographical elements to various characters and situations in her novels. In *An Innocent Gentleman* she reimagines her experience of the fury that haunted the Knight family household, in the process reaffirming that whether some, none, or all of the characters in the novel are innocent or guilty is, for her, a secondary concern at best. As Elaine Lindsay writes, judgement is anathema to Jolley because 'the circumstances of peoples' lives are so far beyond their control that it is impossible to condemn anyone outright for their behaviour'. Or as her father would say, to know all is to forgive all. But that did not stop Jolley from continuing to circle and lick at the wound.

An Innocent Gentleman reaches back to the project Jolley conceived as *Eleanor Page* more than fifty years previously, a novel to feature 'the old house and the upstairs nursing home'. That image finds expression in *Milk and Honey* through Waldemar's one-room asylum in the attic provided by his Aunts Rosa and Heloise and then again in *Mr Scobie's Riddle* in the nursing home where Price and Hailey live; and it finds other expression in Fairfields, White Pines and Trinity College, all schools run by live-in Principals or Headmistresses and their companions. Even when ironic, those novels are utopian for their focus on the struggle to create and maintain an ideal family unit which reaches out to homeless and loveless deracinated people in the world. Jolley's British experiences made her hypersensitive to people who needed various kinds of special care, like the refugees her mother took in during the 1930s, the children she met at Sibford and Pinewood, and the patients she dealt with in the Pyrford and the Queen Elizabeth Hospitals. In Australia her impulse to care sometimes manifested itself in confronting ways: there were dying men she bathed—Andrew Dungey, Joseph Lamb, the husband of the customer on her Watkins rounds, her Curtin student and her teaching colleague with HIV/AIDS—and women in need that she attended to—Edith Lamb, Mrs Dreery, Ludmila Blotnicki, and the women she visited in Bandyup Prison. Those experiences suffuse her early novels. Then, from *My Father's Moon* on, Jolley came progressively to realise that her parents were also in need of special understanding, if not special care. Unlike the end-of-career writers Edward Said speaks of, in *An Innocent Gentleman* Jolley's imagination created a home not unlike the one previewed for *Eleanor Page*, a home where her biological and honorary parents—Wilfrid and Margarete Knight and Kenneth Berrington—enact their own ways of doing life. It was an understanding and loving vision of Monica Knight's family home, one that only after Vera Wright's painful meditations could Jolley at last write about without judgement but with empathetic understanding.

> Elizabeth Jolley has had perhaps the most meteoric rise to fame of any Australian writer during the last quarter of the twentieth century.
>
> Laurie Clancy, 'Elizabeth Jolley'

Andrew E. was right. In the late 1990s Elizabeth Jolley seemed to be everywhere.

In the first half of the 1990s she was robust, acute and active, even choosing to have a pelvic floor repair in November 1991 while she was strong enough not to be too much knocked around by it, although it took more out of her than she expected. Typically, she wrote about that too, in 'Manchester Repair', calling it by the name used in her QEH days. In 1992 she lectured for a fortnight at the University of Melbourne in August and continued making country tours. In 1993 she gave three lectures at the University of Sydney in March and attended the Canberra Word Fest in April, in November meeting with twenty book clubs that had gathered together in Albany. And in 1994 she read at the Sydney Writers' Festival and spoke to the Australian National University/*Canberra Times* Literary Luncheon.

After the success of the Vera trilogy and *The Orchard Thieves*, the continuing appearance of another novel every other year or so until 2001 kept her image in the public's mind. And her willingness to perform at literary festivals, to address professional societies, schools and community groups—providing such good value when she did so—maintained her momentum. Although she only received one more award, the TDK Australian Audio Book Award for *An Accommodating Spouse* in 2000, *Lovesong* was shortlisted for the 1998 Miles Franklin Award and was second on the *Age's* best-selling fiction list in July 1997, the *Weekend Australian's* number eleven in August and in the *Australian Book Review's* top ten in September.[40]

As a result, between 1995 and 2000 her talks, lectures, workshops, readings, launching of others' books and judging competitions averaged one every three weeks. They included an overseas trip—in 1996, to give the keynote address at the conference of the European Association for Commonwealth Literature and Languages Studies (EACLALS) in Oviedo, Spain—and two or three interstate trips per year to the major writers' festivals in Canberra and all of the states, concluding with the Melbourne Writers' Festival in 2001. Her functions also included a great many community presentations: as an example, in March 1995, in addition to appearing on a panel at the Perth Writers' Festival, her other activities in Perth were giving a talk to the Austcare Refugee Literary Program, addressing work-in-progress seminars at the University of Western Australia, running workshops for teachers at Scarborough Senior High School and presenting a lecture to the students at Presbyterian Ladies' College. She declined an offer to speak and read at the week-long Hong Kong International Festival of Literature held in 2002 because she did not want to travel overseas again. The period also included Margaret Throsby's ABC FM interview with her in 1997, two interviews with Ramona Koval and one with Phillip Adams in 1999—as Andrew E. rightly recalled.

A turning point was the 1996–97 period. Her dear friend Hannah Levey from Perth in the 1960s died in Melbourne in January 1996. A year later, on Monday 3 January 1997, a fire swept through the hills east of Perth, destroying a dozen residences, including the bush block and cottage the Jolleys bought in the hills in the 1970s. She did not keep any books or manuscripts at Wooroloo, but there were mementos only she knew the value of, including a piece of silverware from the train she travelled on with her mother and Mr Berrington sixty years before. She received dozens of letters of consolation from friends and from people she did not know. Then her sister's husband Tony Blackmore died in May of 1997, rendering Jolley helpless as she tried to console Madelaine by telephone.

The same period was also a watershed professionally. While no doubt it is a high honour to be named one of Australia's Living National Treasures, as Jolley was in 1997, or named a State Living Treasure, as she was in 1998, any such a honour might also be an omen. That is particularly so if followed by a citation as an Outstanding Citizen by the Claremont Liberal Party and a Commonwealth Recognition Award for Senior Citizens for her 'significant contribution to the community' in 2000, and by a Centenary Medal in 2003 to commemorate 'those who contributed to Australia's first hundred years as a federal nation' and also a commissioned portrait by Mary Moore for the National Portrait Gallery in Canberra. Jolley made light of those honours in a self-deprecating but not disrespectful way. Yet she was aware of an irony in government bestowing honours on someone best remembered for writing novels about lesbians and paedophiles, even if they were prize-winning novels, and even if she were a grandmother from one of the better suburbs.

Even Ramona Koval was caught in the irony about how Jolley and her books were perceived: in an interview after the publication of *Lovesong*, she described Dalton Foster as a paedophile, and Jolley simply replied, 'I don't say he is a paedophile at all in the book'. She said she was inspired to write the book by work she did some twenty years before with women inmates of Perth's Bandyup Prison and male prisoners in Fremantle's maximum-security jail; she was moved when she thought of the loneliness such men faced when they returned to the community. Naturally Koval back-pedalled, acknowledging that Jolley's and the reader's sympathy was with Dalton 'who is doing his best to overcome something over which he has very little control'. But she had read what wasn't written, like the ladies of the Tuart Club who could only think of lesbians when they read *Miss Peabody's Inheritance*, and she had broadcast it nationally. Then Koval went on to distance herself from Rosemary Sorenson's on-air review on the same program which began by saying *Lovesong* is '[t]oo wispy and it's much too queer ... It is just too slippery to be grabbed and held and cared about'.

The program took on quite a different tone when call-in listener Lisa of Torquay said she appreciated how Jolley did not take the 'darkness' out of Dalton's character, did not make a moral judgement about 'deviancies that we all have'. What interested her was 'the progression of the character's own insight'. Then a Helen said reading Jolley's books was one of the great highlights of her life. 'You stagger me', she told Jolley, 'and I love to be staggered . . . I like the way the characters are such a mix of vulnerability and frailty, knowledge, insights, resilience and beauty. Nobody is ever cheapened or scorned . . .' Jolley's call-in listeners knew about Dalton's loneliness.

> *Writing is an act of love carried out in such a way that every aspect of the personality can be examined, not for criticism but for an endless questioning towards a hoped for understanding.*
>
> 'A Timid Confidence' (175–6)

> *She was in the middle of a sentence when she died.*
>
> Matron Flourish, of Diana Hopewell in *Miss Peabody's Inheritance* (145)

> *Wer spricht von Siegen? Überstehn ist alles.—Who talks of victory? To hold out is all.*
>
> 'Who Talks of Victory?' (59)

When Elizabeth Jolley's three-year professorial appointment expired at the end of 2001, Vice Chancellor Lance Twomey asked if she would like it renewed for two years. She said that she would, repeating what she had often said previously, that she wanted to teach as long as possible but wanted colleagues to tell her when she should stop; and so it was renewed. During the first semester of 2001, instead of having face-to-face classroom work, she chose to make herself available to honours and graduate students for consultations in second semester. During the first semester of 2002 a colleague drove her to Curtin whenever she chose to come to the office to attend to her mail and socialise with colleagues and students. Barbara Milech helped her compose her last essay, 'The Little Dance in Writing', that appeared in a Curtin publication in mid 2002. Her last public function was to attend the Annual Elizabeth Jolley Lecture given by Barry Humphries in June of 2002.

She entered the Alfred Carson Hospital on Tuesday 20 August 2002. Some time earlier she had surrendered her driver's licence but kept her automobile—she had had trouble driving at night and thought it wise to have the vehicle for times when it might be convenient for friends to use it to take her places. The proximate cause of her admission to the Alfred Carson was that she had become unsteady on her feet and had a tendency to become confused. Her doctors imagined that she might, unnoticed, have suffered TIA's (transient ischaemic attacks) or 'little bleeds' from blood vessels in her brain, their cumulative effects causing one or both of those problems.

Her confusion was episodic, or at least varying in its severity, and at times it had the quality of lucid dreaming. At one point, while being driven back from Wooroloo where she had made ritualistic checks of her orchard and cottage, she said that she did not want to be late returning home because Leonard would be concerned. Having said that, she immediately explained that she knew Leonard was dead but at times it seemed as if he were not, and those times seemed as real to her as the other ones; she felt that she had to be true to both times. Similarly, reality and imagination conflated in a recurrent dream of this period: in the middle of the night someone brought a busload of Aboriginal children to her home; they rummaged through the drawers in her room, then sat in the lounge room in the dark where their bright eyes stared at her throughout the night; and in the morning the man who had brought them took them away again.

She told her son Richard she fell down the laundry steps and that a Curtin colleague suggested she have her heart checked, which she said she did, receiving a favourable diagnosis. But she did not seem to have any injuries, and Richard was unable to decide whether or not the fall or the subsequent events she described had actually occurred. Another time, while a friend was waiting to take her to lunch, the friend and Richard heard a crash in Jolley's room which turned out to be the television falling over, the VCR on top of it smashing into the fireplace. This time a doctor diagnosed a Vitamin B_{12} deficiency which could cause falls, for which she prescribed regular injections. Around this same time Richard arranged for her to have a discussion with the family doctor, the three of them reluctantly agreeing that it would be best for her to take up residency in the Alfred Carson, something the doctor undertook to arrange. During the early hours a week before she was scheduled to move, she fell during the night and Richard put her back in bed. When he called the Alfred Carson in the morning, they agreed to receive her that day.

During her four-and-a-half year stay there, Richard was her daily caretaker, monitoring her health and treatment, and her daughter Ruth visited with her husband and boys. Jolley had many visitors, their numbers dwindling with her further decline, until her main ones were Delys Bird, a friend and colleague from the University of Western Australia, Barbara Milech and Brian Dibble, both from Curtin, and Nancy McKenzie, Jolley's typist for more than thirty years. Lucy Frost of the University of Tasmania visited, as well as Barry Humphries the year after his Elizabeth Jolley lecture, Caroline Lurie, and Helen Garner, Garner writing touchingly of her experience afterwards.[41]

In 'Who Talks of Victory?' (59) Jolley wrote, 'No one comes out on top in my fiction—not even Miss Thorne—but they all—Weekly, Miss Peabody and Mr Scobie—would endorse the apostle's injunction, "and having done all, to stand".[42] Having become unresponsive to her carers, she stopped eating a week or two before she died in her sleep in the early morning of Tuesday 13 February 2007. The following Friday there was a private ceremony of a dozen friends and family members at Karrakatta Cemetery. They read from *Cymbeline*, Psalm 39 and *Mr Scobie's Riddle* and listened to passages from Brahms' *German Requiem*, which she had wanted, Mozart's *Requiem*, and Schubert's *Winterreise*.

In memory of Elizabeth Jolley, Peter Craven wrote what many felt: 'She was the sublime master of the point where comic capering and human desolation meet and she was also a calm chronicler of the quiet ways the human heart gets its scars'.[43]

Epilogue—Friendship has a meaning that goes both ways...

Friends have the power to find, together, a philosophy that can make human life endurable.
Elizabeth Jolley, 'More than Just Mates' (1)

Elizabeth Jolley was especially preoccupied with love, its possibility and potential, including its potential for failure and what happens then. She knew that what love and war had in common was that each would come to an end and that in each people inevitably suffered. If pacifism was her preferred alternative to war, friendship, not withdrawal, was her alternative to love. Like pacifism, friendship required work and had its own strengths and liabilities.

Just as Kenneth Berrington underscored Robert Louis Stevenson's remark in *Virginibus Puerisque*, that love is 'a business of some importance', Jolley came to emphasise friendship as a matter of importance, 'one involving kindness and goodwill'. 'An acquaintance', Jolley wrote, 'should not be confused with a friend'.[1] Nor should her idea of friendship be confused with the compassion she often felt for others, for example, for the Lambs and Andrew Dungey, fellow feeling that made *caritas*—caressing, cherishing—virtually imperative for her. That imperative had roots in the feelings of homelessness she experienced across twenty years, from Wells Road to Paisley Crescent, and in the question of who-loves-whom-more that she encountered both in her family home and during her days as an unwed mother in Birmingham and at Pinewood. Similarly, Jolley's sense of friendship is not be confused with the sort of dependency she displayed in several of her relationships as a young woman, especially with her mentors Gertrude Whele and Joyce and Leonard Jolley.

In a late essay, she cites Ralph Waldo Emerson's description of a friend as 'a person with whom ... I may think aloud', concurring with his saying that 'the only way to have a friend is to be one'.[2] 'Friendship, like love', she concludes, 'has to be sincere. It requires complete trust between the people and it requires the ability to give and to accept without reservation'. Her writing came to distinguish friendship from love for its neither demanding love's desire for a perfect, exclusive, unending harmony, nor its ignoring another's foibles and failings. Rather, Jolley's imagination of friendship involves a form of John Keats' negative capability, a capacity to appreciate someone else's qualities. Such capacity—an ability to recognise another's sameness and difference from oneself—allowed her to establish and to maintain boundaries, boundaries that distinguish friendship from love's ideal of an at-oneness with the other. Those boundaries were important in several ways. They validated Jolley's having her own life and trusting others to have theirs, although that element of friendship sometimes was at odds with her disposition to compassion, as in the case of Ludmila Blotnicki. They accommodated the failure or dissolution of a friendship. And they provided the structure for a rich substitute for love when love failed: thus Elizabeth's description in the mid-1980s of her marriage to Leonard—it was, she said, a 'total trusting friendship'.[3]

In Australia her first such friend was Hannah Levey. She and Hannah were two of many UWA acquaintances who looked after each others' children and drove them here and there in the early days in Perth. They were, however, more than acquaintances. 'Hannah is the one person to whom I can turn for advice', Jolley said. 'She sees straight through things while I blunder around'. And Levey said of Jolley that she 'helped me to see things. She has made me much more aware'—'The word friendship has a meaning that goes both ways, Elizabeth and I'.[4]

When Stuart Reid asked in 1988, 'Are you really friendless ... ? Jolley said that, beyond her husband, she was 'not intimate with a great number of people', nominating Perth biographer Julie Lewis, poet and novelist Tom Shapcott, and her agent Caroline Lurie as three people she could confide in.[5] What is significant in that brief, tactful catalogue of intimate friendships is that both Shapcott and Lurie were largely epistolary friends—just as Helen Garner, who wrote one of the best early appreciations of Jolley's work, became an epistolary friend[6]—a mode of friendship that carries with it built-in boundaries that sustain intimacy.

The more widely known Jolley became through her fiction, her work with book clubs and her teaching, the more readers and students wrote to her. In time, given the availability of her books in Australia and overseas (a number translated into various languages), and given her many publicity tours and attendance at writers' festivals and academic conferences, she received letters from people she did not know or had only met briefly. They included a German soi-disant aristocrat who promised to favour her in his will if she would only copy out a paragraph for him from one of her novels; an Italian woman who, Jolley said, was 'growing up' by writing to her; and, increasingly, graduate students who wrote to her wanting to be told such things as why she quoted Brahms on page 21 of *Foxybaby*. There was also a James Jolley in England, a man she did not know, who for reasons she never could fathom faithfully posted her newspaper clippings about writers and occasional photographs of paintings he had done, and a lonely Sibford old scholar who, retired from the navy and living in Sydney, sent her packets of overlong poems he had written. And often there were packets of appreciative letters from teachers and students from the schools where she gave talks. Except for the German man, everyone received an answer, however brief, even if Jolley addressed some of the young students through their teachers. When the poet received Jolley's response, he would send her more poems by return mail.[7]

Along with such correspondence, she maintained epistolary friendships with people she had known from childhood, such as her Sibford teacher, Gladys Burgess, until Burgess died, and the Naylors, her English and Art teachers, for the rest of her life. Similarly, her Sibford schoolmates Libby Wood-Thompson and Edith Worrall corresponded regularly, leading to their visiting Jolley in Perth in the 1990s, fifty years after they had last seen each other. In addition, she corresponded with friends like Fairlie Sezacinski (pronounced Sez-inski) whom she met when Sezacinski visited Perth from Melbourne in the 1960s to look after her sister's children while she and her husband were away—her sister Prue and Dick Joske lived two doors from the Jolleys in Parkway. Jolley, still unpublished, took Sezacinski to a meeting of the Fellowship of Australian Writers which interested Sezacinski who, though ten years younger, already had a publication record. Writing served as the basis of their subsequent correspondence which lasted forty years, until Jolley's death.

Her letter-writing had three key elements. She responded to the matters raised in the letter last received, sharing in the other's joys and successes, sympathising with concerns and offering practical advice as she could—'A quick word to ask if you are all right', her 2 July 1993 letter to Fairlie Sezacinski began. Next, she often responded in kind with information about the recent events of her own life. This second part of her letters sometimes shaded into the third aspect of Jolley's epistolary friendships, to ruminating on matters of concern to her, to what Sezacinski, unconsciously echoing Emerson, called 'thinking out loud'. Thus, for example, on 13 September 1995, she told Sezacinski she had been 'helped by our friendship, your friendship, over all these years', going on to meditate on Leonard's unhappiness after he moved to the Alfred Carson Home and his wanting to return to his own home:

> When he described <u>his house</u> he had stairs in it and a billiard room (the house in Glasgow where we lived) and a view of the Firth of Forth (the house in Edinburgh where we lived) and he thought the verandah, where we were sitting, belonged to a lady who might not like us to be sitting there. So you see I have plenty of thoughts at 3 a.m.

Thus her letter-writing could be an occasion for intimacy and self-healing.

Like Hannah Levey, Fairlie Sezacinski became Jolley's friend before she was any sort of public figure and, like Hannah, found that Jolley's fame did not change a long friendship based on trust and the knowledge that the other would 'understand'. Sezacinski always looked forward to receiving a letter from Jolley, after which she would put on the kettle, make a cuppa and then sit down and read. For her, a letter from Jolley was 'a wave from afar'.[8]

The intimate, ruminative aspect of Jolley's epistolary friendships was closely tied to her writing. In more than one place, Jolley tells how corresponding with her father enabled her to begin writing a piece of fiction: 'I would often write to my father what I was writing about, then I would leave his letter and start writing. That was a great help'.[9] After her father died, she felt a 'curious bereavement ... of not writing letters' and, years later, said, 'I go on talking to him in my head, now, even when I am grown up and old'.[10] Confident from childhood of her father's love and guidance, in adulthood Jolley found a kind of friendship in their correspondence, a space to think out loud with someone trusted. And, tellingly, she found a kind of rapprochement with her mother through letters: '. . . we didn't get on very well. We got on better in letter-writing than we did when we were together'.[11]

After her father's death, Jolley reflected on leaving her family behind in England when migrating to Australia, concluding, 'It's funny, I never really missed my family, but I missed the letter-writing'.[12] Being half-way around the world and decades away from her family home gave her one sort of distance, but being in touch with her parents through letters gave her boundaries that enabled her to re-imagine the central drama in her life: her mother's and father's life with Kenneth Berrington. Like writing fiction, friendship conducted through letters was effective in 'arriving at unexpected conclusions'.[13] Those conclusions produced the stunning sequence of the Berrington essays, the Vera novels, the Bewdley essay, and her last novel, *An Innocent Gentleman*.

Jolley was a remarkable essayist, as well as novelist, who often spoke eloquently about her sense of fiction's purpose. She spoke about wanting to write 'with tenderness and hopefulness and a kind of optimism' about 'the inside of people's survival'; and she thought the purpose of fiction was to 'increase awareness of human life', and so it had to be 'larger than life'.[14] She frequently said that writing was a 'stepping off into imagination' from experience and memories, and she thought that readers took a comparable step into imagination, that 'reading was very creative'.[15] Thus her habit of telling stories through juxtapositions of narrative events, and the resultant 'sophisticated spaces' she provided readers.[16] Those sophisticated spaces are akin to the space provided by friendship's boundaries—a space one person provides for another in which to think things that are important to each. Elizabeth Jolley's fiction provides its readers 'a sort of a gift'—the gift of friendship.

NOTES

Introduction—That little art which is family life . . .
1. 'Should a book . . . have a message'. From the opening pages of a manuscript by Elizabeth Jolley begun 15 Mar. 1956, alternately called *A Feast of Life* or *The Feast of Life*, and written until the early 1960s across eight notebooks.
2. Hazel Rowley. In conversation.
3. 'Scenes', and 'intimate epic'. Sisman, pp. 170-2, and Huntington, p. 72.
4. 'Complexly remembered'. See Wilson, p. 16.
5. Don't ask questions. Fonseca, p. 14.

1 'Flowermead'—The fury haunting the family . . .
1. Freud and Knight. Michael Hill told both anecdotes to Brian Dibble. The family story is that Wilfrid Knight met his wife in Vienna while with a Quaker relief mission, but Quaker archives at Friends House in London do not support this, neither the British Quaker weekly *The Friend* for 1921 or 1922, nor Clark, Fry or Spielhofer's authoritative books. The typed index of the Friends Relief and Emergency Committee Workers lists a Charles Knight who went from England to Poland on 21 Feb. 1921, returning via Austria 21 Apr. and going back to Poland 21 June, but this is likely a Charles Knight more than a decade older than Charles Wilfrid Knight. The two stories are compatible: whether Wilfrid Knight's meeting with Freud was successful or otherwise, it is not at all unlikely that he would have joined such a mission while there.

Notes

2   The Sermon on the Mount. Letter from W. Knight to E. Jolley, c. 1936.

3   Margarete. Her German spelling of her Austrian Christian name was Margarethe, and her Austrian nickname was Grete, pronounced 'Gray-tuh'. In England she dropped the 'h' to form Margarete, pronounced 'Mar-ga-ray-tuh', and sometimes used Margaret. In England she discouraged the use of her shortened name because it was variously pronounced 'Gree-ta', 'Greet-a', or (by her mother-in-law) 'Gret-ta'. For the most part, Margarete is used here throughout '(e.g., in her letters to Gabriel Horn)'.

4   *Ein stadtbekannter Sonderling.* Rotter, p. 264.

5   Karl, Alexander, Joseph and Walter Fehr's military records. Held in the Kriegsarchiv and the Arkiv der Republik in Vienna. According to Chisholm, 'The crushing victory won by Admiral von Tegetthoff over the Italian fleet in 1866 [at Lyssa] had the same mystique for the Habsburg navy as Trafalgar had for the Royal Navy'.

6   Austrian Rear Admiral. In the Australian Army context, Alexander Fehr would have been about four levels below Lieutenant-General Peter Cosgrove.

7   Never served on the bench. There is no record in Vienna's Palais Justiz of Joseph Edward Fehr having been a judge; in fact, there is no record of him at all.

8   Joseph Edward Fehr. A man of strongly held beliefs, he joined the Altkatholisch Kirche, a breakaway group founded in the 1870s by Austria's Roman Catholics who disagreed with Pope Pius IX who declared popes to be infallible when speaking ex cathedra. On the terminal illness of his wife when he was forty-four, he stopped work and became a 'house father', looking after his five children with the help of the oldest, Johanna. He championed the beneficial effects of cold-water baths, building one in the basement of Florianigasse 2 and encouraging the other residents to use it. During his peregrinations about Vienna he also practised what he preached, sometimes being arrested for swimming naked in the Danube where it flows through central Vienna. He was, in other words, the sort of relative who achieves mythic stature in family history, a condition often enhanced by early death. He died of tuberculosis at fifty-six, eight years before Margarete Fehr was born.

9   'But not in those words'. But love lived in those words in the first scene of Steiner's play *Die Pforte der Einweihung* (roughly, *The Portal of Consecration*) when Johannes Thomasius remembers the girl he left behind who wastes away from having her hopes dashed. See Lindenberg, p. 138. Radegunde was born in 1868; her death date is unknown. She is last recorded as living at Florianigasse 2 in 1904.

10 Quarrel. Madelaine Knight Blackmore in conversation with Dibble.

11 Margareta. This spelling of her name may have been her actual birth name, and her use of Margarete in England a convenience of her choice.

12 'I will bless you...' 1 Moses 12:2. The bible was in the possession of Madelaine Knight Blackmore.

Notes

13   'Be kind to her...' Madelaine Knight Blackmore in conversation with Dibble.
14   Mrs Moore. In 'My Sister Dancing' Jolley writes of visiting Mrs Moore with her sister Madelaine in Charlbury, Oxfordshire, when she was ten.
15   Monica. Letter from W. Knight to E. Jolley, 16 Oct. 1967.
16   Grandfather's letters. Letters from C. Knight ostensibly to Monica Knight: 24 Dec. 1923—the expectation that she will attend Girton or Newnham (Cambridge colleges), waste not/want not, hope her father will return to preaching and her mother mend her ways; 23 Dec. 1924—will give her father £50 to take an honours degree, her parents should have no more children; and, 3 June 1926—stay away from the pond ('if you die, it would break my heart') and ask her mother to take her to church.
17   'Flowermead'. They did not own it, although it might have been built for them to rent.
18   Knight writing books. Jolley says in '"What Sins"' that '[h]e wrote two textbooks for school children. The one on heat had a red cover and the one on light was blue' (p. 1). A copy of the heat book is held in the British Library.
19   A sleeping grandmother, horses and manure. Reid, p. 3.
20   The farthings. Reid, p. 3.
21   The boiling water. Reid, p. 2.
22   What Daisy did. According to a letter from Patti Knight to her husband's nephew, Ewart Knight, 17 Nov. 1938, Daisy taught Art. In a 14 Oct. 1936 letter to him she said Daisy had bilious attacks at least weekly along with depression and headaches of long standing; and in a 17 Nov. 1938 letter she wrote that Daisy 'is not very strong' and does not like her mentioning the fact.
23   Auntie Maud. Letter from C. Knight to Monica Knight, 3 June 1924, about how shocked Auntie Maud will be to hear that she has not been christened. Auntie Maud's/Anti Mote's identity remains problematic. Charles Knight mentions Maud in his 3 June 1924 Christmas letter, and 'Auntie Maud' wrote to Monica Knight from Oakbridge House, Ilkley, Leeds, on 19 May 1925, to thank her for sending presents, Leeds being where her half-sister Patti Knight was from. Yet both Jolley and her sister remembered her as having a German accent, and she is represented that way in 'One Christmas Knitting' where she speaks German ('*Guten Tag! Grüss Gott...*' [129]) whereas her letter to Monica contains no suggestion of being written by anyone but a native English-speaking person. The fact that the narrator of 'One Christmas Knitting' also says Maud is a baroness (123) rings warning bells, perhaps suggesting that she admired Margarete Knight and mimicked her speech and other characteristics.
24   Sheldon household, speech and knickers. Jolley in conversation with Dibble, Aug. 1996.

Notes

25 '727 Chester Road'. This is the title of a subsection of the essay 'Strange Regions There Are', pp. 118–20.
26 Saints are very nice. Ilse Gaugusch in conversation with Dibble, July 1997.
27 Rowing on the Severn. Ilse Gaugusch in conversation with Dibble, July 1997.
28 Marx's Credo. Letter from W. Knight to E. Jolley, 31 July 1977.
29 His opposition to sexism. Letter from W. Knight to E. Jolley, 20 Dec. 1970.
30 If someone attacked Knight's granddaughter. Ilse Gaugusch in conversation with Dibble, July 1997.
31 Atheist or agnostic. Madelaine Knight Blackmore in conversation with Dibble said her mother 'believed in something' but never joined anything.
32 Wilfrid Knight's overcoats. Cotton, 'Wordly Wise', p. 14.
33 'Glad to live in a monarchy'. Letter from M. Knight to G. Horn, 16 Nov. 1978.
34 Grumbling. Letter from M. Knight to E. Jolley, 18 Nov. 1973.
35 'I am not very fond of women...' Wilfrid and Margarete Knight, audiocassette, 9 June 1978.
36 Poor Nazis/good anti-Semites. Ignatieff, p. 24.
37 Blacks, and Jews. Postscripts on letter from W. Knight to E. Jolley, 16 Dec. 1973, and 4 Apr. 1940.
38 Striking dustmen. Letter from W. Knight to E. Jolley, 11 Oct. 1970, with a postscript from M. Knight.
39 Enoch Powell. M. Knight in a postscript on a letter from W. Knight to E. Jolley, 24 Apr. 1968.
40 Margarete Knight and racism. Letter from M. Knight to G. Horn, 19 Aug. 1978.
41 Hitler. Sorenson, 'Jolley Reveals Idyllic Time in Hitler Camp', p. 3.
42 Phone call to Hitler. Letter from W. Knight to E. Jolley, 25 Sept. 1941.
43 Hitler's speech. See also 10 Oct. 1939.
44 Blowing a fuse over Hitler. Letter from M. Knight to E. Jolley, 1 Nov. 1939.
45 The anti-Semitic tradition. Ignatieff, p. 24.
46 School lunches, German language and fieldtrips at Bilston. Reid, p. 25.
47 Caring for students, memorable to them. In conversation with Dibble, Michael Hill told of praying with Knight, and Bob Hazlehurst spoke of Knight's behaviour in the classroom.
48 Mr Jones the piano teacher. Jolley in conversation with Dibble. The event prefigures Martin Scobie's apparent indiscretion as a piano teacher with a young girl in *Mr Scobie's Riddle*.
49 Anger in the household. Reid, p. 22.
50 Sparks from his boots, and Melanie Klein. Jolley's memory of her father's boots striking sparks as he walked is a recurrent one, most evocatively remembered in 'One Christmas Knitting', p. 119. Perhaps a gesture toward sex education, around the same time Wilfrid Knight took Monica to visit

257

Notes

	Melanie Klein, he took her to hear Margaret Mead speak, an exercise she found embarrassing (Jolley in conversation with Dibble).
51	How well Madelaine was doing. Letter from Patti Knight to Ewart Knight, 14 Oct. 1936.
52	Wanting to be just like Margarete. Doris Horobin in conversation with Dibble.
53	Arriving/departing au pairs. Reid, p. 7.
54	Ilse Fehr in tears, Margarete reproaching Madelaine. Jolley and Madelaine Knight Blackmore in conversations with Dibble.
55	Refugees in the home, Wilfrid Knight helping them from the station, the girls unhappy. Reid, p. 15–6.
56	Margarete not happy in England. Esther Roitman von Wartburg in conversation with Dibble.
57	The best teacher. Gottfried Leiser in conversation with Dibble.
58	'You were taking cups...' Letter from M. Knight to G. Horn, 1 Apr. 97. The line is Tamino's in Mozart's *Die Zauberflöte*: 'Help... Otherwise I'm lost'.
59	Passing judgement. Gottfried Leiser in conversation with Dibble.
60	'No woman is good enough...', and 'you looked so handsome'. Letter from M. Knight to G. Horn, 7 Jan., and 10 June 1977.
61	*Virginibus Puerisque*. The underlined passage appears on p. 119, along with the marginal note 'very important!'
62	Berrington's military service. Madelaine Knight Blackmore in conversation with Dibble. Conscription did not start until 1916. Various people refused or avoided commissions for different reasons, like H. H. Munro ('Saki') who claimed it would be inappropriate for him to lead men into battle without having any experience of it. Berrington entered the Army on 14 September 1915 and was discharged on 13 June 1919 when he was transferred to Army Reserve Class Z. His decorations were routinely awarded for service rather than for distinction.
63	Berrington as a KC. He is not listed in Sainty's authoritative *List* which is based on original patent rolls in the Public Record office, nor did he maintain an office in London which KCs were required to do.
64	Jolley's understanding of the relationship. She talked of 'Mr Berrington, you know the lover she had—well I presume he was her lover', Reid, p. 67; and she said, '[m]y mother went out on her own because she had a lover, a person that she taught German to', Willbanks, p. 125.
65	Paulo and Francesca. See Sayers, p. 103, footnote. The reference is complex. Paolo and Francesca are mutually seduced when reading a book: in the story they read, Galleot acts as an intermediary between Lancelot and Guinevere, and so his name, like Pandarus in Chaucer's tale of *Troilus and Cressida*, became a synonym for a go-between. The sense of the passage is that 'the book was a pander or tempter and so was he who wrote it'.

66 'Margarete's adulterous relationship'. Wimmer, p. 55.
67 £23,659 7s 10d. The 1954 £23,700/2008 $1,000,000+ equivalence is based on May 2008 Australian Bureau of Statistics data. If the sums sound incommensurate, consider: from January 1954 Leonard Jolley's salary as a not-highly-paid RCP Librarian was £1000/year or 4.2% of £23,700; and the May 2008 Australian average salary was $58,874/year or 5.9% of $1,000,000, not a significant discrepancy. Berrington's bequest (probated 8 September 1953) was more than twenty times an annual average salary.
68 Assault. After the trip to Conway, Wales, Ron (the boy called Ronnie or Daffydd in 'Clever and Pretty') wrote a barely literate puppy-love letter to Madelaine; there was no assault. Madelaine Knight Blackmore in conversation to Dibble.
69 Oxford Group. Patti Knight told Cousin Ewart she had been wishing her children could join the Oxford Group. The Oxford Group was founded by Frank Buchman (1878–1961). A lecturer at the Hartford Foundation Seminary in Connecticut, he later became controversial at Princeton but ultimately won support at Oxford where his movement encouraged people to remain in their own churches, committing themselves to the four 'moral absolutes'—hence another name, Moral Rearmament (MRA). (The Oxford Group is not to be confused with the nineteenth-century Oxford Movement supported by John Henry [later Cardinal] Newman to protect the Church of England's privileged position vis-à-vis the state.) The capacity of the Oxford Group to turn people's lives around is testified to by the work of William Griffith (Bill) Wilson (1895–1971) who took such strength from the movement that he was able to quit his destructive drinking and found Alcoholics Anonymous in 1935 (see Cheever).
70 No German classes at the beginning of 1939. Letter from M. Knight to E. Jolley, 1 Nov. 1939.
71 'All that is over'. Letter from W. Knight to E. Jolley, 3 Oct. 1938.
72 A brilliant teacher. Michael and Patricia Hill in conversation with Dibble.
73 A changed woman. Letter from W. Knight to E. Jolley, 26 Dec. 1974. The woman's throat was fine, but she died in the morning after breakfast (letter from W. Knight to E. Jolley, 28 Aug. 1968).
74 'A better place'. Letter from Tony Goring to Dibble, 28 Apr. 2004.
75 Frightened about an accident. M. Knight's postscript on a letter from W. Knight to E. Jolley, 5 June 1969.
76 Aching joints. Letter from M. Knight to E. Jolley, 9 Jan. 1975.
77 Doesn't mind if the house falls down. Letter from M. Knight to E. Jolley, 17 Feb. 1977.
78 'I cannot cope . . .' Letter from M. Knight to E. Jolley, 17 Feb. 1977.
79 Wilfrid Knight's letter. The central part of his unfinished letter suggests forgetfulness consistent with his age.
80 Civilisation stops. Letter from M. Knight to G. Horn, 13 Oct. 1977.

81	Wilfred Knight's death notice. Wolverhampton *Express and Star*, 14 Oct. 1977, following a 12 Oct. article ('Poor Hearing Led to Accident').
82	Christmas invitation. Letter from M. Knight to E. Jolley, 2 Nov. 1977.
83	Destroying letters. M. Knight to G. Horn, 16 Nov. 1978.
84	Leaving The Woodlands. Ilse Gaugusch in conversation with Dibble, July 1997.
85	17 July air letter. Jolley wrote it in response to an audio-cassette letter from her mother (see Audio-cassette)
86	Disappointed in her daughters. Jolley in conversation with Dibble, 2 June 1996. In her will Margarete Knight nearly rivalled Aunt Daisy with her ten beneficiaries, leaving £1000 to: Helen Marsh, her housekeeper from the mid-1970s; each of her three grandchildren; her neighbours Mr/Mrs Morris and Mrs Hall; Ilse Gaugusch in Austria; and to Mr Cotterell she left her National Panasonic Music Centre. Of the remainder of the £66,948, the rest went to her daughters, two thirds to Madelaine and one third to Monica (about $42,000 or three times the average wage for an adult Australian man). Each was surprised to know their mother had so much money.

2 Sibford—If she can swim it does not matter how deep the water is . . .

1	Letters to Hitler. Jolley in conversation with Dibble said the other student was Libby Holden who got to keep the envelope addressed to Monica Knight. The 'Hitler' cards were unsigned but accompanied by a long letter from Hitler's office staff telling what the Führer allegedly was doing. Knight got to keep the letter but her mother later threw it away.
2	Howling in the changing light. 'One Christmas Knitting', pp. 120–1. See also Baker, p. 218.
3	Sibford history. Baily, 'The Sibford Centenary', p. 45. A BBC broadcaster between the world wars, Leslie Baily was the would-be editor of the proposed history, which was indefinitely postponed because of World War II. Also see his interesting film on the history of Sibford which, among other things, addressed the issue of music and other amusements.
4	Golden Age. Finch, p. 36.
5	Harrod's educational experiment. 'Three Great Headmasters', p. 43.
6	Better known/less liked Jessie. Jessie Johnstone aggravated staff and students alike, for example, by defining herself as the French Mistress when another colleague should have taught the subject.
7	Blankenstein's comments. Quoted in Finch, p. 36.
8	Eddington's interview with Johnstone. Eddington, pp. 17, 19. Also see Farr, 'Paul Eddington'.
9	Newspapers and instruments. Randall, p. 46.
10	Lakeman's approval. Lakeman, p. 47. He left Sibford in 1875 and immigrated to Alabama some ten years after the American Civil War.

Notes

11 Burgess and Shakespeare. Eddington, p. 28.
12 Monica Knight's dramatic roles. Presumably the horse in Jolley's photograph of the Sibford stage production is animated by an 'understudy'.
13 Ugly head. Jolley in conversation with Dibble, 2 June 1996.
14 Love of music. Jolley to Worrall in a postcard of 25 Mar. 1993.
15 Johnstone's endurance. Jolley in communication with Sibford Old Scholars' Association. See 'The Passion and the Prose', p. 116, for an example of Jolley's articulating the value of endurance in her life, a theme that pervades her fiction.
16 Sadler's comments. Quoted in Baily, p. 46.
17 Refugees. See Farr, 'Yesterday's Refugees', p. xvii.
18 Herbert. For a profile of Roland Herbert, see 'Fifty Years Ago', p. xii.
19 Friends. Eleven of thirteen were Friends in 1940; see 'Mental Soup', p. 10.
20 Burgess. She also inspired the character Vanburgh, who has an affair with a 'Jacko' Jackson, in Jolley's never-published novel *A Feast*. See Taylor for a tribute to Brigham.
21 Fresh air and food at Sibford. Eddington, pp. 25.
22 Starving, and dry bread. Reid, pp. 11, 25.
23 Complaints about butter and eggs. Sheppard, pp. 46, 48.
24 An egg per week. Sheila MacPherson Naylor in conversation with Dibble.
25 Sex, homosexuals, and chivalry. Eddington, pp. 26-7.
26 Bullying. Eddington, p. 23.
27 Baxter. Born in 1926, he died in 1972.
28 Baxter shocked. Oliver, p. 19.
29 Sapphic relationship. Jolley in conversation with Dibble.
30 Being ragged. Reid, p. 11.
31 'Plan.' Its tone suggests it was written after Knight's reconversion to Methodism and his commitment to the Oxford Group (see the emphasis on absolute honesty and love).
32 Johnstone's reaction. Reid, p. 26.
33 First publication. See Jolley (M. Knight), 'Vitamins' and 'Growth of Plants'. The first article is on Vitamins A, B, C, D, and E, and the second on aquaculture, being the results of an experiment to assay their need for eleven elements.
34 'Animals and Mankind'. Sheppard, p. 47, says in her day 'some of us from different Friends' schools wrote essays on 'Kindness to Animals', something she attributes to an anti-vivisection influence in Quaker schools.
35 The quick note. Reid, p. 14.
36 'Bunny School' stories. They respectively contain 1,200, 750 and 1,200 words and begin, 'It was free walks...', 'Behind the Pine Tree Knoll...', and 'Sunday afternoon...' They would have been written or revised around

the time she was confined to The Ark in January 1938, after which her father praised them in a letter of 14 Feb. 1938.
37 Head and toes. Jolley in conversation with Dibble.
38 Splendid description. Letter from W. Knight to Monica Knight, 14 Feb. 1938.
39 Long golden summer. For a slightly more elaborate account of the trip, see Reid, p. 18.

Causal experience. Madelaine Knight Blackmore's January 1938 assault likely did not affect Jolley's work in a school year that began nine months later, nor could Madelaine's arrival at Sibford, for that was not until the start of the following academic year.
40 Wilfrid Knight/Shining Knight. The pun is originally Jolley's, used as the title of one of her essays, 'Good Knight, Sweet Prince'. In her novel *My Father's Moon* the narrator dreams that her surname is Chevalier, French for Knight, p. 54.
41 'If she can swim . . .' Letter from M. Knight to E. Jolley, 27 Aug. 1969.
42 BDM. It was founded in 1930 as a counterpart to the *HJ* or *Hitlerjugend* that Hitler had started for boys in the 1920s. Both were normally charged with Nazi ideology, but the summer camps were largely free of that—the summer camps were not unlike Girl Scout camps, their common denominator being *Lagerfeuerromantik*, the romantic campfire that imprints camaraderie on everyone and disposes them to think positive thoughts about hard beds and bad food. Margarete Knight's motives for sending her daughter to the camp would have included wanting her daughter to improve her German, to learn about Germany and German culture, to make new friends and to meet Marie Stapf Kemmeter from 'Flowermead' days. The *BDM* is not to be confused with the *Jungmädelführerinnenlager*, an organisation for more senior *BDM* girls where the focus was on training in leadership; the *BDM* was sometimes jokingly called the *Bubidrückmich* or 'Boyo-Squeeze-Me' organisation, so named because it was where middle-class girls got to meet with boys while temporarily outside of their normally sheltered home environments.
43 High jump. Jolley also liked the gymnastics and running; see 'Of Butchers', p. 41.
44 Postcard to her parents. 6 Aug. c. 1939.
45 Invasion of Poland. Hitler declared war on Poland 3 Sept. 1939 and invaded at 4:45 am the following morning.
46 Praying. Reid, p. 16.
47 Realisation. In Reid, p. 17, Jolley reflects, 'I think both [Knight and Berrington] tolerated the other because I think both of them loved my mother. I think that was the most important thing and both probably recognised it. But it took me years to understand that. I've only understood that much later on'.
48 Steffi Kanagur Bauer. Born in 1913 in Tarnow, Poland, she was being housed rather than held, for there were no guards or other barriers to exit

at La Distillerie which was more like a hostel than a prison. A plaque in Vienna commemorates her role as a freedom fighter. See Perruchon; also Sugarman.

3 Pyrford—A nurse should be unable to make a mistake . . .

1 Preparing to study medicine. Jolley acknowledges such an alternative in Reid, p. 26.
2 Doctor and nurse. Gordon Hadfield and Gina Linday McKenzie in conversation with Dibble.
3 Two servants. 'What Sins', p. 2. See also Headon, p. 43.
4 Unable to make a mistake. Quoted in 'The Little Herb of Self-Heal', p. 49.
5 Looked after. Reid, p. 15.
6 Crowded hospital. Reid, p. 27.
7 New type of fear. Reid, p. 27.
8 The learning curve. Reid, p. 27. A related account appears in 'Only Connect! (Part 1)', p. 25.
9 Worst joint to shoot. Reid, p. 29.
10 First impression. Pacifist patient's Diary 11 Feb. 1941.
11 Sweet, young, girlish. Pacifist patient's Diary 13 Feb. 1941.
12 Fresh air, boyfriends and innocent youth. Out for fresh air. Reid, p. 31.
13 Jean Sapcote. Monica Knight wrote in her Form V Biology Notes: 'am afraid Sapcote doesn't really want me at her home nor does she want to come home with me of that I feel certain. Why?'
14 Battle axes. Reid, p. 28.
15 Matron Daisy Zunz. Reid, p. 30.
16 Zunz and Dawson. Jolley in conversation with Dibble.
17 Meal times. Reid, p. 30.
18 Bristow and Furlong. Jolley in conversation with Dibble. Bristow and Furlong were in fact very skilled and highly regarded surgeons. Rowley Bristow (1882–1947) was President of the British Orthopaedic Association in 1936–37, and after his death the hospital was renamed the Rowley Bristow Orthopaedic Hospital. Ronald Furlong (1909–2002) started as an underage apprentice to Bristow, served with the Royal Army Medical Corps in World War II (becoming a brigadier), and after the war was Director of Orthopaedics at St Thomas Hospital in London where he had an international reputation for hand surgery and as a pioneer in hip replacements.
19 Nurses did everything. Reid, p. 29.
20 Emmi/Emmy. Letter from M. Knight to E. Jolley 28 Jan. 1941: 'Hilde Emmy [her friend] made some linen table mats for me as a present'.
21 War was wrong. Reid, p. 26–7.

4 Birmingham—The most powerful thing in this life . . .

1. QEH details. Clifford, p. 21.
2. Salary. For comparison, her mother bought a new radiogram in 1944 for £36. Jolley indirectly supports Pyrford Matron Zunz's view of the QEH as a marriage factory when she spoke of the disadvantage of being 'the daughter of a teacher nursing in a hospital at a time when probationer nurses needed a well-to-do background in order to survive on twenty eight shillings a month and frugal "keep"' ('Self-Portrait', p. 305). Both Pat Goode and Norah Harvey, Knight's QEH friends, married patients.
3. Hours/days, hygiene/public behaviour, and curfew/roll call. Clifford, pp. 89–90, 79, and 26.
4. Like Queen Elizabeth. Clifford, p. 91.
5. Effigy. Norah Harvey Barnes in conversation with Brian Dibble.
6. Block Training System. Smaldon quoted in Clifford, p. 46.
7. Advantages/disadvantages. Clifford, p. 47.
8. QEH beds and sudden influx. Clifford, pp. 74–5.
9. Emptiness, convoys, casualties. Diary 6 July 1944, Clifford, pp. 79, 33.
10. Looking busy, other tasks, and testing urine. Clifford, pp. 85, 80, and 85 (emphasis hers).
11. Infected thumb. Clifford, p. 80.
12. No right names. Reid, p. 35.
13. 'The priest continued . . .' From Dryden's *The Hind and the Panther*, III, line 1685: 'the priest will soon be here. Nurse said so before'.
14. Serious reading. Also Charlotte Brontë, Samuel Butler, Hugo, Mann, Melville, George Moore, Poe, Theodor Storm, Synge, Tolstoy, Woolf, Wilde and Zola.
15. Smaldon's opinions. In QEH records, communicated to Dibble by Clifford on 13 July 1997.
16. Geoffrey Raynor (1913–1983). See Cottrell. Jean Raynor was born in 1918 and died in 1996.
17. Humiliation in the eyes of QEH colleagues. According to Norah Barnes in a 20 Mar. 2005 conversation with Dibble, Mary considered Leonard Jolley to be 'unsuitable' and Jolley's pregnancy 'such a disgrace'.
18. Clarissa. Richardson, p. 1206.
19. Fleetwood-Walker (1893–1965). He was a member of the Royal Academy of the Arts. See Seddon, also see Walker and Quink.
20. Guy Walker. He started to study at the Birmingham School of Art in 1941 but then joined the Navy in 1946, later studying Architecture. He died in late 1998, as did his stepmother Peggy Frazer; Jolley stayed cordially in touch with both of them in later years.
21. Joint writing projects. Leonard Jolley also had a talk on toys broadcast on the BBC—see L. Jolley, 'Toys'.
22. Selly Oak colleagues. Alan Cass in conversation with Dibble.

5 Pinewood—Herts requires Staff: Matron, Teacher, Handyman/Gardner . . .

1. London to Amwell Berry. See Fiennes.
2. Attending a play with Guy. The play was *The Marvelous History of St Bernard* (1938) by Henri Gheon, a pseudonym of Henri Leon Vangeon (1875–1944).
3. *Bless the Bride*. A musical based on A. P. Herbert's book.
4. Chanting monks. See 'Weather'.
5. Argued with mother. Reid, p. 40.
6. Neill's notions. See his *Summerhill* and *Freedom, Not License!*
7. Elizabeth Strachan. She was born in 1890 to a Scottish import–export agent trading with South Africa, Edward and Hannah Balfour Strachan (which in Scotland rhymes with 'bracken'). Of the eight siblings, two died young, and two girls emigrated to South Africa, as did a boy who was never heard from again; one girl played in the quarter finals at Wimbledon, one did not marry until seventy-five, and Strix never married. After a cancer recurrence, she went to live with her youngest sister and her family in Somerset, dying there in 1962.
8. Edna Grace Clarke Kenyatta (1910–1995). Edna and Kenyatta became close after her parents were killed in an air raid in May 1941, and they married in May 1942; Kenyatta was already married to Grace Wahu. See Murray-Brown, p. 213.
9. Work done. Reid, p. 41.
10. Looking forward. Reid, p. 41.
11. Daughter with grandparents. Reid, p. 40.
12. Reviews of Smart. Quoted in Sullivan, pp. 78, 329—the first review is by Frank Scott, the latter by George Woodcock.
13. Smart and Paalen/Rohan. Sullivan, pp. 128–34.
14. Smart and Wickham. Sullivan, pp. 240–3.
15. Sorry for Smart. Later, when asked, Jolley told Smart's biographer that Smart was someone who 'worked very hard and seemed to me to be a wonderful mother, very fond of her children, devoted' (Sullivan, p. 247).

6 Scotland—The horror of marriage lies in its 'dailiness' . . .

1. Suffering fools. Laura Jolley Welton in correspondence to Dibble, 1989.
2. Selly Oak Colleges Library versus the RCP Library. Selly Oak had 70,000 monographs versus the RCP's 50,000. In addition, the RCP Library held 1,000 periodicals and 1,000 manuscripts.
3. Forbidding Joyce. Joyce told Jolley's sister Laura, who was her friend, but his brother Harry claimed not to have found out until he visited Australia in 1961.
4. Invited to few functions. His Sydney Watson Smith Lecture on Archibald Pitcairn on 12 Dec. 1952 at the RCP was an exception.

Notes

5   Hopeful for a confession. In that book Charles Swann idealises Odette in terms of a Botticelli painting he has seen, and Odette, although without looks, brains, or class, is cunning enough to capture and hold him in thrall while continuing to have other lovers male and female.

6   Untidy worker. E. Jolley in *Gardening Diary* 15 Mar. 1953.

7   *Otium* and *dignitas*. On *otium* (leisure/ease), see Curtius, p. 37. *Dignitas* refers to a range of qualities, including moral worth and authority (see Balsdon).

8   The truth. Virginia Woolf is refuting Arnold Bennett's claim that the horror of marriage lies in its 'dailiness'.

9   John Broom. Born in 1925, he died, unmarried, in 1992. He was Librarian at Stromness, and also owned Orkney's best bookshop, Stromness Books and Prints in the 1970s—the motto over the door read 'A book in one hand, a broom in the other'—which he sold to Tam McPhail later in the 1970s; in 1973 he wrote *John Maclean*, a biography on a well-known Scottish Communist; and in 1987 performed in *Edwin Muir and the Labyrinth* at the Edinburgh Festival Fringe, a play written for him by his fellow Orcadian poet-friend George Mackay Brown (see Campbell). Broom discusses his alcoholism under the pseudonym A. Adams in *Another Little Drink*.

10   'Convertion'. 'Convertion' is the Scottish spelling of the word.

11   *The Bibliotheck*. Leonard Jolley conceived this journal in Edinburgh, where its first number was printed, although it was launched in Glasgow. Jolley edited Volume I, Numbers i–iv.

12   Films with students. The first a Nigerian film by Ifoghale Amata and Abay-Ifaa Karbo, on 13 Mar. 1958, then the film version of John Osborne's *Look Back in Anger*, on 15 Mar. 1958, and finally Giraudoux's *Duel of Angels* (*Les Anges du péché*), on 22 Mar. 1958.

13.   Margaret Sprott. In the early 1960s the Jolleys sponsored Sprott's immigration to Western Australia, where she now lives with her Australian farmer-husband in Busselton, Western Australia.

14   Coleridge quotation. Written in the first pages of the first notebook containing *A Feast of Life*.

15   Interleaved manuscripts. By the time Jolley left Glasgow, *A Feast* filled five notebooks. After Jolley left Glasgow the draft grew to fill three more notebooks.

16   Fantasy in *Orlando*. Gilbert, p. xxxvi.

17   Heterosexual couple. Gilbert, p. xxxvi.

18   Recommendation, and not suffering fools. Letter from R. O. MacKenna to the University of Western Australia Personnel Manager, 16 Dec. 1958. In conversation with Dibble, MacKenna volunteered that Jolley did not suffer fools gladly.

7 1960s—After the flight of the cockatoos . . .

1. Newspaper notice. *West Australian*, 25 Nov. 1959, p. 29.
2. Fred Alexander, CBE (1899-1996). See de Garis. Appointed to the University in 1924, he was Professor and Foundation Head of the Department of History and at one time or another Dean of Arts, Director of Adult Education, founder of the Festival of Perth, and Chair of the Professorial Board. The Western Australia State Library is named after him.
3. Malvina Evalyn Wood (1893-1976). See Alexander, *Campus*, pp. 367-9; also Metcalf. Familiarly called 'Emmy', a combination of the initials of her forenames, she was a capable woman, with a BA and MA from the UWA as well as a librarianship qualification. In a 9 Nov. 1959 letter to Leonard Jolley, Alexander made it clear that Emmy Wood had been asked 'to greet you officially'.
4. James Sykes Battye (1871-1954). The Chief Librarian of the Perth Public Library, 1895-1953, effectively the first State Librarian of Western Australia. Alexander summarises Battye's UWA activities in *Campus*, pp. 248-52, 280 inter alia. The Western Australian Library of History is named after him.
5. Ali Sharr (1914-2002). See 'Francis Aubie Sharr'. He was Western Australia's second State Librarian, 1953-1976. His autobiography is not helpful regarding his entry qualifications for the UCL librarianship program.
6. Margaret Thorkildson. Born in Newcastle (England) in 1899, her father was a Danish sea captain. She had no Danish accent and was 'very British'.
7. Student and staff numbers. See Alexander, *Campus*, pp. 233, 711-2 and 795.
8. 'Everyone looked after us'. Reid, p 50.
9. The Leveys. Harris Charles Levey (1923-1966) and Hannah Lasica Levey (1924-1996) were raised in Melbourne, she having emigrated with her parents from Poland at two years of age.
10. Ad eundum gradum. The degree recognises the equivalence of degrees received elsewhere (i.e., Jolley's UCL MA in English). A new university, the UWA's reason for granting it was to increase the membership of Convocation, comprised of graduates; what would have interested Jolley was Convocation's capacity to nominate candidates for election to Senate. On ad eundum gradum qualifications, see Alexander, *Campus*, pp. 288-95; also see 'Convocation'.
11. Dorothy Lucie Sanders/Lucy Walker (1907-1987). She was a prolific writer, with more than fifty novels published in the 1950-80s.
12. Jolley and the Library. Alexander, *Campus*, p. 740.
13. 'Wisdom crieth . . .' From Proverbs 1:10-24; the quotation appears in Leonard Jolley's *Annual Report 1975*, p. 1.
14. Andrew Osborn (1902-1997). See Radford and Whyte. Osborn was the Fisher Library's Librarian for just three years, 1959-62, resigning after

	quarrels with the Vice Chancellor. The tale of the Warragamba Dam epic contest was related by Jean Whyte in conversation with Dibble.
15	Frederick Bert Vickers (1903–1985). Vickers, from the Black Country like Jolley, immigrated to Australia in 1925. In Australian terms, he was a 'battler', serving in the AIF (Australian Imperial Force), working in shearing sheds, running a poultry farm and such. He was President of the local writers' group, the Fellowship of Australia Writers or FAWWA 1953-55 and 1965–66.
16	Tuart Club. The Tuart Club, founded in 1948, is now defunct. It was also called the University Wives' Club.
17	Jolley and fashion. By contrast, her sister Madelaine was clothes-conscious and always carefully dressed and coiffed. In 'My Sister Dancing' Jolley, who never could and always regretted not being able to dance, recalls feeling so proud at Sibford when watching Madelaine dance.
18	Tuart Club. Reid, p. 55.
19	*Cooking by Degrees*. Her editorial colleagues were Mirlwyn Hood, Hannah Levey, and Judith Silberstein.
20	C-Class hospital. C-class hospitals were for patients regarded as largely able to look after their own needs, as in a nursing home.
21	Reasons for working. Jolley in conversation with Barbara Milech, 17 May 1995.
22	Andrew Dungey. Andrew Beeching Betteridge Dungey was born 2 Jan. 1890 in Port Pirie, South Australia, to Florence Lavinia Betteridge and Andrew Beeching Dungey, originally a proofreader and/or journalist known for being opinionated and a flashy dresser and later a farmer in Jitaring, WA—and for giving all but one of his nine children Beeching Betteridge or Betteridge Beeching as middle names. In *Mr Scobie's Riddle* Martin Scobie lived in Rosewood East; Andrew Dungey lived in Parkerville, at what today is 1190 Johnstone Road, near 610 Johnstone Road which in his day was the site of the biggest rose nursery in Western Australia. People who knew Dungey and his three-room cottage remember that he was very religious, played the piano, always spoke to children as adults (advising them to get a good education, to eat fruit, to avoid alcohol), won the lottery for £300 (some say £8,000), always rode a motorcycle with a dog box for his black Pomeranian who was injured and had to be put down, and that he had a cat who was run over and killed—he blamed the 'villain' across the road, accusing him of murdering the cat who was named Scobie. He died 20 Mar. 1965.
23	Gift of £400. Wilfrid Knight gave Madelaine the same amount at that time.
24	Last and longest-lived. Her niece Dr Ilse Fehr died 15 Dec. 1975; they referred to her as 'Ourilse' so as not to confuse her with Ilse Gaugusch, a more distant relation.

25 'Night Runner'. A chapter by that name appears in her novel *My Father's Moon*, p. 61–78.
26 Watkins products. See 'Watkins'. Watkins was founded on Dr Wards Liniment in 1868, the first product ever to carry a money-back guarantee; by the 1940s had over a hundred overseas branches, including Australia where 'Watkins' was a household name comparable to Tupperware today. On Jolley's using the money for typing and postage, see Kitson, 'Elizabeth Jolley', p. 46.
27 Suspect products. Counter-testimony comes from a satisfied, if suggestive, user in Wolverhampton, England, who wrote that the Watkins liniment cured his chapped hands 'in ONE application'.
28 On her knees. Alan and Joyce Billings in conversation with Dibble, 15 Apr. 2006.
29 *The Cardboard Diary*, *The Leila Family*, and *The Prince of a Fellow*. They would become *Palomino*, *The Sugar Mother*, and *Milk and Honey*.
30 Literary output. The following stories were abandoned, amalgamated with one or more others, absorbed into novels, or published as is: 1961—'The Pelican', 'The New Clothes'; 1962—'A Hedge of Rosemary', 'Something to Wear', 'A Day at the River', 'Baldpate'; 1963—'The Sick Vote'; 1964—'*De Profundis* of Dr Ward', 'Eva's Story from the Concrete Palace', 'The Talking Bricks'; 1966—'Night Runner'; 1967—'A New World', 'Edna on the Medway Town'; 1968—'May I Rest My Case on Your Table?' 'Bill Sprockett's Land', 'Lovely Old Christmas', 'Sad Souvenir', 'Poppy Seed and Sesame Rings', 'Hilda's Wedding', 'Arthur's Visit ['true story' Jolley added]'; 1969—'The Travelling Entertainer', 'Night Report', 'A Matter of Speed', 'A Cock Fight', 'Bean Flowers', 'Outink to Uncle's Place'; 1970—'Mr Parker's Valentine', 'Another Holiday for the Prince'.
31 'The Talking Bricks'. See *Mr Scobie's Riddle*, pp. 10–11, 29, 31–4, 92–3, and 104–5.
32 Tuart Club speech. When Jolley became President early in the year, her predecessor Clarissa Fox wrote that Elizabeth was 'the right one in the right place', encouraging her to support the controversial idea of serving less elaborate food but exhorting her to oppose the radical one of breaking into small groups at tea. History does not record how Jolley acted on those issues.

8 1970s—I was sort of on the market . . .

1 Publishing/business. Ellison, p. 189. Her remark that she was 'sort of on the market' appears in Reid, p. 85.
2 Intellectual infrastructure. Dessaix, *Speaking*, p. 212.
3 Challenge for migrants. Andrew Riemer is eloquent on the challenge for migrants in his book *Inside Outside*.
4 Jolley on Waten. 'Living on One Leg like a Bird', p. 140. Jolley talks about Waten in several interviews.

Notes

5 Theme of exile. Many critics have followed Elizabeth Jolley's cue in 'Self-Portrait: A Child Went Forth' and commented on the theme of exile in her work. Of special interest are Riemer's three pieces, 'Between Two Worlds' (1983), 'Displaced Persons—Some Preoccupations in Elizabeth Jolley's Fiction' (1986) and 'Elizabeth Jolley' (1991); Daniel's essay on Elizabeth Jolley in her *Liars*; and Thomson's 'Landscapes of Memory'.

6 Tolstoy story. The experience with Dr Phillip Goatcher and his solicitor was likely the inspiration for Jolley's 'A Gentleman's Agreement', with its reference to the 29-mile peg on the Great Southeast Highway and to Medulla Brook.

7 One-legged escapee. Lyn Blasgund, Superintendent of the Wooroloo Prison Farm, in conversation with Dibble, 14 Nov. 2007.

8 The 4,500 acres to the east of Green Road was the Wooroloo Tuberculosis Sanatorium from 1915–'60, then a district hospital until 1970 when it became a medium-security prison farm run by the Department of Corrections.

9 'The fruit picked . . .' 'Sunday 24th February 1973', *Diary of a Weekend Farmer*, p. 81.

10 Sinister possibility. Jolley pointed out that the only other time she wrote about a bad person was in the 'Worcester Sauce Queens' which became 'The Fellow Passenger'.

11 Feckless. In 'The Jarrah Thieves' Martha defines 'feckless' in terms of 'people who need help all the time, you could give everything to them and they would still need', p. 90. The word/concept appears elsewhere in *Five Acre Virgin* (e.g., 'A Gentleman's Agreement' [p. 14] and 'The Wedding of the Painted Doll' [p. 22]). 'Feckless' is a highly charged word for Jolley, one that designates people the antithesis of those who 'cherish' or are 'cherished', the opposite of those who caress or are caressing.

12 'Quiet in all he did'. Jolley in conversation with Barbara Milech.

13 The woman and her husband appear as Mr and Mrs Morton in Jolley's 'The Goose Path: A Meditation', p. 164, and in various entries in her *Diary of a Weekend Farmer*.

14 'What Men Live By'. See Tolstoy.

15 Władysław 'Steve' Błotnicki (1903–1967) and Ludmiła Baranowska Blotnicka (1907–1981). According to Sylvia Fordymacka in conversation with Dibble. The Blotnickis met at the University of Warsaw where he took a degree in forestry and she in veterinary medicine—she worked in the medieval forest of Białowieża on the Ukrainian border with European *wisent* (bison) which had become extinct in the wild during World War I. When Hitler invaded Poland in 1939, they escaped first to Hungary, then to Yugoslavia and Greece, ending up in Haifa and Jerusalem where he joined the Polish military forces. Always emotionally fragile, the stress of her various migrations increased until she was unable to pursue her profession, turning to painting and writing essays, stories, and poems. They were to be published by one of the several overseas

Polish publishing houses producing books for the Polish military forces and schools but all such outlets closed after World War II, in 1948. Her work was finally published at the end of 2007. The Błotnickis arrived in Perth in March 1950, at first living in Wundowie where he worked in the charcoal and steel factory, frequently contracting pneumonia on account of his weak chest, eventually moving to the new Wandana flats in Thomas Street, Subiaco, in 1954, becoming citizens in 1955. Unhappy because he could not find work commensurate with his intelligence and training, they were thrilled when he was Leonard Jolley's first appointee, hired in January 1960 to work in the Engineering library. Wladyslaw was profoundly devoted to Ludmiła, supporting her in every way, and thus she was hopeless and helpless during the dozen years after his death, when she had open-heart surgery in the late 1960s, and when periodically institutionalised before and after that. From the mid-1970s, she was looked after by Polish immigrants Sylvia Fordymacka and her mother. Fordymacka secured Ludmila's release from the Graylands Mental Hospital and put her in Nazareth House in Hilton in the late 1970s where she remained until she died. Many of these details appear in Jolley's *Newspaper of Claremont Street*, like Ludmiła's being a painter, p. 44, a poet, p. 45, and Wladyslaw's pulmonary problems, p. 47.

16   Flying Domestic. On using the money for typing and postage, see Kitson, 'Elizabeth Jolley', p. 46.

17   Stories published 1970–1973. The stories indebted to Wooroloo for their settings were 'Outink To Uncle's Place' (1970), 'Bill Sprockett's Land' (1971), 'Dingle the Fool' (1972), 'Another Holiday for the Prince' (1973) and 'Uncle Bernard's Proposal' (1973), and the one indebted for its characters was 'A New World' (1973).

18   Eastern-states publishers. Jolley in conversation with Milech.

19   Employment with the Education Department and Channel 9. Jolley briefly wrote for the *School Newsletter* but was unsuccessful in gaining regular employment, and her application to Channel 9 did not result in any opportunities.

20   'The Caretaker'. Templeman's poem appeared in *Westerly*, vol. 13, no. 3, 1968, and was republished in his first book, *Poems*. Templeman described his first meeting with Jolley in '"A Timid Confidence"', his 8 Feb. 2008 launch speech for Elizabeth Jolley Research Collection.

21   Gluck's aria. From *Orfeo ed Euridice*, in the middle of Act 3. '*Che farò senza Euridice*' / '*J'ai perdu mon Euridice*'.

22   'I Am, I Said'. Katherine plays the song for Hester in *The Well*, p. 105.

23   Battleaxes. First-term Literature in 1976, Fremantle Arts Centre classes. 'Battleaxes' was the term Jolley used for some of the nurses at Pyrford where she was first introduced to sex kittens in the form of Snorter and Diamond. It was also the name of a short story she worked on in 1977.

24   Shakespeare and Jolley's writing. See Lear's 'Let copulation thrive' speech (act 4, scene 6, line 116 ff.) and Caithness' claim that Macbeth 'cannot

Notes

buckle his distempered cause / Within the belt of rule' (act 5, scene 2, lines 15–16). Jolley's work in progress became her novel *Palomino* where a belt functions to symbolise the exchange of love (e.g., pp. 2, 103, 122 and 259).

25 Templeman and the FACP. He was Director of the Fremantle Arts Centre, with the Fremantle Arts Centre Press under its umbrella, such that he was effectively its publisher. He appointed Terry Owen as the FACP's Manager, who took up her position mid-1975.

26 First FACP books. There were two collections, *Soundings* (poems edited by Veronica Brady, 1976) and *New Country* (stories edited by Bruce Bennett, 1976). The second book in the single-author series was Alan Alexander's book of poems, *In the Sun's Eye* (1976).

27 Print runs. Figures given by Clive Newman of the Fremantle Press in conversation with Dibble, Dec. 2007.

28 Reappearing characters. Templeman in conversation with Dibble, 19 Dec. 2007.

29 Previous experience. Faculty spouses—a wife in 'Mr Parker's Valentine' and a husband in 'The Travelling Entertainer'; country landowners—'The Performance', 'The Outworks of the Kingdom', 'A New World', 'Grasshoppers'; homes/hospitals—'The Performance', 'The Agent in Travelling', 'A New World'; door-to-door selling—'The Agent in Travelling', 'The Travelling Entertainer'; country lecturing—'The Long Distant Lecture'.

30 The Pages. The wife is named Eleanor Page, the heroine of the novel Jolley began in Birmingham.

31 Valentine. Jolley's father gave her the idea for the story when he wrote of a local farmer finding an unopened valentine a labourer hid in the barn in the crack of a beam forty years previously and who refused to identify the sender when the farmer discovered it. Knight wrote, 'When you get an insight, like this, into people's lives you feel you want to put your arms around them in love' (Letter from W. Knight to E. Jolley, 6 Aug. 1969).

32 Hats and sweets. Hats on p. 144 of 'Grasshoppers', sweets on pp. 142–3, bullying clothing on pp. 172–3 and money on pp. 155 and 162–3.

33 Evil versus foolish. Jolley in conversation with Dibble.

34 Three epigraphs. The one from Ecclesiastes represents death as ubiquitous and inevitable, mourners choosing their own paths afterwards; and the unnamed verses beginning 'Now you lie hard across my lap', another pietà image, can refer to the loss of Bettina or her daughter Kerry or to passion/desire.

35 Foot operation. When he returned to Australia his physician was Dr Phyllis Goatcher who with her husband owned the Jarrahdale bush block the Jolleys considered buying a few years before.

36 Dawkins' positions. Dawkins was Minister for Finance and then Minister for Education in the Hawke Labor government of the 1980s and then was Treasurer under Paul Keating's Labor government in the 1990s.

37	Letter to Editor. 17 Nov. 1973.
38	Ending cleaning/starting teaching. Ian Templeman said he might ask her to speak to a group on the short story.
39	'Where Do I Look . . .' See 'The Changing Family—Who Cares?'
40	Chaplains' Conference and 'God's loving kindness'. Jo Robertson in correspondence with Dibble, 11 Jan. 2008.
41	Western Australian Institute of Technology. Also called WAIT, it became Curtin University of Technology in 1987.
42	1978 Adelaide Festival. It ran from 29 February through 16 March. Hungerford, a respected Western Australian novelist, had recently been dropped by his publisher Angus and Robertson. A press officer in Premier Charles Court's government, he had told Court that there was a publishing log jam in the state preventing Western Australia writers from being published, as a result of which Court made an election promise to establish the FACP. Hungerford's collection of stories, *Wong Chu and the Queen's Letterbox*, the third in the single-author series, had been published by the FACP in 1977. Information about Jolley travelling to and being at the Festival is from Terry Owen in conversation with Dibble.
43	'Writerly' writers. Π O. (Peter Oustabasidis, born 1954), a radical socialist performance/concrete poet, dates the advent of performance poetry to a 1978 Adelaide debate about a speech by David Malouf on modern Australian poetry. 'A group of us objected to the "writerly" bias being expressed, which didn't represent current poetry practices, such as the out-loudness of a poem.' See Baum.
44	Brissenden. Quoted in Starke, frontispiece.
45	First half of the decade. Edith Emily Lamb died at ninety-three on 6 Oct. 1983. Joyce Broom died 13 Jan. 1974 (letter from her husband, J. Broom to E. Jolley, 19 Jan. 1974). 'The Dreerys', Elsa Ada Marsh and Douglass Edwin Marsh, died respectively on 6 July 1973 at age fifty-eight and he on 16 Sept. 2003 at eighty-two.
46	Bill Cotterell. W. Cotterell to E. Jolley, 10 Nov. 1977. Of Margarete Knight he wrote, 'For your mother there has been no outburst of sobbing nor any sense of steeled repression but a great understanding of even such a sudden death as natural like the seasons. She shared with me some passages by Heroditus + I shared with her some words of Chuang Chu'.
47	Parents' deaths. For a 'bereavement of not writing letters', see Willbanks, p. 119; and for her mother not wanting her letters, see Diary 21 Aug. 1979. See also Grenville and Woolfe, p. 163—'I would often write to my father what I was writing about, then I would leave his letter and start writing. That was a great help'.

9 1980–84—The inside of people's survival . . .

1	Published in US/UK, and five translated. *Five Acre Virgin* was not translated; others translated into Dutch, French, German, Icelandic, Polish, and

Notes

       Spanish—*Scobie's Riddle*, translated into Danish as part of a 2007 Curtin Universal doctoral thesis by Dr Anne Ryden, has not been published.

2   Publishing exclusively. Between *Mr Scobie's Riddle* and *Woman in a Lampshade* in 1983 and *The Well* in 1986, Jolley published *Milk and Honey* and *Stories* (*Five Acre Virgin* and *Travelling Entertainer* combined) with the FACP and *Foxybaby* with UQP.

3   Publication history of *Palomino*. Jolley sent the manuscript to Outback Press on 8 Mar. 1997 and received the acceptance on 11 May; she met the publisher in Adelaide on 28 Feb. 1978 and then on 1 Mar. she had the three-hour meeting which left her so happy.

4   Thirty-nine rejection slips. The thirty-nine rejections story becomes a leitmotif of articles on and interviews with Jolley. One example: 'I've had as many as thirty-nine rejections in one year. But everything that was rejected has been accepted. Some pieces have been reworked. Others are just as they were' (Ellison, p. 179).

5   ABC indecision. Bird, p. 145, letter from Shan Benson to E. Jolley, 15 Dec. 1980.

6   Being thick-skinned. The first rejection in her list was from Contempa Publications, Armadale, Vic.; the following ones through to the ABC are reported by Jolley in Reid, pp. 60–1.

7   Lurie meeting Jolley. See Koval, 'Elizabeth Jolley Dies'.

8   Lurie on Jolley. Lurie, 'Tribute', p. 16.

9   Albany summer school. The school ran 3–12 January, and she drove there with a potter.

10   'Starvation of family life'. See, for example, 'The Changing Family—Who Cares' where Jolley remarks, 'Most of all the mother fears starvation, physical, spirtual and emotional, for the child' (85).

11   Better to be the lover, origins of love, and complementary half. In Plato's *Symposium* (189b ff.) Aristophanes speaks of human beings originally being spherical and of three genders, as if they were modern human beings joined back-to-back in female–female, female–male and male–male pairs. In the Greek equivalent of Adam and Eve's 'Fall' in the Garden of Eden, through arrogance they scaled the heavens where Zeus cut them in half and they fell to earth again. The originals were natural pairs, Aristophanes argued, because the Sun, Earth and Moon are three: men made of the Sun, women of the Earth, and the Moon equally of the Sun and the Earth.

12   Optimistic/pessimistic. Jolley often described her writing and herself in these terms, sometimes relating that dual outlook to her tragi-comic sensibility. For example, she told one interviewer that 'looking back I realise that I was tremendously cherished by [my mother] and by my father. I think this cherishing helped me to be optimistic and pessimistic, to see the ridiculous and the grotesque' (Baker, p. 229). See also Kavanagh, p. 445; Grenville and Woolfe, p. 161; and Willbanks p. 116, along with Craven in Dessaix, 'Elizabeth Jolley', p. 48.

Notes

13 Recycled characters, and writing as exploration. In interviews Jolley concurred she recycled characters, and just as often described her writing as an exploration of character. Thus she told one interviewer that 'I have been writing all my life and my characters overlap, weaving in together, one leading on to another in exploring human nature' (quoted in Byrski, p. 97). For writing as exploration, see Baker, p. 220, and Grenville and Woolf, p. 157; for starting with character, see Willbanks, p. 115, and 'Self-Portrait', p. 306.

14 Belongs to no movement. In an early author's statement in 1981, [Author's Statement], p. 214, Jolley comments that 'I write about human beings and their needs and feelings. This must involve society and morality. I do not respond to politics. The morality of my writing is the morality of the single person against the crowd. I cannot associate myself with any movement'. Thus Jolley's reiterated demurrals in the interviews of the 1980s in regard to both feminist and queer readings of her fiction—she always welcomed any reading of her work, but resisted identification with any cohort.

15 '[T]wo women appear to love each other'. Quoted in Britton, p. 55. See also Reid, p. 61.

Palomino, begun in Edinburgh, was originally set in the lowlands of Scotland. The inspiration for Laura was Susanne Jean Paterson (1900-84), an obstetrician and gynaecologist twenty-three years older than Jolley who saw her in Edinburgh for the children and for her irritable bowel syndrome. According to the *British Medical Journal* (Vol. 288 [1994]), Paterson worked in India and then was a research fellow at the Mayo Clinic in the United States before returning to practice medicine in Edinburgh in the 1930s; she was elected to the Fellowship of the College of Obstetricians and Gynaecologists in 1948.

16 *Palomino* and *Scobie* as tiresome. Grenville and Woolfe, p. 163. Though *Milk and Honey* was Jolley's fifth published novel, it and *Mr Scobie's Riddle* were the two novels Jolley first crafted in Australia when, in the early sixties, she set about becoming a published writer (Reid, p. 56).

17 Negative reviews. See, for example, Shapiro, Monson, and McDonald. As Jolley remarked to an interviewer, 'Some reviewers didn't care for the book. It was as if I had touched something in them which disgusted them' (Baker, p. 222).

18 Scrabble game. Monson remarks on 'the brilliant scrabble scene', noting it 'glimpses around the corners at suicide'—a peculiar sort of suicide, given the body is rolled up in a rug.

19 How Madge died. Baker, p. 232. See also Kavanagh, p. 447, where Jolley tells of a woman phoning her to ask who killed Madge, and her replying, so as not to be disappointing, that it seemed like a woman's murder.

20 Norm as in 'normal'. Leisure-loving, beer-bellied couch-potato Norm was the antihero of a national television and poster campaign run by the federal government from 1977 in order to encourage Australians to be more

Notes

diet- and exercise-conscious. See 'Life. Be in it.' Jolley might have taken the character's name from those ads, just as she took biblical quotes-for-the day from the editorial page of the *West Australian*, like the quotation from Proverbs in '"Surprise! Surprise!" from Matron', p. 44.

21 *Scobie* as lament. See Ellison, p. 156.

22 The Morgans. As in '"Surprise! Surprise!" from Matron', Price works to get permission for Mr Morgan to be brought from jail to attend Mrs Morgan's hundredth birthday party (p. 81). Presumably the 'M' in the night sister's forename stands for the Mary, Margarite or Margie of the early short stories; her surname speaks for itself.

23 Comedy/tragedy. Cornford, pp. 190–220.

24 'Plato, [Hopewell] wrote . . .' At a literary luncheon Jolley quoted the same passage, attributing it to Plato in his *Aeon* (or *Ion*) (['Chocolate'], p. 22).

25 Realism. '[N]owhere do I strike out from realism, apart from hysteria and fantasy in *The Well*' (Willbanks, p. 117).

26 Diathermy burn. The letter mimics drafts from Leonard Jolley to his rheumatologist Dr Phyllis Goatcher complaining about such a burn, although there is no evidence that he finally sent any such letter.

27 London to Perth. Hopewell sends Peabody honey made from the flowers of red gum (marri), white gum and blackbutt trees which are endemic to Western Australia. *Palomino* would likewise be set in Perth on account of its iconic jarrah trees (p. 30).

28 Literary journals and jargon. Webby, p. 29–31.

29 Submitting radio plays, and mailing from England. Jolley in conversation with Dibble; and Madelaine Knight Blackmore in conversation with Dibble.

30 Fulminating about Carter. The third member of the clique was D. M. Thomas.

31 Rushdie, and bed full of millipedes. She was pleased to see Rushdie, Russell Hoban and Tom Shapcott at breakfast but preferred to be with others during the festival; see Boucher for the story of the bed full of millipedes. By contrast, two years later at the Commonwealth Writers' Conference held in conjunction at the Edinburgh Festival, Jolley abandoned the dormitory room the organiser had provided because of its dirty, unisex bathroom; without fanfare and at her own expense, she took a hotel in the city (Hanrahan, p. 145).

32 Carter on *Foxybaby*. 'Dreams of Reason', p. 1.

33 1985 book choices. The other two were Kate Grenville's *Lilian's Story* and David Malouf's *Antipodes* ('Books for Christmas').

34 'You're sick . . .' Quoted in Cadzow, p. 16. Colleagues of Astley would point out that she was merely speaking in character, something Jolley did not understand at the time.

35 Enema of writers. Jolley in conversation with Dibble and Milech, Sept. 2001.

10 1985–89—Optimistic and fond . . .

1 Early professional life. Reid, pp. 56–5.
2 Climactic Curve and 'Dingle the Fool'. Reid, p. 62.
3 Ruth's contributions. Dibble in conversation with Ruth Jolley Radley 8 Mar. 2008. 'Boiled egg' is from '"Surprise! Surprise!" from Matron', p. 44; the double collarbones, and breastbone, from 'The Wedding of the Painted Doll', p. 18; and the joke—the answer is a nervous wreck—appears in both 'Five Acre Virgin', p. 11, and *Milk and Honey*, p. 86–7. Jolley said that the collar/breastbone image applied to a large-bosomed woman they both knew (Jolley in conversation with Dibble).
4 Dingo, Dingle, Dino. The Jolleys' dog was named after the Flintstones' pet Dino; see Reid, p. 62.
5 Life she wanted. Reid, p. 56.
6 'The Shed' and East Anglia. Reid, p. 77; also Grenville and Woolfe, p. 164.
7 Sophisticated spaces. Ellison, p. 187.
8 Readers' discoveries. Moran, p. 5.
9 Readers' creativity/hope. Willbanks, pp. 119 and 122.
10 Exact feeling. Gardiner, p. 12.
11 Learning from students, and Waten. Grenville and Woolfe, p. 162, and Smith, p. 116. For other things Jolley thought could be demonstrated in the classroom, see 'Habit of Art', pp. 121–4.
12 Students. See Winton, Epanomitis and Burstow. Parry and Rossetti in conversation with Dibble, Feb. 2008, during the WA Writers' Week.
13 Learning from students. 'I was the one who was gaining all the information' (Reid, p. 63).
14 Teaching load. Reid, p. 90.
15 Conferences. Eastern states conferences: Adelaide Festival in 1980, 1982 and 1984 and the annual conference of the South Pacific and Commonwealth Languages and Literatures Society in Sydney in 1984; the Word Festival in Canberra and the Warana Festival in Brisbane in 1985; and the annual conference of the Association for the Study of Australian Literature (ASAL) at James Cook University in Queensland, Spoleto (precursor of the Melbourne International Festival of the Arts), and the Salamanca Festival of the Arts in Hobart in 1986; and the ASAL conference at the University of Sydney in 1988. Overseas conferences: the Harborfront International Festival of Artists in Toronto in 1983; the Commonwealth Writer's Conference held in conjunction with the Edinburgh Festival in 1986; and International PEN (Poets, Essayists, Novelists) readings at the Folger Shakespeare Library in Washington, DC, and at the YMCA in New York City in 1988.
16 *Foxybaby's* dream. In a 23 Nov. 1984 letter to Patricia Mulcahy, Jolley's literary editor at Viking Penguin in New York, she included sixty-six '[k]ey sentences and fragments of sentences which could be placed in the front of the novel

Notes

Foxybaby as the Guide to the Perplexed is in *Mr Scobie's Riddle*. She also included a shorter list, the first and last two items of which were (ellipses and emphases Jolley's): first, '*so full of sleep was I . . . that I left the true way*' (p. 13), and 'leaning her forehead against the cool window of the bus . . . felt extremely tired. Sensibly she told herself she was suffering from shock' (p. 17); and last, 'leaning her forehead against the cool window the bus' (p. 248), and 'There was the feeling of moving forward and being held back at the same time. The rhythm of travelling had changed. Miss Porch raised her head from the window where her forehead rested on the soothing glass. She felt dazed as she always did if she slept during the day or on a journey. Her knees ached . . .' (p. 260). Photocopy given by Jolley to Dibble.

A complementary classical allusion is to 'a town by the rocks where the sea meets another sea', pp. 10, 89. It is from Sophocles' *Antigone* (line 968 ff.), anticipating the events in Porch's dream which are fantasies of the sort that Freud used as the basis of his theories about sexuality. Peycroft urges the students not to lose sight of the Oedipal and Electra complexes (p. 142).

17 Life with both hands. Ellison, p. 174. Peycroft, however, can be seen as more aggressive than Thorne, as suggested by what she would do to Paisley—'Sometimes, you know, I have this great wish to hold her dangling by the scruff of the neck over a cauldron of something, nothing too painful, but absolutely deadly. I actually visualize the scene and see her horrible little legs kicking helplessly over the morass' (p. 106–7).

18 'Little line of balance', and 'spread some evenness'. Ellison, p. 173, and Baker, p. 222.

19 Snowdon/Viggars type. Baker, p. 222.

20 Conception to final draft, and typing *The Well*. Dibble in conversation with Nancy McKenzie, July 2007.

21 Characters flat on the page. Willbanks, p. 124.

22 Original visions of *The Well*. Willbanks, p. 120.

23 Europe. The waiters standing behind their chairs is one overlapping detail; see 'Of Butchers and Bilberries', p. 43.

24 Hester's endurance. Jolley was 'interested in the power of endurance' (Kitson, 'Elizabeth Jolley', p. 47), something related in the writing to her preoccupation with people's loneliness and need, and in her life to her World War II experiences of refugees and nursing patients. Mr Scobie is perhaps her most powerful image of endurance as he suffers the loss of 'all the things we think will restore us if there are enough of them during one's life . . . to carry with us' (Kavanagh, p. 439). For Jolley, *Mr Scobie's Riddle* was both a celebration of life and of death (Baker, p. 225).

25 Lost manuscript. Elsewhere Jolley despaired of rewriting *The Leila Family*. Sheldon was a figure from Jolley's childhood, the daughter of Acheson

Notes

Sheldon, the nudist who visited Jolley and acted over-familiarly when she worked as a domestic for the Fleetwood-Walkers. Jolley also sent her a manuscript of *Scobie's Riddle*, which Sheldon dropped in the bathtub and had to salvage by hanging up the pages to dry around the house.

26   Manuscript begun/finished, but continued. She was working on the new version, still called *The Leila Family*, in 1984, keep setting it aside in favour of *Shepherd's Well/The Well*, and bringing a final draft—by then called *The Sugar Mother*—to be typed in 1987.

27   Novel as dream. *The Sugar Mother* gestures to the opening of *Foxybaby* and its allusion to Dante: Edwin Page eats an egg which leaves him feeling quite sick (p. 22); and, when he hears a rapping at the window, he meets Mrs Bott who has broken branches of bushes 'in her haste to leave the little path' (p. 25); when friend of the family Daphne calls 'Anyone for tennis?' to him from the window, he hears her 'as if in his dream' (p. 36); and near the end, when he again hears rustling and tapping at the window, Daphne tells him, 'it's that woody old hibiscus and broom you've got out there' (p. 207–8). In other words, once more no one is there. In her interview with Paul Kavanaugh, Jolley affirmed his suggestions that all is told from the point of view of Edwin, who is confused and imagines things, and that a number of details cast doubt 'on all the central narrative' (p. 450).

28   Daphne as Viggars/Tiresias. The comparison goes on: Tiresias was a hermaphrodite, and Daphne's dog Prince, thought to be male at the beginning, is found to be female when it gives birth. Daphne, a schoolgirl friend of Cecilia's, might be bisexual.

29   Vorwickl. A Hilde Vorwickl figured in Knight-family mythology as a Viennese friend of Margarete Knight who visited Wells Road after World War II Madelaine Knight Blackmore in conversation with Dibble).

30   Edwin's fantasy. The oedipal fantasy implicit in these configurations of there being a special relationship between the child and one parent only (the rival relationship between the parents somehow obliterated) is echoed in Edwin's approval of Jason's sentiment in Euripides: *'If only children could be got some other way without the female sex! If women didn't exist, Human life would be rid of all its miseries'* (pp. 19–20, emphasis Jolley's).

31   Daphne. Daphne is a minor deity amorously pursued by Apollo until the river god turns her into a laurel on the banks of the river. Years ago, when they were all on holiday in England, Daphne and Cecilia stripped off to swim in a river, Edwin slower to do so because of embarrassment—the memory of Daphne rising naked from the water never left him, p. 84. If Daphne equates with Viggars, Peycroft's counterpart is Mrs Bott. In her 1960s *Leila Family* draft, Jolley thought of the Bott character as 'a woman [who] tries at all cost to get the best for herself and then has to make the best of what she gets'. The draft manuscript is held in the Mitchell Library.

32   Focus on marriage. Kavanagh, p. 438.

Notes

33   Story and play awards. FAW (Vic.) awards for 'Two Men Running' (1980) and 'The Libation' (1981) and an award from the South Pacific Association for Commonwealth Literature and Language Studies (SPACLALS) for 'Hep Duck and Hildegarde the Meat' (1982), along with an AWGIE (Australian Writers' Guild) prize for the best original radio play for 1982 with 'Two Men Running'.

34   WA Literary Award. The predecessor of Western Australia's Premier's Book Award, the WA Week Literary Awards were given in generic categories without an overall prize being awarded.

35   'Realms of distinction'. This was her goal around the time of writing *Milk and Honey*.

36   Most reviewed authors. Shapcott, *Literature Board*, p. 49.

37   WA Governor General. Professor Gordon Reid (Politics) and his wife Ruth were UWA friends of the Jolleys. Ruth bought Watkins products from Elizabeth (who warned her that the Simply Elegant Coconut Oil Shampoo was no good for her hair) and attended her FAC creative writing classes; and they remained close after the deaths of their husbands.

38   Income and other support in the 1990s. The book-per-year/$4500-per-book formula crudely assumes that each book sells out in the year of publication and is not reprinted. Note that not all of the money her work generated came to her. For example, when actor Noel Ferrier optioned the film rights for *The Well*, that money went to Jolley, and comparably when Martin Field optioned the film rights for *Milk and Honey*; but when Australian Film Commission committed $20,000 for development of the *Milk and Honey* project, that money went to the project itself. Similarly, the Bicentennial Committee committed $45,000 to the *Sugar Mother* writing–publishing project: $20,000 as a writer's grant to Jolley and $25,000 as a publisher's grant to the Fremantle Arts Centre Press. By the end of the 1980s, the Literature Board of the Australia Council had spent $60,000 on her fellowships and nearly $30,000 in publication subsidies on her books. WAIT/Curtin paid her more than $100,000 over the decade, the NSW Premier's award was for $5,000, the *Age* Book of the Year Awards $2,000 for 1983 and $3,000 for 1989, and the Canada–Australia prize $3,000. During the 1980s Australian professors averaged about $55,000 per year.

39   Bilston Bunny. The phrase was one Leonard Jolley used in the 1950s by way of criticising her manners and upbringing, Bilston being one of the areas where her parents lived in the 1930s and where her father taught until his retirement.

11   1990–2007—Who talks of victory . . .

1   *Voices of the Eighties*. The other women were Jessica Anderson, Beverly Farmer, Kate Grenville, Barbara Hanrahan and Olga Masters.

2   Conceptual portrait. Peter Kendall's *Portrait of Elizabeth Jolley* (oil on canvas).

In conversation with Dibble Kendall said his intention was to show 'how she was interested not interesting'. The portrait won the 1986 WA Australia Day Portrait Prize.

3   Stage productions. Other pieces included PACT Youth Theatre's adaptations of six of her stories under the title *Uncle Bernard's New World*—'Outink to Uncle's Place', 'The Outworks of the Kingdom', 'The Agent in Travelling', 'A New World', 'Uncle Bernard's Proposal', and 'The Representative' (1990); *Tell Tales*, which included 'Lorelei in the Wheat' (1993); *Supermarket Pavane* (1996).

4   '*Poms Go Home*'. Jolley, 'Who Would Throw?' p. 64.

5   Orthodoxy, sexist society. Bird, 'New Narrations', pp. 196–7.

6   'Who elected Jolley . . . ?' Pierce, p. 354, referring to Brenda Walker's essay in *New Critical Essays*. Among a number of comparisons to White, Peter Craven, cited by Walker, several times compared Jolley to White, once saying she is the writer 'who some people think is the most significant in this country' ('Writers' Tales', p. 7); and Elizabeth Ward, writing in the *Washington Post*, said that Jolley and White were Australia's 'most eminent writers', and that *Scobie's Riddle* 'touches on greatness'.

7   Three Elizabeths, and the 1995 NSW Premier's Awards. E. Webby in correspondence with Dibble, Mar. 2008. See also Anderson, and Wilcox.

8   Alfred Carson. Letter from E. Jolley to Dibble and B. Milech, 7 Jan. 1991.

9   More tolerance, distanced from passion. Baker, p. 221.

10 Trust and friendship. Willbanks, p. 115. She said elsewhere that theirs was a 'total trusting friendship' (Reid, p. 82).

11 Reading to Leonard. Baker, p. 231.

12 '*Liebes-Lied*'. Lines 1–2, 8–11 and 13 appear on *Lovesong*'s right-hand frontispiece page and on p. 241. The prose translation here of is from Forster, pp. 398–9.

13 Missing Leonard. Barrowclough, p. 16.

14 Child psychology. Facetious paediatric advice to Marion Kingston, now Professor Emeritus M. K. Stocking, Keats–Shelley scholar and long-time editor of the *Beloit Poetry Journal*, in conversation with Dibble in Mar. 2008.

15 Jolley's father made her a writer. Quoted in Craven, 'Writers' Tales', p. 7. Craven goes on to say 'it was he who cared about literature and believed in her capacity to achieve it'. It might be more accurate to say that Wilfred Knight cared about what his daughter wrote and believed in her capacity to be a success at writing it.

16 *Time*, no fixed viewing point. Modjeska, pp. 15-6.

17 Time/age/profession. Given Vera is a boarding-school girl who wore dresses a full-sized adult refugee would steal in the mid-1930s, then she was born in the first half of the 1920s—say 1923 (Jolley's date of birth); she is thirty-four when she arrives in Australia; she attends a medical conference

Notes

in New York in the 1980s where AIDS (discovered in the US in 1981) is mentioned but not on the main agenda (*Cabin Fever* 91); and so she is at least in her late fifties.

18 *Roman-fleuve*. A French term for a long novel in several volumes, the best-known modern example being Marcel Proust's seven-volume *À la Recherche du temps perdu*, a favourite of Jolley's. Lynette Felber, in the only book-length study of the *roman-fleuve*, uses Hélène Cixous and Luce Irigaray to argue that, for the reasons above and still others, the genre affiliates to *écriture féminine* (see Rado, p. 159). Jolley said '*Cabin Fever* is not so much a sequel to my last book as a companion volume. *My Father's Moon* is really an homage to the father of the central character, Vera Wright. *Cabin Fever* moves on, and is an homage to Vera and the mother' (Moran, 'Jolley', p. 5).

19 Moral insanity. It was defined in 1835 by British Dr J. C. Prichard as 'a form of mental derangement in which the mental faculties [are uninjured], while the disorder is manifested principally or alone in the state of feelings, temper, or habits... and the individual is... incapable... of conducting himself with decency and propriety in the business of life' (Ozarin, p. 21).

20 Suffering in marriage. Jolley remarked that her father 'was an idealist... I think he suffered quite a bit, from his marriage' (Kavanagh, p. 443–4).

21 *My Father's Moon* about the father. 'The father in *My Father's Moon* is modelled very closely on my own father' (Reid, p. 67).

22 'Death of the Beloved'. Rilke, '*Der Tod der Geliebten*', Arndts' translation, p. 108. In German, the line Ramsden quotes is '*Und Ihrer weise Wohlzutun*'.

23 Senior Nurse Ramsden. Ramsden reappears throughout the Vera trilogy like an avatar. Most likely she is based at least in part on Eleanor Ann Ellwood, a Senior Nurse with whom Jolley was infatuated for a time. Born 25 July 1922, Ellwood started nurse training at the Queen Elizabeth Hospital in Birmingham in 1940, leaving in 1946 to join the Queen Alexandria Imperial Nursing Service. She served with the QAINS for several years, in Mogadishu, the capital of Somalia, meeting Captain/Doctor Alex C. Jacob of the Royal Army Medical Corps. She married him in 1949 in Sandal, near Wakefield in Yorkshire, where she ran their home and helped in the surgery; they had no children; and in later life she became a Justice of the Peace and a Prison Visitor. She died of cancer in 1981 at age fifty-nine. Jolley last saw Ellwood in March 1945 in the post office at Five Ways, near the QEH; on 2 February 1949, when living with the Fleetwood-Walkers in Birmingham, she urgently wrote to Ellwood in care of her mother but received no response, to her bitter disappointment; and she tried to reach her again from Edinburgh in 1953, with no result.

24 Grandchildren. Matthew, Daniel and Sam were born to Bert and Ruth Jolley Radley in 1982, 1984 and 1988, Alice to Brian and Sarah Jolley Nelson in 1987.

25 Myth of Ceres. The details of the Ceres story mesh tellingly with *The Orchard Thieves*. When Ceres, disguised as an old woman, searches for her daughter Persephone, she is welcomed into the home of King of Eleusis, whose two sons she then nurses. Grateful for his hospitality, she plans to turn one of the sons into a god by making him immortal through burning his mortal spirit away in the family hearth.

26 Is/is not autobiographical. 'Cloisters', p. 531; '"What Sins"', p. 7; Moran, 'Drawing', p. 9 (emphasis added); Kavanagh, p. 440; and the last two quotes, Willbanks, p. 118. See also Glover, p. 64. These and other examples are collected in Milech, 'A Novel', p. 187.

27 Fiction is not autobiography. 'Little Herb', p. 51.

28 'If my purpose was autobiographical . . .' Ronan quoted in Milli, p. 218.

29 Not fictional autobiography, confession or disclosure. Hugo, p. 10, Daniel, 'Plotting', p. 33, and McKernan, p. 93.

30 Trent in fact and fiction. Moran, 'Jolley', p. 1.

31 *Autobiographical* fiction, and 'literary *fiction*'. Craven, 'Writers' Tales', p. 7.

32 Bewdley. 'Summer Memories', p. 7.

33 Assuaging the deep wound. Daniel's phrase is 'licking an old wound', in 'Plotting', p. 33.

34 Bird on Jolley, and Said. Bird, 'Elizabeth Jolley's Late Work', and Said, p. 7.

35 Dalton's 'leanings'. Koval, 'Interview'.

36 Paedophile. Kitson, p. 27.

37 Hawthorne, KC. Henry Bell refers to Hawthorne as 'the Officer, the Gentleman, the Barrister, the Church-going Tennis and Bridge-player . . . he knew had been a cad' (p. 206).

38 Jolley's own line. The last words of the essay are 'that both my father and Mr Berrington loved my mother very much'.

39 Non-judgemental. E. Lindsay, p. 200.

40 *Lovesong* a bestseller. *Age* (Melbourne), Saturday Extra, p. 8; *Weekend Australian Review*, Books, 23–24 Aug. 1997, p. 10; and *Australian Book Review*, Sept. 1997, p. 52.

41 Garner's visit. Garner, p. 14.

42 Apostle's injunction. Ephesians 6:14. Rilke's question and answer are: *Wer spricht von Siegen? Überstehn ist alles* ('Who talks of victory? To hold out is all').

43 The sublime master. Craven, 'Black Humour', p. A2. See also Lurie's 'Fine Friendship'.

Epilogue—Friendship has a meaning that goes both ways . . .

1 An acquaintance is not a friend. Jolley, 'More than Just Mates', p. 1.

2 Emerson on friendship. Quoted in Jolley, 'More than Just Mates', p. 1.

Notes

3   Total, trusting friendship. Reid, p. 82.
4   Jolley and Levey on friendship. Finlay, p. 3.
5   Special friends. Reid, p. 83.
6   Garner's essay, and correspondence. Garner, 'Elizabeth Jolley: An Appreciation', and 'To My Dear Lift-Rat'.
7   Letters from aristocrats and others. Jolley told Dibble about the German man and also alludes to him in her 14 May 1996 letter to Sezacinski; the other examples are from her letters to Sezacinski.
8   A wave from afar. Sezacinski in conversation with Dibble.
9   Writing to her father. Grenville and Woolf, p. 163.
10 The grief of not being able to write to her father. Willbanks, p. 119.
11 Rapprochement with her mother through letters. Baker, p. 229.
12 Missed the letter-writing. Baker, p. 228.
13 Unexpected conclusions. Jolley to Sezacinski, 12 Nov. 1944.
14 Jolley on writing. Gardiner, p. 13; Ellison, p. 176; James, p. 98; and, Willbanks, p. 124.
15 'Stepping off into imagination'. Grenville and Woolfe, p. 157; Kavanagh, p. 447.
16 Sophisticated space. See Milech, 'Sophisticated Spaces'.

ACKNOWLEDGEMENTS

During the course of researching and writing this biography I was often, to paraphrase Leonard Jolley's biblical allusion, like Ignorance crying at the gates, in the streets and at the coming in of the doors. Over time, several hundred people answered my calls. Their names appear below, so many of them that I am sure to have omitted others: I apologise to them. Some are recorded simply, some with comments, some with an indication of what they provided for use in this book. I sincerely thank those who helped; this work was not a solo effort.

I would like especially to foreground the names of some people whose contribution felt personally motivated, in support of me, Elizabeth Jolley, or both. At Edith Cowan University, Senior Music Librarian Ken Gasmier, a friend of both Leonard and Elizabeth Jolley, quietly tracked the research and shared his musical knowledge as it related to Elizabeth Jolley's life and work. At the University of Western Australia, Associate Professor Delys Bird, long-time friend and colleague of Elizabeth Jolley, over the years shared her knowledge and impressions of Jolley and her work; university archivists Christine Bapty, Maria Carvalho and Miriam Congdon found information on Leonard Jolley and a number of other UWA key figures; and Jenny Wildy, Music Librarian, answered many questions about Leonard and Elizabeth Jolley's musical interests. At Curtin University, Professor Colin Brown, Dean of Media, Society and Culture, was continually supportive, and Professor Linda Kristjanson, Pro Vice-Chancellor for Research, provided a grant to aid in its completion; Linda Browning, Irene Faulks, Helen Mumme, Noreen Richards and Sally Worth, Communication and Cultural Studies staff colleagues, supported me and formed and maintained close personal friendships with Elizabeth Jolley; Bruce Ridley found and secured difficult-to-locate permissions for two photos; Sara Buttsworth, Gemma Edeson, Christine Houen, Deborah Hunn, Gillian Martin, Helen Mulroney (who also scanned dozens of photos for possible inclusion), Anne-Marie Newton, Anne Ryden and Jane Scott—dedicated, talented and imaginative researchers—worked on one or more of three overlapping projects, this biographical one, another on Leonard Jolley, and the one driven by Barbara Milech, an on-line bibliography of Elizabeth Jolley and her work housed in the John Curtin Prime Ministerial Library; Rachel Robertson provided editorial assistance and initiated the process of securing permissions to quote from Jolley's work, all to a high standard; Associate Professor Franz Oswald helped with German translations and advised on Hitler's influence in Germany. At the University of Klagenfurt in Austria, Associate Professor Adi Wimmer advised on details of turn-of-the-last-century Austrian life, described the origins of, and distinctions among, the *Hitler Jugend*, *Bund Deutscher Mädel* and *Jungmädelführerinnenlager* organisations, and shared his insights on Elizabeth Jolley's life and fiction. University of Chicago Emeritus Professor of Slavic and Comparative Literature, Edward Wasiolek, advised on Tolstoy and his work. Barry Humphries, who worked for several years to schedule an Elizabeth Jolley Lecture into his Australian itinerary and visited Jolley at home and in hospital on two different visits, shared the story of their friendship. Joan Peters, Perth, an arts and media lawyer (and an ex-Jolley student), and her colleague Robert Garton Smith, Fremantle, of Garton Smith & Co., drafted documents and authorities and provided legal advice throughout the project. And Jo Robertson, former student, colleague and long-time friend of mine and Elizabeth Jolley, reread all of Jolley's work in order to correct details and critique the thrust of my discussions of it.

'Flowermead'—The fury haunting the family...

AUSTRIA Ilse Gaugusch, Oberwölz, described the Fehr family in Austria (one related to her own), Margarete Fehr in England, and the Jolleys in Scotland. Felix Gundacher, Vienna, Institut für Historische Familienforschung, explained the Fehr family tree and speculated on the family's life in the late 1800s–early 1900s. Pfarrer Christian Halama, Vienna, Curator of St Salvator's Altkatholisch Church, provided documentation on Joseph Edward Fehr's affiliation with the Altkatholisch Church. Pfarrer Josef Haracz of St Michaelskirchen in Fischamend offered access to the church's births/deaths/marriages records that yielded essential information on

Joseph Xavier and Joseph Deri Fehr and their families. Doreen Hopwood, and Paul Taylor, Birmingham, Birmingham Central Library Local Studies and Family History Librarians, helped with Knight and Berrington family history questions. Herr Huemer, Vienna, Wiener Stadt- und Landesarchiv, made Joseph Edward Fehr family birth/marriage/death records available. Irene Kirchof, Fischamend, Loba Feinchemie (current owners of the original Fehr factory), outlined the history of the site and provided a tour of the remains of original Fehr textiles factory. Ian Jackson, Woodbrooke Quaker Study Centre, Birmingham, helped on the topic of Quaker pacifism. Kriegsarchiv and Arkiv der Republik staff, Vienna, made records available on the naval careers of Alexander, Karl and Joseph Edward Fehr and also the medical records of Walter Arnold Fehr. Lydia Marinelli, Vienna, Research Director of the Sigmund Freud Foundation, advised on Wilfrid Knight's possible visit to Freud in the 1920s. Professor Adalbert Melichar, Fischamend, local historian, explained Joseph Xavier Fehr's introduction of 'Manchester' fabric to Austria. Palais Justiz staff, Vienna, determined that Joseph Edward Fehr had not been a judge. Esther Roitman von Wartburg, Vienna, Irma Roitman's daughter, spoke about her mother and her friendship with Margarete Fehr and her (Irma's) continuing contact with Madelaine Knight Blackmore whom she had met and with whom she was a friend. Cardinal Christoph Schönborn, Vienna, aided with the search for Margarete Fehr's *Klosterschule*. Sheila Spielhofer, Vienna, helped with research on Fischamend. Rev. Helmut Nauzner of the Methodist Church in Vienna provided documentation on the marriage of Wilfrid and Margarete Knight. **AUSTRALIA** University of Western Australia Emeritus Professor Reg Appleyard (Economics) advised on calculating the 2007 Australian dollar equivalent of Kenneth Berrington's bequest to Margarete Knight. Lieutenant Ian Harvey, Royal Australian Navy, Melbourne, advised on Austrian military matters, including Admiral von Tegetthoff and Alexander and Karl Fehr's naval service, and he also advised on Kenneth Berrington's beliefs and military status. Archbishop Barry Hickey (and his secretary Jane Pilkington), Perth, secured Vienna's then-Archbishop/now-Cardinal Schönborn's help with this research. Dorothy Mali, Perth, an Austrian/Australian colleague, charmed her way through red tape in Vienna's Rathaus. Dr Peter Stanley, Canberra, Principal Historian, and Brad Manera, Senior Research Officer, Australian War Memorial, analysed Kenneth Berrington's war service. Paul Roitman, Melbourne, provided information on his family and his experiences in England. Professor John Scott, University of Western Australia, helped with the Dante references. Dr Ingeborg Zoll, Perth, WAIT/Curtin friend and colleague, helped with German translations and explanations. **BORNEO** Raymund Tan told of studying with

Acknowledgements

Wilfrid Knight in England in the 1960s. **ENGLAND** Ray Annetts, Salisbury, Charles Knight's sister Eliza's grandson, provided a tour of the Knight family's three farms near Salisbury. Margaret Baker, Brentwood, Essex, genealogist, found information on Kenneth Berrington and the Knight families, and advised on Wilfrid's Knight's imprisonment. Joy Knight Blacklock, Swindon, Ewart Knight's daughter, spoke about mysterious Aunt Dorothy. Caroline Brown, Keighley, Librarian and Information Officer, Keighley Local Studies Library, found information on Maud Thrippleton. Hilary Clark, Wolverhampton. Gillian Knight Cauthery, Stowmarket, Charles Knight's brother Arthur's granddaughter, helped with the genealogy. Dr/Reverend Nigel Collinson, Southampton, minister at Beckminster Methodist Church when Wilfrid Knight died, retailed Margarete Knight's story of Wilfrid Knight's trip to meet Freud. Constance 'Betty' Sheldon Cruikshank, Harpenden, Hertfordshire, spoke of her family's stories about their relationship with the Knights and of her continuing contact with Jolley in Australia, advising her regarding publishing opportunities in England. Ursula Garman, University of London, provided access to Wilfrid Knight's BSc and MSc records. Doctor R. B. J. (Bruce) Goldie, Wolverhampton, the Knight family's physician (as was his father before him), advised as he could about the relationship with his Knight family patients. Tony Goring, Tettenhall, Wilfrid Knight's young spastic friend, told of their friendship. Guy Holborn, London, Librarian, Lincoln's Inn Library, supplied information on Berrington's law qualifications and experience. Sir/Professor Gabriel Horn, Cambridge, Margarete Knight's student in the 1940s, kindly supplied photocopies of a 1948 and ten 1976–78 letters from her to him and told of their friendship. Doris Horobin, Wolverhampton, the Knights' Wells Road neighbour, explained her admiration for Margarete Knight. Josef Keith, London, Friends House Library, helped determine there were no Quaker records showing that Wilfrid Knight had gone with Friends to Vienna in the 1920s. John Moxham, Finchfield, Methodist lay preacher with Wilfrid Knight, studied and explained the records of Knight's qualifying to become a lay preacher after his 1938 reconversion. Margaret O'Gorman, Wolverhampton. Norman Reed, Wolverhampton. Keith Munns, London, Governor, HMP Wormwood Scrubs, sent copies of Wilfrid Knight's court and prison records. Matt Perry, Newcastle University, explained the background of those who marched in the Jarrow Crusade and how/where people joined/left it en route. J. S. Ringrose, Cambridge, Honorary Archivist, Pembroke College, supplied information on Kenneth and Leslie Berrington's university education and qualifications, and Dr M. M. N. Stansfield, Durham University Library, Assistant Keeper, Archives and Special Collections, sent further information on the latter.

Acknowledgements

Alice Steel and Sylvia Stanyer, Penn, Wolverhampton, The Woodlands Rest Home, the former for impressions of the Knight family, the latter for information on Margarete Knight's stay at The Woodlands in the 1970s. Trixie Thrift, Penn, Wolverhampton, and Eric and Pip Turner, Wolverhampton, Quaker friends of Wilfrid Knight in the 1930s and 1940s. Arthur Vernon, Warrington, Wilfrid Knight's Bilston Grammar teaching colleague. Jim Washbourne, Oxford, Wilfrid Knight's student in the 1950s. Helen Marsh Wellington, Wolverhampton, Margarete Knight's house helper in the 1970s, told of working for her and of the contretemps around the time of Wilfrid Knight's death. Mary Wynn, Malvern, Worcestershire, spoke of her family's stories about their relationship with the Knights and of Margarete Knight's early days in England. Michael Youett, Birmingham, Quaker Religious Society of Friends. Wolverhampton Local Studies Department, researched information on the Knights and Berrington. **FRANCE** Anne-Marie Soulier, University of Strasbourg, pointed out that the dust jackets of Jolley's European translations represented her mother as a baroness. **GERMANY** Max Knöffel, Ennepetal-Rüggeburg, and Gottfried Leiser, Munich, POWs befriended by the Knights in the 1940s, spoke of visits to their home and their impressions of Wilfrid and Margarete Knight; and Herr Leiser provided a list of dates and events from his time as a POW in England and of the Knights' subsequent visits to see him in Germany. Professor Horst Priessnitz and Cornelia Schulze, Wuppertal, helped contact and interview Herr Knöffel. **NEW ZEALAND** Roger Baker, South Canterbury, Wilfrid Knight's Bilston Grammar student. **WALES** Caroline Jones, Dyfed, Llanelli, French teacher with Wilfrid Knight at Bilston. Michael (and Patricia) Hill, Swansea, Wilfrid Knight's student in the 1960s, recounted Knight's sparrow-killing incident, the Freud trip, and his post-retirement teaching. **UNITED STATES** Long-time friend and colleague Professor G. Thomas Tisue, then with the International Atomic Energy Agency, with his wife Krys Neumann provided accommodation in Vienna, he helping to interview the *BDM* women in Hamburg, and she helping to interview Ilse Gaugusch in Oberwölz.

Sibford—If she can swim, it does not matter how deep the water is . . .

AUSTRALIA Patricia Franz-Cullen, Echuca, Victoria, pointed the way to Rose Marie Haccius Salfeld in Goslar, Germany. Jenny Lamb Wilson, Perth, spoke of her mother Edith Lamb from Jolley's Sibford days. Norman Smith, Sydney, and Brian Southall, Perth, Sibford old scholars from the 1930s, told of their experiences at Sibford. **ENGLAND** Jennifer Barraclough, Selly Oak, Director of the Woodbrooke

Acknowledgements

Quaker Study Centre, provided accommodation and facilitated study on the Society of Friends as it related to Wilfrid Knight's commitment to Quaker principles. John Dunston, Sibford Ferris, Banbury, Oxfordshire, Sibford Headmaster (1990–96), and Ann Stephenson, Secretary, Sibford School, welcomed me to Sibford and provided access to its records. Michael Finch, Churchill, Chipping Norton, Oxfordshire, Sibford School Historian and long-time officer of Sibford Old Scholars' Association, answered many questions, as did Ashley Shirlin, Thorpe Bay, Essex, Sibford School website designer and master (skoolties.co.uk). Sibford students contemporary with Jolley: Tony Mannesah, Penzance, Cornwall; Jean Mills Deardon, Selly Oak, Birmingham; John Osborne and Jean Sinclair Osborne, Selly Oak, Birmingham; Margaret Perry Sargent, Carlisle, Cumbria; Libby Holden Wood-Thompson, Stony Stratford, Buckinghamshire; and Edith Worrall, Bournemouth, Dorset, shared their rich memories of Sibford and Monica 'Beaky' Knight. **FRANCE** Jacques Perruchon, Bernay-Saint Martin, identified records of Steffi Bauer's stay in France. **GERMANY** Inge Edelmann, Hamburg, provided information about the summer camp Jolley attended in 1939. Britta Kuhlenbeck, Hamburg, researched the 1939 timetables of *Der Schwan* and *MS Caribia*. Professor Rose Marie Hacchius Salfeld, Goslar. **WALES** Barrie and Sheila Macpherson Naylor, Near Chepstow, Gwent (and later Sheila Naylor in Portskerritt, Monmouth), Sibford English and Art teachers from the 1930s, shared their memories of Monica Knight and her school friends, provided photographs of Sibford and copies of James K. Baxter's Sibford poems.

Pyrford—A nurse should be unable to make a mistake . . .

ENGLAND Alex Attewell, London, then-Curator of the Florence Nightingale Museum, facilitated contact with others knowledgeable about St Nicholas and St Martin's Hospitals. Gordon Hadfield, Woking, Surrey, Emeritus Consultant Trauma and Orthopaedic Surgeon at the Sir Rowley Bristow Hospital in Pyrford and at St Peter's Hospital in Chertsey—a surgeon at St Nicholas and St Martin's from 1955—spoke about both Bristow and Furlong whom he had known and also said why he thought young women could not start training to be a general nurse before they were seventeen. Gina Linday MacKenzie, Leatherhead, Surrey, who was at St Nicholas and St Martin's in the 1945–46 period (and at the Queen Elizabeth Hospital in Birmingham, 1939–45, in the 10th PTS), reported Zunz's low opinion of the QEH but did not agree with it, and she also said why she thought young women could not start training to be a general nurse before they were seventeen. Barbara Provis, Woking, Surrey, sometime patient, long-time volunteer at St Nicholas and

Acknowledgements

St Martin's, and now unofficial archivist for those two institutions which were demolished in 1990 provided information on them from records in her possession.

Birmingham—The most powerful thing in this life . . .

ENGLAND Norah 'Sticker' Harvey Barnes (15th PTS), Bournemouth, Dorset, provided biographical information on fellow trainee nurse Mary Doyle whom she knew until Doyle's death in 2004. Alan Cass, Sheffield, South Yorkshire, Leonard Jolley's Selly Oak Colleges Library friend and colleague, explained how Jolley ran his library. Jack Chapman, Winchester, Hampshire, founder of the Charney Bassett commune Leonard Jolley joined when he left Pyrford in the early 1940s, recalled Jolley's time there. Professor Collette Clifford, University of Birmingham, and her QEH colleague Doreen Tennant from the 19th PTS, were generous with their time and ingenuity in finding various records of Jolley's years at the QEH. Jeff and Dorothy Davies Woods, Much Wenlock, Shropshire, from the QEH's 35th and 49th PTSs, contacted other women who trained with Jolley at the QEH. Lloyd and Margaret Jolley Edmonds, Manchester, she the daughter of Leonard Jolley's older brother Harry and friendly with his sister/her aunt Laura—in addition to her father's sister, she was the main source of information on the Jolley children's childhood, providing photographs of them as young scholars. Dr Peggy Frazer/Mrs Fleetwood-Walker, London, shared her memories of Monica Knight/Fielding and her daughter Sarah from the 1940s—Jolley kept in touch with her until Frazer died in 1998, shortly before her son Guy. Guy Walker's widow Winifred Walker, Stratford-on-Avon, was also very helpful, as were her children: Tim Walker, London, provided biographical information on his grandparents and a photograph of Guy Walker and his brother Colin Fleetwood, and Nicola Walker, Guy Walker's daughter Head of Collections Care and Access, The Whitworth Art Gallery, University of Manchester, provided the image of Peggy Frazer. Peggy's stepson Colin Fleetwood's widow Patricia Fleetwood, Birmingham, and her brother Dominican Father Jonathan Fleetwood, Stowe, Staffordshire, were also helpful (by chance their family name was also Fleetwood, the name Colin chose to use). Lesley Lam, Exmouth, Devon, spoke about Leonard Jolley's Charney Bassett experience when she and her husband were there in the 1930s and 1940s, and about Joyce Hancock who sometimes visited there. Janet Leonard and Meline Nielsen, Birmingham, Selly Oak Colleges Head Librarians, the one preceding and the other succeeding Leonard Jolley, spoke of his reputation. Duncan Raynor, the King Edward's School in Birmingham, son of Geoffrey and Jean Raynor, spoke of his parents and their professional lives. Marion

Acknowledgements

Sprague, Seisdon, Wolverhampton, Gertrude Whele's daughter and Sibford student, recalled Jolley's visits. Laura Jolley Welton, Exmouth, Devon, wrote about her brother Leonard Jolley and their family background. Father Gregory Winterton, The Oratorio/Church of the Immaculate Conception, Birmingham, provided the contact for Colin Walker's surviving family. Staff at the Birmingham Registry Office. **UNITED STATES** Pat Goode Hertzog (15th PTS), Puyallup, Washington, who was at the QEH with Jolley, Barnes and Doyle, gave her perspective on Elizabeth Jolley and her relationship with Leonard Jolley.

Pinewood—Herts requires Staff: Matron, Teacher, Handyman/Gardner . . .

AUSTRALIA Tim Hanbury, Sydney, whose parents owned Amwellbury House from the 1960s to the 1990s, supplied photographs of it. Christina Martin, Melbourne, Pinewood student from the 1950s and now a psychologist, shared her insights about Pinewood. **CANADA** Professor Rosemary Sullivan, Toronto, University of Toronto, Elizabeth Smart's biographer, spoke of her correspondence with Jolley about her time at Pinewood. **ENGLAND** Margaret Arnold, Frogmore, Near Kingsbridge, Devon, a family friend of Elizabeth Strachan, explained the origins and peregrinations of Pinewood and provided photographs of Elizabeth Strachan. Moona Richardson Beswick, London, daughter of the Ralph Richardsons who in the 1950s owned the estate where Pinewood was located. John Bridges, Ware, Hertfordshire, friend of Pinewood staff member painter Melville Hardiment. Ben McKenzie, Ware, Hertfordshire, Deputy Head of Pinewood, a nearby school of the same name but otherwise unrelated, volunteered to study voting roles from the 1950s and to determine who was working/living at the school during the period Fielding/Jolley was there. Pinewood staff from the 1950s—Arthur Pickford, Stoke-by-Nayland, Suffolk; Rosemary Pohl, Hertford; Tessa Spackman Chestnut, Hertford Heath; and Pinewood students from the 1950s—Georgina Barker and Peter Kenyatta, London (who kindly provided a photograph of his mother from her days at Pinewood); Angela Pleasence, Weybridge, Surrey; Julyan Wickham, London; Anna Wilson, West High Wycombe, South Buckinghamshire. Dr David and Antonia Preston, Ware, Hertfordshire, current owners of Amwellbury House, generously provided a tour of their historic home and told of its history. Su Miller, London, daughter of Elizabeth Strachan's youngest sister Irene (Reenee), a Pinewood student in 1947–48, provided a photograph of Strachan and much information about her. Rev. A. and Jean Walker, Great Amwell, Hertfordshire, of St John the Baptist Anglican church in the 1950s, spoke of Edna Kenyatta and her son. **JAPAN** Ian Channing, Tokyo, journalist interested in Celia Fiennes and her uncle's Amwellbury House. **SWITZERLAND** Alistair Scott, Gland, a Pinewood student in the 1950s.

Scotland—The horror of marriage lies in its 'dailiness' . . .

AUSTRALIA Margaret Sprott Coates, Busselton, friend of the Jolleys from Glasgow days. Geoff Gallop, Perth, then-Leader of the Western Australian (Labor) Opposition and university friend of Tony Blair, served as liaison with Blair's office. **CANADA** Emeritus Professor Geoffrey Pendrill, Jolley's successor at the Royal College of Physicians. **ENGLAND** Tony Blair, London, via his Special Assistant Anji Hunter. Jo Clogg, Selly Oak, Librarian at the Woodbrooke Quaker Study Centre. Martyn Turnbull, London BBC, provided typed and audio copies of Elizabeth Jolley radio plays. **SCOTLAND** Margaret D. Bell (ret.), Edinburgh, Librarian of the Central Library of the University of Edinburgh (co-author of an article with Leonard Jolley). Donald Campbell, Edinburgh, Scottish writer, director and theatre historian, described John Broom's later life in Edinburgh. Roger and Diana Bland, Edinburgh (he the son of Bill and Nora Bland, and younger brother of Richard) recalled the Jolleys' life in Paisley Crescent in the early 1950s. Professor Iain Donaldson, Edinburgh, Honorary Librarian of the RCP. Dr Robert Donaldson, Edinburgh, explained the early days of *The Bibliotheck*. Kenneth Dunn, Edinburgh, Senior Manuscripts Curator of the National Library of Scotland, described the Edinburgh Bibliographical Society and Leonard Jolley's involvement with it—as serendipity would have it, in 1964 Dunn lived in the Jolleys' old house in Jordanhill, where, he said, some of his older neighbours still referred to the conservatory as 'Mrs Jolley's sewing room'. Peter Grant (ret.), Aberdeen, Head of the Central Library and friend of John Broom, provided images of him. Joan Ferguson, MBE, Edinburgh, Geoffrey Pendrill's successor at the RCP. R. O. MacKenna (ret.), Glasgow, Librarian for the University of Glasgow, described Leonard Jolley's appointment as Deputy Librarian and his contribution to reorganising the library. Iain Milne, Edinburgh, Librarian of the Royal College of Physicians, helped in a variety of ways regarding the RCP, Leonard Jolley's work environment and his accomplishments there. Tam McPhail, Stromness, proprietor of Stromness Books and Prints, told of John Broom's history before and after he ran Stromness Books and Prints in the 1970s. Andrew Wale, Glasgow, then-Director for the University of Glasgow Library, defined the changes and the significance of them that Leonard Jolley made to the library.

Acknowledgements

1960s—After the flight of the cockatoos . . .

AUSTRALIA G. G. Allen (ret.), Perth, Head Librarian, WAIT. Dr Lynn Allen, Perth (ret.), CEO and State Librarian (1989-2001), Alexander/State Library of Western Australia. Professor John Barnes (ret.), La Trobe University. Lyn Beard, Parkerville, WA, teacher and history enthusiast, shared her local history research which helped in constructing the Andrew Dungey story. Professor Alan Billings (Engineering) and Joyce Billings (Mathematics), Perth, both retired from the University of Western Australia, provided anecdotes on staff life in the 1960s and 1970s, on Elizabeth Jolley's work with Watkins Products, and loaned a copy of *Cooking by Degrees*. Wendy Birman (ret.), Perth, librarian. Carol Blacklett, Claremont Museum, Perth, for information on Hedges Store and the Victoria Nursing Home. Judy Brown Bottomley (ret.), Perth, librarian, University of Western Australia. Harrison Bryan (ret.), Sydney, Librarian of the Australian National Library spoke of Leonard Jolley's reputation as a scholar-librarian and of his not suffering fools gladly. Merle Schock Campbell, daughter of the Headmaster of the Parkerville School, recalled the experience of riding her bicycle past Andrew Dungey's place every day. Noreen and Malcolm Campbell, Parkerville, current owners of Sunnybrook Farm, immediately east of Dungey's home. Eric Crumb (ret.), Sawyers Valley, teacher and naturalist. Diane Costello, Canberra, Executive Officer of CAUL (Council of Australian University Librarians). Dr Andrew Domahidy (ret.), Perth, Librarian, University of Western Australia. Dungey relatives and in-laws too numerous to mention, in New South Wales, South Australia and Western Australia, whose help individually and collectively was invaluable. Murdoch University Emeritus Professor Brian de Garis, Perth, provided information on Fred Alexander and Leonard Jolley. Joan Feathers (ret.), Perth, Manager, Alfred Carson Lodge. F. D. O. Fielding (ret.), Brisbane, Librarian of the University of Queensland. Earl Gow (ret.), Adelaide, Chief Librarian, La Trobe University. Professor Selwyn Grave (ret.), New Zealand, University of Western Australia. Rob Greenwood and his family, Perth, Sunnybrook Farm neighbours of Andrew Dungey during the 1940s–1960s. Barbara M. Hale (ret.), Perth, Deputy Librarian, University of Western Australia. University of Western Australia Emeritus Professor (Law) Richard Harding, Perth, now Inspector of Custodial Services, recalled the 'Hopalong Acidly' epithet for Leonard Jolley. Professor John Legge (ret.), Adelaide, Monash University historian. Professor (History) J. M. Lindsay (ret.), Adelaide, formerly of the University of Western Australia. Hannah Levey, Melbourne, the first person to be interviewed for this book; and Ruth Levey Alexander, Melbourne, Harry and Hannah Levey's daughter, who contributed information in the 2000s. Professor Roy Lourens (ret.), Perth, Vice Chancellor of Edith Cowan University. John McIver, Parkerville, Parkerville Boys' Home boy, recalled Andrew Dungey from the mid-1930s through the mid-1960s; and comparably his sister Pat McIver Hahnel. Nancy McKenzie, Perth, Jolley's long-time typist and friend. Claire McLisky, University of Melbourne, Dorothy Sanders/Lucy Walker scholar. Julie Smith Maxam (ret.), Sydney, Librarian, University of Western Australia. Kevin Mountain (ret.), Midland, WA, Western Australian Government Railroad, found information on Dungey's friend Fred Medcraft. Gil Nicol (ret.), Margaret River, WA, Partner, Cameron Chisholm and Nicol. Neil Radford (ret.), Sydney, Librarian of the Fisher Library, University of Sydney. Vivienne Rowney, Perth, Editor of *Country Woman*, the magazine of the Country Women's Association of WA. Robert Sharman (ret.), Perth, State Librarian (1976-89), Alexander/State Library of Western Australia. F. A. Sharr (ret.), OBE, State Librarian (1953-76), Alexander/State Library of Western Australia. Fairlie Sezachinski, Melbourne, provided copies of her correspondence with Elizabeth Jolley and permission to quote from them. Professor Phil (Mathematics, ret.) and Judith Silberstein, University of Western Australia, loaned a home movie of UWA colleagues (including Elizabeth Jolley) socialising together. Ingrid Sims (ret.), Perth, Librarian, University of Western Australia. Colonel (ret.) Cecily Sinclair Smith, Perth, a genealogist with extensive knowledge of the Dungey family. Dr Sian Supski, Perth, Australian Research Institute Lotteries West Historical Research Fellow, Curtin University, researched information on Andrew Dungey's £300 lottery win. Professor David Tunley (ret.) Music, University of Western Australia. Ian Viner, QC, Perth, prosecutor in the case of *The State of Western Australia v. Vladimir Nabokov's Lolita*, relayed with good humour how a number of UWA academics were successfully deployed to undermine his case, Leonard Jolley among them. E. D. ('Ted') Watt (ret.), University of Western Australia. Professor Jean Whyte, Adelaide, Library Studies, Monash University. **ENGLAND** Lyndall Florence Pearce Dunne, Tavistock, Devon, object of Leonard Jolley's infatuation at University College London in the 1930s. Trevor Todd, London, Royal Institute of British Architects, Information Unit.

1970s—I was sort of on the market...

AUSTRALIA Jill Belbin described Jolley's discussions with her about mothers and daughters while Jolley worked in the Belbin home. Lyn Blasgund, Perth, Superintendent of the Wooroloo Prison Farm. Pam Burgoyne, Perth, student in

Acknowledgements

Jolley's first Fremantle Arts Centre classes. Sylvia Fordymacka, Perth, Ludmila Blotnicki's informal carer in the 1970s and 1980s, prepared biographical information about the Blotnickis and offered a photograph for use in this book (provided in digitised form by Bogumiła Żongołowicz, Melbourne—it appears in her edition of Blotnicki's posthumous book *Przez zieloną granicę* [2008]). Sir/Justice Francis Burt, Perth, recalled presiding over the case involving John Dawkins, Leonard Jolley and WA Newspapers. Dr Phillip Goatcher, Cottesloe, owner (with his wife Phyllis) of the Jarrahdale bush block Leonard Jolley wanted to buy in the 1970s (his permission given via their daughter Jane Goatcher Storey). Clive Newman, Fremantle, Business Manager of the original Fremantle Arts Centre Press, provided sales details of Jolley's early books. Terry Owen, Claremont, Foundation Manager of the Fremantle Arts Centre Press, related events from the early days of the FACP. Joslyn Summerhayes described Jolley's days cleaning in the Summerhayes' home at 3 The Coombe, Mosman Park. Ian Templeman, Canberra, Foundation Director of the Fremantle Arts Centre and CEO of the Fremantle Arts Centre Press, explained how he first met Jolley. Louise Clark Tyson (ret.), Perth, Leonard Jolley's secretary. Helen Wade, Canberra, Senior Research Librarian, the National Library of Australia.

1980–84—The inside of people's survival . . .

AUSTRALIA: Connie Gregory, Melbourne, Darwin Community College staff member in the 1980s when Jolley judged the Northern Territory Literary Awards. Dr Beate Josephi, Perth, Edith Cowan University, member of the Adelaide Festival Writers' Week Committee 1982–88 and its Chair 1986–88. Associate Professor Joan Kirkby, University of New South Wales, recounted Jolley's visit when *Milk and Honey* was launched. Dr Elaine Lindsay, Sydney, Program Manager, Literature and History, Arts NSW. Ruth Reid, Perth, Jolley's long-time friend. Maree Roberts, Curtin University, Manager of Remuneration Services, reported professorial salaries in the 1980s. Susan Ryan, Canberra, Penguin's Publications Director in 1988. University of Adelaide Emeritus Professor Tom Shapcott, Melbourne, poet/novelist and Director of the Literature Board of the Australia Council (1983–90). Jason Steger, Literary Editor, and Monica Simpson, Manager of the Research Library, Melbourne *Age*. Irene Stevens, Sydney, Project Officer for the Literature Board (1970s–96). **ENGLAND**: Margaret Coutts, University of Leeds, Librarian and Keeper of the Brotherton Collection, on Leonard Jolley's interest in B. S. Page, a prominent British librarian.

Acknowledgements

1990–2007—Who talks of victory . . .

AUSTRALIA Louise Angrilli, Melbourne, Festival Administrator, and Rosemary Cameron, Director of the Melbourne *Age* Writers' Festival. Dr Peter Chapman, Curator, National Portrait Gallery, Canberra. Curtin ex-students Fotini Epanomitis Harvey, Sydney, Glen Parry, Perth, Tracy Ryan, Perth and Cambridge (England), and Sarah Rossetti, Perth, fine writers all, shared their experiences of being in Elizabeth Jolley's classes, Rossetti agreeing to hers being published. Mary Moore, Perth, painter of the portrait of Elizabeth Jolley in the National Portrait Gallery. Peter Kendall, Perth, artist. Sharon Rundle, Bucketty, NSW, a Jolley friend and correspondent from the early 1990s. University of Sydney Emeritus Professor Elizabeth Webby, Sydney, on the 'Three Elizabeths' confusion at the 1993 ASAL conference. **ENGLAND** Ruth Ellwood Pearce, Costock, Loughborough, Leicestershire, Eleanor Ellwood's sister. Margaret Pearce Jacob, Eleanor Ellwood's widowed husband's second wife, Wakefield, Yorkshire. Dr M. E. Scott, Wakefield, Yorkshire, who pointed the way to Margaret Jacob. Capt. (ret.) Peter H. Starling, Ash Vale, Hampshire, Director, Army Medical Services Museum, offered information on how to access Eleanor Ellwood's Army records. **SCOTLAND** Susan McCann, Edinburgh, Archivist, Royal College of Nursing, for information on Eleanor Ellwood's nursing career. **UNITED STATES** Photographer Ann Arbor and Professor John Rosenwald, Farmington, Maine, friends and colleagues, provided fine photographs from their 1996 meeting with Elizabeth Jolley. Beloit College Emeritus Professor Marion Kingston Jolley, Lamoine, Maine, for her provocative second-hand advice on parenting. **WALES** David Britton, Cardiff, playwright and friend of Jolley who (with Alan Becher) adapted her novel *The Newspaper of Claremont Street* for the stage in the 1990s.

General

Kevin Leamon, Copyright Librarian, Mitchell Library, State Library of New South Wales, made difficult deadlines possible by the speed with which he located and digitised archival photographs of Jolley and her family; and likewise Mirage Photographic Laboratory, Perth, digitised other photographs at remarkably short notice. Kay Mumme, expert genealogist and web navigator, against the odds found information on a number of people key to the Jolley story.

LIST OF ILLUSTRATIONS

1: Fehr family home, Florianigasse 2, Vienna, VIII, late 19th century (water colour by 'Riffler').
2: Wilfrid Knight in his late twenties.
3: Margarete Fehr in her early twenties.
4: 'Flowermead', the Knights' first home of their own, c. 1925–1928.
5: Monica holding Madelaine at 'Flowermead'.
6: Madelaine and Monica and their father's Ariel, July 1931.
7: Margarete Fehr Knight, 1932.
8: Wilfrid Knight, 1932.
9: Kenneth Berrington.
10: "The Hill", Sibford School, 1939.
11: *Drei Führerinnen*, Inge Edelmann, Monica Knight and Lenchen Haake, August 1939.
12: Sibford scholars, Libby Holden, Ishbel Whittaker and Monica 'Beaky' Knight, 1939.
13: 'Waldhof' youth hostel, Wingst, Germany.
14: Monica Knight, c. 1939—'Soon that smile will be wiped from my face'.
15: St Nicholas and St Martin's orthopaedic and tubercular patients in courtyard, Pyrford, c. 1940–1942.
16: Father Rudolph listening to music with Leonard Jolley.
17: Close friend Joyce Broom with patient.

List of Illustrations

18: Monica Knight with child, Summer 1940.
19: Monica Knight, trainee nurse, c. 1943.
20: Gertrude Whele (1904–1957), Monica Knight's friend and mentor.
21: Eleanor Ann Ellwood, 1940, a senior QEH nurse Knight much admired.
22: Fleetwood-Walker Home, 91 Hagley Rd, Edgbaston, Birmingham.
23: Guy Walker and Colin Fleetwood, in the late 1940s.
24: Peggy Frazer.
25: Edna Kenyatta (1910–1995), Monica Knight/Fielding's friend and confidante, early 1950s.
26: Elizabeth 'Strix' Strachan (1890–1962), late 1930s, proprietor of Pinewood from the early 1940s.
27: 48 Paisley Crescent, Edinburgh, the Jolleys' home, 1950–1956.
28: John Broom, friend of the Jolleys, before a painting based on Robert Burns' poem 'The Deil's Awa Wi' The Exciseman'.
29: The Jolleys' home at 62 Abbey Drive, Glasgow, 1956–1959.
30: Jolley after publishing her first book (*Five Acre Virgin*, 1976), portrait by Meg Padgham, 1977.
31: Leonard Jolley on his retirement, portrait by Ben Joel, 1979.
32: Quilt by Lesley Fitzpatrick (1999) based on Jolley's 'Pear Tree Dance'.
33: Ludmila Blotnicki, 1948, model for Nastasya in *The Newspaper of Claremont Street* (1981).
34: Hannah Levey—'the person who showed me how to live in Australia', with the Jolleys.
35: Jolley with her 1980–1993 agent Caroline Lurie at Southbank readings where she performed with Edna O'Brien, London, 1991.
36: Elizabeth Jolley at Wooroloo, 1986.
37: Jolley at her Federation home in Claremont, 1988.
38: The Jolleys' cottage in Wooroloo.
39: Jolley at Wooroloo, 1996.
40: 'Woman in a Lampshade', Ruth Cracknell with Peter Giutronich, from Christina Wilcox's film *The Nights Belong to the Novelist* (1986).
41: Jolley with Ingle Knight, winner of a WA Premier's award for his script of the 1998 stage adaptation of *Milk and Honey* (briefly called *A Prince of the Cello*).
42: L–R, scriptwriter Laura Jones, producer Sandra Levy, actors Pamela Rabe and Miranda Otto, director Samantha Lang and cinematographer Mandy Walker, people involved with the film version of Jolley's *The Well*,

List of Illustrations

      Australia's only film accepted for the 1997 Cannes International Film Festival.
43: State Living Treasure (Robert Garvey©1998).
44: Barry Humphries with Jolley at his 2002 Curtin University Elizabeth Jolley Lecture, 'My Life As Me'.
45: Curtin honorary doctorate, 1987, Jolley's first of four.
46: Portrait by Ben Joel, 1995.

Image Credits

I am grateful to the following photographers for allowing me to use their work:

24	Chris Quirk
27	Linda Browning
29	John Shade
37	Richard Hann
39	Ann Arbor
41	Frances Andrijich
43	Robert Garvey

I also thank the following people/organisations for allowing pictures from their collections/archives to appear here (the photographer's name, when known, appears in parentheses following the picture number):

1-3	Madelaine Knight Blackmore
4	Elizabeth Jolley
5	Madelaine Knight Blackmore
6-7	Mitchell Library, Library of New South Wales
8	Sarah Jolley Nelson (Elliott & Fry, photographers, London)
9	Mitchell Library, Library of New South Wales
10	Elizabeth Wood-Thompson
11-21	Elizabeth Jolley
22	Brian Dibble and Barbara Milech
23	Tim Walker for the estate of Mrs P Walker
24	Nicola Walker for the estate of Mrs P Walker; www.fleetwood-walker.co.uk — Study of Peggy for 'Peggy and Jean', 1939, Ref. 400
25	Peter Kenyatta
26	Su Miller
28	Gordon Wright's Scottish Photo Library (Gordon Wright)

List of Illustrations

30	Brian Dibble and Barbara Milech (Hans Versluis)
31	University of Western Australia
32	John Curtin Prime Ministerial Library (Hans Versluis)
33	Sylvia Fordymacka
34	Ruth Levey Anderson
35	Caroline Lurie
36	Christina Wilcox, director of the film *The Nights Belong to the Novelist*
38	Elizabeth Jolley
40	Christina Wilcox, director of the film *The Nights Belong to the Novelist*
42	Newspix (Marco del Grande)
44	Curtin University (GFP Studios)
45	Curtin University (Gillian Forsyth)
46	Robert Finlay-Jones (Ben Joel)

Every effort was made to contact the photographers of these images; anyone omitted who contacts us will be appropriately acknowledged in any subsequent edition.

WORKS CITED

Elizabeth Jolley—Novels and Collections

Citations to works by Elizabeth Jolley refer to *Elizabeth Jolley—A Bibliography, 1965–2007*, compiled by Barbara Milech and Brian Dibble, and published online through the Elizabeth Jolley Research Collection, John Curtin Prime Ministerial Library, Curtin University of Technology, Perth, WA, at <http://john.curtin.edu.au/jolley>.

Jolley, E., *An Accommodating Spouse*, Viking, New York, 1999; Penguin–Putnam, New York, 1999; Penguin, Ringwood, Vic., 1999.
——*Cabin Fever*, Viking, New York, 1990; Viking–Penguin, New York,1991; Penguin, Ringwood, Vic., 1991; Perennial-HarperCollins, New York, 1991; Sinclair-Stevenson, New York, 1991.
——*Central Mischief: Elizabeth Jolley on Writing, Her Past and Herself*, ed. and introd. Caroline Lurie, Viking, New York, 1992; Viking–Penguin, New York, 1993; Penguin, Ringwood, Vic., 1993.
——*Diary of a Weekend Farmer*, paintings by E. Kotai, Fremantle Arts Centre Press, Fremantle, WA, 1993.
——*Fellow Passengers: Collected Stories*, ed. and introd. B. Milech, Viking–Penguin, New York, 1997; Penguin, Ringwood, Vic., 1997.
——*Five Acre Virgin and Other Stories*, drawings by S. Grey-Smith, Fremantle Arts Centre Press, Fremantle, WA, 1976.

Works Cited

——*Foxybaby*, University of Queensland Press, St. Lucia, Qld., 1985.
——*The Georges' Wife*, Viking, New York, 1993; Viking–Penguin, New York, 1994; Penguin, Ringwood, Vic., 1994.
——*An Innocent Gentleman*. Viking, New York, 2001; Penguin–Putnam, New York, 2001; Penguin, Ringwood, Vic., 2001.
——*Learning to Dance: Elizabeth Jolley—Her Life and Works*, ed. and introd. C. Lurie, Viking, New York, 2006; Penguin, Camberwell, Vic., 2006.
——*Lovesong*. Viking, New York, 1997; Viking–Penguin, New York, 1997; Penguin, Ringwood, Vic., 1997.
——*Milk and Honey*, Fremantle Arts Centre Press, Fremantle, WA, 1984.
——*Miss Peabody's Inheritance*, University of Queensland Press, St. Lucia, Qld., 1983.
——*Mr Scobie's Riddle*, Penguin, Ringwood, Vic., 1983.
——*My Father's Moon*, Viking, New York, 1989; Viking–Penguin, New York, 1989; Penguin, Ringwood, Vic., 1989.
——*The Newspaper of Claremont Street*, drawings by M. Browne, Fremantle Arts Centre Press, Fremantle, WA, 1981.
——*Off the Air: Nine Plays for Radio by Elizabeth Jolley*, comp. and introd. D. Bird, Penguin, Ringwood, Vic., 1995.
——*The Orchard Thieves*, Viking, New York, 1995; Viking-Penguin, New York, 1997; Penguin, Ringwood, Vic., 1997.
——*Palomino*, Outback Press, Collingwood, Vic., 1980.
——*Stories—Five Acre Virgin, The Travelling Entertainer*, Fremantle Arts Centre Press, Fremantle, WA, 1984.
——*The Sugar Mother*, Fremantle Arts Centre Press, Fremantle, WA, 1988; Harper and Row, New York, 1988.
——*The Travelling Entertainer and Other Stories*, photographs by R. Jolley, Fremantle Arts Centre Press, Fremantle, WA, 1979.
——*The Well*, Viking, New York, 1986; Penguin, Ringwood, Vic., 1986.
——*Woman in a Lampshade*, Penguin, Ringwood, Vic., 1983.

Elizabeth Jolley—Short Stories, Poems, Essays, Reviews, Radio Plays, Adaptations

Jolley, E., 'The Adventures of George Henry the Caterpillar', *Children's Hour*, BBC Midland Region, 23 Aug. 1947.
——'The Agent in Travelling', *Travelling Entertainer*, pp. 48–55.
——'Another Holiday for the Prince', *Five Acre Virgin*, pp. 1–6. First published,

Works Cited

—— *Sandgropers: A Western Australian Anthology*, ed. D. Hewett, University of Western Australia Press, Perth, 1973, pp. 138–4.

—— [Author's Statement], *Australian Literary Studies*, vol. 10. no. 2, 1981, pp. 213–5.

—— 'Bill Sprockett's Land', *Five Acre Virgin*, pp. 63–8. First published, *Westerly*, vol. 16, no. 2, 1971, pp. 11–4.

—— 'Books for Christmas', *Sydney Morning Herald*, 7 Dec. 1985, Saturday Review, p. 41.

—— 'By the Waters of Babylon', *Central Mischief*, pp. 155–62. First published as '1983 Autumn[,] Summer 1950[,] 1983 Autumn', *Scripsi*, vol. 6, no.1, 1990, pp. 191–8.

—— 'The Changing Family—Who Cares?' *Central Mischief*, pp. 80–92. First published as 'Where Do I Look for Help?' *The Changing Family . . . Who Cares?* Proceedings of the First Australian Conference on the Family and Health, 14–19 Aug. 1977, University of Western Australia, Royal Australian College of General Practitioners, 1977, pp. 84–93.

—— ['Chocolate Has Its Own Melancholy'], *An Eloquent Sufficiency: 50 Writers Talk about Life and Literature over Lunch*, ed. S. Wyndham, S[ydney] M[orning] H[erald]–John Fairfax, Sydney, 1998, pp. 22–7.

—— 'Clever and Pretty', *Woman in a Lampshade*, pp. 182–200. First published, *Celebrations: A Bicentennial Anthology of Fifty Years of Western Australian Poetry and Prose*, ed. B. Dibble, D. Grant and G. Phillips, University of Western Australia Press, Perth, 1988, pp. 40–54.

—— 'Cloisters of Memory', *Meanjin*, vol. 48, no. 3, 1989, pp. 531–9.

—— 'Country Towns and Properties', *Diary of a Weekend Farmer*, p. 11. First published in 'Orchard (7 poems)', *Westerly*, vol. 18, no. 3, 1973, pp. 42–7.

—— 'Dead Trees in Your Absence', *Diary of a Weekend Farmer*, p. 39. First published in 'Orchard (7 poems)', *Westerly*, vol. 18, no. 3, 1973, pp. 42–7.

—— 'Dear Diary: The Absorbing Journals of Elizabeth Smart', review of *Necessary Secrets: The Journals of Elizabeth Smart*, ed. Alice Van Wart, *Sunday Age* (Melbourne), 12 May 1991, Agenda, p. 11.

—— 'Decidedly Pointing to Central Mischief', *Central Mischief*, 93–7. First published, *Australia and New Zealand Journal of Psychiatry*, vol. 24, no. 3, 1990, pp. 309–11.

—— 'Dignity, Composure and Tranquillity in Old Age', *Central Mischief*, pp. 180–4. Address at the Annual General Meeting of The Homes of Peace, Perth, 26 Oct. 1989.

—— 'Dingle the Fool', *Woman in a Lampshade*, pp. 157–70. First published, *Quadrant*, vol. 16, no. 1, 1972, pp. 67–74.

——'The Fellow Passenger', *Travelling Entertainer*, pp. 70–85.

——'A Gentleman's Agreement', *Five Acre Virgin*, pp. 13–7.

——'Good Knight, Sweet Prince', *Central Mischief*, pp. 125–31. First published, in a fuller version, *Sunday Herald* (Melbourne), 8 Oct. 1989, Sunday Plus, p. 31.

——'The Goose Path: A Meditation' *Central Mischief*, 163–73. First published, *Encounter*, vol. 73, no. 3, 1989, pp. 9–13.

——'Grasshoppers', *Travelling Entertainer*, pp. 133–181. First published, *Westerly*, vol. 24, no. 2, 1979, pp. 62–9.

——'Great Branches Fall', *Diary of a Weekend Farmer*, p. 87. First published in 'Orchard (7 poems)', *Westerly*, vol. 18, no. 3, 1973, pp. 42–7.

——(M. Knight), 'The Growth of Plants in "Water Cultures"', *The Owl: A Journal of Popular Science*, Sibford School Science Society, vol. 3, 1938 (Winter Term), pp. 8–9 (560 words).

——'The Habit of Art', *Central Mischief*, pp. 121–4. First published, *Curtin Gazette* Curtin University of Technology, Perth, June 1989, pp. 9–10.

——'A Hedge of Rosemary', *Five Acre Virgin*, pp. 69–75. First published, *Westerly*, vol. 12, no. 2, 1967, pp. 18–22.

——'Hep Duck and Hildegarde The Meat', *Westerly*, vol. 27, no. 1, 1982, pp. 25–30.

——'Hilda's Wedding', *Woman in a Lampshade*, pp. 39–46. First published *Loose-Licks: A Bi-Monthly Review of Music, Media, Drugs and Lifestyles*, vol. 2, no. 2, 1976, pp. 26+.

——'Interruption from the Fencing Wire, Neighbour Woman Sucking Her Teeth', *Diary of a Weekend Farmer*, p. 69.

——'The Jarrah Thieves', *Five Acre Virgin*, pp. 76–91.

——'The Last Crop', *Woman in a Lampshade*, pp. 208–29.

——*The Last Crop*, dir. S. Clayton, adapted by R. Burridge and M. O'Hanlon, Zenith Productions (UK) with Film Australia and the Australian Film Commission, 1990.

——'Lehmann Sieber', early story c. 1940, ed. and transcribed B. Dibble, *Overland*, vol. 163, 2001, pp. 59–60. Published with *'Plus Ça Change . . .*: An Early Elizabeth Jolley Short Story', pp. 53–8.

——'The Libation.' *Woman in a Lampshade*, pp. 105–17. First published, *Australian Book Review, Tabloid Story* feature, Dec. 1982–Jan. 1983, pp. 13–6.

——'The Little Dance in Writing', *Learning to Dance*, pp. 267–70. First published, *Cite*, Curtin University of Technology, Perth, Dec. 2002, p. 28.

Works Cited

—'The Little Herb of Self-Heal', *Central Mischief*, pp. 46–52.

—'Living on One Leg Like a Bird', *Central Mischief*, pp. 132–41. First published, in a slightly different form, as 'On Being an Australian Author: "Living on One Leg Like a Bird"', *Island Magazine*, issue 30, 1987, pp. 25–31.

—'The Long Distant Lecture', *Travelling Entertainer*, pp. 66–79.

—'Lorelei in the wheat', dir. L. Taylor. Dolphin Theatre, Perth, 9–28 Feb, 1993. Part of the *Tell Tales* stage collection.

—'Manchester Repair', *Learning to Dance*, pp. 283–90. First published as 'Diary: A Personal Note', *Independent Monthly* (Sydney), Dec. 1990–Jan. 1991, p. 3.

—'Mark F', *Patterns*, vol. 7, no. 3, 1981, pp 7–8.

—'May I Rest My Case on Your Table?', prod. M. Hartley, BBC World Service, 10 Jan. 1970. Rebroadcast by the BBC World Service 13 Jan. 1970.

—'Mr Berrington', *Central Mischief*, pp. 31–8. First published, *Australian*, 18–19 Apr. 1987, Literary Quarterly, pp. 1–2.

—'Mr Parker's Valentine', *Travelling Entertainer*, pp. 84–95. First published, *Pinup*, a literary poster, Fremantle Arts Centre, Fremantle, WA, July 1975.

—'More Than Just Mates', *The Weekend Australian*, 4–5 Jan. 1997, p. 14.

—'My First Editor', *Central Mischief*, pp. 27–30. First published as 'Schooldays', *Age* (Melbourne), 16 July 1988, Saturday Extra, pp. 1–2.

—'My Sister Dancing', *Sisters*, ed. D. Modjeska, Angus and Robertson–HarperCollins, Pymble, NSW, 1993, pp. 165–83.

—'Neighbour Woman on the Fencing Wire', *Diary of a Weekend Farmer*, p. 28. First published in 'Orchard (7 poems)', *Westerly*, vol. 18, no. 3, 1973, pp. 42–7.

—'A New World', *Travelling Entertainer*, pp. 96–104. First published, *Australian New Writing*, ed. O. Mendelsohn and H. Marks, Nelson, Melbourne, 1973, pp. 73–9.

—'Night Runner', *Meanjin*, vol. 42, no. 4, 1983, pp. 419–30.

—'No Date Required', *Diary of a Weekend Farmer*, pp. 89–90.

—'Of Butchers and Bilberry Baskets', *Central Mischief*, pp. 39–45. First published, *Sydney Morning Herald*, 20 Jan. 1988, p. 13.

—'On War', *Central Mischief*, pp. 13–5. First published as 'No Winners or Losers—Only Humanity', *Age* (Melbourne), 6 Mar. 1991, Tempo Magazine, p. 5.

—'One Bite For Christmas', *Five Acre Virgin*, pp. 31–5.

—'One Christmas Knitting', *Woman in a Lampshade*, pp. 118–29. First published,

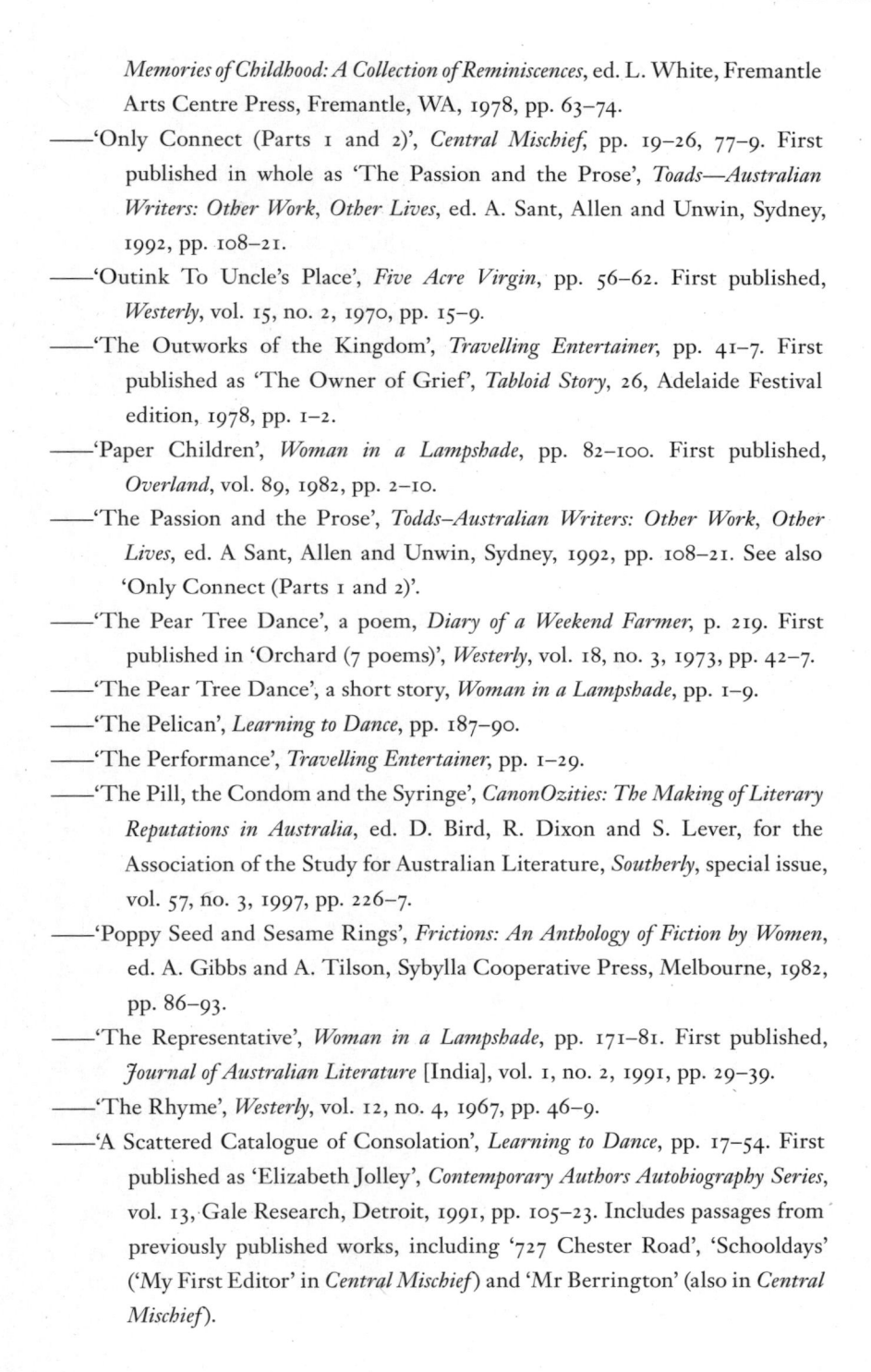

Memories of Childhood: A Collection of Reminiscences, ed. L. White, Fremantle Arts Centre Press, Fremantle, WA, 1978, pp. 63-74.

——'Only Connect (Parts 1 and 2)', *Central Mischief*, pp. 19-26, 77-9. First published in whole as 'The Passion and the Prose', *Toads—Australian Writers: Other Work, Other Lives*, ed. A. Sant, Allen and Unwin, Sydney, 1992, pp. 108-21.

——'Outink To Uncle's Place', *Five Acre Virgin*, pp. 56-62. First published, *Westerly*, vol. 15, no. 2, 1970, pp. 15-9.

——'The Outworks of the Kingdom', *Travelling Entertainer*, pp. 41-7. First published as 'The Owner of Grief', *Tabloid Story*, 26, Adelaide Festival edition, 1978, pp. 1-2.

——'Paper Children', *Woman in a Lampshade*, pp. 82-100. First published, *Overland*, vol. 89, 1982, pp. 2-10.

——'The Passion and the Prose', *Todds–Australian Writers: Other Work, Other Lives*, ed. A Sant, Allen and Unwin, Sydney, 1992, pp. 108-21. See also 'Only Connect (Parts 1 and 2)'.

——'The Pear Tree Dance', a poem, *Diary of a Weekend Farmer*, p. 219. First published in 'Orchard (7 poems)', *Westerly*, vol. 18, no. 3, 1973, pp. 42-7.

——'The Pear Tree Dance', a short story, *Woman in a Lampshade*, pp. 1-9.

——'The Pelican', *Learning to Dance*, pp. 187-90.

——'The Performance', *Travelling Entertainer*, pp. 1-29.

——'The Pill, the Condom and the Syringe', *CanonOzities: The Making of Literary Reputations in Australia*, ed. D. Bird, R. Dixon and S. Lever, for the Association of the Study for Australian Literature, *Southerly*, special issue, vol. 57, no. 3, 1997, pp. 226-7.

——'Poppy Seed and Sesame Rings', *Frictions: An Anthology of Fiction by Women*, ed. A. Gibbs and A. Tilson, Sybylla Cooperative Press, Melbourne, 1982, pp. 86-93.

——'The Representative', *Woman in a Lampshade*, pp. 171-81. First published, *Journal of Australian Literature* [India], vol. 1, no. 2, 1991, pp. 29-39.

——'The Rhyme', *Westerly*, vol. 12, no. 4, 1967, pp. 46-9.

——'A Scattered Catalogue of Consolation', *Learning to Dance*, pp. 17-54. First published as 'Elizabeth Jolley', *Contemporary Authors Autobiography Series*, vol. 13, Gale Research, Detroit, 1991, pp. 105-23. Includes passages from previously published works, including '727 Chester Road', 'Schooldays' ('My First Editor' in *Central Mischief*) and 'Mr Berrington' (also in *Central Mischief*).

Works Cited

——'Self-Portrait: A Child Went Forth', *Stories—Five Acre Virgin, The Travelling Entertainer*, pp. 301–8. First published, *Australian Book Review*, Nov. 1983, pp. 5–8.

——'The Shed', *Woman in a Lampshade*, pp. 201–7. First published, *New Country: A Selection of Western Australian Short Stories*, ed. B. Bennett, Fremantle Arts Centre Press, Fremantle, WA, 1976, pp. 64–8.

——'Shepherd on the Roof, *Five Acre Virgin*, pp. 46–55.

——'The Sick Vote', *Quadrant*, vol. 12, no. 5, 1968, pp. 43–6.

——'The Silent Night of Snowfall: Tales of Christmas Past', *Learning to Dance*, pp. 79–86. First published, *Age* (Melbourne), 24 Dec. 1994, Saturday Extra, pp. 1+.

——'A Sort of Gift', *Central Mischief*, pp. 69–76. First published as 'A Sort of Gift: Images of Perth', *Bulletin*, 26 Jan. 1988, pp. 188–90.

——'Strange Regions There Are', *Central Mischief*, pp. 103–20. First published as 'Strange Regions There Are (for Robert Finlay Jones)', *Australian*, 14 May 1990, n. pag.

——'Summer Memories: Outlines and Shadings', *Age* (Melbourne), 6 Jan. 1995, Summer Age, p. 7. Also published as 'A Summer to Remember', *Learning to Dance*, pp. 73–8.

——*Supermarket Pavane*, stage adaptation of a short story by E. Jolley, adapt. S. Rider, et al., dir. S. Rider, La Boite Theatre, Brisbane, 14 Sept. – 5 Oct. 1996.

——'"Surprise! Surprise!" from Matron', *Five Acre Virgin and Other Stories*, pp. 36–44.

——'The Talking Bricks', *Summer's Tales* 2, ed. Kylie Tennant, Macmillan, Melbourne, 1965, pp. 158–68.

——*Tell Tales*, stage adaptation of 'Lorelei in the Wheat', dir. L. Taylor, Dolphin Theatre, Perth, 9–28 Feb. 1993.

——'The Travelling Entertainer', *Travelling Entertainer*, pp. 105–31.

——'Tricked or Treated?' *Central Mischief*, pp. 66–8. First published, *West Australian*, 26 Jan. 1988, 200 Years On Special Bicentennial Supplement, p. 18.

——'Turning Points', *Age* (Melbourne), 18 June 1994, Saturday Extra, pp. 1+.

——'Two Men Running', *Woman in a Lampshade*, pp. 47–70. First published, *Bulletin Literary Supplement*, 21 Apr. 1981, pp. 8–17.

——'Two Men Running', *The Sunday Play*, prod. J. Howard, ABC Radio 2, 13 June 1982.

——*Uncle Bernard's New World*, stage adaptation of six stories by E. Jolley, adapt. and dir. P. Dwyer and PACT Youth Theatre, Erskineville, Sydney, 10 Aug – 2 Sept. 1990.

——'Uncle Bernard's Proposal', *Woman in a Lampshade*, pp. 71–81. First published, *Landfall: A New Zealand Quarterly*, vol. 27, no. 3, 1973, pp. 202–10.

——(M. Knight), 'Vitamins', *The Owl: A Journal of Popular Science*, Sibford School Science Society, vol. 1, 1937 (Autumn Term), p. 10 (350 words).

——'The Wedding of the Painted Doll', *Five Acre Virgin*, pp. 18–30.

——'Wednesdays and Fridays', *Woman in a Lampshade*, pp. 150–6. First published, *Quadrant*, vol. 25, no. 1–2, 1981, pp. 105–7.

——'The Well–Bred Thief', *South Pacific Stories*, ed. C. Tiffin and H. Tiffin, *SPACLALS* (South Pacific Association for Commonwealth Literature and Language Studies) with the Department of English, University of Queensland, St. Lucia, 1980, pp. 122–31.

——'"What Sins to Me Unknown Dipped Me in Ink?"', *Central Mischief*, pp. 1–12. First published, *The Writer on Her Work: New Essays in New Territory*, vol. 2, ed. J. Sternburg, Norton, New York, 1991, pp. 125–39.

——'Who Talks of Victory', *Central Mischief*, pp. 53–9, First published, *Meanjin*, vol. 46, no. 1, 1987, pp. 4–15.

——'Who Would Throw Streamers and Sing to a Container?' *Central Mischief*, pp. 60–65. First published as 'Voyagers Together to a New World', *Age* (Melbourne), 16 Jan. 1988, Saturday Extra, pp. 3–4.

——'Winter Nelis', *Travelling Entertainer*, pp. 30–40. First published as 'Winter Nellis [sic]', *Stories of Her Life: An Anthology of Short Stories by Australian Women*, ed. S. Zurbo, Outback Press, Collingwood, Vic., 1979, pp. 71–82.

Jolley, Elizabeth (ed.), *Cooking by Degrees*, University Branch of the Save the Children Fund, n.p. (University of Western Australia, Perth), c. 1962.

Elizabeth Jolley — Archival Material

Archival material drawn on here derives from two sources: papers lodged by Elizabeth Jolley in the Mitchell Library, State Library of New South Wales in 1987; and materials given by Elizabeth Jolley to Dibble for the duration of his research/writing.

Citations to manuscripts, refer to *Papers of Elizabeth Jolley, c. 1939; 1957–1987*, MLMSS 4880, Mitchell Library, State Library of New South Wales. The collection includes literary manuscripts, correspondence, diaries, and pictorial material, with some materials embargoed. All of these resources have been accessed but the embargoed materials have not been directly quoted in this biography. An online finding-aid to the collection, 'Guide to the Papers of Elizabeth Jolley', is located at <http://findaid.library.uwa. edu.au/cgi-bin/nph-dweb/dynaweb/findaid/jolley/@Generic__BookView; cs=default;ts=default>.

There is also a hard-copy finding aid, located at the beginning of the collection: *Guide to the Papers of Elizabeth Jolley in the Mitchell Library, State Library of NSW,* arranged and described by J. Andrighetti, Mitchell Library, MLMSS 4880/1, 1987. Access to the full collection was made available to Dibble by permission from Elizabeth Jolley.

Materials given by Elizabeth Jolley to Dibble for the duration of his research/ writing include:

Letters

There are some 300 core letters to Monica Knight/Elizabeth Jolley.
- Grandparents. Charles Knight—four undated letters/poems/prayers c. 1923–25, four others from him on 24 Dec. 1923, 3 June and 23 Dec. 1924 and 3 June 1926. Patti Knight—June 22 (c. 1923–25) and 1 June 1943.
- Parents, 1934–45. Wilfrid Knight—7 Mar. 1924 (to baby Monica 'Lieserli' in Vienna with her mother), an undated letter (to 'Crocodile Lieserli' in Vienna, c. 1924), 14 Feb., 10 June and 3 Oct, 1938, his undated 'Plan for VICTORIOUS LIVING' (c. 1938, after his Oxford Group conversion), 24 Jan. 1939, undated letter about his conviction and imprisonment as a conscientious objector (c. 1940), 12 Mar. 1939, 6 Dec. 1940, 13 Dec. 1940 ('Splendid New World') and 18 Dec. 1940 (proposing reading bible together), 25 and 28 Jan., 3 Feb. and 22 July 1941. Margarete Knight— 25 Mar. and 10 Oct. 1938, 28 Jan. 1941 and 5 Mar. 1945.
- Other family/friends:
  Madelaine Knight under the pseudonym of 'Bobby' (the family dog), one undated from the mid-1930s, and another 22 Feb. 1938.
  Honorary Uncle Otto Stapf. Christmas 1923.
  Aunt Maud (Thrippleton). 19 May 1925.
  Aunt Johanna ('Gross Tante') Fehr Bukowsky. 12 Sept. 1926, and Silly

Works Cited

[sic] Neumann and Mina [illegible], n.d., from Vienna, both unknown.

Lunds, Hamburg. 12 Aug. 1939.

Charly Mews, Germany. 20 Apr. [n.d.], 2 May [n.d.], 9 and 20 Nov. 1938, 19 Jan. 1939, 10 and 14 Mar. 1939, 8 Aug. 1939.

Félix Thérond, France. 13 May 1937, 20 Aug. 1937, 2 Oct. 1937, 8 Nov. 1937, 2 Jan. 1938, 2 Feb. 1938, 14 May 1938, 21 Oct. 1938, 22 Sept. 1938, 15 Dec. 1938, 3 Jan. 1939, 10 Mar. 1939, 13 Apr. 1939, 23 June 1939, 13 July 1939, Christmas 1940.

Margaret 'Pecker' Sargent. Undated letter c. 1939–40.

Marie Stapf Kemmeter, Germany. n.d., after mid–1946.

Mildred [Joyce] Broom, 21 Feb. 1941, 'Potrait of Knight', whimsical 12-line poem.

Kenneth Berrington. 14 Dec. 1952.

- Leonard Jolley. To L. Jolley from Leslie Clarke of the Coopers' Company, explaining Jolley's eligibility for the 'freedom of the company', 7 Feb. 1936. From L. Jolley to Monica Fielding/Knight—26 Aug. 1950 (to Monica Jolley at Wells Road), 28 May 1952, undated from the Royal College of Physicians in Edinburgh, and 23 Aug. c. 1957, written in Glasgow;
- Parents from 1962 onward (200 letters). Wilfrid Knight—26 May 1962 through 5 Oct. 1977, some of those with postscripts by Margarete Knight. Margarete Knight—12 and 22 Nov. 1977; 26 Dec. 1977; 8, 19 and 22 Jan. 1978; 2, 11 and 24 Feb. 1978; 6 and 15 Mar. 1978; 26 Apr. 1978; 8 May 1978; 25 and 31 Oct. 1978; 5, 14 and 23 Nov. 1978; 8 and 25 Dec. 1978; 3 and 10 Jan. 1979.
- Audio-cassette letter from the parents, recorded for them by friend Bill Cotterell, 9 June 1977, five days after Margarete Knight's eighty-first birthday.
- Bill Cotterell to E. Jolley 10 Nov. 1977 on the death of Jolley's father.

Sibford School Notebooks

- Sibford Poems (Spring Term 1939, ends July 1939)
- Sibford English Prep.
- Sibford Form U.III English (includes horse-beating story).
- Sibford Form U.III English Essay Book 18 May–29 Oct. 1937 (includes family story, 'A Miner's Cottage').
- Sibford Form IV English Essay Book (includes Kemmeter 'Her First Minuet Story' and 'Scholar Gypsy' essay).

Works Cited

- Sibford Form VI Housecraft (9 Nov. 1939).
- Sibford Form V/Pyrford Biology Notes (Oct. – Nov. 1942)

St Nicholas and St Martin's Hospital Notebooks

- Nursing, Anatomy and Physiology, 1941.
- Orthopaedic Nursing, c. 1942.

Queen Elizabeth Hospital (QEH) Notebooks

- QEH First–year Nursing Notes, Class A (from 9 Jan. 1943).
- QEH First–year Physiology Notes, Class A (from 15 Mar. 1943).
- QEH Second–year Lectures Medicine, Children's Diseases, and Materia Medica (26 Sept. – 30 Oct. 1944).
- QEH Anatomy Notes, Class A (6 Jan. – 11 Mar. 1943).
- QEH Anatomy Notes (25 Oct. – 26 Nov. 1943).

Leonard Jolley Notebooks

Diary (Hackney), 30 May – 27 July 1940
Diary (Pyrford), 29 July – 6 Sept. 1940
Diary (Pyrford), 19 Sept. – 20 Nov. 1940
Diary (Pyrford), 2 Dec. 1940 – 9 Jan. 1941
Diary (Pyrford), 12 Jan. 1941 – 14 Feb. 1941
Diary (Pyrford), 19 Feb. – 18 Apr. 1941
Diary (Pyrford), 24 Apr. – 21 July 1941
Diary (Pyrford), and Charney Bassett: 26 July – 28 Nov. 1941
Diary (Charney Bassett and Selly Oak), 1 Dec. 1941 – 24 Jan. 1942
Diary (Selly Oak), 4 Apr. – 14 July 1942
Gardening Diary (Scotland): 1952 entries—1 Jan.–20 Dec.; 1952 entries—27 Jan.–6 Dec.; 1954 entries—28 Feb.–19 May; 1958–59 entries—one-page list of bulbs planted.

Sundry

- The Nelson Letters and the Watkins Affair. A Gordon exercise book of some 235 unnumbered pages, 86 written on, 6 recording Jolley's Watkins sales, with interleaved carbon copies of letters from Elizabeth Jolley to her daughter Sarah Jolley Nelson in Cambridge (not consulted).

Works Cited

- Other varied items of memorabilia, including 'Monica's prayer', Margarete Knight's list of Monica's 1923 Christmas presents, Margarete Knight's 15 Apr. 1941 list of birthdays for her daughter to remember, dozens of photographs, dozens of received and blank postcards, concert programs, and such, along with dozens of letters from writing colleagues and from people Jolley met after she started publishing, including cards and letters from people she met at book clubs, in workshops and when running classes for schools.
- Correspondence between Jolley and friends/colleagues, including the author, Barbara Milech, Shiela MacPherson Naylor, Jo Robertson, Sharon Rundle, and Fairlie Sezacinski.

General

Citations to published works on Elizabeth Jolley refer to *Elizabeth Jolley— A Bibliography, 1965–2007*, compiled by Barbara Milech and Brian Dibble, and published online through the Elizabeth Jolley Research Collection, John Curtin Prime Ministerial Library, Curtin University of Technology, Perth, WA, at <http://john.curtin.edu.au/jolley>. Analyses in the text may draw without specific reference on entries listed for Dibble and/or Milech.

Citations to *SOSA*, *Sibford* and *S.O.S.O* relate to publications of Elizabeth Jolley's secondary school, Sibford School. *SOSA* was the journal of the Sibford Old Scholars' Association, published from 1903–71; thereafter *SOSA* was published as part of the school magazine *Sibford*, which after the mid-1990s was titled *S.O.S.O.*

A[ustralian] B[roadcasting] C[ompany], 'Author Elizabeth Jolley Dies, Aged 83', 20 Feb. 2007, <http:/www.abc.net.au/news/newsitems/200702/s1851723.htm>, viewed 20 Feb. 2007.

Adams, A. (John Broom), *Another Little Drink . . .*, Scotia, Caithness, Scotland, 1973.

Adams, P. 'Wild Minds', interview with Elizabeth Jolley. Late Night Live, ABC Radio National, 8 Sept. 1999.

Alexander, F., 'Battye, James Sykes (1871–1954)', *Australian Dictionary of Biography*, vol. 7, Melbourne University Press, 1979, pp. 212–4.

——*Campus at Crawley: A Narrative and Critical Appreciation of the First Fifty Years of the University of Western Australia*, Cheshire, for the University of

Works Cited

Australia Press, Melbourne, 1963.

Alighieri, Dante, *The Divine Comedy of Dante Alighieri: The Inferno*, vol. 1, trans. and ed. R. M. Durling, Oxford University Press, London, 1996.

Anderson, D., 'The Bunfight at the O.K. Corral', *National Times* (Sydney), 20–25 Sept. 1985, On His Selection, p. 30.

Andrew E., 'About ten years ago you couldn't move for Elizabeth Jolley...' <larvatusprodeo.net/2006/10/10/online-opinion-article-australian-literature-on-the-nose/-165k>, viewed 18 Jan. 2008.

Australia Council, 'Vale Elizabeth Jolley', 20 Feb. 2007, <http://www.ozco.gov.au/news_hot_topics/news/vale_elizabeth_jolley/>, viewed 20 Feb. 2002.

Baily, L., 'The Sibford Centenary', *SOSA*, Sibford School, Sibford Ferris/Banbury, Oxfordshire, 1939, pp. 43–6.

——(dir. and prod., with M. Braithwaite), *The Sibford Story*, 16-mm film, 36 mins., Sibford School, Sibford Ferris, Banbury, Oxfordshire, 1948. The film incorporates footage from a 1928 film on the school.

Baker, C., 'Elizabeth Jolley', *Yacker: Australian Writers Talk About Their Work*, interview with Elizabeth Jolley, Pan, Sydney, 1986, pp. 210–33.

Balsdon, J. P. V. D., *'Auctoritas, Dignitas, Otium'*, *The Classical Quarterly*, new series, vol. 10, 1960, pp. 43–50.

Barrowclough, N., 'Secrets and Lines', interview with Elizabeth Jolley, *Age* (Melbourne), 28 June 1997, Good Weekend, pp. 12–8.

Baum, C., '"Rap Poets" Society', *Sydney Morning Herald*, 3 Jan. 2004, <http://www.smh.com.au/articles/2004/01/02/1072908895037>, viewed 3 Jan. 2007.

Bedford, J., 'Adversity in Detail', review of *Five Acre Virgin and Other Stories* by E. Jolley, *Australian*, 5 Mar. 1977, p. 28.

Bennett, T. R. (ed.), *Investigating Penn: A Brief History of a Staffordshire Village Now Part of Wolverhampton*, Workers' Educational Association (Wolverhampton Branch) in association with the University of Birmingham Department of Extramural Studies, Wolverhampton, West Midlands, 1975. Described as '[p]apers submitted by members of an evening class'.

Bird, D., 'Elizabeth Jolley's Late Work', *Australian Literary Studies*, in press.

——'New Narrations: Contemporary Fiction', *The Cambridge Companion to Australian Literature*, ed. E. Webby, Cambridge University Press, 2000, pp. 183–208.

——*Off the Air: Nine Plays for Radio by Elizabeth Jolley*, Penguin, Ringwood, Vic., 1995.

Birman, W., 'Francis Aubie Sharr: Librarian Extraordinaire', *Australasian Public Libraries and Information Services*, vol. 4, no. 2, 1991, pp. 68–70.

Blackmore, Madelaine Knight, 'Alan Proudfoot's Obsession', *Morning Story*, BBC, narr. Bill Wallis, 15 mins., Radio 4, 11 Aug. 1983. Transcript available from BBC.

——'Kindred Spirits', *Morning Story*, BBC Radio 4, narr. Bill Wallis, 15 mins., 8 Dec. 1983. Transcript available from BBC.

——'Night Work', *Morning Story*, BBC Radio 4, narr. Jill Balcon. 15 mins., 25 July 1984. Transcript available from BBC.

——'Gnomic Verses', *The Poetical Works of William Blake*, ed. J. Sampson, Oxford University Press, London, 1913.

Blake, W., *William Blake, The Complete Poems*, ed. A. Ostriker. Penguin, Ringwood, Vic., 1977.

Błotnicka, L., *Przez zieloną granicę: Wyboru dokonała, opracowała I napisała przedmowę (In Search of a Refuge . . .)*, ed. B. Żongołłowicz, Toruń, Melbourne, 2007.

Boucher, B., 'A Stuttering Start but It's All Go', *Advertiser* (Adelaide), 5 Mar. 1984, n. pag.

Bradley, J., 'The Fuss over Super-fine Fiction', <http://www.theaustralian.news.com.au/story/0,20867,20459847-25132,00.html>, viewed 15 Dec. 2007.

Britton, D., 'Elizabeth Jolley's Years of Triumph', *The West Australian*, 26 May 1987, p. 55.

Broom, J., *John Maclean*, Macdonald, Edinburgh, 1973.

Brown, D., Publishing Culture: Commissioning Books in Australia, 1970–2000, PhD, Victoria University, 2003.

'The Bruderhof: An Introduction', <http://www.bruderhof.org.html>, viewed 14 June 2004.

Bullock, A., *Hitler: A Study in Tyranny*, Harper, New York, c. 1952.

Burstow, S. (prod.), 'IOU: Elizabeth Jolley', *Artscape*, ABC TV, 26 Feb. 2008.

Byrski, L., 'Elizabeth Jolley: West Australian Woman Achiever', *Skywest Inflight*, Apr. 1985, p. 97. Part of a regional column, Achievement Profile.

Cadzow, J., 'A Compulsive Writer Who Sifts Shadows from Another World', *Weekend Australian*, 22–23 Sept. 1984, Magazine, p. 16.

Campbell, D., 'Greenness in Every Line: The Drama of George Mackay Brown', *International Journal of Scottish Theatre*, vol. 1, no.1, 2000, <http://www.arts.gla.ac.uk/ScotLit/ASLS/ijost/Volume1_no1/D_Campbell.htm>.

Works Cited

Carter, A., 'Dreams of Reason . . . And of Foxes', review of *Foxybaby* by Elizabeth Jolley, *New York Times Review of Books*, 24 Nov. 1985, pp. 1+.

——'Writers' Reading in 1984', *Guardian*, 13 Dec. 1984, p. 18.

Carter, D., 'Boom, Bust or Business as Usual? Literary Fiction Publishing', *Making Books: Contemporary Australian Publishing*, ed. D. Carter and A. Galligan, University of Queensland Press, St. Lucia, Qld, 2007, pp. 231–46.

Chesterton, R., 'Literature Loses Heroine', *The Daily Telegraph* (Sydney), 21 Feb. 2007, <http://www.news.com.au/dailytelegraph/story/0,22049,21258699-5001031,00.html>, viewed 28 Feb. 2007.

Cheever, S., 'The Healer: Bill W.', *Time* (Australia), 14 June 1999, pp. 147–9.

Chisholm, J. F., '1870–1914—The Austro–Italian Naval Race', http://www.worldwar1.com/tlainr.htm>, viewed 20 June 2007.

Clancy, L., 'Elizabeth Jolley', <http://biography.jrank.org/pages/4474/Jolley-Monica-Elizabeth.html>, viewed 31 Mar. 2008.

Clark, H. *War and Its Aftermath: Letters from Hilda Clark from France, Austria and the Near East, 1914–1924*, ed. Edith M. Pye, Friends Book Centre/Virago, London, 1956.

Clifford, C., *QE Nurse, 1938–1957: A History of Nursing at the Queen Elizabeth Hospital, Birmingham*, Brewin Books, Studley, Warwickshire, 1997.

Coleridge, S.T., *The Letters of Samuel Taylor Coleridge*, ed. E. Hartley, Heinemann, London, 1895.

'Convocation: Powers, Duties and Functions', *Gazette*, University of Western Australia, vol. 10, no. 1, 1960, pp. 7–8.

Cooper, W. S., *Comfortable Houses, Middle-class People: The Story of Agett Road, Claremont*, Research Institute for Cultural Heritage, Curtin University of Technology with the Claremont Museum, Perth, 2000.

Cornford, F. M., 'Comedy and Tragedy', *The Origins of Attic Comedy*, Edward Arnold, London, 1914, pp. 190–220.

Cotton, P., 'Worldly Wise', *Age* (Melbourne), 17 Dec. 1994, Good Weekend, p. 14.

Cottrell, A., 'Geoffrey Vincent Raynor: 1913–83', *Bibliographical Memoirs of Fellows of the Royal Society*, vol. 30, 1984, pp. 547–63.

Craven, P., 'Black Humour, Jolley Heart', obituary, *The Saturday Age*, 24 Feb. 2007, pp. A2.

——'Writers' Tales Writing with Gentle Dignity', review of *The Georges' Wife* by E. Jolley, *Age* (Melbourne), 2 Oct. 1993, Saturday Extra, p. 7.

Crawford, P. and M. Tonkinson, *The Missing Chapters: Women Staff at the*

University of Western Australia 1963–1987, Centre for Western Australian History, University of Western Australia, Perth, 1988.

Curtius, E. R., *European Literature and the Latin Middle Ages*, trans. W. R. Trask, Harper, New York, 1963.

Daniel, H., 'Double Cover: Frankly, Miles . . . ' *Age* (Melbourne), 7 May 1994, Saturday Extra, p. 8.

——'Eighth Dialogue: A Literary Offering', *Liars: Australian New Novelists*, Penguin, Ringwood, Vic., 1988, pp. 263–300.

——'Painful Passage into Memory', review of *My Father's Moon* by E. Jolley, *Age* (Melbourne), 15 Apr. 1989, Saturday Extra, p. 11.

——'Plotting (3): A Quarterly Account of Recent Fiction', *Overland*, vol. 115, 1989, pp. 31–6.

Davis, M., 'The Decline of the Literary Paradigm in Australian Publishing', *Ten Years, HEAT* 12, new series, pp. 91–108.

De Garis, B., 'The Department of History in the University of Western Australia, 1913–65', *Fred Alexander: A Tribute, Studies in Western Australian History*, vol. 6, Department of History, University of Western Australia, Perth, 1988, pp. 1–21.

Dessaix, R., 'Elizabeth Jolley: A Formidable Sensibility', interview with Peter Craven, *24 Hours*, Aug. 1992, pp. 48–9.

——'In the Spotlight', *CanonOzities: The Making of Literary Reputations in Australia*, ed. D. Bird, R. Dixon and S. Lever, for the Association of the Study for Australian Literature, *Southerly*, special issue, vol. 57, no. 3, 1997, pp. 216–8.

——*Speaking Their Minds: Intellectuals and the Public Culture in Australia*. ABC Books, Sydney, 1998.

Dibble, B., 'Dream–crowded Inferno', review of *Foxybaby* by E. Jolley, *Australian Book Review*, Dec. 1985 – Jan. 1986, pp. 29–30.

——'Elizabeth Jolley', *A Reader's Companion to the Short Story in English*, ed. E. Fallon, et al., Greenwood Press, Westport, Connecticut, 2001, pp. 214–4.

——'Elizabeth Jolley: Books with Words in Them', *Lines in the Sand: New Writing from Western Australia*, ed. G. Phillips and J. van Loon, Fellowship of Australian Writers (WA), Swanbourne, WA, 2008, 23–7.

——'Fruit Cake of Life', review of *The Well* by E. Jolley, *Overland*, vol. 106, 1987, pp. 83–4.

——'Jolley Excellent', review of *The Newspaper of Claremont Street* by E. Jolley, *Australian Book Review*, May 1982, pp. 29–30.

―― 'Mothers, Daughters and Elizabeth Jolley's Ethic of Hope', *Journal of the Association for the Study of Australian Literature*, vol. 4, 2005, pp. 63–76.

―― *Mr Scobie's Riddle*, review of a novel by E. Jolley, *Westerly*, vol. 28, no. 1, 1983, pp. 85–7.

―― 'On Mr Berrington and the Geometry of Love in Elizabeth Jolley's Family Home', commemorative essay, *Westerly*, vol. 52, no. 2, 2007, pp. 35–45.

―― '*Plus Ça Change*...: An Early Elizabeth Jolley Short Story', *Overland*, vol. 163, 2001, pp. 53–8. Published with 'Lehmann Sieber' by E. Jolley, c. 1940, ed. and transcribed B. Dibble, pp. 59–60.

Dibble, B. and B. Milech, '"A Timid Confidence": Elizabeth Jolley—Bibliography in Progress', *Elizabeth Jolley: New Critical Essays*, ed. D. Bird and B. Walker, Collins-Angus and Robertson, North Ryde, NSW, 1991, pp. 220–32.

Dryden, J., 'The Hind and the Panther', *The Poetical Works of John Dryden*, ed. G. R. Noyes, Cambridge edn, Houghton Mifflin, Boston, 1909.

Eddington, P., *So Far, So Good: The Autobiography*, Hodder and Stoughton, London, 1995.

Ellison, J., 'Elizabeth Jolley', *Rooms of Their Own*, interview with Elizabeth Jolley, Penguin, Ringwood, Vic., 1986, pp. 172–91.

Epanomitis, F., 'Classy Masters', *Sydney Morning Herald*, 26 July 1997, Spectrum, p. 9.

Farr, M., 'Paul Eddington, CBE, 1927–1995', *Sibford 1995–1996*, Sibford School, Sibford Ferris, Banbury, Oxfordshire, c. 1996, pp. 50–2.

―― 'Yesterday's Refugees', *Sibford 1998–1999*, Sibford School, Sibford Ferris/Banbury, Oxfordshire, c. 1999, p. xvii.

Felber, L., *Gender and Genre in Novels without End: The British* Roman–Fleuve, University Press of Florida, Gainesville, 1995.

'Fifty Years Ago', *SOSA*, Sibford School, Sibford Ferris/Banbury, Oxfordshire, 1998–1999, pp. xii–xiii.

Finch, M., 'Heads—Its [sic] Sibford', *Sibford, 1989–1990*, Sibford School, Sibford Ferris/Banbury, Oxfordshire, c. 1990, p. 36.

Finlay, L., 'Extended Hand from Australia', *West Australian*, 8 Feb. 1992, Big Weekend, p. 3. Part of a feature article, 'Best of Mates'.

Fiennes, C., *The Illustrated Journeys of Celia Fiennes, 1685–1712*, ed. C. Morris, MacDonald, London, 1982.

Flower, N., *Franz Schubert: The Man and His Circle*, Cassell, London, 1928.

Fonseca, I., *Bury Me Standing: The Gypsies and Their Journey*, Vintage, New York, 1995.

Forster, L. (ed.), *The Penguin Book of German Verse*, Penguin, Ringwood, Vic., 1959.
'Francis Aubie Sharr', *Western Perspectives: Library and Information Services in Western Australia*, ed. R. C. Sharman and L. A. Clyde, Australian Library and Information Association, Perth, 1990.
Freud, S., 'Creative Writers and Day-dreaming', *Art and Literature*, Pelican Freud Library, vol. 14, ed. A. Dickson, trans. J. Strachey, Penguin, London, pp. 131–41.
Fry, A. R., *A Quaker Adventure: The Story of Nine Years' Relief and Reconstruction*, Nisbet, London, 1926.
Garner, H., 'Elizabeth Jolley: An Appreciation', *Meanjin*, vol. 42, no. 2, 1983, pp. 153–7.
——'To My Dear Lift–Rat', *Sunday Age* (Melbourne), 26 June 2005, Saturday Extra, p. 14.
Gardiner, K., 'The Love Song of Elizabeth Jolley', *Lip—The Lesbian Magazine*, vol. 2, 1997, pp. 11–3.
Gilbert, S. M., Introduction, '*Orlando*: Virginia Woolf's *Vita Nuova*', *Orlando, a Biography* by V. Woolf, ed. B. Lyons, Penguin, New York, 1993.
Glover, R. C., 'The Good, the Bad and the Jolley', *Sydney Morning Herald*, 15 Apr. 1989, Good Weekend, pp. 62–4.
Gray, D. B. and F. R. Barlow, *Woodbrooke, 1953–1978: A Documentary Account of Woodbrooke's Third 25 Years*, Sessions with Woodbrooke College, York, 1982.
Grenville, K. and S. Woolfe, 'Elizabeth Jolley: *Mr Scobie's Riddle*', *Making Stories: How Ten Australian Novels Were Written*, Allen and Unwin, St Leonards, NSW, 1993, pp. 154–83.
Greve, T., *Fridtjof Nansen, 1905–1930*, Glydenal Norsk Forlag, Oslo, 1974.
Hanrahan, B., *The Diaries of Barbara Hanrahan*, ed. E. Lindsay, Queensland University Press, St Lucia, Qld., 1998.
Harte, N., *The University of London: 1836–1896, An Illustrated History*, Athlone Press, London, 1986.
Hazlehurst, B., *Copthorne Road: A Short History*, Copthorne 2000 Millennium Festival, Wolverhampton, West Midlands, 2000.
Headon, D., 'Elizabeth Jolley', interview, *Meanjin*, vol. 44, no. 1, 1985, pp. 39–46.
Hinshaw, D., *Herbert Hoover: An American Quaker*, Farrar Strauss, London, 1950.

Works Cited

Hugo, G., 'Jolley—Crossing Pages as She Comes to Them', *The Mercury* (Hobart), 22 Apr. 1989, Weekend Review, p. 10.

Humphries, B., 'Maroan (for Elizabeth Jolley)', *Neglected Poems and Other Creatures*, Angus and Robertson, Pymble, NSW, 1991, pp. 103–4.

Huntford, R., *The Explorer as Hero*, Gerald Duckworth, London, 1997.

Huntington, T., 'James Boswell's Scotland', *Smithsonian*, Jan. 2005, pp. 72–7.

Ignatieff, M., 'The Rise and Fall of Vienna's Jews', *The New York Review of Books*, 29 June 1989, pp. 21–5.

James, Neil (ed.), 'The Writer and the Central Mischief', *Writers on Writing*, Halstead Press, Rushcutters Bay, NSW, 1999, pp. 97–100.

Jolley, L., *Principles of Cataloguing*, Crosby Lockwood, London, 1960.

——'Toys', *Children's Toys*, BBC Midland Home Service Radio, 2 Feb. 1948.

'Jolley's Diary Entries to be Kept a Secret for a Time Yet', *AAP General News Wire* (Sydney), 21 Feb.2007, Channel 9 News, <http://news.ninemsn.com.au/article.aspx?id=228222&print=true, viewed 21 Feb. 2007.

Jones, J., *The Mayors of Wolverhampton*, vol. 2, Whitehead Brothers, Wolverhampton, West Midlands, 1893.

Kauffmann, W. (ed. and trans.), *Twenty-five German Poets: A Bilingual Collection*, Norton, New York, 1975.

Kavanagh, P., 'The Self the Honey of All Beings—A Conversation with Elizabeth Jolley', *Southerly*, vol. 49, no. 3, 1989, pp. 438–51.

Kent, J., *A Certain Style: Beatrice Davis, A Literary Life*, Viking, Melbourne, 2001; Penguin, Scoresby, Vic., 2001.

Kitson, J., 'Elizabeth Jolley: The Art of Writing and the Art of Living', *24 Hours*, Aug. 1992, pp. 44–7.

——'Jolley's Orchestration', review of *Lovesong* by E. Jolley, *Australian Book Review*, July 1996, pp. 27–9.

Knight, Charles Wilfrid, *School Researches in Heat . . . Pupil's Book (Teacher's Handbook)*, G. P. Philip, London, c. 1928.

Koval, R., 'Elizabeth Jolley Dies', obituary, *The Book Show*, ABC, Radio National, 20 Feb. 2007, <http://www.abc.net.au/rn/bookshow/stories/2007/1851909.html>, viewed 20 Feb. 2008.

——'Interview with Ramona Koval and Sandy McCutcheon [on *Lovesong*]', *Australia Talks Books*, ABC, Radio National, 26 Mar. 1999.

——'National Treasures'. Books and Writing, ABC Radio National, 22 October 1999.

Lawson, B. G., *Vienna: A City in Distress*, Anglo–American Society of Friends Publicity Department, Vienna, 1920.

Lakeman, E. P., quoted in 'Alabama Sibfordian', unsigned article, *SOSA*, Sibford School, Sibford Ferris, Banbury, Oxfordshire, 1937, pp. 45–8.

The Law List, Stevens, London, annual publication.

Lehmanns Allgemeiner Wohnungs–Anzeiger nebst Handels und Gewerbe–Adressbuch für Wien (*Lehmanns General Directory of Domiciles with a Directory for Trade and Commerce for Vienna*), Alfred Hölder, Wien, 1928.

'Life. Be in It.', <http://www.lifebeinit.org/index.php?uri=media/2000.11.22>, viewed 1 Dec. 2007.

Lindenberg, C., *Rudolf Steiner*, Rowohlt, Hamburg, 1992.

Lindsay, E., *Rewriting God: Spirituality in Contemporary Australian Women's Fiction*, Cross/Cultures—Readings in the Post/Colonial Literatures in English, vol. 45, Rodopi, Amsterdam, 2000.

Lurie, C., 'A Fine Friendship', *Good Reading Magazine*, July 2006, pp. 23–3.

——'Tribute: Elizabeth Jolley', *Australian Book Review*, Apr. 2006, p. 16.

McDonald, J., 'Jolley Disturbing', review of *Milk and Honey* by E. Jolley, *NSWIT*, New South Wales Institute of Technology, Sydney, 29 July 1985, n. pag.

McKernan, S., Review of *Elizabeth Jolley: New Critical Essays*, ed. D. Bird and B. Walker, *Westerly*, vol. 37, no. 1, 1992, pp. 92–3.

McMullin, B., 'Yadlamalka Library Girl [Jean Whyte] Shaped Australian Librarianship', *Australian Library Journal*, vol. 52, no. 2, pp. 105–8.

McRae, A., 'Female Mobility and National Space in Restoration England: The Travel Journals of Celia Fiennes', *Women Writing: 1550–1750*, ed. J. Wallwork and P. Salzman, La Trobe University, English Program, Bundoora, Vic., 2001, pp. 105–13.

'Mental Soup', *SOSA*, Sibford School, Sibford Ferris, Banbury, Oxfordshire, 1940, pp. 9–10.

Meredith, 'Elizabeth Jolley—A Wee Sketch', obituary, 22 Feb. 2007, <http://sarsaparillablog.net/?p=496>, viewed 10 Apr. 2007.

Metcalf, M., 'Wood, Malvina Evalyn (1893–1976)', *Australian Dictionary of Biography*, supplementary vol., Melbourne University Press, 2005, pp. 411–2.

Milech, B. H., 'Becoming "Elizabeth Jolley": The First Twenty Years in Australia', *Australian Literature and the Public Sphere*, ed. A. Bartlett, R. Dixon and C. Lee, Association for the Study of Australian Literature with the University of Queensland, Toowoomba, Qld., 1999, pp. 132–41.

Works Cited

———'Elizabeth Jolley, Mr Berrington and the Resistance to Monogamy', *Journal of the Association for the Study of Australian Literature*, vol. 3, 2004, pp. 67–79.

———'The Erotics of Friendship in Elizabeth Jolley's Fiction', *Hungarian Journal of English and American Studies*, vol. 12, no. 1–2, 2006, pp. 263–84.

———'Friendship in a Time of Loneliness', *Australian Literary Studies*, in press.

———'"A Novel I Believe In": Reading Elizabeth Jolley', *Proceedings of the 1994 Association for the Study of Australian Literature*, ASAL with the Department of English, Australian Defence Force Academy, Canberra, 1995, pp. 187–95.

———'"On the Edge"—An Idea Central to *Central Mischief*', review of *Central Mischief* by E. Jolley, *Antipodes*, vol. 6, no. 2, 1992, pp. 169–70.

———'"Sophisticated Spaces": Fiction, Autobiography, and Reading Elizabeth Jolley', *A/B: Auto/Biography Studies*, vol. 12, no.1, 1997, pp. 90–105.

Milech, B. and B. Dibble, 'Aristophanic Love–Dyads: Community, Communion, and Cherishing in Elizabeth Jolley's Fiction', *Antipodes*, vol. 7, no. 1, 1993, pp. 3–10.

———'Elizabeth Jolley's Cross–cultural Life in Writing', *Australian Studies: Journal of the British Australian Studies Association*, in press.

Milli, V., 'A Novel Is a Lengthy Question: An Interview with Frank Ronan', *Estudios Irlandeses*, vol. 2, 2007, pp. 218–25.

Modjeska, D., 'Extra to Real Life', *Australian Book Review*, Apr. 1995, pp. 15–16.

Molfenter, E., 'Bürger und Mitmachen des Dorfes Fischamend vom Jahre 1786', *Fischamend: Ein Heimatbuch* ('Citizens and Others of the Village Fischamend in 1786', *Fischamend: A Native Book*), Vlg. der Marktgemeinde, Fischamend, 1964.

Monson, K., 'An Eerie Tale with Music, Marriage and Surprises', review of *Milk and Honey* by E. Jolley, *Baltimore Sunday Sun*, 25 May 1986, n. pag.

Moran, R., 'Drawing Life from a Deep Well', *Fremantle Arts Review*, vol. 3, no. 2, 1988, pp. 8–9.

———'Jolley: Optimist to the Point of Despair', *West Australian*, 11 May 1991, Big Weekend, p. 5.

Murray–Brown, J., *Kenyatta*, Allen and Unwin, London, 1972.

Mwangi, M., 'Police Stop VP's Bid for Kenyatta Papers', *Daily Nation on the Web*, <http://www.nationaudio.com/News/DailyNation/20102003/News/News6.html>, viewed 1 Oct. 2004.

Neill, A. S., *Freedom, Not License!* Hart, New York, 1966.

——— *Summerhill: A Radical Approach to Child Rearing*, Hart, New York, 1960.

Oliver, W. H., *James K. Baxter: A Portrait*, Port Nicholson Press, Wellington, 1983.

Ozarin, L., 'Moral Insanity: A Brief History', *Psychiatric News*, vol. 36, no. 10, 18 May 2001, p. 21.

Papers of Elizabeth Jolley, ca.1939; 1950–1987, MLMSS 4880, Mitchell Library, State Library of New South Wales.

Perruchon, J., *Le Centre d'étrangers de Montguyon, Réfugiés espagnols en Charente–Maritime (et Deux–Sèvres), 1936–1945* (*The Centre for Foreigners in Montguyon, Spanish Refugees in the Charente–Maritime and Deux–Sèvres Regions, 1936–1945*), Crois vif, Paris, 2000, pp. 151–72.

Perry, M., *The Jarrow Crusade: Protest and Legend*. University of Sunderland Press, 2005.

Pierce, P., 'Narcotic Entanglements: Recent Works of Australian Literary Criticism', review of *Elizabeth Jolley: New Critical Essays*, ed. by D. Bird and B. Walker, *Helplessly Tangled in Female Arms and Legs: Elizabeth Jolley's Fictions* by P. Salzman, and several others, *Australian Literary Studies*, vol. 16, no. 3, 1994, pp. 352–5.

Plato, 'Symposium', *The Dialogues of Plato*, vol. 1, ed. and trans. B. Jowett, Random House, New York, 1937, pp. 301–45.

Prior, M., *The Literary Works of Matthew Prior*, ed. H. Bunker Wright and M. K. Spears, 2 vols., Clarendon Press, Oxford, 1959.

Radford, N. A., 'Jean Primrose Whyte AM', obituary, *AARL (Australian Academic and Research Libraries)*, vol. 34, no. 3, Sept. 2003, <http://www.alia.org.su/publishing/aar/34.3/obituaries.html>, viewed 10 Oct. 2006.

Radford, N. and J. Whyte, 'Librarian Built up Uni Collection', obituary for Andrew Osborn, *The Australian*, 7 May 1991, p. 14.

Rado, L., Review of *Gender and Genre in Novels without End: The British Roman-Fleuve* by L. Felber, *Tulsa Studies in Women's Literature*, vol. 16, no. 1, 1997, pp. 159–61.

Randall, H. J., 'I Remember', *SOSA*, Sibford School, Sibford Ferris, Banbury, Oxfordshire, p. 46–8.

Reid, S., *Dr Elizabeth Jolley: Early Life in England, Migration to Australia 1959, Development as a Writer since 1960s, Publications to 1989, Tutoring and Lecturing in Creative Writing*, verbatim transcript of an interview with Elizabeth Jolley (6 x 60 min. tapes), Library Board of Western Australia,

Works Cited

J. S. Battye Library, Perth, 1989.

Richardson, S., *Clarissa: or, The History of a Young Lady*, ed. A. Ross, Viking Penguin, New York, 1985.

Riemer, A. P., 'Between Two Worlds—An Approach to Elizabeth Jolley's Fiction', *Southerly*, vol. 43, no. 3, 1983, pp. 239–52.

——'Displaced Persons—Some Preoccupations in Elizabeth Jolley's Fiction', *Westerly*, vol. 31, no. 2, 1986, pp. 64–79.

——'Elizabeth Jolley: New Worlds and Old', *International Literature in English: Essays on the Major Writers*, ed. R. L. Ross, Garland, New York, 1991, pp. 371–82.

——*Inside Outside: Life between Two Worlds*, Angus and Roberston, Pymble, NSW, 1992.

Rilke, R. M., *The Best of Rilke: 72 True-Verse Translations*, ed. and trans. W. Arndt, University of New England Press, Lebanon, New Hampshire, 1989.

Rodriguez, J., 'Elizabeth and Red Socks in Perth', *Meanjin*, vol. 56, no. 3, 1987, p. 356–7.

Rosner, R. and W. Meindl, *Loba Feinchemie: 1957–1997*, LOBA Feinchemie AG, Fischamend, 1997.

Rotter, H., *Die Josephsstadt: Geschichte des 8 Wiener Gemeindebezirkes (The Josephsstadt: History of the 8th Viennese District)*, Gemeinderat der Stadt, Wien (Municipal Council of Vienna), 1918.

Rowley, H., 'The Ups, the Downs: My Life as a Biographer', *Australian Book Review*, July–Aug. 2007, pp. 29–35.

Russell, B., *The Autobiography of Betrand Russell—1872–1914*, [vol.1], Allen and Unwin, London, 1967.

Said, E., *On Late Style: Music and Literature Against the Grain*, Pantheon, New York, 2006.

Sainty, Sir John C., *List of English Law Officers, King's Counsel and Holders of Patents of Precedence*, Selden Society, London, 1987.

Sapegno, N. (ed.), *La Divina Commedia: Inferno*, vol. 1, Nuova Italia, Firenze, 1955.

Sayers, D. L. (ed.), *The Comedy of Dante Alighieri the Florentine, Cantica I, Hell (L'Inferno)*, trans. and intro. D. L. Sayers, Penguin, Harmondsworth, Middlesex, 1949.

Seddon, R. B., Introduction, *B. Fleetwood–Walker: Memorial Exhibition, 1893–1963*, catalogue, Royal Birmingham Society of Artists, Birmingham, c. 1963.

Shapcott, T., 'Aubade: For Elizabeth Jolley', *Weekend Australian*, 21–22 June 2003, Review, p. 9.

——'Cape Lilacs', *The City of Empty Rooms*. Salt Publishing, Cambridge, Eng., 2006, p. 10. Also published in *Blue Dog: Australian Poetry*, vol. 5, no. 10, 2006, p. 8.

——*The Literature Board: A Brief History*, University of Queensland Press, St Lucia, Qld., 1988.

Shapiro, N., 'The Darker Truths of Love', review of *Milk and Honey* by E. Jolley, *St Louis Post–Dispatch*, 25 May 1986, n. pag.

Sharr, F. A., *Recollections: Forty Years of Public Library Service*, Auslib Press, Adelaide, 1992.

Sheppard, T., 'The War Years at Sibford', *SOSA*, Sibford School, Sibford Ferris, Banbury, Oxfordshire, 1935, pp. 45–8.

Sisman, A., *Boswell's Presumptuous Task: The Making of the Life of Dr Johnson*, Farr, Strauss and Giroux, New York, 2003.

Smart, E., *By Grand Central Station I Sat Down and Wept*, Granada, London, 1966 (1945).

Smith, A., 'Elizabeth Jolley', *Publishers Weekly*, 7 Apr. 1989, pp. 115–6

Sorenson, R., 'Jolley Reveals Idyllic Time in Hitler Camp', *Courier–Mail* (Brisbane) 29 June 2001, p. 3.

——'The Power of the Prize', *Weekend Australian* (Canberra), 16 June 2007, Features, p. 4.

——'A Prolific, Peculiar Voice', obituary, *Australian*, 20 Feb. 2007, p. 12.

Soulier, A., 'Elizabeth Jolley et le Pays des Autres' ('Elizabeth Jolley and the Country of Others'), *Commonwealth: Essays and Studies* (France), vol. 17, no. 1, 1994, pp. 45–50.

Spielhofer, S., *Stemming the Dark Tide: Quakers in Austria, 1919–1942*. William Sessions, York, 2001.

——'To Vienna, with Love: Quaker Relief Work, 1919–1922', *The Woodbrooke Journal*, vol. 4, 1999, pp. 1–19.

Starke, R., *Writers, Readers and Rebels: Upfront and Backstage at Australia's Top Literary Festival*, Wakefield Press, Kent Town, SA, 1998.

Steger, J., 'Literary Peers Mourn Mischievous Mistress of Black Humour', obituary, *Age* (Melbourne), 20 Feb. 2007, p. 3.

Stevenson, R. L., Virginibus Puerisque *and Other Papers*, Chatto and Windus, London, 1903 (1881).

Sugarman, M., 'Jews in the Spanish Civil War (Part 3)', <http://www.us–israel.org/jsource/History/sugar12b.html>, viewed 10 June 2004.

Sullivan, R., *By Heart: The Life of Elizabeth Smart*, Flamingo, London, 1991.

Works Cited

Taylor, A. S., 'Dorothy Brigham 1906–1995', *Sibford, 1995–1996/S.O.S.O*, ed. M. D. T. Farr, Sibford School, Sibford Ferris, Banbury, Oxfordshire, pp. 52–3.

Templeman, I., '"A Two Book Wonder": A Decade of Publishing—Fremantle Arts Centre Press—1976–1986', *Westerly*, vol. 31, no. 4, 1986, pp. 78–86.

——*Poems*, Freshwater Bay Press, Claremont, WA, 1979.

Thackeray, W. M., *The Pocket Thackeray*, ed. A. H. Hyatt, Chatto and Windus, London, 1906.

Thomson, A., 'Landscapes of Memory', *Meanjin*, vol. 61, no. 3, 2002, pp. 81–96.

'Three Great Headmasters', *SOSA*, Sibford School, Sibford Ferris, Banbury, Oxfordshire, 1937, p. 43.

Throsby, M. Interview with Elizabeth Jolley. ABC Classic FM, 28 February 1997; rebroadcast 23 March 2007.

Tolstoy, L., 'What Men Live By', *Twenty-Three Tales*, trans. L. Maude and A. Maude, Oxford University Press, London, 1906, pp. 55–82.

Walker, H. and C. Quirk, 'B. Fleetwood-Walker: Drawings from the Artist's Studio', <http://www.fleetwood-walker.co.uk/biography.php>.

Ward, E., 'Moments of Vision', review of *Miss Peabody's Inheritance* and *Mr. Scobie's Riddle* by E. Jolley, *Washington Post*, 4 Nov. 1984, Book World, pp. 1–2.

'Watkins', <http://www.watkinsonline.com>, viewed 20 Oct. 2007.

'Weather Dependant [sic]=Paranormal Database Records', <www.paranormaldatabase.com/calendar/Pages/weather.php>, viewed 20 Sept. 2004.

Webby, E., 'Jolley Marvellous', review of *My Father's Moon* by E. Jolley, *Sydney Morning Herald*, 15 Apr. 1989, Books, p. 89.

——'The Uses of Fiction: Some Recent Novels from the South Pacific Region', *SPAN (Journal of the South Pacific Association for Commonwealth Literature and Language Studies)*, vol. 21, 1985, pp. 29–37.

White, Terri–ann, 'A Fine Line Between Truth and Fiction', interview with Christina Wilcox, *Fremantle Arts Review* vol. 3, no. 2, 1988, p. 12.

Whitlock, G. (ed.), *Eight Voices of the Eighties: Stories and Criticism by Australian Women*, University of Queensland Press, St Lucia, Qld., 1989, pp. 334–44.

Whyte, J., 'Librarians and Scholars', *Australian Academic Libraries in the Seventies: Essays in Honour of Dietrich Borchardt*, ed. H. Bryan and J. Horacek, University of Queensland Press, St Lucia, Qld., pp. 243–62.

Wilcox, C., (dir.), *The Nights Belong to the Novelist: The Imaginative World of*

Elizabeth Jolley, prod. Nigel Williams, written by J. Kirby and C. Wilcox, Yowie Films, Sydney, 1986.

Willbanks, R., 'Elizabeth Jolley', interview, *Speaking Volumes: Australian Writers and Their Work*, Penguin, Ringwood, Vic., 1991, pp. 111–27.

Williams, G., 'Elizabeth Jolley', *Studio Collections*, Aug.–Sept. 1987, p. 282+.

Wilson, F., 'Ordinary Lives Writ Large', review of *Two Lives* by V. Seth, *The Observer*, 21 Oct. 2005, p. 16.

Wimmer, A., 'Don't Forget Electra', review of *An Innocent Gentleman* by E. Jolley, *Australian Book Review*, Sept. 2001, pp. 55–6.

Winton, T., 'Remembering Elizabeth Jolley', commemorative essay, *Westerly*, vol. 52, no. 2, 2007, pp. 27–34.

Woolf, V., *The Diary of Virginia Woolf, Vol. III: 1925–1930*, ed. A. Oliver Bell, assisted by A. McNeillie, Hogarth Press, London, 1980.

——*The Letters of Virginia Woolf. Vol. II. 1912–1922*, ed. N. Nicholson, Harcourt Brace Jovanovich, New York, 1976.

——*To the Lighthouse*, Harcourt Brace, New York, 1955.

INDEX

Bold type indicates works discussed; underlined type indicates photo number.

ABC (Australian Broadcasting Corporation)
competitions, 199
interviews, 221, 243–4
radio plays and readings, 167, 184, 193, 199, 240, 276, 280
TV, 220, 221
Adams, Phillip, 221, 244
Adelaide Festivals, 180–1, 184, 185, 199, 207, 273, 277
Age Book of the Year awards, 218, 238, 239, 280
Alexander, Fred and Gretha, 137–9, 144, 224, 267
Andrew E., blogger, 220, 224
Anti Mote *see* Thrippleton, Annie Maud
Aristophanes, 187, 241, 274
Astley, Thea, 199, 200–1, 220, 222, 276
Augustine, Saint, 9, 18, 88, 229
Australian letter competition, 155–6
Australian Literature Board, Senior Fellowship, 218, 280
Australian Society of Authors, President, 218
autobiographical fiction, 236–8

BBC (British Broadcasting Corporation) radio plays and broadcasts, 26, 93–4, 154, 166–7, 193, 199, 260, 264
of Madelaine's stories, xv
Barker, George, 111
Barker children, 105, 111–12, 133, 207
Barthes, Roland, 'death of the author', 198
Bauer, Steffi, 39–40, 62, 261
Baxter, James K., 48–9, 51, 57
Belbin, Jill, 167

bereavement, 227, 232–3, 234
Berrington, Kenneth, x, xii, xv, 28–30, 258-9, 283, 287, <u>9</u>
bequest to Margarete, 15, 32, 125
in Jolley's works *see* 'Mr Berrington'; Vera trilogy; *and under* Knight household
payment of school fees, 32, 34
travels with Margarete and Monica, 30–1, 58–9, 213
Bicentennial Grant, 215, 218, 280
Bildungsroman, 228
Billings, Alan and Joyce, 140
biography, xi–xvi
Bird, Delys, 222, 240, 241, 248
Blair, Tony, 122
Bland, Bill and Nora, 123, 127, 131
Bloomsbury ethos, 110, 134
Blotnickis, Wladyslaw and Ludmila, 269; Ludmila, 164–5, 174, 176, 178, 182, 186, 226, 250, 271, <u>33</u>
Bond, Alan, 167
Boswell, James, xii
Brigham, Dorothy, 45, 46
Bristow, Sir Rowley, 71–2, 263
Brittain, Vera, 52
Broom, John, 123–4, 127, 131, 132, 139, 266, <u>28</u>
Broom, Joyce, 70, 181, <u>17</u>
Bund Deutsches Mädel (BDM), 60, 73, 262
Burgess, Gladys, 43, 45–6, 54, 56, 98, 251, 261
Cadbury, Edward, 90
Canada–Australia prize, 218, 279
Carter, Angela, 199–200, 201
Centenary Medal, 245
Chaplains' Conference,

paper, 179, 223
characters
drawn from life, 15, 25, 73, 102, 152, 167, 241–2, 282
explorations of, 154, 195, 238, 240–1, 245–6
migrants as 154, 155, 172–3, 175, 192, 241
names, 236
recycling of, 154–5, 173–4, 275
sexual outsiders, 240–1
Vera Wright *see* Vera Wright
'[Chocolate Has Its Own Melancholy]', 188
Christina Stead Prize, 218
Churchill, Winston, 17–8
Clarissa, Samuel Richardson, 90
classical music: Beethoven, *Violin Concerto*, 69; Brahms, *Deutsches Requiem*, 69; Mozart, *Eine Kleine Nachtmusik*, 69; Schubert, *Winterreise*, 247
Coleridge, Samuel Taylor, 132
Cornford, F. M., 194, 276
community, ix, 148, 173
conferences and arts festivals, 277
see also names of specific events
Cotterell, William 'Bill', 181, 260, 273
Craven, Peter, 228, 236, 237, 248
Curtin University of Technology
Elizabeth Jolley Lecture Series, 221, 246
Honorary Degree, 219, 239, <u>45</u>
writing classes, 179, 206, 246–7

Daniel, Helen, 188, 220, 239
Dante's *Inferno*, 32, 203, 208, 279

328

Davis, Beatrice, 153, 184,
    200–1, 218, 239
Dawkins, John, 181, 272
    sued Jolley and WA
        Newspapers, 179
Dawson, Sister, 262
Dessaix, Robert, 158, 221,
    269
Deutsche Jungmädel, 60–1
Diamond, Neil, 170
Dickens, Charles, 54, 102
Dickens, Monica, 83
distress, as theme, 44, 259
Doyle, Mary, 82, 84, 87,
    159
dreams, in plots, 208–9,
    215, 217, 278
Dungey, Andrew, 149–50,
    164-5, 243, 249, 268

écriture féminine, 228
Eddington, Paul, 42–3, 46,
    48, 51, 57–8
Ellmann, Richard, xi
Ellwood, Eleanor Ann,
    282, 21
endurance, as theme, 44,
    214, 259, 277
Epanomitis, Fotini
    (Harvey), 206, 277
Euripides, *Medea*, 170
Eurydice, 233
evil, potential for, 162–3,
    175, 178
Ewer, Monica, 9, 63
Ewers, John K., 154
exile, 157, 172
    experienced, 21, 88,
        158–9, 172
    as theme, 159, 173, 270

families, as theme, x, xii,
    57, 73, 74, 96, 106–7, 134,
    191, 235–6
    unhappy, x, 120, 124,
        231, 232
    training for love, 226,
        232
fecklessness, 162, 270
Fehr, Ilse, 24, 268
Fehr, Margarethe *see*
    Knight, Margarete Fehr
Fehr family, x–xi, 5–7, 8, 9,
    150, 255, 285–6
    Joseph Edward Fehr,
        6–7, 12, 29, 255
    Walter Fehr, 5–7, 9, 29
    Florianigasse
        apartments, 5–6, *1*

Felber, Lynette, 228
Fellowship of Australian
    Writers, 168
    awards and prizes, 153,
        172, 202, 218
    life membership in WA,
        218–19
Fidelio, Beethoven, 32, 241
Fiennes, Celia, 97, 99
Finlay–Jones, Robert and
    Judy Mary, 161
Flaubert, Gustave, 164
    (*Julian the Hospitaller*),
        227, 238
Fleetwood–Walker,
    Bernard, 91, 92
    drawing of Sarah, 92–3,
        97
Fonseca, Isobel, *Bury Me
    Standing*, xv
Franz Josef, Emperor, 17
Frazer, Peggy Levi, 90, 91,
    93, 97, 136, 291, 24
Fremantle Arts Centre,
    169
    summer schools, 170–1,
        185
    writing classes, 169, 203
Fremantle Arts Centre
    Press, 171, 183
    publication and launch
        of *Five Acre Virgin*,
        171–2
    at Writers' Weeks,
        180–1, 185
Friends, Society of,
    see Quakers
friendships, 248–50
    and closeness, 176, 182
    as theme, 188, 189
    through letters, 132, 196,
        250–1
Freud, Sigmund, xvi, 3, 5,
    22, 68, 74, 139, 228, 254
Furlong, Ronald, 71, 262

gardening, 86, 116, 119–21
Gardening Diary, 119–120,
    121
Garner, Helen, 220, 248,
    251
Gauguach, Ilse, 15, 16, 125,
    286
Germans, attitudes to,
    79–80
Glaskin, Gerry, 154
Goatcher, Phillip and
    Phyllis, 160, 270, 272,
    276

Goethe, Johann,
    *The Sorrows of Young
    Werther*, 3
Gollancz, publisher, 122
Goring, Tony, 35

Hancock, Joyce Ellen,
    see Jolley, Joyce
Hanrahan, Barbara, 200
Harborfront International
    Festival of Artists, 199,
    207, 277
Hitler, Adolph, xi, 17–18,
    61, 75
    postcards from, 39, 259
Hitler Jugend (HJ), 261
Holden (Wood–
    Thompson), Libby, 69,
    260, 298, 12
homelessness, 103, 112–13,
    158, 159, 248–9
    as theme, 208, 227, 241
homosexuality, 176
    between women
        see between women
        under 'love as theme'
Honorary doctorates, 219,
    221, 239
Hope, A. D., 154, 200
hope as theme, 170, 187,
    191, 198, 206, 217, 235
Horn, Gabriel, 25, 26–7,
    36
Horne, Donald, 218
Horobin, Doris, 23
house cleaning, 166–8, 179
Humphries, Barry, 221–2,
    246, 248, 286, 44
Hungerford, Tom, 154,
    180

idyllic times, 48, 73, 120
    in novels, 189, 194–5,
        196, 212, 213
Ignatieff, Michael, 18

Joel, Ben and Eveline
    Kotai, 221
Johnson, Samuel, xii
Johnstone, E. Arthur and
    Jessie, 42–4, 48, 260
    girls' encounter with
        soldiers, 52–3, 75
    quick note practice,
        56–7
Jolley, Bertha, 94
Jolley, Elizabeth/Monica
    Elizabeth Knight,
    xvi–xvii, birth 8, early

329

Index

home life 9–34, <u>4</u>, <u>5</u>, <u>6</u>, <u>11</u>, <u>12</u>, <u>14</u>
Her life
school at Sibford *see under* Sibford
archives, xv, 204, 309–13
awards and honours, 218–19, 221, 238–9, 280
Berrington's presence, 2–3, 30–3, 35, 40, 51, 58–9, 96, 121, 237
care of refugees, 19, 24
closeness with Madelaine, 21–2, 41, 82
compassion and caring, 152, 162–5, 187–8, 225–6, 249
correspondence, 251–2, 310-11
deaths of family and friends, 181–2, 273
domestic workload, 146–7, 148, 156, 202, 204
door-to-door selling, 151–2
dress, 145, 147
driver's licence and car, 142, 152
Edinburgh house purchase, 106, 108–9
employment, 148, 151, 166–7, 168
family life, 20–2, 82–3
in Jolley's fiction, 15, 21–2, 25, 236, 241–2
films about, 220, 221
at 'Flowermead', 10–11, 15, 133, 255, <u>4</u>, <u>5</u>
German girls' youth camp, 56, 59–61, 262, <u>12</u>
health issues, 129–30, 145, 146, 181
marriage to Leonard, 121
move to Scotland, 114–15
music, 44, 54–5, 69, 82–3
names, name changes, xvi–xvii, 9, 97, 108, 112–13, 116, 128
optimism, 44, 117, 121, 130, 131, 136, 159, 205, 253
pacifism, 75, 79–80
placatory, 3, 117, 118, 135

portraits, 220–1, 245, 280, <u>30</u>, <u>46</u>
pregnancy and birth of Sarah, 88–91
professorial appointment, 221, 222
prominence and public persona, 220–1, 222–3
psychoanalysis, 22–3
recipes, 146
relationship with father, 11, 22–3, 33, 34, 107, 181, 226, 252, 257–8, 281
relationship with grandparents, 9–10, 41, 82, 256
relationship with Jolleys, 85–6, 87, 88, 91, 93, 96, 159, 250
relationship with Leonard Jolley, xvi, 88, 94–5, 112, 130, 131, 134, 159, 161, 203, 224–5, 250
relationship with mother, 23, 38, 40, 59, 74, 89, 97, 100, 107–8, 112, 121, 124–6, 150, 181, 226, 253
religious beliefs, 51–2, 65
schooling, 15, and home schooling, 21
social circle, 12–16
sought work in schools, 98–100
youthful literary interests, 51, 54–5
Her work
Essays
Central Mischief ix, 221, 238–9, 281, *Learning to Dance* 221; 'Where Do I Look for Help' 179, 'By the Waters of Babylon' **207**, 'The Changing Family' 12, 19, 106, 204, 273, 'Decidedly Pointing to Central Mischief' 227, 'Good Knight, Sweet Prince' 17, 262, 'Manchester Repair' 243, 'My First Editor' 52, 54, 56, '"My Sister Dancing" 21, 'Of Butchers and Bilberry Baskets' 33, 39, **58–61**, 75, 83, 242, 'On War' 12, 'One

Christmas Knitting' xiii, 10, 13, 24, 256–7, 260, 'Only Connect!' 22, 63, 152, 'The Pill, the Condom and the Syringe' 172, 'Poppy Seed and Sesame Rings' 153, 'Self-Portrait: A Child Went Forth' 54, 'A Sort of Gift' 20, 153, 'Strange Regions There Are' 14, 'Tricked or Treated' 159, '"What Sins to Me Unknown ..."' ix–x, 1, 3, 11, 88

Novels
A Feast of Life ix, 76, 111, 127, **129–33**, 147, 153, 254, 266, *An Accommodating Spouse* 240–3, *Cabin Fever* 90, 207, 227, **228–33**, *Eleanor Page* 96, 106–7, 122–3, 214, *Foxybaby* 102, 200 (review Carter's review) 203, **207–11**, 215, 234, 277–8, *The Georges' Wife* 133–4, 190, **233–4**, *An Innocent Gentleman* 31–3, **240–2**, 252, *Lovesong* 225, 227, **240**, **244–5**, *Milk and Honey* (*The Prince of a Fellow*) 153, 268) 24, 173, 185, 188–9, **191–2**, 195, 199–200, 221, *Miss Peabody's Inheritance* 46, 77, 102, 183, **195–8**, 201, 207, 211, 223, 245, *Mr Scobie's Riddle* 102, 110, 149, 153, 183, **193–5**, 230, 257, 268, 278, *My Father's Moon* 15, 50, 70, 86, 89, 102 105, 109–10, 181, 218–9, 228, 230–2, 236, **239–40**, 269, 282, *The Newspaper of Claremont Street* 22, 161, 165–7, 172, **177–78**, 182–6, 239, 271, *The Orchard Thieves* 175–6, 218, 226, **234–5**, 240, 244, 283, *Palomino* (*The Cardboard Diary* [153]) 25, 161, 172, **188–90**, 192, 195, 200, 202, 211–2, 214, 240, 274–5, *The Sugar Mother* (*The Leila*

330

Index

Family 151, 153, 184, 214–5 [manuscript lost 214–5, 278–9]) 24, 203, **214–7**, 239–41, 279–80, 221 (stage production), *The Well* 183, 195, 211–4, 218, 221, 227, <u>42</u>

Plays
Off Air: Nine Plays for Radio 240

Poems
Diary of a Weekend Farmer ix, 223, 239, 270; 'Dead Trees in Your Absence' 223, 'The Goose Path: A Meditation' 270, 'Great Branches Fall' ix

Stories
Another Holiday for the Prince 167, *Fellow Passengers* 221, 239, *Five Acre Virgin* xvi, 161, 167, 171–2, 177, 270, *The Travelling Entertainer* 172–75, 177, 182, 185, *Woman in a Lampshade* 173, 183, 193, 200, *40*; 'The Adventures of George Henry the Caterpillar' 26, **93–4**, 'The Agent in Travelling in Travelling' 173, 'Another Holiday for the Prince' 167, 174, 239–40, 271, 'Bill Sprockett's Land' 154, 'Bunny School' stories **57–8**, 73, 94, 261, 'Clever and Pretty' 13, 18, 33, 61, 241, **258**, 'The Comforter' 132, 'Dingle the Fool' 204, 271, 'The Disciple' 184, 'The Fellow Passenger' **175–7**, 270, 'Five Acre Virgin' 161, 'A Gentleman's Agreement' 174, 'Grasshoppers' 161–2, **175–6**, 'A Hedge of Rosemary' **153–5**, 'Her First Minuet' 15, 56, 73, 'Hilda's Wedding' 184, 'The Jarrah Thieves' 74, 270, 'Lehmann Sieber' **73–5**, 'Little Herb of Self Heal' 73, 'The Man Who Was Poor' 83, 87, 'Mark F' 180, 'May I Rest My Case on Your Table' 152, 154, 'Mr Berrington' x, 21–2, 28–32, 37, 59, 61, 91, 'Mr Parker's Valentine' 170, **174**, 271, 'The New Clothes' 148, 'A New World' 151, 154, 'Night Runner' 150–1, 'Outink to Uncle's Place' 173', 'The Owner of Greif' 180, 'The Pear Tree Dance' (poem and story) **165–6**, <u>32</u>, 'The Pelican' 153, 'The Performance' 170, 177, **185–7**, 188–9, 215, 'The Return' 132, 'The Rhyme' 153–4, 158, 'The Shepherd on the Roof' **174**, 'The Sick Vote' 149, 154–5, 'The Silent Night of Snowfall' 14, 'The Spruce Tree' 122, 'The Talking Bricks' 150, 153–4, 'The Travelling Entertainer' 152, 154, 'Waterloo Mouse' **93–4**, 122, 'The Well–Bred Thief' 173, 214

Others
Cooking by Degrees, 148, 268, *Travelling Notebooks* 171

Jolley, Joyce Ellen Hancock, 85–96, 108, 116–7, 121, 130–1, 134–6, 159, 225, 236, 250, 265
Jolley, Leonard, xvi, xvii, 67–8, 84–5, <u>31</u>, <u>34</u>
  arrogance, 115, 138, 139, 182
  controlling nature, 115, 118, 119, 131–2,
  editor of *The Bibliothek*, 129
  estranged from family, 124, 130–1
  as flirt, 68–9, 84, 119, 132, 142, 145–6
  health issues, 144–5, 146, 179, 186, 203
  in hospital at Pyrford, 67, 68–9, 71, 72, 84, *16*
  intolerance, 115, 135, 164, 174
  librarian: for Selly Oak Colleges, 84, 88; at RCP, Edinburgh, 106, 108, 115–16, 118, 126; at University of Glasgow, 126–7, 128–9, 135; at UWA, 135–6, 137, 144–5, 295
  marriage to Joyce, 85–6, 106, 116–17
  marriage to Monica, 121
  in nursing home, 223–5
  The Principles of Cataloguing, 135
  procrastination over marriages, 97, 98, 106, 108, 225
  retirement, 181–2, 203–4
  study leave, 150, 178–9, 181
  study tours, 95–6
  sued by John Dawkins, 179, 181
  visitors discouraged, 118–19, 122
  at Wooroloo, 161
Jolley, Richard, xv, 121, 125, 130, 145, 204
  care of mother, 247–8
Jolley (Radley), Ruth, xv, 121, 130, 145, 166, 282;
  her children, 236, 282
Jolley (Nelson), Sarah, 91, 96, 114, 145, 156, 282;
  her daughter, 282
Jolley family life, 120–1, 128, 129–30, 131–2, 136, 186
  bush block, 159–61
  see also Wooroloo property
  house in Perth, 142, *37*
  houses in Scotland, 122, 123, 129, *27*, *29*
  in England for Leonard's sabbatical, 150–1
  move to Perth, 135–6, 137, 139
  social life, 139–43
Jones, Mr, piano teacher, 21
Jungmädelführerinnenlager, 262

331

Index

Kadova Arab horse stud, 161
Kemmeter, Marie Stapf, xi, 14, 15, 26, 56, 73, 74, 80, 262
Kendall, Peter, 220–1, 280
Kenyatta, Edna Grace Clarke, 102–4, 109–10, 119, 131, 265, 25
Kenyatta, Jomo, 102
Kenyatta, Peter, 102, 105, 119
Kirkby, Joan, 200
Kitson, Jill, 221, 239, 240
Klein, Melanie, 22–3
Knight, Charles, 3, 4, 12
  letters to Monica (Elizabeth), 9–10, 256
Knight, Daisy, 3–4, 10, 12–13, 150, 256
  relationship with Monica, 95, 107
Knight, Dorothy, 12–3
Knight, Ingle, 41
Knight, Madelaine (Blackmore), xiv–xv, 2–3, 8–9, 16, 21–2, 23, 24, 82, 121, 5, 6
  assault incident, 33, 262
  attitude to Berrington, 27, 29, 31, 32, 241
  dancing, 114, 267
  death of mother 37–8i
  death of husband Tony, 245
  in Glasgow, 114–15
  Jolley's competition entries, 199
  own radio plays, xv
  at Sibford, 32, 34, 47
Knight, Margarete Fehr, x, 5, 8–9, 11–12, 16–18, 88, 255, 3, 7
  aging, 35–6, 37
  attitude to Hitler, 17–18, 259
  attitude to men, 25–6, 27
  attitude to women, 17, 23–5
  concern over relationship with Leonard, 87, 112
  death, 37, 181
  early life, 2, 5–7, 10
  exile, 158
  relationship with Berrington, 2–3, 27–8, 29–32, 237
  as tutor, 26, 29, 35

Knight, Martha 'Patti' Elizabeth Thrippleton, 3, 4, 33, 256, 258–9
Knight, Wilfrid (Charles Wilfrid), ix, 2, 3–4, 8–10, 11, 16, 18, 54, 2, 8
  conscientious objection and jailing, 4, 11, 51
  death, 36–7, 181
  distressed by Berrington, 31, 237
  Methodist lay preacher, 34, 35, 288
  Oxford Group commitment, 33–4, 50–1, 261
  relationship with Margarete, 1–2, 19, 40, 51
  teacher, 3–4, 4–5, 19–20, 35
  in Vienna, 3, 5, 8, 254
Knöfel, Max, 26
Koval, Ramona, 221, 245

Lamb, Edith, 98–9 and Joseph, 163–4, 225
Lamb, Theodore, 47
Larkin, Philip, 126–7, 136
Lehmann, Ingeborg, 73
Lehrer, Tom, 141
Leiser, Gottfried, 25–6, 29, 107, 288
Levey, Harry and Hannah, 140–2, 147, 150, 244, 250, 252, 267, 34
Lewis, Julie, 250
Lindsay, Elaine, 242
Living Treasure, 245, 43
loneliness, 187, 193, 214, 227, 241
  of single motherhood, 91, 95, 159, 250–1
  as theme, 155, 191–2, 197, 207–8, 212, 214
love as theme, xvi, 83, 155, 186–91, 194–5
  age disparities, 196, 212, 240, 245
  between women, 76, 146, 176–7, 188–90, 193–4, 196–7, 229
  and dependency, 191–2
  ending of, 176, 249
  hidden relationships, 91
  incest, 189–90, 207, 209, 215–6
  of the land, 165–6, 177, 178, 186

  parental, 50, 234–5
  quest for complementarity, 217–18
  and restraint, 141, 189–90, 209, 214
  triangular relationships, 83, 213–14, 215–17, 229–30, 231, 237, 241
lovelessness, 173, 207–8, 227, 241
  and sexuality, 173, 177
Lund, Hans and Denie, 59–60, 75, 80
Lurie, Caroline, ix, xiv, 184–5, 219, 221, 248, 250, 273, 35

MacKenna, R.O., 129, 135
MacPherson, Sheila see Naylor
Macswiney, Alix, 82, 119, 136, 150
Mamer, Gladys, 121
Marsh, Helen, 36
McCauley, James, 154, 184
McKenzie, Nancy, 247
Mead, Margaret, memory, 227, 228, 229, 233–6
Mews, Charles-Fleury, 39, 62, 80
migrants
  as characters, 154, 155, 172–3, 175, 192, 241
  as writers, 158
Milech, Barbara, xv, 246, 248, 286
Miles Franklin Award, 218, 238
  ineligible works, 222, 239
Modjeska, Drusilla, 228, 281
Moore, Margaret, 8, 11
Moore, Mary, 245
Moorhouse, Frank, 222, 239
moral insanity, 229, 231–2, 282
mother–daughter relationships as theme, 167–8, 234–5

National Book Council Banjo Award, 239
Nansen, Fridtjof, 5
Naylor, Barry and Sheila

332

MacPherson, 45, 46, 57, 251
Neill, A. S., Summerhill
New York Times Review of Books, 200, 218
Norris, Mrs, 109–10
Noster, Aloisia, 7
  child Johanna 'Hansi' Noster Fehr 7

Orfeo ed Euridice, Gluck, 170, 271
Orpheus and Eurydice, 232–3
Osborn, Andrew, 145–6
Outback Press, 183, 184, 185, 274
Oxford Group, 33–4, 259

Paalen, Wolfgang, 112
pacifists and conscientious objectors, 14, 28, 29, 32
  Kenneth Berrington, 29, 32
  Arthur Johnstone, 44
  Leonard Jolley, 68, 84, 85, 138
  Monica Knight, 75, 79–80
  Wilfrid Knight, 4, 11, 32, 51
Parry, Glyn, 206
Pearce, Evelyn, 65
Penguin Australia, 183
Pinewood school, 98, 99–100, 292, 26
  abuse at, 104–5
  Monica's experience of, 103–4, 105–6, 107, 159
  source material for writings, 102–3, 105, 109–11
  staff, 102–3
  students, 103–4, 105
Π O (Peter Oustabasidis), 180, 273
Plato, on love, 187, 274
Pleasance, Angela, 103, 105
Powell, Enoch, 52
Prestcott, Ann, 110
Prestcott, Stanley, Sir, 166
Pride and Prejudice, 52
Prior, Dorothy, 44, 45, 46
Proust, *À la Recherche du temps perdu*, 119, 127–8, 282
publishers, 183–4, 274

publishing, 157, 171–2, 183–4, 193, 201, 239–40
  rejections, 153, 184, 202, 274

Quadrant, 154, 184
Quakers, 4, 8, 14, 254
  meetings at Sibford Gower, 47, 51
  schools, 41, 44–5, 64, 261
Queen Elizabeth Hospital, Birmingham, 66, 76–8, 80–2, 263
  Monica's experiences at, 77, 78, 81–2, 87, 262
  nursing training, 78, 290
  wartime pressure, 78–9
quick notes, 56–7, 107, 167, 205

Raynor, Emily and Geoffrey, 88–90
refugees, 19, 24–5, 39–40
Reid, Gordon and Ruth, 218, 280
Reid, Stuart, xiv, 250
Riddell, Elizabeth, 223
Rilke, quotes from, 176, 225, 232–3
Rodriguez, Judith, 221
Roitman, Irma, 24–5, 181
roman à clef, 236, 241–2
roman à thèse, 236, 241–2
roman-fleuve, 228, 229, 282
Rohan, Alice, 112
Ronan, Frank, 236
Rossetti, Sarah, 206, 277
Rowley, Hazel, x, xii
Royal College of Physicians, Edinburgh, 106, 108, 115, 118, 126
Russell, Bertrand, on loneliness, 214, on pleasure 134

St Nicholas and St Martin's Hospitals, Pyrford, 65–6, 71–2, 15–18
  Monica's experiences at, 66–7, 69–70, 76, 159, 19
St Thomas Hospital, London, nursing application, 64–5
Sanders, Dorothy, aka

Lucy Walker, 144, 199, 222
Sapcote, Jean, 70, 84
Schumann, Elizabeth, 54
Seneca, 5
Sessions, Robert, 222
Seth, Vikram, xiii
Sezacinski, Fairlie, 251–2
Shapcott, Tom, 250–1
Sheldon, Acheson and Mary, 13–5, 95, 256; 278;
  Betty Sheldon, 13, 15, loses ms 214,
short stories and essays, ix, 83, 122, 179, 253, 269, 282
  awards for, 153
  competitions, 122, 127, 153, 184
  themes and plots, 154, 173, 174–7
  see also titles of individual stories and collections under Jolley, Elizabeth
Sibford school, 41–8, 222, 260, 10
  bullying and teasing, 48–50
  friendships maintained, 250
  influences on Jolley's writing, 56–7
  Monica's experiences at, 23, 39, 40–1, 43–4, 48, 49–50, 53–4
Siebert, Ilse, 73
Sinclair, Jean, 64
Smaldon, Catherine, 77, 78, 88
Smart, Elizabeth, 111–12, 207
Society of Women Writers, award, 239
Sorenson, Rosemary, 245, 257
SPACLALS Conference, 200–1
Southall, Brian, 41
speaking engagements, 179, 205, 206–7, 243–4
Sprott, Margaret, 132
stage productions, 221, 281
Stapf, Marie *see* Kemmeter, Marie Stepf
Stapf, Otto and Martha, 14, 23
Stevenson, Robert Louis, *Virginibus Puerisque*, 27, 28, 249

333

Index

Stewart, Douglas, 200
Strachan, Elizabeth, 100–2, 104, 105, 106, 265, 26
Sturge, Amy, 23, 65
Summerhayes, Geoffrey and Joslyn, 167

teaching creative writing, 179, 185, 205–6
  for FAC, 169–71, 185
  in prisons, 206, 245
  successful students, 206
  at WAIT/Curtin, 179, 206, 246–7
Templeman, Ian, 169, 171, 180, 271
von Tegetthoff, Admiral Wilhelm, 106
Thrippleton, Annie Maud, xii, xiii, 13, 256
Thrippleton, Martha 'Patti' Elizabeth *see* Knight, Martha
Throsby, Margaret, 221, 244
Tolstoy, Leo, 114, 120, 124, 160, 163
  Anna Karenina, x, 74, 107
  'How Much Land Does a Man Need', 160
translations, 183, 239, 251, 273
Tuart Club, 147–8, 152, 168
  Elizabeth as office bearer, 147, 156
  reactions to Jolley's works, 205, 245
Tybussek, Renate, 60

University of Edinburgh 'Art of Writing' course, 122
University of Glasgow library, 128–9
University of Queensland Press, 183, 184
University of Western Australia, 143–4
  community life, 139–40, 147–8
  library, 135–6, 137, 144

Vera Wright
  in *Cabin Fever*, 228–9
  in *A Feast of Life*, 76, 132–4
  in *The Georges' Wife*, 132–3, 224,
  in *My Father's Moon*, 50, 70, 89, 103, 105, 109, 229
  in *Orchard Thieves*, 234–5
  as self-examination, 236–8
  throughout the trilogy, 229–34, 280–1
Vickers, Bert, 146, 154, 268
Victoria Nursing Home, 148, 168
Virgil, 32, 120 (*Georgics*), 208, 210, 234
Voltaire, 156
Vorwickl, Hilde, 24, 279;
  in *Sugar Mother*, 24, 215

Walker home, 22
  Monica as domestic 92–6
  relationship with Guy Walker 95, 97–8, 108, 263, 264, 23
Walli, Gretl, 22
Walsh, Richard, 184
Waten, Judah, 158, 206, 222
Watt, A. P., literary agent, 122
Webby, Elizabeth, 228
'The Wedding of the Painted Doll', 11
Watkins products, 151–2, 269
Westerly, 153, 154, 168, 184
Western Australia Week Literary Award, 218
Wheeler, Les and Louise, 130–1, 136
Whele, Gertrude, 82, 86–7, 131, 155, 250, 20
White, Patrick, 222, 281
Whitlock, Gillian, 220
Whyte, Jean Primrose, 145
Wickham, Michael, wife Tanya and son Julyan, 103
Wickham, Michael and Elizabeth Smart, 112
Wimmer, Adi, 32
Winton, Tim, 206, 277
women writers, 55, 220, 228
Wood, Malvina Evalyn 'Emmy', 137–8, 267

Woodward, Jessica, 112
Woolf, Virginia, 121,
  Orlando, 134,
Wooroloo property, 160–1, 244, 36, 38, 39
  as burden for Elizabeth, 162, 163
  entertaining at, 161, 163
  neighbours, 162–3
  as source material, 168, 270
Worrall, Edith, 44, 95, 163, 251
Wran, Neville, 223
Writers' Weeks *see* Adelaide Festivals
writing, 128, 147, 153, 156, 188
  as a business, 219, 280
  development over time, 227, 240, 279
  early writings, 15, 22, 54, 55–7, 73, 83, 261
  from experience of life, xv, xii, xvi, 56–7, 154, 155, 186–8, 208, 238, 275
  with Leonard, 93, 94
  metafiction technique, 195, 196, 198, 207, 211
  narrative modes, 188, 195–6, 203–4, 211
  while nursing, 83, 87
  as a profession, 157, 168–9, 170, 201, 202, 205
  first publication, 26, 93–4
  recycling of earlier works, 154–5, 173, 175–6, 177, 211
  sophisticated spaces, 205, 253
  techniques, 204, 205–6
Wynn, William 'Will', his wife Elsie and daughter Margaret, 8–9, 14–15, 95, 136

Yeoman, Peggy, 66, 69, 71

Die Zauberflöte, Beethoven, 26–7, 32, 258
Zunz, Daisy (Matron), 70–1, 263
Zwicky, Fay, 144